# Lecture Notes in Computer Science 12449

More information about this subseries at http://www.springer.com/series/7412

Seyed Mostafa Kia ·
Hassan Mohy-ud-Din et al. (Eds.)

# Machine Learning in Clinical Neuroimaging and Radiogenomics in Neuro-oncology

Third International Workshop, MLCN 2020,
and Second International Workshop, RNO-AI 2020
Held in Conjunction with MICCAI 2020
Lima, Peru, October 4–8, 2020
Proceedings

 Springer

*Editors*
Seyed Mostafa Kia 🆔
Donders Institute
Nijmegen, The Netherlands

Hassan Mohy-ud-Din 🆔
Lahore University of Management Sciences
Lahore, Pakistan

Additional Volume Editors *see next page*

ISSN 0302-9743  ISSN 1611-3349 (electronic)
Lecture Notes in Computer Science
ISBN 978-3-030-66842-6  ISBN 978-3-030-66843-3 (eBook)
https://doi.org/10.1007/978-3-030-66843-3

LNCS Sublibrary: SL6 – Image Processing, Computer Vision, Pattern Recognition, and Graphics

This Springer imprint is published by the registered company Springer Nature Switzerland AG
The registered company address is: Gewerbestrasse 11, 6330 Cham, Switzerland

# Additional Volume Editors

**MLCN 2020 Editors**

Ahmed Abdulkadir
University of Pennsylvania
Philadelphia, PA, USA

Mohamad Habes
The University of Texas Health Science
Center at San Antonio
San Antonio, TX, USA

Chantal Tax
CUBRIC
Cardiff, UK

Thomas Wolfers
University of Oslo
Oslo, Norway

Cher Bass
King's College London
London, UK

Jane Maryam Rondina
University College London
London, UK

Hongzhi Wang
IBM Almaden Research Center
San Jose, CA, USA

**RNO-AI 2020 Editors**

Madhura Ingalhalikar
Symbiosis Institute of Technology,
Pune, India

Saima Rathore
Eli Lilly Pharmaceutical Company
Philadelphia, PA, USA

# MLCN 2020 Preface

Recent advances in machine learning and neuroimaging provide an exceptional opportunity for researchers to discover complex relationships between biology, brain, and behavior. Neuroimaging techniques such as structural and functional magnetic resonance imaging (s/fMRI) can measure non-invasively the morphology as well as properties related to the function of brain networks. While classical univariate statistics are unable to exploit complex patterns present in neuroimaging data, advanced machine learning approaches can be employed to benefit from this wealth of information to provide a deeper understanding of the underlying neurobiological mechanisms. Unfortunately, even though machine learning techniques were first successfully applied to clinical neuroimaging data about two decades ago, to date, there has been very limited translation to the clinic. This is mainly because of the lack of generalization of existing approaches to new populations due to 1) the underlying biological heterogeneity in both clinical and healthy populations, and 2) inherent limitations of neuroimaging data including high dimensionality and low signal-to-noise ratio.

The 3rd International Workshop on Machine Learning in Clinical Neuroimaging (MLCN 2020) was held in conjunction with MICCAI 2020 and aimed to bring together experts in machine learning and clinical neuroimaging to address two main challenges in the field: 1) development of methodological approaches for analyzing complex and heterogeneous neuroimaging data; and 2) filling the translational gap in applying existing machine learning methods in clinical practices.

The call for papers for the MLCN 2020 workshop was released on May 8, 2020, with the manuscript submission deadline set to July 10, 2020. The received manuscripts went through a double-blind review process by MLCN 2020 program committee members. Each paper was thoroughly reviewed by at least three reviewers and the top 18 papers were selected for publication. The accepted papers present novel contributions both in developing new machine learning methods and in applications of existing methods to solve challenging problems in clinical neuroimaging.

To end, we would like to thank the MLCN 2020 steering committee for their enlightening guidance in organizing this event. We also wish to thank all the authors for their valuable contributions and the MLCN 2020 program committee for their precious effort in evaluating the submissions.

October 2020

Seyed Mostafa Kia
Ahmed Abdulkadir
Cher Bass
Mohamad Habes
Jane Maryam Rondina
Chantal Tax
Hongzhi Wang
Thomas Wolfers

# MLCN 2020 Organization

## Steering Committee MLCN 2020

| | |
|---|---|
| Christos Davatzikos | University of Pennsylvania, USA |
| Andre Marquand | Radboud University Medical Center, The Netherlands |
| Jonas Richiardi | Lausanne University Hospital, Switzerland |
| Emma Robinson | King's College London, UK |

## Organizing Committee MLCN 2020

| | |
|---|---|
| Ahmed Abdulkadir | University of Pennsylvania, USA |
| Cher Bass | King's College London, UK |
| Mohamad Habes | UT Health San Antonio, USA |
| Seyed Mostafa Kia | Radboud University Medical Center, The Netherlands |
| Jane Maryam Rondina | University College London, UK |
| Chantal Tax | Cardiff University, UK |
| Hongzhi Wang | IBM Almaden Research Center, USA |
| Thomas Wolfers | NORMENT, Norway |

## Program Committee MLCN 2020

| | |
|---|---|
| Ehsan Adeli | Stanford University, USA |
| Andre Altmann | University College London, UK |
| Luca Ambrogioni | Radboud University, The Netherlands |
| Özgün Çiçek | University of Freiburg, Germany |
| Richard Dinga | Radboud University Medical Center, The Netherlands |
| Florian Dubost | Erasmus University Medical Center, The Netherlands |
| Fabian Eitel | Bernstein Center for Computational Neuroscience Berlin, Germany |
| Guray Erus | University of Pennsylvania, USA |
| Pouya Ghaemmaghami | Concordia University, Canada |
| Thomas Hope | University College London, UK |
| Hangfan Liu | University of Pennsylvania, USA |
| Tommy Löfstedt | Umeå University, Sweden |
| Marco Lorenzi | Université Côte d'Azur, France |
| Emanuele Olivetti | Bruno Kessler Foundation, Italy |
| Pradeep Raamana | University of Toronto, Canada |
| Saige Rutherford | University of Michigan, USA |
| Mortiz Seiler | Charité-Universitätsmedizin Berlin, Germany |
| Maurício Serpa | University of São Paulo, Brasil |
| Haykel Snoussi | UT Health San Antonio, USA |
| Sourena Soheili Nezhad | Radboud University Medical Center, The Netherlands |

Rashid Tanweer          University of Pennsylvania, USA
Sandra Vieira           King's College London, UK
Tianbo Xu               University College London, UK
Mariam Zabihi           Radboud University Medical Center, The Netherlands

# RNO-AI 2020 Preface

Due to the exponential growth of computational algorithms, AI methods are poised to improve the precision of diagnostic and therapeutic methods in medicine. The field of radiomics in neuro-oncology has been and will likely continue to be at the forefront of this revolution. A variety of AI methods applied to conventional and advanced neuro-oncology MRI data can do several tasks. The first essential step of radiomics generally involves lesion segmentation, which is generally preceded by image preprocessing steps including skull stripping, intensity normalization, and alignment of image volumes from different modalities. A variety of methods have been used for segmentation, ranging from manual labeling and/or annotation and semiautomated methods to more recent deep learning methods. The next step of radiomics with traditional machine learning involves the extraction of quantitative features, including basic shape, size, and intensity metrics, as well as more complex features derived from a variety of statistical approaches applied to the images, for example, histogram-based features, texture-based features, fitted biophysical models, spatial patterns, and deep learning features. A variety of different machine learning models can then be applied to the intermediate quantitative features in order to "mine" them for significant associations, allowing them to predict crucial information about a tumor, such as infiltrating tumor margins, molecular markers, and prognosis, which are relevant for therapeutic decision making. Alternatively, deep learning approaches to radiomics in neuro-oncology generally necessitate less domain-specific knowledge compared with the explicitly engineered features for traditional machine learning, allowing them to make predictions without explicit feature selection or reduction steps.

Radiogenomics has also advanced our understanding of cancer biology, allowing noninvasive sampling of the molecular environment with high spatial resolution and providing a systems-level understanding of underlying heterogeneous cellular and molecular processes. By providing in vivo markers of spatial and molecular heterogeneity, these AI-based radiomic and radiogenomic tools have the potential to stratify VI patients into more precise initial diagnostic and therapeutic pathways and enable better dynamic treatment monitoring in this era of personalized medicine. Although substantial challenges remain, radiologic practice is set to change considerably as AI technology is further developed and validated for clinical use.

The second edition of the **Radiomics and Radiogenomics in Neuro-oncology using AI (RNO-AI 2020)** workshop was successfully held in conjunction with the 23rd International Conference on Medical Image Computing and Computer-Assisted Intervention (MICCAI 2020) in Lima, Peru on October 8, 2020. The aim of RNO-AI 2020 was to bring together the growing number of researchers in the field given the significant amount of effort in the development of tools that can automate the analysis and synthesis of neuro-oncologic imaging. Submissions were solicited via a call for papers by the MICCAI and workshop organizers, as well as by directly emailing more than 400 colleagues and experts in the area. Each submission underwent a double-blind review by two to three members of the Program Committee, consisting of researchers actively contributing in the area. Three invited papers were also solicited from leading experts in the field. RNO-AI 2020 featured three keynote talks and eight oral presentations. The duration of the workshop was approximately 4 hours.

We would like to extend warm gratitude to the members of the program committee for their reviews; to the keynote speakers, Prof. Ulas Bagci, Prof. Thomas Booth, and Prof. Jayashree Kalpathy-Cramer, for illuminating talks; to the authors for their research contributions; and to the MICCAI Society for their overall support.

October 2020                                          Hassan Mohy-ud-Din
                                                     Saima Rathore
                                                     Madhura Ingalhalikar

# RNO-AI 2020 Organization

## Organizing Committee RNO-AI 2020

Hassan Mohy-ud-Din      Lahore University of Management Sciences, Pakistan
Saima Rathore           Eli Lilly, USA
Madhura Ingalhalikar    Symbiosis Institute of Technology, India

## Program Committee RNO-AI 2020

Ulas Bagci              University of Central Florida, USA
Nicolas Honnorat        SRI International, USA
Ahmad Chaddad           McGill University, Canada
Niha Beig               Tempus Labs, USA

# Contents

## RNO-AI 2020

MLCN 2020

# Surface Agnostic Metrics for Cortical Volume Segmentation and Regression

Samuel Budd[1]([⊠])(iD), Prachi Patkee[2], Ana Baburamani[2], Mary Rutherford[2], Emma C. Robinson[2], and Bernhard Kainz[1]

[1] Department of Computing, BioMedIA, Imperial College London, London, UK
samuel.budd13@imperial.ac.uk
[2] Centre for the Developing Brain, School of Biomedical Engineering and Imaging Sciences, King's College London, ISBE, London, UK

**Abstract.** The cerebral cortex performs higher-order brain functions and is thus implicated in a range of cognitive disorders. Current analysis of cortical variation is typically performed by fitting surface mesh models to inner and outer cortical boundaries and investigating metrics such as surface area and cortical curvature or thickness. These, however, take a long time to run, and are sensitive to motion and image and surface resolution, which can prohibit their use in clinical settings. In this paper, we instead propose a machine learning solution, training a novel architecture to predict cortical thickness and curvature metrics from T2 MRI images, while additionally returning metrics of prediction uncertainty. Our proposed model is tested on a clinical cohort (Down Syndrome) for which surface-based modelling often fails. Results suggest that deep convolutional neural networks are a viable option to predict cortical metrics across a range of brain development stages and pathologies.

## 1 Introduction

Irregularities in cortical folding and micro-structure development have been implicated in a range of neurological and psychiatric disorders including: Autism, where disruptions to folding cortical and thinning of the cortex has been found in regions associated with social perception, language, self-reference and action observation [21]; Down Syndrome, where smoother cortical surfaces and abnormal patterns of cortical thickness are linked to impaired cognition [14]; Epilepsy, where malformations in cortical development are associated with seizure onset [15] and psychosis, which is associated with abnormal functional behaviour of the pre-frontal cortex [18].

There is a strong need to model cortical development in at-risk neonatal populations. However, due to the heterogeneous and highly convoluted shape of the

**Electronic supplementary material** The online version of this chapter (https://doi.org/10.1007/978-3-030-66843-3_1) contains supplementary material, which is available to authorized users.

S. M. Kia et al. (Eds.): MLCN 2020/RNO-AI 2020, LNCS 12449, pp. 3–12, 2020.
https://doi.org/10.1007/978-3-030-66843-3_1

cortex, it has proved highly challenging to compare across populations. Recent consensus has been that cortical features are best studied using surface-mesh models of the brain [10], as these better represent the true geodesic distances between features on the cortex. However, these require running of costly multi-process pipelines which perform intensity-based tissue segmentation, followed by mesh tessellation and refinement.

For developmental cohorts, the fitting of surface mesh models is even more challenging due to the relatively low resolution and likely motion corruption of these datasets. This leads to artifacts and partial volume effects or blurring across tissue boundaries. Methods to tackle these problems individually exist [16] but they are highly tuned to high-resolution, low motion research data sets and do not always transfer well to clinical populations as outlined in Fig. 1.

As an alternative, several groups have proposed techniques for extracting cortical surface metrics from volume data directly [4,5,20]. Specifically, Tustison et al. [5,20] show that an ANTs-based extension for the estimation of cortical thickness from volumetric segmentation generates thickness measures which out-perform FreeSurfer (surface) metrics when applied to predictive tasks associating thickness with well-studied phenotype relations such as age and gender. Never-theless, volumetric fitting approaches such as [20] have not yet been validated on developmental data and their slow run times limit their utility for clinical appli-cations. In this paper we therefore seek to develop a novel algorithm for cortical metric prediction from clinical, developmental data, through Deep Learning.

**Contribution:** The key contributions of this paper are: 1) We propose the first probabilistic Deep Learning tool for cortical segmentation and metric learning. 2) We validate the method against cortical thickness and curvature prediction for data from the Developing Human Connectome Project (dHCP); 3) The tool is used to predict cortical metrics for a Down Syndrome cohort in which surface-based analysis often fails; 4) Our probabilistic approach returns confidence maps which can inform clinical researchers of areas of the brain where measurements are less reliable.

## 2    Related Work

The cerebral cortex is a thin layer of grey-matter tissue at the outer layer of the brain. Studying it is important for improved understanding of cognitive and neurological disorders but doing so is challenging due to it's complex shape and patterns of micro-structural organisation.

Currently, most studies of the cortex use surface mesh models [7,9,16], which fit mesh models to inner and outer cortical boundaries following pipelines which perform tissue segmentation, followed by surface tessellation with intensity based refinement (Fig. 1). Summary measures of cortical thickness and curvature may then be estimated from the Euclidean distance between mesh surfaces, and prin-cipal curvatures of the white-matter surface respectively.

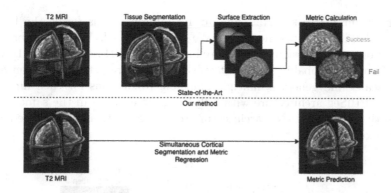

**Fig. 1.** Overview figure of current state-of-the-art approach to extracting cortical metrics from MRI volumes showing a success and failure case vs. our method. The segmentation and surface extraction components of the pipeline are prone to fail, thus to produce artifacts as displayed in the fail case above.

By contrast, ANTs (Advanced Normalisation Tools) and CAT (Computational Anatomy Toolbox) propose volume-based pipelines for cortical thickness estimation. Specifically, the ANTs pipeline estimates cortical thickness in five steps: 1) Initial N4 bias correction of input MRI; 2) Segmentation/Registration based brain extraction; 3) Alternating prior-based segmentation and weighted bias correction using Atropos and N4; 4) DiReCT-based cortical thickness estimation; 5) Optional normalisation to template and multi-atlas cortical parcellation [5,20]. CAT uses segmentation to estimate white matter (WM) distance, and then projects the local maxima (equal to cortical thickness) to other grey matter voxels by using a neighbour relationship defined by the WM distance [4].

## 3    Method

**Segmentation and Regression Network:** Our proposed network architecture augments the popular U-Net architecture into a 3D Multi-Task prediction network [19]. We introduce a branch of fully connected layers prior to the final convolution of the U-Net as shown in Fig. 2. The network predicts a cortical segmentation through the standard U-Net architecture while simultaneously regressing a cortical metric value for every voxel in the image [3]. These two tasks are strongly coupled and as such we design the regression branch of our network to see a large amount of information from the segmentation path. We use a cross-entropy loss function for the segmentation task and consider two different loss functions for the regression task: Mean squared error (MSE) and Huber/L1 Loss, the latter is considered to encourage smoothness of regression predictions across neighbouring pixels by being robust to outliers [11], a property that should hold for cortical metric predictions.

We propose a probabilistic extension of our network in which we introduce Dropblock to our network during training and test time, this approach ensures

variation in our network predictions during inference, this forms the baseline
for our probabilistic experiments [8]. We propose an alternative probabilistic
segmentation and regression architecture based on the PHiSeg network [1], which
extends from the probabilistic U-Net [13] to model prediction variation across
multiple scales and generate multiple plausible predictions for each input. We
extend the PHiSeg architecture with fully connected layers in the same way we
extended the initial 3D U-Net architecture to regress cortical metrics predictions
for each voxel.

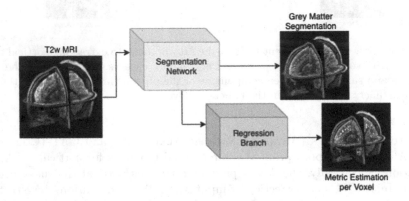

**Fig. 2.** Architecture Diagram for the proposed simultaneous segmentation and regression network: The network predicts a cortical segmentation through the chosen segmentation architecture while simultaneously regressing a cortical metric value for every
voxel in the image via the fully connected regression branch

We generate confidence maps for each prediction by sampling multiple times
from each probabilistic network. This results in a range of segmentations and a
range of metric predictions for each voxel. We argue that the larger the range
of values predicted for a given voxel, the less confidence our network has in
predicting a value for that voxel. We quantify the confidence of each prediction
as the variance of each prediction made during inference. We seek the confidence
map with the greatest correlation to prediction accuracy. From each range we can
also define a metric 'Percentage in range' where we measure the percentage of
voxels for which the ground truth value lies within the predicted range of values,
where we seek the smallest ranges for which the ground truth is contained [2].

## 4 Experimental Methods and Results

**Data:** Data for this study comes from the Developing Human Connectome
Project (dHCP) acquired in two stacks of 2D slices (in sagittal and axial planes)
using a Turbo Spin Echo (TSE) sequence [12]. The used parameters were:
TR=12s, TE=156ms, SENSE factor 2.11 (axial) and 2.58 (sagittal) with overlapping slices. The study contains 505 subjects aged between 26–45 weeks. Tissue

segmentations and surface metrics for training are derived form the dHCP surface extraction pipeline [16][1].

A second clinical Down Syndrome cohort of 26 subjects was collected with a variety of scanning parameters, aged between 32–45 weeks, most subjects were acquired in the sagittal and transverse planes using a multi-slice TSE sequence. Two stacks of 2D slices were acquired using the scanning parameters: TR=12 s, TE=156 ms, slice thickness = 1.6 mm with a slice overlap = 0.8 mm; flip angle = 90° and an in-plane resolution: 0.8×0.8 mm.

**Preprocessing:** We project surface-based representations of cortical biometrics into a volumetric representation using a ribbon constrained method[2] provided by the HCP project [17]. This operation is performed for both hemispheres of the brain and then combined into a single volume, where overlapping metric values are averaged. These volumes (together with the tissue segmentations) represent the training targets for the learning algorithm. T2w input volume and corresponding metric volumes are then resampled to a isotropic voxel spacing of 0.5 to ensure a prediction of physically meaningful values for each subject, *i.e*, each voxel of our input image represents the same physical size in millimetres. Each T2 volume is intensity normalised to the range [0,1].

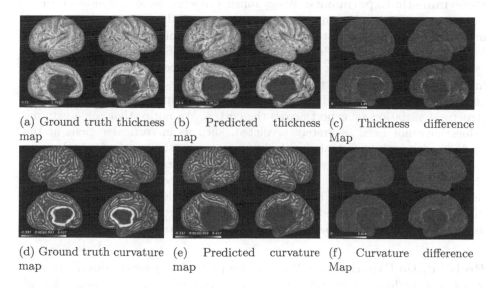

(a) Ground truth thickness map

(b) Predicted thickness map

(c) Thickness difference Map

(d) Ground truth curvature map

(e) Predicted curvature map

(f) Curvature difference Map

**Fig. 3.** Qualitative results on a dHCP subject: Here we have used ground truth surfaces to re-project our predicted metric volumes and difference map back into a surface representation for ease of comparison.

---

[1] https://github.com/BioMedIA/dhcp-structural-pipeline.
[2] https://www.humanconnectome.org/software/workbench-command/-metric-to-volume-mapping.

**Table 1.** Results for metric prediction: Metric error calculated as average voxel-wise difference between prediction and ground truth only for voxels within the cortex. Dice score is reported over the segmentation.

| Experiment | Dice | Mean error (mm) | Median error (mm) |
|---|---|---|---|
| Thickness (mm) | | | |
| **UNetMSE** | **0.946 ± 0.010** | **0.179 ± 0.025** | **0.125 ± 0.021** |
| UNetHuber | 0.939 ± 0.012 | 0.197 ± 0.027 | 0.139 ± 0.022 |
| Curvature | | | |
| **UNetMSE** | **0.945 ± 0.010** | **0.0424 ± 0.005** | **0.0304 ± 0.003** |
| UNetHuber | 0.935 ± 0.011 | 0.0498 ± 0.006 | 0.0361 ± 0.004 |

**Training:** 400 subjects are used for training; 50 for validation; 55 for test. During training we sample class-balanced 64×64×64 patches (N=12) from each subject's volume pair. We test on the entire volume of the image using a 3D sliding window approach. We conduct our experiments to predict two different cortical metrics: Thickness and Curvature.

**Deterministic Experiments:** We establish a baseline for simultaneous estimation of cortical segmentation and metric regression. Table 1 reports performance measures for all deterministic experiments. We find minimal difference in performance using the Huber loss function instead of MSE loss on the regression task module. Figure 3 show example outputs produced by our best performing model in comparison to the ground truth. Our network successfully extracts accurate cortical metric predictions directly from the input MRI, maintaining the structural variation we expect across the cortex. We notice that some extreme values have not been accurately predicted, such as in cortical regions at the bridge between the two brain hemispheres (for curvature prediction). However the extreme values that are present in the ground truth data are an artifact of the surface based metric prediction method, hence it is less important to replicate this precisely. In Fig. 6 we report test-set wide metrics comparing predicted global metric distributions in comparison to ground truth distributions, our method predicts a similar distribution of results to the ground truth.

**Probabilistic Experiments:** We consider probabilistic extensions of our previous best performing method. Table 2 reports performance measures for all probabilistic experiments. We find that introducing DropBlock layers into our network has improved segmentation accuracy, but metric estimation accuracy has declined. PHiSeg has not improved either segmentation or metric estimation performance. In these experiments, PHiSeg training was often unstable, and took much longer to converge than other methods. While our error has increased, the ability to generate confidence maps for these predictions increases their value. Figure 4 shows a generated confidence map using PHiSeg.

**Table 2.** Probabilistic Prediction results: We show dice scores and the mean metric error when taking mean and the median of multiple (N = 5) predictions as the final output.

| Experiment | Dice | Mean Mean error | Mean Median error | Percent in range |
|---|---|---|---|---|
| Thickness (mm) | | | | |
| **UNetDropBlock** | **0.945 ± 0.009** | **0.268 ± 0.017** | **0.373 ± 0.017** | **59.83%** |
| PHiSeg | 0.774 ± 0.075 | 0.567 ± 0.096 | 0.550 ± 0.052 | 19.60% |
| Curvature | | | | |
| **UNetDropBlock** | **0.946 ± 0.009** | **0.0538 ± 0.004** | **0.0705 ± 0.003** | **56.19%** |
| PHiSeg | 0.796 ± 0.022 | 0.102 ± 0.006 | 0.102± 0.006 | 24.98% |

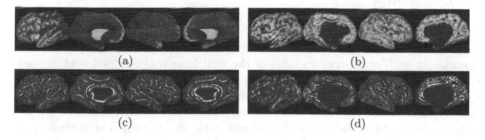

**Fig. 4.** Confidence map generated with PHiSeg for a dHCP subject. Brighter areas indicate decreased confidence.

(a)  (b)

(c)  (d)

**Fig. 5.** Qualitative results on Down Syndrome dataset: a) dHCP predicted thickness; b) Our method predicted thickness; c) dHCP predicted curvature; d) Our method predicted curvature.

**Down Syndrome Experiments:** We assess the performance of our method on a challenging Down Syndrome MRI dataset for which the dHCP pipeline fails to extract metrics correctly for many subjects. Since the 'ground truth' for this dataset is error prone, we demonstrate the performance of our method qualitatively and through population comparisons to the healthy dHCP test set used in previous experiments. Figure 5 shows that our method produces more reasonable estimates of cortical thickness than the dHCP pipeline, thus showing evidence for our method's robustness to challenging datasets. Population statistics indicating that our method produces metric values in a sensible range for cortical thickness are shown in Fig. 6. However our predicted distribution for

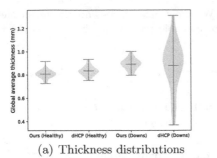
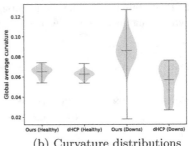

(a) Thickness distributions          (b) Curvature distributions

**Fig. 6.** Global average metric distributions a) Thickness and b) Curvature. Our method produces a sensible distribution of values for the Down Syndrome data set compared to the dHCP pipeline for thickness prediction. However curvature prediction remains challenging. Pathological cases (right two in each plot) cannot be quantitatively evaluated because of missing ground truth.

cortical curvature is not consistent with healthy patients, indicating curvature and other more complex metrics remain challenging.

## 5   Discussion

We propose an automatic, pathology-robust method to predict cortical metric values from any T2w image stack. Our method is fast, robust and precise. We experiment with multi-task variants of the well known U-Net architecture and demonstrate how readily applicable deep learning is to predict cortical metric values in a reproducible way. Many architecture extensions are possible, which can for example be explored with neural architecture search methods [6]. In order to fully utilise the predictions of our network an imminent extension of our method is to automatically extract surface meshes from unseen data to enable proper visualisation of our predictions from images without ground truth surfaces.

Probably the biggest advantage of our method is that we can produce cortical measurements for pathological cases. However, the curvature example in Fig. 6b shows that more complex metrics remain challenging and that we will need to further verify the robustness of our method in a clinical setting. Fine tuning may allow to generate disease-discriminative biomarkers directly from the network's latent space. At present our pipeline optimises cortical curvature and thickness prediction which naturally extends to sulcal depth and myelination prediction. There is potential to combine all metric predictions into a single model as it can be argued that prediction of different cortical properties are strongly correlated and would benefit each other as natural regulariser.

# 6   Conclusion

We offer an open-source framework for the extraction of cortical biometrics directly from T2 MRI images. This is the first of its kind that shows potential to be independent of age, image quality or presence of pathologies, and likely extendable to any cortical properties. We have tested our approach on a challenging pathological dataset for which we have not been able to reliably extract metrics with conventional methods like the dHCP processing pipeline. We expect that our future work will open new avenues for the analysis of cortical properties related to human brain development and disease in heterogenous populations.

**Acknowledgements.** We thank the parents and children who participated in this study. This work was supported by the Medical Research Council [MR/K006355/1]; Rosetrees Trust [A1563], Fondation Jérôme Lejeune [2017b – 1707], Sparks and Great Ormond Street Hospital Children's Charity [V5318]. The research leading to these results has received funding from the European Research Council under the European Unions Seventh Framework Programme (FP/2007–2013)/ERC Grant Agreement no. 319456. The work of E.C.R. was supported by the Academy of Medical Sciences/the British Heart Foundation/the Government Department of Business, Energy and Industrial Strategy/the Wellcome Trust Springboard Award [SBF003/1116]. We also gratefully acknowledge financial support from the Wellcome Trust IEH 102431, EPSRC (EP/S022104/1, EP/S013687/1), EPSRC Centre for Medical Engineering [WT 203148/Z/16/Z], the National Institute for Health Research (NIIIR) Biomedical Research Centre (BRC) based at Guy's and St Thomas' NHS Foundation Trust and King's College London and supported by the NIHR Clinical Research Facility (CRF) at Guy's and St Thomas', and Nvidia GPU donations.

# References

1. Baumgartner, C.F., et al.: PHiSeg: capturing uncertainty in medical image segmentation. In: Shen, D., et al. (eds.) MICCAI 2019. LNCS, vol. 11765, pp. 119–127. Springer, Cham (2019). https://doi.org/10.1007/978-3-030-32245-8_14
2. Budd, S., et al.: Confident head circumference measurement from ultrasound with real-time feedback for sonographers. In: Shen, D., et al. (eds.) MICCAI 2019. LNCS, vol. 11767, pp. 683–691. Springer, Cham (2019). https://doi.org/10.1007/978-3-030-32251-9_75
3. Çiçek, Ö., Abdulkadir, A., Lienkamp, S.S., Brox, T., Ronneberger, O.: 3D U-Net: learning dense volumetric segmentation from sparse annotation. In: Ourselin, S., Joskowicz, L., Sabuncu, M.R., Unal, G., Wells, W. (eds.) MICCAI 2016. LNCS, vol. 9901, pp. 424–432. Springer, Cham (2016). https://doi.org/10.1007/978-3-319-46723-8_49
4. Dahnke, R., Yotter, R.A., Gaser, C.: Cortical thickness and central surface estimation. NeuroImage **65**, 336–348 (2013). https://doi.org/10.1016/j.neuroimage.2012.09.050, http://www.ncbi.nlm.nih.gov/pubmed/23041529
5. Das, S.R., Avants, B.B., Grossman, M., Gee, J.C.: Registration based cortical thickness measurement. NeuroImage **45**(3), 867–879 (2009). https://doi.org/10.1016/j.neuroimage.2008.12.016

6. Elsken, T., Metzen, J.H., Hutter, F.: Neural architecture search: a survey. J. Mach. Learn. Res. **20** (2018). http://arxiv.org/abs/1808.05377
7. Fischl, B., Dale, A.M.: Measuring the thickness of the human cerebral cortex from magnetic resonance images. Proc. Natl. Acad. Sci. United States Am. **97**(20), 11050–11055 (2000). https://doi.org/10.1073/pnas.200033797
8. Ghiasi, G., Lin, T.Y., Le, Q.V.: DropBlock: a regularization method for convolutional networks. In: Advances in Neural Information Processing Systems 2018-December, pp. 10727–10737 (2018). http://arxiv.org/abs/1810.12890
9. Glasser, M.F., et al.: The minimal preprocessing pipelines for the Human Connectome Project. NeuroImage (2013). https://doi.org/10.1016/j.neuroimage.2013.04.127
10. Glasser, M.F., et al.: A multi-modal parcellation of human cerebral cortex. Nat. Publishing Group **536**, 171–178 (2016). https://doi.org/10.1038/nature18933
11. Huber, P.J.: Robust estimation of a location parameter. Ann. Math. Stat. **35**(1), 73–101 (1964). https://doi.org/10.1214/AOMS/1177703732
12. Hughes, E.J., et al.: A dedicated neonatal brain imaging system. Magn. Reson. Med. **78**(2), 794–804 (2017). https://doi.org/10.1002/mrm.26462
13. Kohl, S., et al.: A probabilistic U-Net for segmentation of ambiguous images. In: Advances in Neural Information Processing Systems, pp. 6965–6975 (2018)
14. Lee, N.R., et al.: Dissociations in cortical morphometry in youth with down syndrome: evidence for reduced surface area but increased thickness. Cerebral Cortex (New York, N.Y.: 1991) **26**(7), 2982–2990 (2016). https://doi.org/10.1093/cercor/bhv107, http://www.ncbi.nlm.nih.gov/pubmed/26088974www.pubmedcentral.nih.gov/articlerender.fcgi?artid=PMC4898663
15. Leventer, R.J., Guerrini, R., Dobyns, W.B.: Malformations of cortical development and epilepsy (2008)
16. Makropoulos, A., et al.: The developing human connectome project: a minimal processing pipeline for neonatal cortical surface reconstruction. NeuroImage **173**, 88–112 (2018). https://doi.org/10.1016/j.neuroimage.2018.01.054
17. Marcus, D.S., et al.: Informatics and data mining tools and strategies for the human connectome project. Front. Neuroinf. **5**, 4 (2011). https://doi.org/10.3389/fninf.2011.00004, http://journal.frontiersin.org/article/10.3389/fninf.2011.00004/abstract
18. Mukherjee, P., et al.: Disconnection between amygdala and medial prefrontal cortex in psychotic disorders. Schizophrenia bull. **42**(4), 1056–167 (2016). https://doi.org/10.1093/schbul/sbw012, http://www.ncbi.nlm.nih.gov/pubmed/26908926www.pubmedcentral.nih.gov/articlerender.fcgi?artid=PMC4903065
19. Ronneberger, O., Fischer, P., Brox, T.: U-Net: convolutional networks for biomedical image segmentation. In: Navab, N., Hornegger, J., Wells, W.M., Frangi, A.F. (eds.) MICCAI 2015. LNCS, vol. 9351, pp. 234–241. Springer, Cham (2015). https://doi.org/10.1007/978-3-319-24574-4_28
20. Tustison, N.J., et al.: Large-scale evaluation of ANTs and FreeSurfer cortical thickness measurements. NeuroImage **99**, 166–179 (2014). https://doi.org/10.1016/j.neuroimage.2014.05.044
21. Yang, D.Y., Beam, D., Pelphrey, K.A., Abdullahi, S., Jou, R.J.: Cortical morphological markers in children with autism: a structural magnetic resonance imaging study of thickness, area, volume, and gyrification. Molec. Autism **7**(1), 11 (2016). https://doi.org/10.1186/s13229-016-0076-x, http://molecularautism.biomedcentral.com/articles/10.1186/s13229-016-0076-x

# Automatic Tissue Segmentation with Deep Learning in Patients with Congenital or Acquired Distortion of Brain Anatomy

Gabriele Amorosino[1,2], Denis Peruzzo[3], Pietro Astolfi[1,4],
Daniela Redaelli[3], Paolo Avesani[1,2], Filippo Arrigoni[3],
and Emanuele Olivetti[1,2(✉)]

[1] NeuroInformatics Laboratory (NILab), Bruno Kessler Foundation, Trento, Italy
{gamorosino,olivetti}@fbk.eu
[2] Center for Mind and Brain Sciences (CIMeC), University of Trento,
Rovereto, TN, Italy
[3] Neuroimaging Lab, Scientific Institute IRCCS Eugenio Medea,
Bosisio Parini, Lecco, Italy
[4] PAVIS, Italian Institute of Technology (IIT), Genova, Italy

**Abstract.** Brains with complex distortion of cerebral anatomy present
several challenges to automatic tissue segmentation methods of T1-
weighted MR images. First, the very high variability in the morphology
of the tissues can be incompatible with the prior knowledge embedded
within the algorithms. Second, the availability of MR images of distorted
brains is very scarce, so the methods in the literature have not addressed
such cases so far. In this work, we present the first evaluation of state-of-
the-art automatic tissue segmentation pipelines on T1-weighted images
of brains with different severity of congenital or acquired brain distortion. We compare traditional pipelines and a deep learning model, i.e.
a 3D U-Net trained on normal-appearing brains. Unsurprisingly, traditional pipelines completely fail to segment the tissues with strong
anatomical distortion. Surprisingly, the 3D U-Net provides useful segmentations that can be a valuable starting point for manual refinement
by experts/neuroradiologists.

## 1  Introduction

Accurate segmentation of brain structural MR images into different tissues, like
white matter (WM), gray matter (GM) and cerebrospinal fluid (CSF), is of
primary interest for clinical and neuroscientific applications, such as volume
quantification, cortical thickness analysis and bundle analysis.

Since manual segmentation of the brain tissues is extremely time consuming
it is usually performed by means of well-established automated tools, such as
FSL [7], SPM [1], FreeSurfer [5] and ANTs [15]. Typically, these tools obtain
excellent quality of segmentation in normal-appearing brains.

© Springer Nature Switzerland AG 2020
S. M. Kia et al. (Eds.): MLCN 2020/RNO-AI 2020, LNCS 12449, pp. 13–22, 2020.
https://doi.org/10.1007/978-3-030-66843-3_2

More recently, brain tissue segmentation has been addressed by deep learning algorithms like convolutional neural networks (CNNs) [4,10,11,16], applied directly to T1 or T2 weighted MR images. The quality of segmentation obtained by such methods is again excellent and the computational cost, once trained, is usually greatly reduced with respect to traditional pipelines.

Especially in children, many congenital (e.g. malformations, huge arachnoid cysts) or acquired (e.g. severe hydrocephalus, encephalomalacia) conditions can cause complex modifications of cerebral anatomy that alter the structural and spatial relationship among different brain structures. Automatically segmenting such brains presents multiple challenges mainly due to the high variability of the morphology together with the scarce availability of data. Moreover, the prior knowledge encoded in automated pipelines, or the set of images used to train segmentation algorithms, do not cover such cases. In the literature, the problem of segmenting brain with distorted anatomy, has been addressed in the case of traumatic brain injury [8] or specifically when parcelling ventricles in patients with ventriculomegaly [13,14].

In this work, for the first time, we present results of different well-established whole-brain tissue segmentation pipelines on T1 images of malformed and highly distorted brains in the pediatric age which were congenital or acquired. Unsurprisingly, we observe that the quality of segmentation is highly variable with traditional pipelines, and it fails when the complexity of the brain distortion and the severity of the malformation are high.

Moreover, as a major contribution, we show the results of a CNN for segmentation of medical images, namely the 3D U-Net [3,12], trained on over 800 pediatric subjects with *normal brain*. Surprisingly, the 3D U-Net segments brains with moderate and severe distortion of brain anatomy either accurately or at least to a sufficient level to consider manual refinement by expert radiologists.

The evaluation study of the U-Net presented here is first conducted on a large sample of normal brain images, as a sanity check, to quantitatively assess that the specific implementation and training procedure reaches state-of-the-art quality of segmentation. The evaluation on distorted brains is instead qualitative, because of the small sample available due to the rarity of the condition, as well as the current lack of gold standard segmentation.

If confirmed by future and more extensive studies, this result opens the way to CNNs-based tissue segmentation methods in applications, even in the case of malformed and highly distorted brains. From the methodological point of view, CNNs show a much higher degree of flexibility in tissue segmentation than well-established pipelines, despite being trained on segmentations obtained from those same pipelines.

## 2   Materials

We assembled a dataset of over 900 MR images from subjects and patients in the pediatric age, divided into two parts: normal brains and distorted brains. The first part consists of 570 T1-w images from public databases (C-MIND[1], NIMH[2]) and 334 T1-w images acquired in-house by the authors during clinical activity at IRCCS Eugenio Medea (Italy). The second part comprises 21 patients, again acquired at IRCCS E.Medea.

## 2.1 Normal Brains

### – Public Databases.

- T1-w images from 207 healthy subjects of the C-MIND database (165 from CCHMC site, with average age 8.9 (SD = 5.0) and 42 from UCLA site, with average age 7.6 (SD = 3.8)) both with 3D MPRAGE MRI 3T scan sequence (TR = 8000 ms, TE = 3.7 ms, Flip angle = 8°, FOV=256 × 224 × 160, voxel spacing=1 × 1 × 1 mm$^3$).
- T1-w images from 363 healthy subjects (average age 10.7 (SD = 6.0)) from the *Pediatric MRI* database of NIMH Data Archive [6], MRI 1.5T scanner with two different sequences:

  * 284 subjects acquired with a 3D T1-w Sequence 3D RF-spoiled gradient echo sequence (TR 22–25 ms, TE = 10–11 ms, Excitation pulse =30°, Refocusing pulse 180°, FOV = 160–180 × 256 × 256, voxel spacing=1 × 1 × 1 mm$^3$)
  * 79 subjects acquired with a T1-w Sequence Spin echo (TR = 500 ms, TE = 12 ms, Flip angle = 90°, Refocusing pulse = 180° Field of view = 192 × 256 × 66, voxel spacing = 1 × 1 × 3 mm$^3$)

- **In-House Database: IRCCS E.MEDEA.** T1-w images from 334 subjects with normal brain, acquired in-house with average age 10.6 (SD = 5.2) and 3D T1-w MPRAGE 3T MRI scan sequence (TR = 8000 ms, TE = 4ms, Flip angle = 8°, FOV = 256 × 256×170, voxel spacing = 1 × 1 × 1 mm$^3$).

## 2.2 Distorted Brains

Images from two groups of patients acquired in-house at IRCSS E.Medea with the same MR and scan sequence described above. In detail:

- **Agenesis of Corpus Callosum.** 12 patients with agenesis of corpus callosum (ACC) (average age 5.8 (SD = 5.2)). Callosal agenesis is characterized by colpocephaly, parallel ventricles, presence of Probst bundles and upward extension of third ventricle. See some cases in Fig. reffig:acc.
- **Complex distortions.** 9 patients (average age 7.9 (SD = 3.2)) with severe parenchymal distortion related to complex malformations (4 cases), parenchymal poroencephalic lesions and severe hydrocephalus (4 cases) and massive arachnoid cyst (1 case). See some cases in Fig. 2.

---

[1] https://research.cchmc.org/c-mind, NIH contract #s HHSN275200900018C.
[2] http://pediatricmri.nih.gov.

## 2.3   Pre-processing and Reference Tissue Segmentation

All T1-w images received bias field correction (N4BiasFieldCorrection) and AC-PC alignment. The reference segmentation of *normal brains* was performed with the AntsCorticalThickness.sh script of ANTs [15] with the PTBP (pediatric) prior [2], resulting in a 3D mask with 7 labels (6 tissues): background, Cerebrospinal fluid (CSF), Gray matter (GM), White matter (WM), Deep gray matter (DGM), Trunk and Cerebellum. The results of the segmentations were visually assessed by two experts in pediatric neuroimaging.

## 3   Methods

A standard whole-brain 3D U-Net model [3,12] was implemented to predict the brain masks of 6 tissues plus background from T1-w images. The architecture of the network consists of 3 main parts: the contraction path, the bottleneck and the expansion path. The input and the output layer are for $256 \times 256 \times 256$ isotropic 3D images, resolution to which all input images are initially resampled. The adopted architecture, described below, has minor changes with respect to the literature to reduce the memory footprint and to fit the GPU used during the experiments reported in Sect. 4.

The contraction path consists of 4 blocks, each with two convolutional layers ($3 \times 3 \times 3$ kernel followed by ReLU) followed by MaxPooling ($2 \times 2 \times 2$ filter, stride $2 \times 2 \times 2$) for downsampling. The size of the downsampling over the blocks is $256 \rightarrow 128 \rightarrow 64 \rightarrow 32 \rightarrow 16$, while the application of convolutional layers produces an increasing number of feature maps over the blocks, $12 \rightarrow 24 \rightarrow 48 \rightarrow 96$. The bottleneck consists of 2 convolutional layers both of 192 filters ($3 \times 3 \times 3$ kernel then ReLU), followed by a dropout layer (dropout rate: 0.15) used to prevent overfitting. Similarly to the contraction path, the expansion path consists of 4 blocks, each with transposed convolution for upsampling, followed by concatenation with contraction features (skip connected) and two convolutions. The upsampling size over the blocks is the opposite of the downsampling, i.e. from 16 to 256. All convolutional layers have $3 \times 3 \times 3$ kernel then ReLU, that produce a decreasing number of feature maps from 192 to 12.

Multiclass classification (6 tissues and background), is obtained with a last layer of convolution with 7 $1 \times 1 \times 1$ filters, followed by a softmax activation.

## 4   Experiments

We qualitatively compared the segmentation pipelines of FSL, FreeSurfer, SPM, ANTs and the 3D U-Net on T1-weighted images from patients with agenesis of corpus callosum (ACC) and with complex distortions of brain anatomy, as described in Sect. 2.2. Different pipelines produced different sets of segmented tissues. To harmonize the results, we considered only 3 main tissues: gray matter (GM), white matter (WM) and the cerebrospinal fluid (CSF). These tissues are the ones of greater interest in most of the applications of brain tissue segmentation. Moreover, for the pipelines segmenting the deep gray matter (DGM), we labeled DGM as GM. The technical details of each pipeline are the following:

- **FSL v6** [7]: we used `fsl_anat`[3] with default parameter values.
- **FreeSurfer v6** [5]: we used `recon-all`[4] with default parameter values.
- **SPM12** [1]: we used default parameter values and default prior.
  **ANTs v2.2.0** [15]: we used `AntsCorticalThickness.sh` with default parameter values and the PTBP (pediatric) prior [2]. We considered only the steps till tissue segmentation.
- **3D U-Net.** The model was implemented with TensorFlow 1.8.0 [9] trained on T1-weighted images from the Normal Brains Datasets of $\approx 900$ images described in Sect. 2. We kept apart 90 randomly selected images for a sanity check, i.e., to assess that the trained model could reach state-of-the-art quality of segmentation on healthy subjects. The training (loss: cross-entropy, Adam optimization, learning rate: $10^{-4}$) was performed iteratively, one image at a time taken at random from the training set, looping over the whole set for 60 epochs.

All computations were performed on a dedicated workstation: 6 cores processor Intel(R) Xeon(R) CPU E5-1650 v4 3.60 GHz, 128 Gb RAM, GPU: NVIDIA GeForce GTX 1080TI 11 Gb RAM.

## 4.1 Results

Except for FreeSurfer (`recon-all`), all pipelines carried out all the required segmentations. FreeSurfer failed in all cases of severe anatomical distortion. Specifically, `recon-all` did not converge during either Talairach registration or skull stripping. SPM completed the segmentation task in all subjects. However, its confidence in the prior for the segmentation initialization and optimization leads to many major macroscopic errors. Given the strong limits on the length of this article, we do not illustrate and discuss the uninteresting results of FreeSurfer and SPM.

In Fig. 1, we show a paradigmatic set of axial slices segmented by FSL, ANTs and the 3D U-Net, from patients with ACC, i.e. from 4 of the 12 subjects described in Sect. 2.2. Similarly, in Fig. 2, we report paradigmatic axial slices segmented by those methods, from 4 of the subjects with complex cerebral distortions. For the segmentations of all methods, we re-labeled as CSF all the voxels inside the brain mask of each patient that were incorrectly segmented as background. In both figures in the last row, for each subject, we highlight a detail of the slice for one of the segmentation methods (indicated with a dashed square, above in the same column). Such details are discussed in Sect. 5.

Finally, in Table 1, we report the results of the sanity check, i.e. that the training process of the 3D U-Net on normal brains was successful. The numbers

---

[3] https://fsl.fmrib.ox.ac.uk/fsl/fslwiki/fsl_anat.
[4] https://surfer.nmr.mgh.harvard.edu/fswiki/recon-all.

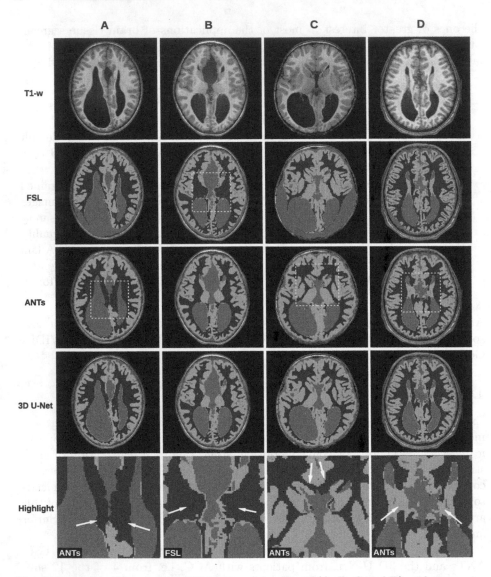

**Fig. 1.** First row: T1-weighted MR images of 4 subjects (A, B, C and D) with *agenesis of corpus callosum*. Below, the related tissue segmentations (GM in green, WM in blue and CSF in red) of the following pipelines: FSL (2nd row), ANTs (3rd row) and 3D U-Net (4th row). In the 5th row, for each subject, we show the enlarged view of one of the segmentations, indicated above with a dashed yellow square. White arrows point to the highlights discussed in Sect. 5. (Color figure online)

represent the average quality of segmentation (DSC, Dice similarity coefficient) obtained by the 3D U-Net for the reference segmentation of the 6 tissues of

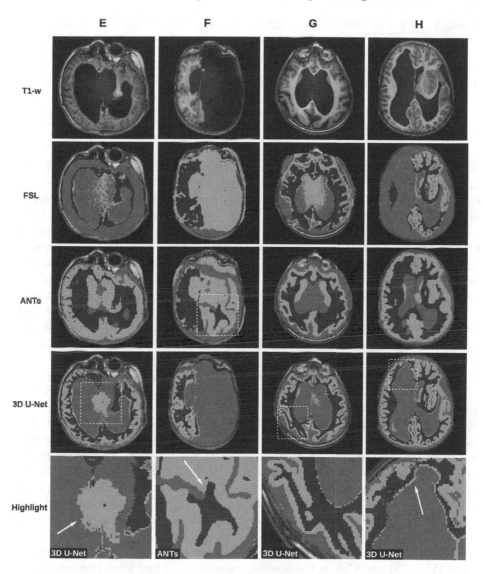

**Fig. 2.** First row: T1-weighted MR images of 4 subjects (E, F, G and H) with *complex cerebral distortions*. Below, the related tissue segmentations (GM in green, WM in blue and CSF in red) of the following pipelines: FSL (2nd row), ANTs (3rd row) and 3D U-Net (4th row). In the 5th row, for each subject, we show the enlarged view of one of the segmentations, indicated above with a dashed yellow square. White arrows point to the highlights discussed in Sect. 5. (Color figure online)

normal brains described in Sect. 2.3. These results are comparable to those in the state-of-the-art [4, 16].

**Table 1.** 3D U-Net: average Dice similarity coefficient (DSC) for segmentations of 6 tissues, plus grand average, on 90 normal brains, after 60 epochs of training.

| Metric | CSF | GM | WM | DGM | Trunk | Cereb | Grand Avg. |
|--------|-----|-----|-----|------|-------|-------|------------|
| DSC | $0.87 \pm 0.06$ | $0.95 \pm 0.04$ | $0.95 \pm 0.03$ | $0.93 \pm 0.02$ | $0.93 \pm 0.03$ | $0.96 \pm 0.02$ | $0.93 \pm 0.03$ |

## 5   Discussion

Figure 1 shows that FSL fails to segment GM and WM in cases of moderate and severe ventricular dilatation with thinning of the WM (case A, C and less evident in D). In one case (B) FSL also misses identifying the thalami as (deep) GM. ANTs performs better in identifying (deep) GM and the cortex at the convexity. However, case A and C show that it may fail in differentiate between GM and subcortical WM on the mesial surface of the hemispheres. This may be related to the prior used by that pipeline, which is based on the anatomy of normal subjects and not designed to recognize spatial reorganization of the cortex, especially in the midline, like in ACC cases. A similar error is in case C where a cortical component close to the head of the caudate is misclassified as WM. Finally in D, Probst bundles, which are abnormal WM tracts running parallel to the medial ventricular wall, are labelled as GM. In contrast, the 3D U-Net performs well in segmenting ACC. The most relevant error in these cases is at the interface between ventricles and WM: the 3D U-Net wrongly identifies a very thin layer of GM along the inner ventricular surface. This is probably related to partial volume effects.

Figure 2 shows that, in case of complex malformations and severe parenchymal distortion, FSL and ANTs are unreliable and incur in major macroscopic errors, as opposed to 3D U-Net which performs vastly better. In cases of severe ventricular dilatation and distortion (E and H), FSL fails to segment the cortex, which is wrongly labelled as CSF. In case F, the CSF collection that replaces the left hemisphere is misclassified as the cortex. In G, FSL fails to properly segment the pachygyric (i.e. with a reduced number of gyri) cortex. Finally, some intensity inhomogeneities in the deep ventricular CSF are misclassified as GM (E and G). With ANTs, which is based on priors, the pipeline is forced to segment WM, GM and CSF in the missing hemisphere (F) or when the anatomy is highly irregular. In all of these cases, the pipeline misplaces structures (E, G, H) or segment structures that are actually missing (F). The 3D U-Net outperforms FSL and ANTs in all cases (e.g. G), with few mistakes. The main issues are: i) the mislabeling of signal inhomogeneities in the deep CSF (E, same as FSL), and the segmentation of a subtle layer of GM at the border between lateral ventricles and WM (H, as done in ACC cases). Care must be used in evaluating CSF/WM interface in cases of brain malformations because, at this level, heterotopic GM nodule may occur.

## 5.1   Conclusions

In this work, we observe a much higher accuracy of the 3D U-Net when segmenting brains with different degrees of anatomical distortion, compared to well-established pipelines. This is surprising given that such cases were not used in the training phase. At the same time, the 3D U-Net can reproduce the high quality of segmentation of ANTs on normal brains. Clearly, the results on distorted brains are not perfect but still a valuable starting point for manual refinement by experts/neuroradiologists. In future work we plan to manually segment T1-w images of the distorted brains, to create a gold standard and to be able to quantify the quality of segmentation of the 3D U-Net and to use some of them during the training process of the network.

**Acknowledgment.** Data used in the preparation of this article were obtained from the C-MIND Data Repository created by the C-MIND study of Normal Brain Development. This is a multisite, longitudinal study of typically developing children from ages newborn through young adulthood conducted by Cincinnati Children's Hospital Medical Center and UCLA and supported by the National Institute of Child Health and Human Development (Contract #s HHSN275200900018C). A listing of the participating sites and a complete listing of the study investigators can be found at https:// research.cchmc.org/c-mind. This manuscript reflects the views of the authors and may not reflect the opinions or views of the NIH.

# References

1. Ashburner, J., Friston, K.J.: Voxel-based morphometry–the methods. NeuroImage **11**(6 Pt 1), 805–821 (2000). https://doi.org/10.1006/nimg.2000.0582
2. Avants, B., Tustison, N., Wang, D.J.: The Pediatric Template of Brain Perfusion (PTBP) (2015). https://doi.org/10.6084/m9.figshare.923555.v20
3. Çiçek, Ö., Abdulkadir, A., Lienkamp, S.S., Brox, T., Ronneberger, O.: 3D U-Net: learning dense volumetric segmentation from sparse annotation. In: Ourselin, S., Joskowicz, L., Sabuncu, M.R., Unal, G., Wells, W. (eds.) MICCAI 2016. LNCS, vol. 9901, pp. 424–432. Springer, Cham (2016). https://doi.org/10.1007/978-3-319-46723-8_49
4. Cullen, N.C., Avants, B.B.: Convolutional neural networks for rapid and simultaneous brain extraction and tissue segmentation. In: Spalletta, G., Piras, F., Gili, T. (eds.) Brain Morphometry. N, vol. 136, pp. 13–34. Springer, New York (2018). https://doi.org/10.1007/978-1-4939-7647-8_2
5. Dale, A.M., Fischl, B., Sereno, M.I.: Cortical surface-based analysis I. Segmentation and surface reconstruction. NeuroImage **9**(2), 179–194 (1999). https://doi.org/10.1006/nimg.1998.0395
6. Evans, A.C.: The NIH MRI study of normal brain development. NeuroImage **30**(1), 184–202 (2006). https://doi.org/10.1016/j.neuroimage.2005.09.068
7. Jenkinson, M., Beckmann, C.F., Behrens, T.E.J., Woolrich, M.W., Smith, S.M.: FSL. NeuroImage **62**(2), 782–790 (2012). https://doi.org/10.1016/j.neuroimage.2011.09.015
8. Ledig, C., et al.: Robust whole-brain segmentation: application to traumatic brain injury. Med. Image Anal. **21**(1), 40–58 (2015). https://doi.org/10.1016/j.media.2014.12.003

9. Abadi, M., et al.: TensorFlow: Large-Scale Machine Learning on Heterogeneous Systems (2015)
10. Moeskops, P., Viergever, M.A., Mendrik, A.M., de Vries, L.S., Benders, M.J.N.L., Išgum, I.: Automatic segmentation of MR brain images with a convolutional neural network. IEEE Trans. Med. Imaging **35**(5), 1252–1261 (2016). https://doi.org/10.1109/TMI.2016.2548501
11. Rajchl, M., Pawlowski, N., Rueckert, D., Matthews, P.M., Glocker, B.: NeuroNet: Fast and Robust Reproduction of Multiple Brain Image Segmentation Pipelines (2018)
12. Ronneberger, O., Fischer, P., Brox, T.: U-Net: convolutional networks for biomedical image segmentation. In: Navab, N., Hornegger, J., Wells, W.M., Frangi, A.F. (eds.) MICCAI 2015. LNCS, vol. 9351, pp. 234–241. Springer, Cham (2015). https://doi.org/10.1007/978-3-319-24574-4_28
13. Roy, S., et al.: Subject-specific sparse dictionary learning for atlas-based brain MRI segmentation. IEEE J. Biomed. Health Inf. **19**(5), 1598–1609 (2015). https://doi.org/10.1109/JBHI.2015.2439242
14. Shao, M., et al.: Brain ventricle parcellation using a deep neural network: application to patients with ventriculomegaly. NeuroImage Clin. **23**, 101871 (2019). https://doi.org/10.1016/j.nicl.2019.101871
15. Tustison, N.J., et al.: Large-scale evaluation of ANTs and FreeSurfer cortical thickness measurements. NeuroImage **99**, 166–179 (2014). https://doi.org/10.1016/j.neuroimage.2014.05.044
16. Yogananda, C.G.B., Wagner, B.C., Murugesan, G.K., Madhuranthakam, A., Maldjian, J.A.: A deep learning pipeline for automatic skull stripping and brain segmentation. In: 2019 IEEE 16th International Symposium on Biomedical Imaging (ISBI 2019), pp. 727–731 (2019). https://doi.org/10.1109/ISBI.2019.8759465, iSSN: 1945-7928

# Bidirectional Modeling and Analysis of Brain Aging with Normalizing Flows

Matthias Wilms[1,2,3(✉)], Jordan J. Bannister[1,2,3], Pauline Mouches[1,2,3],
M. Ethan MacDonald[1,2], Deepthi Rajashekar[1,2,3], Sönke Langner[4],
and Nils D. Forkert[1,2,3]

[1] Department of Radiology, University of Calgary, Calgary, Canada
`matthias.wilms@ucalgary.ca`
[2] Hotchkiss Brain Institute, University of Calgary, Calgary, Canada
[3] Alberta Children's Hospital Research Institute, University of Calgary,
Calgary, Canada
[4] Institute for Diagnostic and Interventional Radiology, Pediatric and
Neuroradiology, University Medical Center Rostock, Rostock, Germany

**Abstract.** Brain aging is a widely studied longitudinal process throughout which the brain undergoes considerable morphological changes and
various machine learning approaches have been proposed to analyze it.
Within this context, brain age prediction from structural MR images and
age-specific brain morphology template generation are two problems that
have attracted much attention. While most approaches tackle these tasks
independently, we assume that they are inverse directions of the same
functional bidirectional relationship between a brain's morphology and
an age variable. In this paper, we propose to model this relationship with
a single conditional normalizing flow, which unifies brain age prediction
and age-conditioned generative modeling in a novel way. In an initial
evaluation of this idea, we show that our normalizing flow brain aging
model can accurately predict brain age while also being able to generate
age-specific brain morphology templates that realistically represent the
typical aging trend in a healthy population. This work is a step towards
unified modeling of functional relationships between 3D brain morphology and clinical variables of interest with powerful normalizing flows.

**Keywords:** Brain aging · Normalizing flows · Conditional templates

## 1 Introduction

Many machine learning (ML) tasks in neuroimaging aim at modeling and exploring complex functional relationships between brain morphology derived from
structural MR images and clinically relevant scores and variables of interest [17].

**Electronic supplementary material** The online version of this chapter (https://
doi.org/10.1007/978-3-030-66843-3_3) contains supplementary material, which is available to authorized users.

S. M. Kia et al. (Eds.): MLCN 2020/RNO-AI 2020, LNCS 12449, pp. 23–33, 2020.
https://doi.org/10.1007/978-3-030-66843-3_3

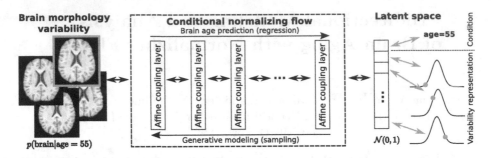

**Fig. 1.** Graphical overview of the proposed modeling approach based on a conditional normalizing flow composed of affine coupling layers. The bidirectional flow maps brain morphology variability to a structured latent space. It solves the brain age prediction problem (left to right) and can be utilized to sample from the distribution of brain morphology conditioned on age (right to left). The first component of the latent space encodes brain age while all other dimensions represent variability. See text for details.

In this context, the aging process of the brain throughout which it undergoes considerable morphological changes is a widely studied example. Many prediction models have been proposed to estimate a brain's biological age from a patient's structural MRI data (see overview in [6]). The potential difference between a patient's predicted biological brain age and the true chronological age is an early indicator for neurodegenerative disorders like Alzheimer's disease [7].

In contrast, modeling the inverse direction of this classical regression task allows the study of morphological changes associated with a certain age on a population level, which can be useful to assist basic research [7], or for patient-specific brain aging simulation [20,22]. This generative modeling problem is closely related to the numerous atlas (a.k.a. template) building approaches that aim at computing a model of a population's average anatomy conditioned on age [13,18]. Several recent papers model the joint distribution of brain morphology and age with deep learning (DL) techniques such as variants of Generative Adversarial Networks (GANs), Variational Autoencoders (VAEs), or related concepts [8,20,22,25]. However, most of them only focus on single slices or small 3D regions of the brain due to the high computational costs of these DL techniques.

Despite the volumes of literature available on brain age prediction and age-conditioned generative brain modeling, the fact that these tasks constitute inverse directions of the same bidirectional functional relationship between age and morphology is usually ignored, and independent or loosely coupled models for each problem are created. A notable exception is [25], where a VAE is equipped with a linear regression model that maps the VAE's latent space representation of a brain to its age. This component allows the use of the VAE's encoder for age prediction and the decoder can generate age-conditioned brains. However, this extension still does not guarantee that the encoder and the decoder are inverses of each other, which potentially leads to inconsistencies. Additionally, training a VAE is usually difficult due to intractable likelihoods and posterior collapse.

In this work, we propose to model the bidirectional functional relationship between brain morphology and brain age in a unified, consistent way using conditional normalizing flows. Normalizing flows (NFs) [14] learn invertible functions between a complex probability distribution of interest and a simple base distribution. In contrast to GANs and VAEs, they can be trained directly via maximum likelihood estimation, they do not suffer from posterior collapse, sampling is very efficient, and both directions are the exact inverses of each other [14].

Our bidirectional NF-based brain aging model is based on ideas about unifying regression and generative modeling using NFs described in [1]. Our model (1) learns the distribution of brain morphology conditioned on age of a population, which can be sampled to generate age-conditioned brain templates, and (2) is able to predict a brain's biological age given its structural MR image (see Fig. 1). Moreover, we propose pre-processing steps to encode morphological variability based on diffeomorphic transformations that allow us to directly handle whole 3D images. To our knowledge, this is the first conditional NF for bidirectional modeling and analysis of brain aging directly utilizing 3D structural MRI data.

## 2   Problem Formulation and Pre-processing

We will first introduce our notation and the modeling problem, then two pre-processing steps are described in Sect. 2.1 and Sect. 2.2. These steps help us to efficiently model the brain aging problem described in Sect. 3 with a NF.

For our analysis, we assume a training population $\{(I_i, a_i)\}_{i=1}^{n_{\mathrm{pop}}}$ of $n_{\mathrm{pop}}$ healthy subjects[1] to be given. Each tuple $(I_i, a_i)$ consists of a subject's 3D structural MRI brain scan $I_i : \mathbb{R}^3 \to \mathbb{R}$ and the associated chronological brain age $a_i \in \mathbb{R}$. The goal of this work is to train a combined regression and generative NF model that is able (1) to estimate the brain age $a \in \mathbb{R}$ of a new subject with brain scan $I : \mathbb{R}^3 \to \mathbb{R}$, and (2) to accurately approximate the distribution of plausible brain morphology conditioned on age.

### 2.1   Reference Space and Deformation-Based Analysis

Instead of directly using the structural MR images, our method follows the classical concepts from deformation-based morphometry [4] to represent morphological differences with respect to a common template via non-linear, diffeomorphic transformations. A deformation-based approach is appropriate here as aging mostly results in shape changes of various brain structures (e.g., cerebral atrophy) and it allows our NF to directly focus on shape differences for regression and we avoid typical problems of generative models (e.g., blurry images).

Following standard practice in deformation-based brain aging modeling [18], a template image $\overline{I} : \mathbb{R}^3 \to \mathbb{R}$ with a reference brain morphology serves as a reference space for all further computations. The template can either be computed specifically for the training population or a standard template can also be used.

---

[1] We assume that for healthy subjects, chronological and biological brain age are equal.

We map all the training images non-linearly to this template via diffeomorphic image registration resulting in $n_{pop}$ spatial transformations $\{\varphi_i : \mathbb{R}^3 \to \mathbb{R}^3\}_{i=1}^{n_{pop}}$, which encode the morphological differences between the template and each subject. Here, each diffeomorphic transformation $\varphi_i = \exp(v_i)$ is parameterized via a stationary velocity field $v_i : \mathbb{R}^3 \to \mathbb{R}^3$ where $\exp(\cdot)$ denotes the group exponential map from the Log-Euclidean framework (see [3] for details).

## 2.2  Dimensionality Reduction via PCA on Diffeomorphisms

Directly utilizing the previously computed diffeomorphic transformations for 3D NF-based brain aging modeling is challenging due to the high dimensionality of the data (MRI brain scans usually consist of several millions of voxels $n_{vox}$), which is usually also magnitudes larger than the number of training samples $n_{pop}$. However, it is safe to assume that the transformations, which are vector fields, contain redundant information and noise allowing for dimensionality reduction. Following previous results on brain modeling [12,24], we, therefore, assume that a low dimensional structure of the space of brain shapes exists. More specifically, we assume that all plausible transformations needed for aging modeling lie within a $n_{sub}$-dimensional affine subspace of maximum data variation $\mathcal{A} = \{\overline{\mathbf{v}} + \mathbf{q} \mid \mathbf{q} \in \text{span}(\mathbf{Q})\}$ with $n_{sub} < n_{pop}$ of the velocity fields of the training data. Here, $\overline{\mathbf{v}} \in \mathbb{R}^{3n_{vox}}$ denotes the vectorized mean velocity field of the training data and $\mathbf{Q} \in \mathbb{R}^{3n_{vox} \times n_{sub}}$ is an orthonormal column matrix of the first $n_{sub}$ principal components resulting from a principal components analysis (PCA) of the velocity fields $\{v_i\}_{i=1}^{n_{pop}}$ [3,10]. Performing statistics directly on velocity fields will preserve diffeomorphisms and the projection matrix $\mathbf{Q}$ (with pseudoinverse $\mathbf{Q}^T$) can be directly integrated into the NF model.

# 3  Normalizing Flow Model for Brain Aging Analysis

Applying the pre-processing steps detailed in Sect. 2 to the training data results in a set $\{(\mathbf{v}_i, a_i)\}_{i=1}^{n_{pop}}$. Here, $\mathbf{v}_i \in \mathbb{R}^{n_{sub}}$ denotes a projected velocity field $v_i$ in coordinates of subspace $\mathcal{A}$. Given the training tuples, our goals are two-fold: (1) Learn a function $f(\cdot; \theta)$ with parameters $\theta$ that takes a new morphology-encoding velocity field representation $\mathbf{v} \in \mathbb{R}^{n_{sub}}$ and predicts its age $a \in \mathbb{R}$: $a = f(\mathbf{v}; \theta)$. (2) Train a generative model to efficiently sample velocity fields from the conditional distribution of brain morphologies conditioned on age: $p(\mathbf{v}|a)$.

## 3.1  Bidirectional Conditional Modeling

The innovative idea of this work is to solve both problems with a unified, bidirectional conditional NF model. In general, a NF represents a complex, bijective function between two sets as a chain of simpler sub-functions [14]. At first, the bijective property seems to be incompatible with our setup as we are mapping from $\mathbb{R}^{n_{sub}}$ (velocity fields) to $\mathbb{R}$ (age). However, to model $p(\mathbf{v}|a)$ we also need to encode the (inter-subject) morphological variability associated with brains at the same age. We therefore follow [1] to combine regression and generative modeling with an NF that is conditioned on the regression target.

Our conditional NF model represents a bijective function $f(\cdot;\theta) : \mathbb{R}^{n_{\mathrm{sub}}} \to \mathbb{R}^{n_{\mathrm{sub}}}$ that maps a $n_{\mathrm{sub}}$-dimensional velocity field to a latent space of the same size. Aiming for a structured latent space, we define that one dimension of the latent space accounts for the age $a$ of the input $\mathbf{v}$, solving the prediction task while conditioning the flow. All other dimensions store the age-unrelated information $\mathbf{z} \in \mathbb{R}^{n_{\mathrm{sub}}-1}$ needed to reconstruct the input. In the following, sub-parts of $f(\cdot;\theta)$ mapping $\mathbf{v}$ to $a$ will be named $f_a(\cdot;\theta)$.

Imposing a simple prior on $\mathbf{z} \sim p(\mathbf{z})$ (e.g., Gaussian distribution with diagonal covariance) and assuming that the distribution $p(f_a(\mathbf{v};\theta)|a)$ associated with the age prediction part can be modeled easily and independently (e.g., age-independent Gaussian residuals for squared error) allow us to relate $p(\mathbf{v}|a)$ and the latent space via $f(\cdot;\theta)$ with the change of variables theorem [1,23]:

$$p(\mathbf{v}|a) = p(\mathbf{z})p(f_a(\mathbf{v};\theta)|a)|J|^{-1} \text{ with } J = \det\left(\frac{\partial f^{-1}([a,\mathbf{z}];\theta)}{\partial[a,\mathbf{z}]}\right). \quad (1)$$

Here, $f^{-1}(\cdot;\theta)$ denotes the inverse of $f(\cdot;\theta)$ and $J$ represents the associated Jacobian determinant. Given an invertible function $f(\cdot;\theta)$, samples from the simple priors can be transformed to approximate $p(\mathbf{v}|a)$.

## 3.2 Normalizing Flow Architecture and Training

The challenge resulting from Eq. (1) is to find an easily invertible function $f(\cdot;\theta)$ with a tractable Jacobian. In NFs, this is done by first defining $[a,\mathbf{z}] = f(\mathbf{v};\theta) = f_{n_{\mathrm{lay}}} \circ \cdots \circ f_i \circ \cdots \circ f_1(\mathbf{v})$ as a chain of $n_{\mathrm{lay}}$ simpler, invertible sub-functions $f_i(\cdot,\theta_i)$ (also named coupling layers). Our NF model consists of affine coupling layers [1,9], which are a common choice in previous NF research due to their flexibility and favourable computational properties [14].

Let $\mathbf{u} = [\mathbf{u}_1, \mathbf{u}_2] \in \mathbb{R}^{n_{\mathrm{sub}}}$ and $\mathbf{w} = [\mathbf{w}_1, \mathbf{w}_2] \in \mathbb{R}^{n_{\mathrm{sub}}}$ denote input and output vectors of an affine coupling layer, where $\mathbf{u}_1$ and $\mathbf{w}_1$ represent the first $n_{\mathrm{sub}}/2$ dimensions while $\mathbf{u}_2$ and $\mathbf{w}_2$ cover the second half. Then, an affine coupling layer $\mathbf{w} = f_i(\mathbf{u},\theta_i)$, with $\mathbf{u} = [\mathbf{u}_1,\mathbf{u}_2] \in \mathbb{R}^{n_{\mathrm{sub}}}$ and $\mathbf{w} = [\mathbf{w}_1,\mathbf{w}_2] \in \mathbb{R}^{n_{\mathrm{sub}}}$, defines an element-wise affine transformation parameterized by $\mathbf{u}_2$ that maps $\mathbf{u}_1$ to $\mathbf{w}_1$ [9]:

$$\mathbf{w}_1 = \exp\big(s(\mathbf{u}_2,\theta_i)\big) \odot \mathbf{u}_1 + t(\mathbf{u}_2,\theta_i) \quad \text{and} \quad \mathbf{w}_2 = \mathbf{u}_2 .$$

Here, the scaling function $s(\cdot,\theta_i)$ and the translation function $t(\cdot,\theta_i)$ can be arbitrarily complex neural networks with weights $\theta_i$, which allows the NF to express complex, non-linear transformations. The inverse $\mathbf{u} = f_i^{-1}(\mathbf{w},\theta_i)$ of such a layer can be computed without having to invert $s(\cdot,\theta_i)$ or $t(\cdot,\theta_i)$ via

$$\mathbf{u}_1 = \exp\big(-s(\mathbf{w}_2,\theta_i)\big) \odot \big(\mathbf{w}_1 - t(\mathbf{w}_2,\theta_i)\big) \quad \text{and} \quad \mathbf{u}_2 = \mathbf{w}_2 .$$

The Jacobian of an affine coupling layer is triangular and easy to compute (see [9] for details). In our model, we choose $s(\cdot,\theta_i)$ and $t(\cdot,\theta_i)$ to be fully-connected neural networks composed of $n_{\mathrm{hid}}$ hidden layers and ReLU activations with shared weights $\theta_i$. As each coupling layer only affects half of the inputs, permuting or mixing them after each layer is crucial to allow for interaction between the dimensions. To do so, we simply reverse the order of the inputs after every second layer to make sure that all dimensions are able to contribute. The other coupling layers are linked by random, fixed orthogonal transformations that mix the data in an easily invertible way as proposed in [2].

The parameters $\theta = \{\theta_1, \ldots, \theta_{n_{lay}}\}$ (weights of all $n_{lay}$ scaling/translation functions) of our conditional NF model $f(\cdot; \theta)$ can be directly estimated using maximum likelihood training based on Eq. (1). We choose a multivariate Gaussian distribution with diagonal unit covariance as a prior for $p(\mathbf{z})$ and also assume that the age prediction error $\|f_a(\mathbf{v}; \theta) - a_{gt}\|_2$ with respect to ground-truth value $a_{gt}$ follows an univariate Gaussian distribution with small, user-defined covariance $\sigma^2$. This results in a negative log-likelihood loss term [2,15,23]

$$\mathcal{L}(a, \mathbf{z}) = \frac{1}{2}\left(\sigma^{-2}\|a - a_{gt}\|_2^2 + \|\mathbf{z}\|_2^2\right) - \log|J| \ . \tag{2}$$

It is worth noting that this loss will only focus on correctly mapping velocity fields to the structured latent space (unidirectional training). By representing a bijective function, no two-way training is required to fit the bidirectional NF. Furthermore, replacing age $a$ with a vector would allow to build a conditional model that incorporates factors beyond age.

## 4   Experiments and Results

In our evaluation, we focus on showing that the conditional NF model for brain aging analysis derived in Sect. 2 and Sect. 3 is able to (1) predict the biological brain age of previously unseen structural MR images, while (2) also serving as an age-conditioned, continuous generative model of brain morphology. To illustrate the second aspect, we use our NF model to generate conditional templates for different ages as, for example, also done in [8].

**Data:** Two databases of T1-weighted brain MR images of 3730 healthy adults for which age data is available are used for our evaluation: (1) 3167 scans (age range: 20–90 years) from the Study of Health in Pomerania (SHIP) [19] for training (2684 randomly chosen subjects) and testing (483 subjects not used for training); (2) 563 scans (age range: 20–86 years) from the publicly available IXI database[2] serve as an independent validation set.

For pre-processing (see Sect. 2), we start by computing a SHIP-specific brain template using all 49 scans of subjects younger than 26 years and the ANTs toolkit [5]. We use young subjects here because they have little to no atrophy and a young template seems to be a reasonable starting point when the goal is to analyze and compare different aging effects/trajectories with respect to a single template. This 3D template ($166 \times 209 \times 187$ voxels; isotropic 1 mm spacing)

---

[2] https://brain-development.org/ixi-dataset/.

defines the reference space for our deformation-based modeling approach (see Sect. 2.1). Subsequently, all 3730 scans are mapped to this brain template via non-linear diffeomorphic transformations (parameterized by stationary velocity fields) between the template brain and all subjects, which are computed using ITK's *VariationalRegistration* module [11,21].

The velocity fields of the SHIP data are then used to estimate the affine subspace of maximum data variation via PCA to reduce the dimensionality of the modeling problem (see Sec. 2.2). We choose $n_{sub} = 500$ for our subspace, which covers $\approx 97\%$ of the variability of the training data.

**Experiments:** Using the 2684 SHIP training subjects, we first train a conditional NF model as described in Sect. 3.2 on a NVIDIA Quadro P4000 GPU with 8 GB RAM and a TensorFlow 2.2 implementation. Our architecture consists of $n_{lay} = 16$ affine coupling layers and each scaling/translation function is represented by a fully-connected neural network with $n_{hid} = 2$ hidden layers of width 32. Given an input size of $n_{sub} = 500$, this setup results in $\approx 400k$ trainable parameters $\theta$. Our batch size was selected to be equal to the total number of training samples and we optimize the loss function defined in Eq. (2) with $\sigma = 0.14$ for 20k epochs with an AdamW optimizer and a learning rate/weight decay of $10^{-4}/10^{-5}$. All parameters were chosen heuristically, but we found the results to be relatively insensitive to changes in $\sigma$ and $n_{lay}$.

**Table 1.** Mean absolute errors (MAEs) in years between the known chronological age and the predicted age obtained for the two approaches (MLR model & NF model) when the trained models are applied to the SHIP test data subjects and all IXI subjects. Averaged results are reported for all subjects and six different age groups. See suppl. material for information about the number of subjects per age group.

| Model/ Age range | <40 | 40–50 | 50–60 | 60–70 | 70–80 | >80 | All |
|---|---|---|---|---|---|---|---|
| SHIP data (468 test subjects) | | | | | | | |
| MLR | 5.34 | 4.79 | 5.33 | 4.35 | 6.13 | 7.53 | **5.12** |
| NF (ours) | 5.35 | 4.67 | 5.10 | 4.37 | 6.29 | 6.99 | **5.05** |
| IXI data (563 test subjects) | | | | | | | |
| MLR | 6.54 | 5.44 | 6.19 | 7.84 | 7.71 | 9.86 | **6.73** |
| NF (ours) | 8.47 | 5.37 | 4.92 | 7.11 | 6.57 | 10.17 | **6.93** |

The trained conditional NF model is then first used to predict the brain age of the SHIP test data subjects and all IXI subjects. Prediction accuracy is assessed by computing the mean absolute error (MAE) between the known chronological age and the predicted age. For comparison, we also train and evaluate the MAE of a multivariate linear regression (MLR) model on the same data to predict brain age from low-dimensional velocity field representations. Here, it is important to note that this MLR model also implicitly represents a non-linear map between brain morphology and age due to the non-linear relationship between deformation and velocity fields (group exponential map; see Sect. 2.2 and [3]).

Our conditional NF also provides an age-continuous generative model of brain aging. We show its capabilities by generating age-specific templates of the modeled population for different age values. Here, we assume that the conditional expectation $\mathbb{E}[\mathbf{v}|a]$ is an appropriate morphology template for a given age $a$ and compute velocity vectors $\mathbf{v}$ for ages $a = \{40, 50, 60, 70, 80, 90\}$ via Monte-Carlo approximation with 150k random samples. This is done by fixing the age component of the latent space and sampling from the NF's prior for the variability part. The vectors are then mapped back to the high-dimensional space of velocity fields using $\mathbf{Q}^T$ (see Sect. 2.2) to obtain the associated diffeomorphic transformations. These transformations are then applied to the SHIP-specific brain template to generate structural MR images for the age-conditioned morphology templates.

**Results:** The evaluation results are summarized in Table 1 and Fig. 2. Our NF model achieves an overall MAE of 5.05 years for the SHIP data and a MAE of 6.93 years for the IXI data, respectively. Both results are comparable to the overall accuracy of the MLR model (insignificant differences; paired t-test with $p = 0.79/p = 0.13$). However, their performance differs for certain age groups. Interestingly, for the IXI data, which is known to be a challenging dataset due to its variability [16], the NF clearly outperforms the MLR model for subjects

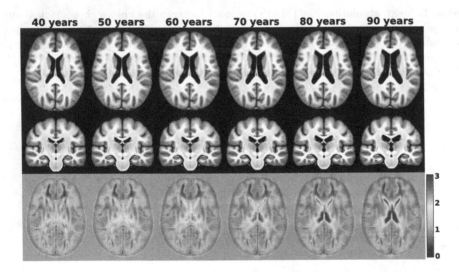

**Fig. 2.** Selected slices of age-specific morphology templates generated using our NF model for different ages. Last row: Corresponding axial slices of the Jacobian determinants for the generated transformations with respect to the (young) reference template, which clearly show the increase in ventricle size (values > 1) and the shrinking trend in other areas (values < 1).

between 50 and 80 years. We believe that this finding indicates that our NF model is able to better capture the general non-linear trend of the aging process.

The conditional templates for different ages displayed in Fig. 2 illustrate that our NF model is able to capture the typical trend of healthy brain aging. For example, the total ventricle volume increases by a factor of 2.02 between age 40 and age 90, while the total putamen volume decreases by a factor of 0.87. Volumes changes were quantified based on segmentations propagated from the template. Furthermore, the general shape characteristics of the different templates are stable across the age range, which indicates that the NF disentangles aging and non-aging factors (see also Fig. 1 of the suppl. material).

## 5   Conclusion

In this paper, we propose a new method to model bidirectional functional relationships between 3D brain morphology and brain age in a unified way using conditional normalizing flows. In an initial evaluation, we showed that our unified model can accurately predict biological brain age while also being able to generate age-conditioned brain templates. Based on the evaluation results, our future work will primarily focus on obtaining more training data and improving our architecture to obtain even more accurate age prediction results. We also plan to compare its performance to different prediction and generative modeling approaches from the literature and to condition the model on additional factors beyond age.

**Acknowledgement.** This work was supported by the University of Calgary's Eyes High postdoctoral scholarship program and the River Fund at Calgary Foundation.

## References

1. Ardizzone, L., Kruse, J., Rother, C., Köthe, U.: Analyzing inverse problems with invertible neural networks. In: 7th International Conference on Learning Representations - ICLR 2019 (2019)
2. Ardizzone, L., Lüth, C., Kruse, J., Rother, C., Köthe, U.: Guided image generation with conditional invertible neural networks. arXiv preprint arXiv:1907.02392 (2019)
3. Arsigny, V., Commowick, O., Pennec, X., Ayache, N.: A log-euclidean framework for statistics on diffeomorphisms. In: Larsen, R., Nielsen, M., Sporring, J. (eds.) Medical Image Computing and Computer-Assisted Intervention - MICCAI 2006. LNCS, vol. 4190, pp. 924–931. Springer, Berlin Heidelberg (2006). https://doi.org/10.1007/11866565_113
4. Ashburner, J., Hutton, C., Frackowiak, R., Johnsrude, I., Price, C., Friston, K.: Identifying global anatomical differences: Deformation-based morphometry. Hum. Brain Mapp. 6(5–6), 348–357 (1998)
5. Avants, B.B., Tustison, N.J., Song, G., Cook, P.A., Klein, A., Gee, J.C.: A reproducible evaluation of ants similarity metric performance in brain image registration. NeuroImage 54(3), 2033–2044 (2011)

6. Cole, J.H., Franke, K., Cherbuin, N.: Quantification of the biological age of the brain using neuroimaging. In: Moskalev, A. (ed.) Biomarkers of Human Aging. HAL, vol. 10, pp. 293–328. Springer, Cham (2019). https://doi.org/10.1007/978-3-030-24970-0_19

7. Cole, J.H., Marioni, R.E., Harris, S.E., Deary, I.J.: Brain age and other bodily 'ages': implications for neuropsychiatry. Molecular Psychiatry **24**, 266–281 (2019)

8. Dalca, A., Rakic, M., Guttag, J., Sabuncu, M.: Learning conditional deformable templates with convolutional networks. Adv. Neural Inf. Process. Syst. **32**, 806–818 (2019)

9. Dinh, L., Sohl-Dickstein, J., Bengio, S.: Density estimation using real NVP. In: 5th International Conference on Learning Representations - ICLR 2017 (2017)

10. Ehrhardt, J., Werner, R., Schmidt-Richberg, A., Handels, H.: A statistical shape and motion model for the prediction of respiratory lung motion. In: Dawant, B.M., Haynor, D.R. (eds.) SPIE Medical Imaging 2010: Image Processing. Proc SPIE, Orlando, USA, vol. 7623, pp. 531–539 (2010)

11. Ehrhardt, J., Schmidt-Richberg, A., Werner, R., Handels, H.: Variational registration - a flexible open-source itk toolbox for nonrigid image registration. Bildverarbeitung für die Medizin **2015**, 209–214 (2015)

12. Gerber, S., Tasdizen, T., Fletcher, P.T., Joshi, S., Whitaker, R.: Manifold modeling for brain population analysis. Med. Image Anal. **14**(5), 643–653 (2010)

13. Huizinga, W., Poot, D., Vernooij, M., Roshchupkin, G., Bron, E., Ikram, M., Rueckert, D., Niessen, W., Klein, S.: A spatio-temporal reference model of the aging brain. NeuroImage **169**, 11–22 (2018)

14. Kobyzev, I., Prince, S., Brubaker, M.: Normalizing flows: an introduction and review of current methods. IEEE Trans. Pattern Anal. Mach. Intell., 1 (2020)

15. Kruse, J., Ardizzone, L., Rother, C., Köthe, U.: Benchmarking invertible architectures on inverse problems. In: Workshop on Invertible Neural Networks and Normalizing Flows, International Conference on Machine Learning 2019 (2019)

16. MacDonald, M.E., Williams, R.J., Forkert, N.D., Berman, A.J.L., McCreary, C.R., Frayne, R., Pike, G.B.: Interdatabase variability in cortical thickness measurements. Cerebral Cortex **29**(8), 3282–3293 (2018)

17. Mateos-Pérez, J.M., Dadar, M., Lacalle-Aurioles, M., Iturria-Medina, Y., Zeighami, Y., Evans, A.C.: Structural neuroimaging as clinical predictor: a review of machine learning applications. NeuroImage Clin. **20**, 506–522 (2018)

18. Sivera, R., Delingette, H., Lorenzi, M., Pennec, X., Ayache, N.: A model of brain morphological changes related to aging and alzheimer's disease from cross-sectional assessments. NeuroImage **198**, 255–270 (2019)

19. Völzke, H., et al.: Cohort profile: the study of health in pomerania. Int. J. Epidemiol. **40**(2), 294–307 (2011)

20. Wegmayr, V., Hörold, M., Buhmann, J.M.: Generative aging of brain MR-images and prediction of alzheimer progression. In: Fink, G.A., Frintrop, S., Jiang, X. (eds.) German Conference on Pattern Recognition - GCPR 2019. LNCS, vol. 11824, pp. 247–260. Springer, Cham (2019). https://doi.org/10.1007/978-3-030-33676-9_17

21. Werner, R., Schmidt-Richberg, A., Handels, H., Ehrhardt, J.: Estimation of lung motion fields in 4D CT data by variational non-linear intensity-based registration: a comparison and evaluation study. Phys. Med. Biol. **59**(15), 4247–4260 (2014)

22. Xia, T., Chartsias, A., Tsaftaris, S.A.: Consistent brain ageing synthesis. In: Shen, D., et al. (eds.) Medical Image Computing and Computer Assisted Intervention - MICCAI 2019. LNCS, vol. 11767, pp. 750–758. Springer, Cham (2019). https://doi.org/10.1007/978-3-030-32251-9_82

23. Xiao, Z., Yan, Q., Amit, Y.: A method to model conditional distributions with normalizing flows. arXiv preprint arXiv:1911.02052 (2019)
24. Zhang, M., Wells, W.M., Golland, P.: Probabilistic modeling of anatomical variability using a low dimensional parameterization of diffeomorphisms. Med. Image Anal. **41**, 55–62 (2017)
25. Zhao, Q., Adeli, E., Honnorat, N., Leng, T., Pohl, K.M.: Variational autoencoder for regression: application to brain aging analysis. Medical Image Computing and Computer Assisted Intervention - MICCAI 2019. LNCS, vol. 11765, pp. 823–831. Springer, Cham (2019). https://doi.org/10.1007/978-3-030-32245-8_91

# A Multi-task Deep Learning Framework to Localize the Eloquent Cortex in Brain Tumor Patients Using Dynamic Functional Connectivity

Naresh Nandakumar[1](✉), Niharika Shimona D'Souza[1], Komal Manzoor[2],
Jay J. Pillai[2], Sachin K. Gujar[2], Haris I. Sair[2], and Archana Venkataraman[1]

[1] Department of Electrical and Computer Engineering, Johns Hopkins University,
Baltimore, USA
nnandak1@jhu.edu
[2] Department of Neuroradiology, Johns Hopkins School of Medicine, Baltimore, USA

**Abstract.** We present a novel deep learning framework that uses dynamic functional connectivity to simultaneously localize the language and motor areas of the eloquent cortex in brain tumor patients. Our method leverages convolutional layers to extract graph-based features from the dynamic connectivity matrices and a long-short term memory (LSTM) attention network to weight the relevant time points during classification. The final stage of our model employs multi-task learning to identify different eloquent subsystems. Our unique training strategy finds a shared representation between the cognitive networks of interest, which enables us to handle missing patient data. We evaluate our method on resting-state fMRI data from 56 brain tumor patients while using task fMRI activations as surrogate ground-truth labels for training and testing. Our model achieves higher localization accuracies than conventional deep learning approaches and can identify bilateral language areas even when trained on left-hemisphere lateralized cases. Hence, our method may ultimately be useful for preoperative mapping in tumor patients.

## 1 Introduction

The eloquent cortex consists of regions in the brain that are responsible for language comprehension, speech, and motor function. Identifying and subsequently avoiding these areas during a neurosurgery is crucial for improving recovery and postoperative quality of life. However, localizing these networks is challenging due to the varying anatomical boundaries of the eloquent cortex across people [1,2]. The language network has especially high interindividual variability because it can appear on one or both hemispheres [3]. The gold standard for preoperative functional mapping of eloquent areas is intraoperative electrocortical stimulation (ECS) of the cerebral cortex during surgery [4,5]. While reliable, ECS is highly invasive and requires the patient to be awake and responsive during surgery.

© Springer Nature Switzerland AG 2020
S. M. Kia et al. (Eds.): MLCN 2020/RNO-AI 2020, LNCS 12449, pp. 34–44, 2020.
https://doi.org/10.1007/978-3-030-66843-3_4

For these reasons, task-fMRI (t-fMRI) is becoming increasingly popular as a noninvasive alternative to ECS. Typically, activation maps derived from t-fMRI are inspected by an expert to determine the regions in the brain that are recruited during the experimental condition. However, t-fMRI can be unreliable for certain populations, like children and the cognitively disabled, due to their inability to complete the paradigm [6,7]. In contrast to t-fMRI, resting-state fMRI (rs-fMRI) captures spontaneous fluctuations in the brain when the subject is lying passively in the scanner. Unlike t-fMRI paradigms, which are designed to activate a single area, correlations in the rs-fMRI data can be used to identify multiple cognitive systems [8]. Recent work has moved towards using rs-fMRI for presurgical mapping to avoid the above issues associated with t-fMRI [7,9].

Automatically localizing the eloquent cortex using rs-fMRI is a challenging problem with limited success in the literature. For example, the authors of [10,11] demonstrate that spatial components identified by group ICA on the rs-fMRI data coincide with the language and motor networks from t-fMRI. While the result is promising, the spatial accuracy is highly variable across patients. The work in [12] describes a multi-layer perceptron architecture that classifies rs-fMRI networks at the voxel level using seed based correlation maps; this method was extended in [13] to handle tumor cases. However, the perceptron is trained on healthy subjects and may not accommodate changes in brain organization due to the tumor. Finally, the method in [9] is the first end-to-end graph neural network (GNN) to automatically localize eloquent cortex in tumor patients. While this method achieves good classification performance, separate GNNs must be trained and tested for each eloquent network [9], which increases the training time, the overall number of parameters, and the required training data.

There is growing evidence in the field that functional connectivity patterns are not static, but evolve over time. In particular, studies have shown that individual functional systems are more strongly present during specific intervals of the rs-fMRI scan [14,15]. Several studies have leveraged these dynamic connectivity patterns for classification. For example, the work in [16] uses a long-short term memory (LSTM) cell to learn time dependencies within the rs-fMRI to discriminate patients with autism from controls. More recent work by [17] and [18] has shown that combining static and dynamic connectivity can achieve better patient versus control classification performance than either set of features alone. However, these works focus on group-level discrimination. We will leverage similar principles in this paper to classify ROIs within a single patient.

We propose a novel multi-task deep learning framework that uses both convolutional neural networks (CNNs) and an LSTM attention network to extract and combine dynamic connectivity features for eloquent cortex localization. The final stage of our model employs multi-task learning (MTL) to implicitly select the relevant time points for each network and simultaneously identify regions of the brain involved in language processing and motor functionality. Our model finds a shared representation between the cognitive networks of interest, which enables us to handle missing data. This coupling also reduces the number of model parameters, so that we can learn from limited patient data. We evaluate our framework on rs-fMRI data from 56 brain tumor patients while using

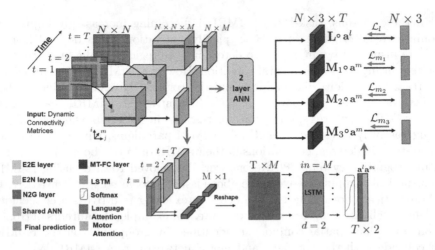

**Fig. 1. Top**: Specialized convolutional layers identify dynamic patterns that are shared across the functional systems. **Bottom**: The dynamic features are input to an LSTM network to learn attention weights $\mathbf{a}^l$ (language) and $\mathbf{a}^m$ (motor). **Right**: MTL to classify the language ($\mathbf{L}$), finger ($\mathbf{M}_1$), foot ($\mathbf{M}_2$) and tongue ($\mathbf{M}_3$) networks.

task fMRI activations as surrogate ground-truth labels for training and testing. Our model achieves higher localization accuracies than a variety of baseline techniques, thus demonstrating its promise for preoperative mapping.

## 2    Eloquent Cortex Localization Using Deep Learning

Our framework makes two underlying assumptions. First, while the anatomical boundaries of the eloquent cortex may shift across individuals, its functional connectivity with the rest of the brain will be preserved [10]. Second, the networks associated with the eloquent cortex phase in and out of synchrony across the rs-fMRI scan [19]. Hence, isolating these key time points will help to refine our localization. Figure 1 illustrates our framework. In the top branch, we use specialized convolutional filters to capture rs-fMRI co-activation patterns from the dynamic connectivity matrices. In the bottom branch, we use an LSTM to identify key time points where the language and/or motor networks are more synchronous. We tie the activations from the LSTM branch of our model into our MTL classification problem via our specialized loss function.

*Input Connectivity Matrices.* We use the sliding window technique to obtain our connectivity matrices [20]. Let $N$ be the number of brain regions in our parcellation, $T$ be the total number of sliding windows (i.e., time points in our model), and $\{\mathbf{W}^t\}_{t=1}^T \in \mathbb{R}^{N \times N}$ be the dynamic similarity matrices. $\mathbf{W}^t$ is constructed from the input time courses $\{\mathbf{X}^t\}_{t=1}^T \in \mathbb{R}^{D \times N}$, where each $\mathbf{X}^t$ is a segment of the rs-fMRI obtained with window size $D$. The input $\mathbf{W}^t \in \mathbb{R}^{N \times N}$ is

$$\mathbf{W}^t = \exp\left[\frac{(\mathbf{X}^t)^T\mathbf{X}^t}{\epsilon} - 1\right] \tag{1}$$

where $\epsilon \geq 1$ is a user-specified parameter that controls decay speed [9]. Recall that our setup must accommodate the presence of brain tumors that vary across patients. Since these tumors represent non-functioning areas of the brain, we follow the approach of [9] and treat the corresponding rows and columns of the similarity matrix as "missing data" by fixing them to zero. This procedure removes the effect of the tumor regions on the downstream convolution operations.

***Representation Learning for Dynamic Connectivity.*** Our network leverages the specialized convolutional layers developed in [21] for static analysis. The edge-to-edge (E2E) layer in Fig.1 acts across rows and columns of the input matrix $\mathbf{W}^t$. Mathematically, let $f \in \{1, \cdots, F\}$ be the E2E filter index, $\mathbf{r}^f \in \mathbb{R}^{1 \times N}$ be the row filter $f$, $\mathbf{c}^f \in \mathbb{R}^{N \times 1}$ be the column filter $f$, $\mathbf{b} \in \mathbb{R}^{F \times 1}$ be the E2E bias, and $\phi(.)$ be the activation function. For each time point $t$ the feature map $\mathbf{H}^{f,t} \in \mathbb{R}^{N \times N}$ is computed as follows:

$$\mathbf{H}_{i,j}^{f,t} = \phi\left(\sum_{n=1}^{N} \mathbf{r}_n^f \mathbf{W}_{i,n}^t + \mathbf{c}_n^f \mathbf{W}_{n,j}^t + \mathbf{b}_f\right). \tag{2}$$

Effectively, the E2E filter output $\mathbf{H}_{ij}^{f,t}$ for edge $(i,j)$ extracts patterns associated with the neighborhood connectivity of node $i$ and node $j$. The edge-to-node (E2N) filter in Fig. 1 is a 1D convolution along the columns of each feature map. Mathematically, let $\mathbf{g}^f \in \mathbb{R}^{N \times 1}$ be E2N filter $f$ and $\mathbf{p} \in \mathbb{R}^{F \times 1}$ be the E2N bias. The E2N output $\mathbf{h}^{f,t} \in \mathbb{R}^{N \times 1}$ from input $\mathbf{H}^{f,t}$ is computed as

$$\mathbf{h}_i^{f,t} = \phi\left(\sum_{n=1}^{N} \mathbf{g}_n^f \mathbf{H}_{i,n}^{f,t} + \mathbf{p}_f\right). \tag{3}$$

The E2E and E2N layers extract topological graph-theoretic features from the connectivity data. Following the convolutional layers in the top branch, we cascade two fully-connected (FC) layers to combine these learned topological features for our downstream multi-task classification. In the bottom branch, we use a node-to-graph (N2G) layer to extract features that will be input to our LSTM network. The N2G filter acts as a 1D convolution along the first dimension of the E2N output, effectively collapsing the node information to a low dimensional representation for each time point. Let $\mathbf{k}^f \in \mathbb{R}^{N \times 1}$ be N2G filter $f$ and $\mathbf{d} \in \mathbb{R}^{F \times 1}$ be the bias. The N2G filter gives a scalar output $q^{f,t}$ for each input $\mathbf{h}^{f,t}$ by

$$q^{f,t} = \phi\left(\sum_{n=1}^{N} \mathbf{k}_n^f \cdot \mathbf{h}_n^{f,t} + \mathbf{d}_f\right). \tag{4}$$

***Dynamic Attention Model.*** Per time point, we define $\mathbf{q}^t = [q^{1,t} \cdots q^{F,t}]$ and feed the vectors $\{\mathbf{q}^t\}_{t=1}^{T}$ into an LSTM module to learn attention weights for our classification problem. The LSTM adds a cell state to the basic recurrent neural network to help alleviate the vanishing gradient problem, essentially by accumulating state information over time [22]. LSTMs have demonstrated both predictive power for rs-fMRI analysis [16,18] and the ability to identify different brain states [23]. We choose $d = 2$ as the output dimension, and perform a softmax over each column of the LSTM output to get the attention vectors $\mathbf{a}^l \in \mathbb{R}^{T \times 1}$ (language) and $\mathbf{a}^m \in \mathbb{R}^{T \times 1}$ (motor). These attention vectors provide information on which input connectivity matrices are more informative for identifying the language or motor networks. The attention model outputs are combined with the classifier during backpropagation in our novel loss function.

***Multi-task Learning with Incomplete Data.*** The black blocks in Fig. 1 show the multi-task FC (MT-FC) layers, where we have four separate branches to identify the language, finger, foot, and tongue areas. Up until this point, there has been an entirely shared representation of the feature weights at each layer. Let $\mathbf{L}^t, \mathbf{M}_1^t, \mathbf{M}_2^t$, and $\mathbf{M}_3^t \in \mathbb{R}^{N \times 3}$ be the output of the language, finger, foot, and tongue MT-FC layers, respectively, at time $t$. The $N \times 3$ matrix represents the region-wise assignment into one of three classes; eloquent, tumor, and background. As in [9], we introduce the tumor as its own learned class to remove any bias these regions may have introduced to the algorithm. We introduce a novel variant of a modified version of the risk-sensitive cross-entropy loss function [9,24], which is designed to handle membership imbalance in multi-class problems. Let $\delta_c$ be the risk factor associated with class $c$. If $\delta_c$ is small, then we pay a smaller penalty for misclassifying samples that belong to class $c$. Due to a training set imbalance, we set different values for the language class ($\delta_c^l$) and motor classes ($\delta_c^m$) respectively. Let $\mathbf{Y}^l, \mathbf{Y}^{m_1}, \mathbf{Y}^{m_1}$, and $\mathbf{Y}^{m_3} \in \mathbb{R}^{N \times 3}$ be one-hot encoding matrices for the ground-truth class labels of the language and motor subnetworks. Notice that our framework allows for overlapping eloquent labels, as brain regions can be involved in multiple cognitive processes. Our loss function is the sum of four terms:

$$\mathcal{L}_\Theta(\{\mathbf{W}^t\}_{t=1}^T, \mathbf{Y}) = \sum_{n=1}^N \sum_{c=1}^3 \Big[ \underbrace{-\delta_c^l \log\Big(\sigma\Big(\sum_{t=1}^T \mathbf{L}_{n,c}^t \cdot \mathbf{a}^{l,t}\Big)\Big) \mathbf{Y}_{n,c}^l}_{\text{Language Loss } \mathcal{L}_l}$$

$$\underbrace{-\delta_c^m \log\Big(\sigma\Big(\sum_{t=1}^T \mathbf{M}_{1n,c}^t \cdot \mathbf{a}^{m,t}\Big)\Big) \mathbf{Y}_{n,c}^{m_1}}_{\text{Finger Loss } \mathcal{L}_{m_1}} \underbrace{-\delta_c^m \log\Big(\sigma\Big(\sum_{t=1}^T \mathbf{M}_{2n,c}^t \cdot \mathbf{a}^{m,t}\Big)\Big) \mathbf{Y}_{n,c}^{m_2}}_{\text{Foot Loss } \mathcal{L}_{m_2}} \quad (5)$$

$$\underbrace{-\delta_c^m \log\Big(\sigma\Big(\sum_{t=1}^T \mathbf{M}_{3n,c}^t \cdot \mathbf{a}^{m,t}\Big)\Big) \mathbf{Y}_{n,c}^{m_3}}_{\text{Tongue Loss } \mathcal{L}_{m_3}} \Big]$$

where $\sigma(\cdot)$ is the sigmoid function. Our loss in Eq. (5) allows us to handle missing information during training. For example, if we only have ground-truth labels for some of the functional systems, then we can freeze the other branches and just backpropagate the known loss terms. This partial backpropagation will continue to refine the shared representation, thus maximizing the amount of information mined from our training data. Note that our formulation is agnostic to the length of the rs-fMRI scan (i.e. $T$), which is useful in clinical practice.

*Implementation Details.* We implement our network in PyTorch using the SGD optimizer with weight decay $= 5 \times 10^{-5}$ for parameter stability, and momentum $= 0.9$ to improve convergence. We train our model with learning rate $= 0.002$ and 300 epochs, which provides for reliable performance without overfitting. We used $D = 45$ and a stride length of 5 for the sliding window. We specified $F = 25$ feature maps in the convolutional branch, and 2 layers in our LSTM. The LeakyReLU with slope $= -0.1$ was used for $\phi(.)$. Using cross validation, we set the cross-entropy weights to $\delta^m = (1.5, 0.5, 0.2)$, and $\delta^l = (2.25, 0.5, 0.2)$. We compare the performance of our model against three baselines:

1. PCA + Multi-class linear SVM on dynamic connectivity matrices (SVM)
2. A multi-task GNN on static connectivity (MT-GNN)
3. A multi-task ANN with LSTM attention model (MT-ANN)

The first baseline is a traditional machine learning SVM approach to our problem. The MT-GNN operates on static connectivity and does not have an LSTM module. We include the MT-GNN to observe the difference in performance with and without using dynamic information. The MT-ANN maintains the same number of parameters as our model but has fully-connected layers instead of convolutional layers. Therefore, the MT-ANN does not consider the network organization of the input dynamic connectivity matrices.

## 3    Experimental Results

*Dataset and Preprocessing.* We evaluate the methods on rs-fMRI data from 56 brain tumor patients who underwent preoperative mapping at our institution. These patients also underwent t-fMRI scanning, which we use to derive pseudo ground-truth labels for training and validation. Our dataset includes three different motor paradigms that are designed to target distinct parts of the motor homunculus [25]: finger tapping, tongue moving, and foot tapping. It also includes two language paradigms, sentence completion and silent word generation. Since the t-fMRI data was acquired for clinical purposes, not all patients performed each task. The number of subjects that performed the language, finger, foot, and tongue tasks are displayed in the left column of Table 1.

The fMRI data was acquired using a 3.0 T Siemens Trio Tim (TR = 2000 ms, TE = 30 ms, FOV = 24 cm, res = $3.59 \times 3.59 \times 5$ mm). Preprocessing steps include slice timing correction, motion correction and registration to the MNI-152 template. The rs-fMRI was further bandpass filtered from 0.01 to 0.1 Hz, spatially smoothed with a 6 mm FWHM Gaussian kernel, scrubbed using the

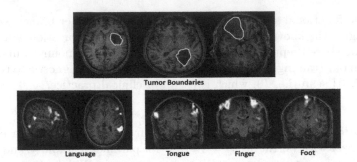

**Fig. 2. Top**: Tumor boundaries for three patients. **Left**: One sagital and axial view of a language network. **Right**: Coronal views of the motor sub-networks for one patient.

**Table 1.** Class accuracy, overall accuracy, and ROC statistics. The number in the first column indicates number of patients who performed the task.

| Task | Method | Eloquent | Overall | AUC |
|------|--------|----------|---------|-----|
| Language (56) | SVM | 0.49 | 0.59 | 0.55 |
| | MT-ANN | 0.70 | 0.71 | 0.70 |
| | MT-GNN | 0.73 | 0.74 | 0.74 |
| | Proposed | **0.85** | **0.81** | **0.80** |
| Finger (36) | SVM | 0.54 | 0.61 | 0.57 |
| | MT-ANN | 0.73 | 0.75 | 0.74 |
| | MT-GNN | <u>0.87</u> | **0.86** | **0.84** |
| | Proposed | **0.88** | <u>0.85</u> | **0.84** |
| Foot (17) | SVM | 0.58 | 0.63 | 0.60 |
| | MT-ANN | 0.72 | 0.77 | 0.74 |
| | MT-GNN | 0.82 | 0.79 | 0.79 |
| | Proposed | **0.86** | **0.85** | **0.82** |
| Tongue (39) | SVM | 0.54 | 0.60 | 0.58 |
| | MT-ANN | 0.74 | 0.76 | 0.73 |
| | MT-GNN | 0.85 | 0.81 | 0.82 |
| | Proposed | **0.87** | **0.83** | **0.84** |

ArtRepair toolbox [26] in SPM8, linearly detrended, and underwent nuisance regression using the CompCor package [27]. We used the Craddocks atlas to obtain $N = 384$ brain regions [28]. Tumor boundaries for each patient were manually delineated by a medical fellow using the MIPAV software package [29]. An ROI was determined as belonging to the eloquent class if a majority of its voxel membership coincided with that of the t-fMRI activation map. Tumor labels were determined in a similar fashion according to the MIPAV segmentations. A general linear model implemented in SPM8 was used to obtain t-fMRI

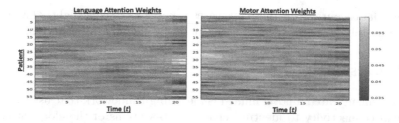

**Fig. 3.** Language (**L**) and motor (**R**) attention weights for all patients.

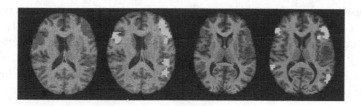

**Fig. 4.** Ground truth (Blue) and predicted (Yellow) language labels for two subjects. (Color figure online)

activation maps. Figure 2 shows representative examples of the tumor boundaries and each of the four cognitive networks of interest obtained from t-fMRI.

***Localization.*** We use 8-fold cross validation (CV) to quantify our eloquent cortex localization performance. Table 1 reports the eloquent per-class accuracy and the area under the receiver operating characteristic curve (AUC) for detecting the eloquent class on the testing data. Each MT-FC branch has separate metrics. Our proposed method has the best overall performance, as highlighted in bold. Even with attention from the LSTM layer, we observe that a fully-connected ANN still is sub-par for our task compared to using the specialized E2E, E2N, and N2G layers. Furthermore, our performance gains are most notable when classifying the language and foot networks. The former is particularly relevant for preoperative mapping, due to the difficulties in identifying the language network even with ECS [1,2]. Figure 3 shows the language (left) and motor (right) attention vectors for all patients across time. We observe that both systems phase in and out, such that when one system is more active, the other is less active. This pattern lends credence to our hypothesis that identifying the critical intervals is key for localization. Hence, our model outperforms the static MT-GNN.

***Bilateral Language Identification.*** Finally, we test whether our model can recover a bilateral language network, even when this case is not present in the training data. Here, we trained the model on 51 left-hemisphere language network patients and tested on the remaining 5 bilateral patients. Our model correctly predicted bilateral parcels in all five subjects. Figure 4 shows ground truth (blue) and predicted language maps (yellow) for two example cases. The mean language class accuracy for these five cases was **0.72**. This is slightly lower than reported in Table 1 likely due to the mismatch in training information.

## 4   Conclusion

We have demonstrated a novel multi-task learning framework that uses dynamic functional connectivity to identify separate sub-systems of the eloquent cortex in brain tumor patients. Our model is extendable to adding more eloquent sub-classes, as it finds a shared representation of the eloquent cortex that can subsequently classify sub-regions of interest. Going one step further, we show that our model can correctly identify bilateral language networks even when trained on only unilateral cases. Finally, our attention features suggest that using dynamic connectivity could be preferred to the traditional static case. Our results demonstrate promise for using rs-fMRI analysis in the preoperative phase for tumor resection procedures.

**Acknowledgement.** This work was supported by the National Science Foundation CAREER award 1845430 (PI: Venkataraman) and the Research & Education Foundation Carestream Health RSNA Research Scholar Grant RSCH1420.

## References

1. Ojemann, G.A., Whitaker, H.A.: Language localization and variability. Brain Lang. **6**(2), 239–260 (1978)
2. Tomasi, D., Volkow, N.: Language network: segregation, laterality and connectivity. Mol. Psychiatry **17**(8), 759 (2012)
3. Tzourio-Mazoyer, N., Josse, G., Crivello, F., Mazoyer, B.: Interindividual variability in the hemispheric organization for speech. Neuroimage **21**(1), 422–435 (2004)
4. Gupta, D.K., Chandra, P., Ojha, B., Sharma, B., Mahapatra, A., Mehta, V.: Awake craniotomy versus surgery under general anesthesia for resection of intrinsic lesions of eloquent cortex-a prospective randomised study. Clin. Neurol. Neurosurg. **109**(4), 335–343 (2007)
5. Berger, M.S., Kincaid, J., Ojemann, G.A., Lettich, E.: Brain mapping techniques to maximize resection, safety, and seizure control in children with brain tumors. Neurosurgery **25**(5), 786–792 (1989)
6. Kokkonen, S.-M., et al.: Preoperative localization of the sensorimotor area using independent component analysis of resting-state fMRI. Magn. Reson. Imaging **27**(6), 733–740 (2009)
7. Lee, M.H., et al.: Clinical resting-state fMRI in the preoperative setting: are we ready for prime time? Top. Magn. Reson. Imaging TMRI **25**(1), 11 (2016)
8. Van Den Heuvel, M.P., Pol, H.E.H.: Exploring the brain network: a review on resting-state fMRI functional connectivity. Eur. Neuropsychopharmacol. **20**(8), 519–534 (2010)
9. Nandakumar, N., Manzoor, K., Pillai, J.J., Gujar, S.K., Sair, H.I., Venkataraman, A.: A novel graph neural network to localize eloquent cortex in brain tumor patients from resting-state fMRI connectivity. In: Schirmer, M.D., Venkataraman, A., Rekik, I., Kim, M., Chung, A.W. (eds.) CNI 2019. LNCS, vol. 11848, pp. 10–20. Springer, Cham (2019). https://doi.org/10.1007/978-3-030-32391-2_2

10. Sair, H.I., et al.: Presurgical brain mapping of the language network in patients with brain tumors using resting-state fMRI: comparison with task fMRI. Hum. Brain Mapp. **37**(3), 913–923 (2016)
11. Tie, Y., et al.: Defining language networks from resting-state fMRI for surgical planning-a feasibility study. Hum. Brain Mapp. **35**(3), 1018–1030 (2014)
12. Hacker, C.D., et al.: Resting state network estimation in individual subjects. Neuroimage **82**, 616–633 (2013)
13. Leuthardt, E.C., et al.: Integration of resting state functional MRI into clinical practice-a large single institution experience. PloS One **13**(6), e0198349 (2018)
14. Dvornek, N.C., Li, X., Zhuang, J., Duncan, J.S.: Jointly discriminative and generative recurrent neural networks for learning from fMRI. In: Suk, H.-I., Liu, M., Yan, P., Lian, C. (eds.) MLMI 2019. LNCS, vol. 11861, pp. 382–390. Springer, Cham (2019). https://doi.org/10.1007/978-3-030-32692-0_44
15. Yan, W., Zhang, H., Sui, J., Shen, D.: deep chronnectome learning via full bidirectional long short-term memory networks for MCI diagnosis. In: Frangi, A.F., Schnabel, J.A., Davatzikos, C., Alberola-López, C., Fichtinger, G. (eds.) MICCAI 2018. LNCS, vol. 11072, pp. 249–257. Springer, Cham (2018). https://doi.org/10.1007/978-3-030-00931-1_29
16. Dvornek, N.C., Ventola, P., Pelphrey, K.A., Duncan, J.S.: Identifying autism from resting-state fMRI using long short-term memory networks. In: Wang, Q., Shi, Y., Suk, H.-I., Suzuki, K. (eds.) MLMI 2017. LNCS, vol. 10541, pp. 362–370. Springer, Cham (2017). https://doi.org/10.1007/978-3-319-67389-9_42
17. Rashid, B., et al.: Classification of schizophrenia and bipolar patients using static and dynamic resting-state fMRI brain connectivity. Neuroimage **134**, 645–657 (2016)
18. El-Gazzar, A., Quaak, M., Cerliani, L., Bloem, P., van Wingen, G., Mani Thomas, R.: A hybrid 3DCNN and 3DC-LSTM based model for 4D spatio-temporal fMRI data: an ABIDE autism classification study. In: Zhou, L., et al. (eds.) OR 2.0/MLCN -2019. LNCS, vol. 11796, pp. 95–102. Springer, Cham (2019). https://doi.org/10.1007/978-3-030-32695-1_11
19. Kunert-Graf, J.M., Eschenburg, K., Galas, D., Kutz, J.N., Rane, S., Brunton, B.W.: Extracting reproducible time-resolved resting state networks using dynamic mode decomposition. Front. Comput. Neurosci. **13**, 75 (2019)
20. Hutchison, R.M., et al.: Dynamic functional connectivity: promise, issues, and interpretations. Neuroimage **80**, 360–378 (2013)
21. Kawahara, J., et al.: BrainNetCNN: convolutional neural networks for brain networks; towards predicting neurodevelopment. NeuroImage **146**, 1038–1049 (2017)
22. Xingjian, S., Chen, Z., Wang, H., Yeung, D.-Y., Wong, W.-K., Woo, W.-C.: Convolutional LSTM network: a machine learning approach for precipitation nowcasting. In: Advances in Neural Information Processing Systems, pp. 802–810 (2015)
23. Li, H., Fan, Y.: Brain decoding from functional MRI using long short-term memory recurrent neural networks. In: Frangi, A.F., Schnabel, J.A., Davatzikos, C., Alberola-López, C., Fichtinger, G. (eds.) MICCAI 2018. LNCS, vol. 11072, pp. 320–328. Springer, Cham (2018). https://doi.org/10.1007/978-3-030-00931-1_37
24. Suresh, S., et al.: Risk-sensitive loss functions for sparse multi-category classification problems. Inf. Sci. **178**(12), 2621–2638 (2008)
25. Jack Jr., C.R., et al.: Sensory motor cortex: correlation of presurgical mapping with functional MR imaging and invasive cortical mapping. Radiology **190**(1), 85–92 (1994)
26. Mazaika, P.K., Hoeft, F., Glover, G.H., Reiss, A.L., et al.: Methods and software for fMRI analysis of clinical subjects. Neuroimage **47**(Suppl 1), S58 (2009)

27. Behzadi, Y., Restom, K., Liau, J., Liu, T.T.: A component based noise correction method (CompCor) for BOLD and perfusion based fMRI. Neuroimage **37**(1), 90–101 (2007)
28. Craddock, R.C., et al.: A whole brain fMRI atlas generated via spatially constrained spectral clustering. Hum. Brain Mapp. **33**(8), 1914–1928 (2012)
29. McAuliffe, M.J., Lalonde, F.M., McGarry, D., Gandler, W., Csaky, K., Trus, B.L.: Medical image processing, analysis and visualization in clinical research. In: Proceedings 14th IEEE Symposium on Computer-Based Medical Systems. CBMS 2001, pp. 381–386. IEEE (2001)

# Deep Learning for Non-invasive Cortical Potential Imaging

Alexandra Razorenova$^{(\boxtimes)}$ (ID), Nikolay Yavich (ID), Mikhail Malovichko (ID),
Maxim Fedorov (ID), Nikolay Koshev (ID), and Dmitry V. Dylov (ID)

Skolkovo Institute of Science and Technology (Skoltech), Moscow, Russia
`alexandra.razorenova@skoltech.ru`

**Abstract.** Electroencephalography (EEG) is a well-established non-invasive technique to measure the brain activity, albeit with a limited spatial resolution. Variations in electric conductivity between different tissues distort the electric fields generated by cortical sources, resulting in smeared potential measurements on the scalp. One needs to solve an ill-posed inverse problem to recover the original neural activity. In this article, we present a generic method of recovering the cortical potentials from the EEG measurement by introducing a new inverse-problem solver based on deep Convolutional Neural Networks (CNN) in paired (U-Net) and unpaired (DualGAN) configurations. The solvers were trained on synthetic EEG-ECoG pairs that were generated using a head conductivity model computed using the Finite Element Method (FEM). These solvers are the first of their kind, that provide robust translation of EEG data to the cortex surface using deep learning. Providing a fast and accurate interpretation of the tracked EEG signal, our approach promises a boost to the spatial resolution of the future EEG devices.

**Keywords:** ECoG · Inverse problem · EEG super-resolution · CNN · FEM · Brain modelling · Neuroimaging

## 1 Introduction

Electroencephalography (EEG) is a common method of non-invasive registration of the brain activity. It has high temporal resolution and has low operational cost. These aspects make the adoption of EEG widespread, including the areas of neurophysiological and cognitive research, non-invasive Brain-Computer Interface (BCI) devices, clinical studies, and diagnostics. However, there are multiple technical limitations to modern EEG technology, with a poor spatial resolution being the major one [20,27]. The low spatial resolution of EEG is primarily caused by the significant difference of conductivity between the skull and the

---

Supported by Skoltech CDISE, Foundation grant 1101-Sk, project 1-RP-11513.

---

**Electronic supplementary material** The online version of this chapter (https://doi.org/10.1007/978-3-030-66843-3_5) contains supplementary material, which is available to authorized users.

© Springer Nature Switzerland AG 2020
S. M. Kia et al. (Eds.): MLCN 2020/RNO-AI 2020, LNCS 12449, pp. 45–55, 2020.
https://doi.org/10.1007/978-3-030-66843-3_5

other tissues. Generally speaking, the conductivity of all tissues composing the head should be taken into account.

In this work, we will consider how to recover the signal from the brain surface given measurements on the scalp, using the most recent arsenal of techniques from the classical and the deep learning disciplines. We proceed with a formal problem statement and with a review of the state-of-the-art.

## 1.1   Statement of the Problem

Let the head be represented by the computational domain $\Omega \subset \mathbb{R}^3$ bounded by a piecewise-smooth boundary $\partial\Omega$. Within the domain, the electric potential $p(\mathbf{x})$ satisfies the following expression [5]:

$$\nabla \cdot (\sigma(\mathbf{x})\nabla p(\mathbf{x})) = \nabla \cdot \mathbf{J}(\mathbf{x}) \text{ in } \Omega, \quad \mathbf{n}(\mathbf{x}) \cdot \nabla p(\mathbf{x}) = 0 \text{ on } \partial\Omega \qquad (1)$$

where $\sigma(\mathbf{x})$ is the conductivity distribution over the head volume, $\mathbf{J}(\mathbf{x})$ represents the volumetric distribution of a primary current source that produces the signal, and $\mathbf{n}(\mathbf{x})$ is the vector normal to the surface $\partial\Omega$ at the point $\mathbf{x} \in \partial\Omega$. The conductivity $\sigma$ is assumed to be known. We also introduce the area of measurements on the scalp $\Gamma \subset \partial\Omega$, and the cortex $C \subset \Omega$. Based on Eq. (1), we can formulate three main mathematical problems (see Fig. 1A for visualizing the concept):

**Forward problem (FP):** *compute the scalp voltages* $p(\mathbf{x})$, $\mathbf{x} \in \partial\Omega$, *given current dipoles or density* $\mathbf{J}(\mathbf{x})$.

**Inverse problem 0 (IP0):** *given known electric voltages* $p(\mathbf{x})$, $\mathbf{x} \in \Gamma$ *on the area of measurements* $\Gamma$, *compute current density* $\mathbf{J}(\mathbf{x})$, $\mathbf{x} \in C$ *on the cortex.*

**Inverse problem 1 (IP1):** *given known electric voltages* $p(\mathbf{x})$, $\mathbf{x} \in C$ *on the cortex, compute current density* $\mathbf{J}(\mathbf{x})$, $\mathbf{x} \in C$ *on the cortex.*

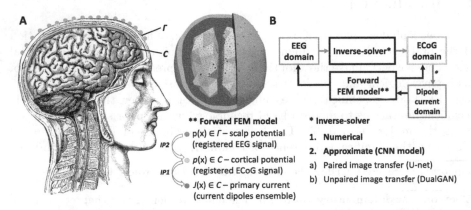

**Fig. 1.** A. Concept of cortical activity registration (left, head image reproduced from [6]) and its physical model implemented in FEM (right). IP stands for "Inverse problem". B. Schematic representation of Forward and Inverse problems solving.

**Inverse problem 2 (IP2):** *given known electric voltages* $p(\mathbf{x}), \mathbf{x} \in \Gamma$ *on the area of measurements* $\Gamma$, *compute the electric voltage* $p(\mathbf{x})$, $\mathbf{x} \in C$ *on the cortex.*

## 1.2 State-of-the-Art

The majority of algorithms proposed in the EEG community are dedicated to *IP0* and formulated in the framework of Tikhonov regularization, including the MNE, LORETA, and LCVM families (see [11,23,29] for a review). The main limitation of these methods is their low spatial resolution due to the head model geometry and the high demand for computational resources (especially, if MRI-based head models are used). The *IP1* is generally considered concerning invasive ECoG measurements. However, solving *IP1* after *IP2* provides an estimate of the cortical current from non-invasive (EEG) data (see Supplementary material). Moreover, *IP2* itself is of great interest since a reconstructed potential on the cortex localizes activation zones. There are algorithms for solving *IP2* [3,9,15] but their spatial resolution is insufficient.

Recent studies propose neural networks as alternative method of the inverse problem solution [13,14,28]. Convolutional neural networks (CNN) are capable of providing both an approximation of the physical model and a sufficient regularization, leading to more accurate inverse-problem solution, stable with respect to noisy inputs. U-Net can serve as an efficient integrator of various numerical modelling solutions to improve the accuracy [19]. An Autoencoder-based CNN was also proposed for EEG super-resolution as a non-linear interpolation method [17]. Finally, the most popular trend today is to use the temporal information as an additional constraint and to apply Markov models, or their approximations, in a recurrent network configuration (e.g. LSTM) [4,12,18].

In this work, we aspire to solve IP2 using deep CNNs. We present a generic methodology for recovering cortical potentials (referred here as extended ECoG) from the EEG measurement using a new CNN-based inverse-problem solver based on the U-Net or the DualGAN architectures (Fig. 1). Paired examples of EEG-ECoG synthetic data were generated via forward problem solving Eq. (1). Thus, we reformulate the problem as an image-to-image translation task and find a way to reconstruct accurate mapping of the cortical potentials to recover the original brain activity beyond the spatial resolution of EEG.

## 2 Methods

**Head Model and Data Generation.** A realistic 3-D head model was used to prepare a synthetic dataset (Fig. 1A). An anatomical head model was constructed from the sample subject data of the MNE package [10]. We extracted triangulated surfaces of the cortex, skull and skin and smoothed them using the iso2mesh toolbox [25]. The volume conductor was meshed into 261,565 tetrahedrons with 42,684 vertices. The conductivity of the cortex surface, the skin, and the skull were assumed to be 0.33 S/m, 0.33 S/m, and 0.01 S/m, respectively [8].

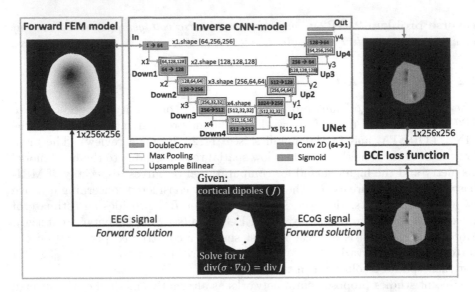

**Fig. 2.** U-Net-solver for imaging cortical potential from the EEG data. The EEG and the ECoG images are modelled via solution to the FP, defined in text.

Source current dipoles were positioned in the centers of the boundary triangles of the cortex mesh. For simplicity, we considered only the upper part of the cortex in order to provide an 2-D representation of the data, resulting in 400 possible locations of the source current dipoles (the number of active dipoles was, however, restricted for each simulation to $n$ dipoles, as described in Sect. 3).

Cortical potential sensors were located in the same manner, leading to 400 measurement probes of the cortex potential (see yellow dots in Fig. 1A, left). Scalp potential sensors (i.e., channels of an EEG device) were uniformly located on the outer scalp surface. We tested different number of EEG channels: 128, 64, or 32.

Our simulation run went as follows. First, a random initialization of $n$ current dipoles with the current values in the range 0.1–0.9 $\mu$A [22] was done. Then, we carried out a calculation of EEG and ECoG data as a numerical solution to the FP (1), discretized with the Finite Element Method (FEM) [1]. The resulting system was solved with preconditioned conjugate gradient method [7]. Thus, EEG and the ECoG pairs were modelled[1]. We converted them into 256×256 float32 images to provide precise topographic representation of the measured activity. Min-max contrast normalization was applied to the image intensities. Thus, each computed output is a pair of the top-view image of the scalp potential distribution and the top view image of the cortical potential distribution.

---

[1] FEM modeling combines high geometrical flexibility, economical matrix assembly and fast solution of the resulting linear system. Thus a single solution took near 1 s.

**Evaluation Details.** Using the head model, a dataset of synthetic EEG-ECoG pairs was generated. It was split into 5000 train, 400 validation, and 600 test pairs. Both the data generation and the training of the neural network were performed on the ZHORES supercomputer using Tesla V100-SXM2 GPUs [31].

To train the topographic translation from EEG to ECoG domain, we did minimal modifications to U-Net [26] (see Fig. 2) to adapt it to the paired image-to-image translation task. The U-Net network was optimized to minimize the Binary Cross Entropy (BCE) loss function between the recovered ECoG image and the corresponding ground truth (GT) ECoG image. The training was performed with the ADAM optimizer, sigmoid activation function, the batch size of 4, and the learning rate of $10^{-4}$.

Additionally, we tested DualGAN architecture [24,30] as an inverse solver, aiming at creating an architecture to handle realistic unpaired EEG-ECoG data samples available in clinical practice, e.g. [2]. Its first generator was trained to translate ECoG images to EEG; and the second generator translated the images from EEG to ECoG domain.

## 3    Experiments

We tested the effectiveness and robustness of the proposed U-Net-solver by varying the complexity of the pattern of cortical activity. For this purpose, the proposed model was trained on four datasets with different number of active dipoles.

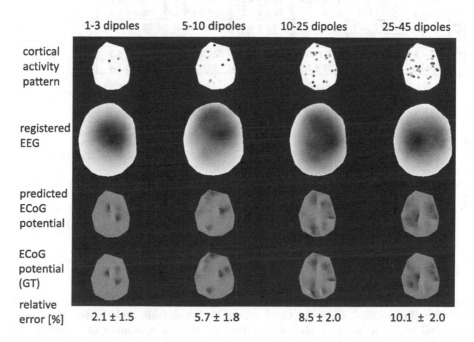

**Fig. 3.** The U-Net-solver results for cortical potential imaging as a function of a random number of randomly located source dipoles (columns from left to right correspond to the increased number of sources).

We started from a subset where the corresponding ECoG and the EEG image representations were generated from a superposition of one, two, or three source current dipoles. Then, we gradually increased the model's complexity to 5–10, 10–25, and 25–45 active dipoles, respectively (see Fig. 3, top row).

As can be seen in the Fig. 3, the U-Net-solver is capable of recovering the original cortical potential distribution pattern given indiscernible EEG data input. The relative error between the ground truth cortical potential distribution and the one obtained via the U-Net-solver is lower than 10%. The error does not increase dramatically as the complexity of the original cortical activity pattern is varied.

We noted that the relative error dynamics can be explained by the number of dipoles and by the variability of this parameter within the training set. In other words, when 1 to 3 dipoles are active simultaneously, the majority of the training examples is separable and the reconstruction of the sources lacks any ambiguity, but when the number of active dipoles rises to 10 to 25 dipoles, the separation of the source dipoles on the ground truth images is less pronounced. This additional ambiguity limits the overfitting of the solver.

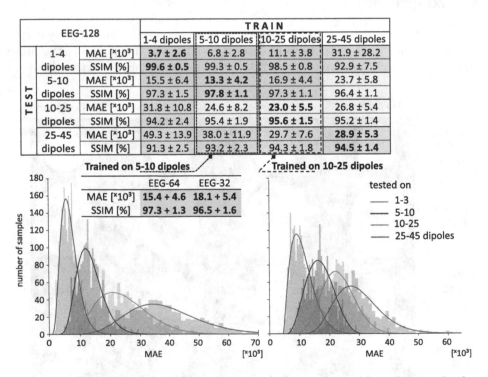

| EEG-128 | | | TRAIN | | | |
|---|---|---|---|---|---|
| | | | 1-4 dipoles | 5-10 dipoles | 10-25 dipoles | 25-45 dipoles |
| **T E S T** | 1-4 dipoles | MAE [×10³] | **3.7 ± 2.6** | 6.8 ± 2.8 | 11.1 ± 3.8 | 31.9 ± 28.2 |
| | | SSIM [%] | **99.6 ± 0.5** | 99.3 ± 0.5 | 98.5 ± 0.8 | 92.9 ± 7.5 |
| | 5-10 dipoles | MAE [×10³] | 15.5 ± 6.4 | **13.3 ± 4.2** | 16.9 ± 4.4 | 23.7 ± 5.8 |
| | | SSIM [%] | 97.3 ± 1.5 | **97.8 ± 1.1** | 97.3 ± 1.1 | 96.4 ± 1.1 |
| | 10-25 dipoles | MAE [×10³] | 31.8 ± 10.8 | 24.6 ± 8.2 | **23.0 ± 5.5** | 26.8 ± 5.4 |
| | | SSIM [%] | 94.2 ± 2.4 | 95.4 ± 1.9 | **95.6 ± 1.5** | 95.2 ± 1.4 |
| | 25-45 dipoles | MAE [×10³] | 49.3 ± 13.9 | 38.0 ± 11.9 | 29.7 ± 7.6 | **28.9 ± 5.3** |
| | | SSIM [%] | 91.3 ± 2.5 | 93.2 ± 2.3 | 94.3 ± 1.8 | **94.5 ± 1.4** |

**Fig. 4.** Performance of the U-Net-solver as a function of a number of active dipoles and a number of EEG channels. Cells, where both the train and the test data were generated with the same number of dipoles and the same number of channels, are marked in bold. Histograms on the bottom show MAE distribution for the data used as the test sample; the models were trained with 5–10 (left) and 10–25 (right) dipoles.

To study the generalization performance of the U-Net-solver all trained models were reciprocally tested on all test sets. The experiments were done for the 128-channel EEG.

We also tested the ability of the solver to process the EEG data, obtained from more commonly used EEG configurations: 64 and 32 channels. For this experiment, pattern of only 5–10 dipoles were considered, and the result is shown in Fig. 4(inset table). Conventional metrics, such as MAE and SSIM, were calculated for ECoG topomaps. Background pixels were excluded. All cells in the tables of Fig. 4 are color-coded using empirical threshold: cells with relatively high performance (MAE<20 c.u. and SSIM>95%) are highlighted in green; cells with relatively moderate performance (MAE<30 c.u. or SSIM>95%) are highlighted in yellow; the other cells are highlighted in red.

We observe that the U-Net-solver trained on 10–25 dipoles yields similar errors for pairs containing 1–3 or 5–10 dipoles and thus is capable of generalizing the input data. Therefore it effectively resolves the EEG signal even if the configuration differs from the source pattern which the solver was trained on. The trade-off between the solver's accuracy and its ability to generalize is demonstrated in the histograms (Fig. 4, bottom panel).

The solver has a better ability to process unseen data when it was trained on a dataset with more variability. However, it does not hold for the model trained on more complex data examples: e.g., ECoG patterns from a superposition of 25–45 dipoles are reconstructed more coarsely and the pre-trained solver fails to resolve the simpler data examples. This is possibly caused by the loss of information incurred by inaccurately representing the complex cortical patterns as 2D images instead of 3D volumes. In contrast, the U-Net-solver effectively deals with EEG data in any available data configuration. The reduction of information in the input data recorded with 32 or 64 EEG channels (instead of 128 full channel set) does not significantly alter the efficiency of the U-Net-solver, as seen in the extended column 2 of the table in Fig. 4.

# 4 Discussion

**Baseline Comparison.** Since to our best knowledge ours is the first DL-based IP2 solution, we compared our U-Net-solver to the numerical solution of the Cauchy problem by the method of quasi-reversibility [15], using identical inputs for both solvers (see Fig. 5A).

Specifically, the same set of 128 EEG-channel data with 5% Gaussian noise was taken as input images for the U-Net-solver, the DualGAN-solver, and the numerical solution of the Cauchy problem. The statistics calculated on 25 test samples (5–10 dipoles superposition) is shown in the table insets of Fig. 5A.

Once fully trained, our deep learning models exhibit better suitability for the future cortical potential images than the numerical method [15]. Their inherent numerical stability shows better results quantitatively (see the scores in Fig. 5) and qualitatively (notice blur patterns in the images).

Unlike direct numerical solutions to the ill-posed problem, our models require no explicit regularization to stabilize the approximating functions, avoiding the

**A**

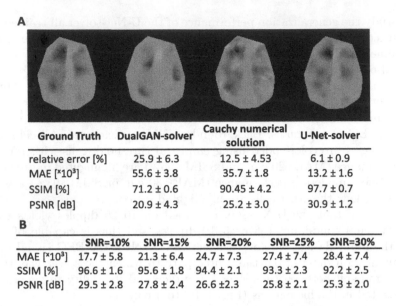

| | Ground Truth | DualGAN-solver | Cauchy numerical solution | U-Net-solver |
|---|---|---|---|---|
| relative error [%] | | 25.9 ± 6.3 | 12.5 ± 4.53 | 6.1 ± 0.9 |
| MAE [×10³] | | 55.6 ± 3.8 | 35.7 ± 1.8 | 13.2 ± 1.6 |
| SSIM [%] | | 71.2 ± 0.6 | 90.45 ± 4.2 | 97.7 ± 0.7 |
| PSNR [dB] | | 20.9 ± 4.3 | 25.2 ± 3.0 | 30.9 ± 1.2 |

**B**

| | SNR=10% | SNR=15% | SNR=20% | SNR=25% | SNR=30% |
|---|---|---|---|---|---|
| MAE [×10³] | 17.7 ± 5.8 | 21.3 ± 6.4 | 24.7 ± 7.3 | 27.4 ± 7.4 | 28.4 ± 7.4 |
| SSIM [%] | 96.6 ± 1.6 | 95.6 ± 1.8 | 94.4 ± 2.1 | 93.3 ± 2.3 | 92.2 ± 2.5 |
| PSNR [dB] | 29.5 ± 2.8 | 27.8 ± 2.4 | 26.6 ±2.3 | 25.8 ± 2.1 | 25.3 ± 2.0 |

**Fig. 5. A.** Comparison of our U-Net-solver to the SOTA method (numerical solution of the Cauchy problem by quasireversibility [15]) and to the DualGAN-solver. **B.** To estimate the stability of U-Net-solver we gradually increased the noise and estimated the error and the image quality scores.

buildup of error, that is frequent to a particular numerical method. The choice of regularization coefficients constitutes a separate engineering problem that we eliminate herein. Our solvers rely on neural networks that provide implicit regularization of the solution and, ultimately, yield superior accuracy with reduced regularization noise. We also observe that the quality of the solution decreases linearly as the data noise is increased (Fig. 5B), suggesting that our solution is stable with respect to SNR.

**Further Research.** Although the U-Net-solver is found to be a better model for reconstructing unseen ECoG patterns, it requires *paired* EEG-ECoG datasets. DualGAN model, to the contrary, could be trained in an *unpaired* manner (Fig. 5A), which increases the amount of readily available *real* data [2]. Preliminary experiments have shown promising results as to the appearence of ECoG topomaps obtained with DualGAN. However, quantitative evaluation demonstrated that the DualGAN architecture cannot be used "as is". The modification of DualGAN for the optimization of MAE, SSIM and PSNR will be the subject of future research.

Another area of further research is the extension of our approach to the translation between corresponding 3-D volumes [21], which may provide a more detailed solution due to avoiding of in-plane projections of the measurements.

3-D synthetic data can be used to pre-train translation models, which in turn can be applied in clinical settings (see, e.g. [16] and references therein).

We prioritize providing complex comparison of the method either with *IP1* or with *IP0* solutions. Conventional methods (MNE, LCVM, etc.) [11,23,29] and novel approaches [4,13,15] will be tested both on modelled and on real data with proper statistical analysis.

## 5   Conclusions

We proposed a new approach to brain activity reconstruction by reformulating it into an image-to-image translation framework. We demonstrated successful 2-D topographical mapping of the EEG data to the cortical potentials. CNNs fine-tuned to directly approximate the inverse-operator, achieved a remarkably low error of reconstruction and high image quality scores, effectively promising a boost to the spatial resolution of the EEG signal. The CNN-based solver demonstrated high stability with respect to noise and to the number of measurements (EEG channels). Due to the flexibility of the solver, it can provide approximations to the solution regardless of the geometries of the scalp and the cortex, mitigating possible anatomical differences in patients. Furthermore, the U-Net-solver approach provides accurate primary current dipole localization either with discrete or with distributed source current activity (see Supplementary material). Our framework can be put at use in areas where high-resolution and high-speed EEG data interpretation is sought after, e.g., in the non-invasive brain-computer interface devices or in localization of epileptogenic foci.

**Conflict of Interest:** The authors declare that the research was conducted in the absence of any commercial or financial relationships that could be construed as a potential conflict of interest.

## References

1. Anderson, R., et al.: Mfem: a modular finite element methods library. arXiv preprint arXiv:1911.09220 (2019)
2. Boran, E., et al.: Dataset of human medial temporal lobe neurons, scalp and intracranial EEG during a verbal working memory task. Sci. Data **7**(1), 1–7 (2020)
3. Bourgeois, L.: Convergence rates for the quasi-reversibility method to solve the Cauchy problem for Laplace's equation. Inverse Prob. **22**(2), 413 (2006)
4. Cui, S., et al.: EEG source localization using spatio-temporal neural network. Chin. Commun. **16**(7), 131–143 (2019)
5. Da Silva, F.L., Hansen, P., Kringelbach, M., Salmelin, R., et al.: Electrophysiological basis of MEG signals. In: MEG: An Introduction to Methods, pp. 1–2. Oxford, Univ. Press (2010)
6. Fischer, A., Kaplan, M., Azéma, L.: La femme, Médecin du Foyer: Ouvrage d'Hygiène et de Médecine familiale, concernant particulièrement les Maladies des Femmes et des Enfants, les Accouchements et les Soins à donner aux Enfants. E. Posselt & Cie, Éditeurs, Bibliothèque nationale de France (1905). http://catalogue.bnf.fr/ark:/12148/cb30437824k

7. Fletcher, R.: Conjugate gradient methods for indefinite systems. In: Watson, G.A. (ed.) Numerical Analysis. LNM, vol. 506, pp. 73–89. Springer, Heidelberg (1976). https://doi.org/10.1007/BFb0080116
8. Fuchs, M., Wagner, M., Kastner, J.: Development of volume conductor and source models to localize epileptic foci. J. Clin. Neurophysiol. **24**(2), 101–119 (2007)
9. Gevins, A., Le, J., Brickett, P., Reutter, B., Desmond, J.: Seeing through the skull: advanced EEGs use MRIs to accurately measure cortical activity from the scalp. Brain Topogr. **4**(2), 125–131 (1991)
10. Gramfort, A., et al.: MEG and EEG data analysis with MNE-Python. Front. Neurosci. **7**, 267 (2013). https://doi.org/10.3389/fnins.2013.00267
11. Hämäläinen, M.S., Ilmoniemi, R.J.: Interpreting magnetic fields of the brain: minimum norm estimates. Med. Biol. Eng. Comput. **32**(1), 35–42 (1994)
12. Hansen, S.T., Hansen, L.K.: Spatio-temporal reconstruction of brain dynamics from EEG with a Markov prior. NeuroImage **148**, 274–283 (2017)
13. Hecker, L., Rupprecht, R., Tebartz van Elst, L., Kornmeier, J.: ConvDip: a convolutional neural network for better M/EEG source imaging. BioRxiv (2020). https://doi.org/10.1101/2020.04.09.033506, https://www.biorxiv.org/content/early/2020/06/10/2020.04.09.033506
14. Jin, K.H., McCann, M.T., Froustey, E., Unser, M.: Deep convolutional neural network for inverse problems in imaging. IEEE Trans. Image Process. **26**(9), 4509–4522 (2017)
15. Koshev, N., Yavich, N., Malovichko, M., Skidchenko, E., Fedorov, M.: Fem-based scalp-to-cortex EEG data mapping via the solution of the cauchy problem. Journal of Inverse and Ill-posed Problems 1(ahead-of-print) (2020). https://www.degruyter.com/view/journals/jiip/ahead-of-print/article-10.1515-jiip-2019-0065/article-10.1515-jiip-2019-0065.xml
16. Krylov, D., Dylov, D.V., Rosenblum, M.: Reinforcement learning for suppression of collective activity in oscillatory ensembles. Chaos Interdisc. J. Nonlinear Sci. **30**(3), 033126 (2020). https://doi.org/10.1063/1.5128909
17. Kwon, M., Han, S., Kim, K., Jun, S.C.: Super-resolution for improving EEG spatial resolution using deep convolutional neural network-feasibility study. Sensors **19**(23), 5317 (2019)
18. Lamus, C., Hämäläinen, M.S., Temereanca, S., Brown, E.N., Purdon, P.L.: A spatiotemporal dynamic distributed solution to the MEG inverse problem. NeuroImage **63**(2), 894–909 (2012)
19. Latvala, J.: Applying neural networks for improving the MEG inverse solution. G2 pro gradu, diplomityö (2017). https://urn.fi/URN:NBN:fi:aalto-201712188173
20. Lopes da Silva, F.: EEG and MEG: relevance to neuroscience. Neuron **80**(5), 1112–1128 (2013). https://doi.org/10.1016/j.neuron.2013.10.017, http://www.sciencedirect.com/science/article/pii/S0896627313009203
21. Milletari, F., Navab, N., Ahmadi, S.A.: V-net: fully convolutional neural networks for volumetric medical image segmentation. In: 2016 Fourth International Conference on 3D Vision (3DV), pp. 565–571. IEEE (2016)
22. Murakami, S., Okada, Y.: Contributions of principal neocortical neurons to magnetoencephalography and electroencephalography signals. J. Physiol. **575**(3), 925–936 (2006)
23. Pascual-Marqui, R., et al.: Imaging the electric neuronal generators of EEG/MEG. Electrical Neuroimaging, p. 49–78 (2009)

24. Prokopenko, D., Stadelmann, J.V., Schulz, H., Renisch, S., Dylov, D.V.: Unpaired synthetic image generation in radiology using gans. In: Nguyen, D., Xing, L., Jiang, S. (eds.) Artificial Intelligence in Radiation Therapy, pp. 94–101. Springer International Publishing, Cham (2019). https://doi.org/10.1007/978-3-030-32486-5_12

25. Fang, Q., Boas, D.A.: Tetrahedral mesh generation from volumetric binary and grayscale images. In: 2009 IEEE International Symposium on Biomedical Imaging: From Nano to Macro, pp. 1142–1145, June 2009. https://doi.org/10.1109/ISBI.2009.5193259

26. Ronneberger, O., Fischer, P., Brox, T.: U-Net: convolutional networks for biomedical image segmentation. In: Navab, N., Hornegger, J., Wells, W.M., Frangi, A.F. (eds.) MICCAI 2015. LNCS, vol. 9351, pp. 234–241. Springer, Cham (2015). https://doi.org/10.1007/978-3-319-24574-4_28

27. Ryynanen, O.R.M., Hyttinen, J.A.K., Malmivuo, J.A.: Effect of measurement noise and electrode density on the spatial resolution of cortical potential distribution with different resistivity values for the skull. IEEE Trans. Biomed. Eng. **53**(9), 1851–1858 (2006). https://doi.org/10.1109/TBME.2006.873744

28. Stadelmann, J., Schulz, H., van der Heide, U., Renisch, S.: Pseudo-CT image generation from mDixon MRI images using fully convolutional neural networks. In: Medical Imaging 2019: Biomedical Applications in Molecular, Structural, and Functional Imaging, vol. 10953, p. 109530Z. International Society for Optics and Photonics (2019)

29. Van Veen, B.D., Van Drongelen, W., Yuchtman, M., Suzuki, A.: Localization of brain electrical activity via linearly constrained minimum variance spatial filtering. IEEE Trans. Biomed. Eng. **44**(9), 867–880 (1997)

30. Yi, Z., Zhang, H., Tan, P., Gong, M.: DualGAN: unsupervised dual learning for image-to-image translation. In: Proceedings of the IEEE International Conference on Computer Vision, pp. 2849–2857 (2017)

31. Zacharov, I., et al.: "Zhores" –petaflops supercomputer for data-driven modeling, machine learning and artificial intelligence installed in Skolkovo institute of science and technology. Open Eng. **9**(1), 512–520 (2019)

# An Anatomically-Informed 3D CNN for Brain Aneurysm Classification with Weak Labels

Tommaso Di Noto[1]([⊠])[iD], Guillaume Marie[1][iD], Sébastien Tourbier[1][iD],
Yasser Alemán-Gómez[1,2][iD], Guillaume Saliou[1][iD], Meritxell Bach Cuadra[1,3,4][iD],
Patric Hagmann[1][iD], and Jonas Richiardi[1][iD]

[1] Department of Radiology, Lausanne University Hospital and University
of Lausanne, Lausanne, Switzerland
tommaso.di-noto@chuv.ch
[2] Center for Psychiatric Neuroscience, Department of Psychiatry, Lausanne
University Hospital and University of Lausanne, Lausanne, Switzerland
[3] Medical Image Analysis Laboratory, Center for Biomedical Imaging,
Lausanne, Switzerland
[4] Signal Processing Laboratory (LTS5), Ecole Polytechnique Fédérale de Lausanne,
Lausanne, Switzerland

**Abstract.** A commonly adopted approach to carry out detection tasks in medical imaging is to rely on an initial segmentation. However, this approach strongly depends on voxel-wise annotations which are repetitive and time-consuming to draw for medical experts. An interesting alternative to voxel-wise masks are so-called "weak" labels: these can either be coarse or oversized annotations that are less precise, but noticeably faster to create. In this work, we address the task of brain aneurysm detection as a patch-wise binary classification with weak labels, in contrast to related studies that rather use supervised segmentation methods and voxel-wise delineations. Our approach comes with the non-trivial challenge of the data set creation: as for most focal diseases, anomalous patches (with aneurysm) are outnumbered by those showing no anomaly, and the two classes usually have different spatial distributions. To tackle this frequent scenario of inherently imbalanced, spatially skewed data sets, we propose a novel, anatomically-driven approach by using a multi-scale and multi-input 3D Convolutional Neural Network (CNN). We apply our model to 214 subjects (83 patients, 131 controls) who underwent Time-Of-Flight Magnetic Resonance Angiography (TOF-MRA) and presented a total of 111 unruptured cerebral aneurysms. We compare two strategies for negative patch sampling that have an increasing level of difficulty for the network and we show how this choice can strongly affect the results. To assess whether the added spatial information helps improving performances, we compare our anatomically-informed CNN with a baseline, spatially-agnostic CNN. When considering the more realistic and challenging scenario including vessel-like negative patches, the former model attains the highest classification results (accuracy$\simeq$95%, AUROC$\simeq$0.95, AUPR$\simeq$0.71), thus outperforming the baseline.

© Springer Nature Switzerland AG 2020
S. M. Kia et al. (Eds.): MLCN 2020/RNO-AI 2020, LNCS 12449, pp. 56–66, 2020.
https://doi.org/10.1007/978-3-030-66843-3_6

**Keywords:** 3D-CNN · Negative sampling · Weak labels · Magnetic resonance angiography · Aneurysm detection

# 1   Introduction

Cerebral aneurysms (CA) are abnormal focal dilatations in brain arteries caused by a weakness in the blood vessel wall. The overall population prevalence of CA ranges from 5% to 8% [1] and CA rupture is the predominant cause of nontraumatic subarachnoid hemorrhages (SAH) [2]. The mortality rate of aneurysmal SAH is around 40% and only half of post-SAH patients return to independent life [3,4]. Considering that the workload of radiologists is steadily increasing [5,6] and the detection of CAs is deemed a non-trivial task (especially for small aneurysms) [7], the development of an automatic tool able to detect aneurysms before they become symptomatic would be highly beneficial, both to reduce false negative cases, and to speed up the daily workflow in radiology departments.

Nowadays, non-enhanced Time-Of-Flight Magnetic Resonance Angiography (TOF-MRA) is routinely used for CA detection because of its high sensitivity ($\simeq$95%) and pooled specificity of 89% [8]. Also, it has the advantage of being non-invasive and without radiation exposure, as opposed to Digital Subtraction Angiography (DSA) or Computed Tomography Angiography (CTA).

In the last few years, several medical imaging tasks such as classification, detection and segmentation have been profoundly revolutionized by the application of deep learning (DL) algorithms [9] which have shown a noteworthy potential. However, DL has to deal with the recurrent challenge of limited availability of (labelled) training examples, for building predictive algorithms that do not suffer from overfitting [10]. This is especially true in radiology where the voxel-wise manual annotation of medical images is commonly considered a tedious and time-consuming task [11] which often takes away precious time from experts.

The task of automated brain aneurysm detection with DL algorithms has already been addressed by several research groups. For instance, [12] used 2D patches and a ResNet-like model to detect aneurysms from TOF-MRA. Similarly, 2D Maximum Intensity Projection (MIP) patches with Convolutional Neural Network (CNN) have been proposed by [7,13]. In [14], 2D nearby projection (NP) images extracted from 3D CTA are fed as input to a Region-CNN (R-CNN) to detect aneurysms. Other works rather use 3D patches to perform aneurysm detection either in MRA or CTA imaging [15,16]. Though many of these works present encouraging results for the development of a Computer-Assisted Diagnosis (CAD) system for aneurysm detection, most of them [7,13,15,16] build their supervised models starting from voxel-wise manual annotations. From these annotations, they either carry out plain aneurysm segmentation [16], or they first perform a segmentation and then refine it with post-processing steps [7,13,15], in order to obtain detection bounding boxes.

Differently from previous approaches, our work investigates the task of brain aneurysm classification exploiting "weak" labels. In our application, these correspond to manual annotations which are not drawn with voxel-wise precision, but rather consist of spheres enclosing the aneurysms which are faster to create for the expert with respect to a slice-by-slice labelling. The concept of "lazy" or "weak" labels has already been used in previous works, in particular for segmentation [17,18], or cell type concentration prediction [19] where full labelling would be infeasible. However, while [17,19] exploited under-labelled data, we use over-labelled (more labelled voxels than actual true positives) data to perform aneurysm classification.

The goal of this study is three-fold: first, we assess the capability of a custom CNN to distinguish 3D TOF-MRA patches positive/negative for aneurysms, using weak labels. Second, we show the substantial impact that negative sampling can have on classification performances. Lastly, we propose an anatomically-driven solution to mitigate the problem of negative sampling for our dataset and for similar medical imaging tasks.

## 2   Materials and Methods

### 2.1   Data Set

A retrospective cohort of 214 subjects who underwent clinically-indicated TOF-MRA between 2010 and 2012 was used. Out of these 214 subjects, 83 had one (or more) aneurysm(s), while 131 did not present any. For the former group, patients with one or more unruptured intracranial aneurysms were included, while patients with treated and ruptured aneurysms were excluded. Different aneurysms of the same patient were treated as independent, but most patients (81%) had only one aneurysm. Similarly, for patients with multiple sessions, we treated each session independently. The overall number of aneurysms included in the study is 111 and their anatomical location distribution is shown in Table 1. A 3D gradient recalled echo sequence with Partial Fourier technique was used for all subjects (see MR acquisition parameter details in Table 2). Aneurysms were annotated by one radiologist with 4 years of experience in neuroimaging. The Mango software was used to create the aforementioned weak labels which correspond to spheres that enclose the whole aneurysm, regardless of the shape (i.e. saccular, fusiform or multilocular). All TOF-MRA subjects included in the study were double checked by a senior neuroradiologist with over 14 years of experience, in order to exclude potential false positives or false negatives that might have been present in the original medical reports. The data set was organized according to the Brain Imaging Data Structure (BIDS) standard [20].

### 2.2   Image Processing

Two preprocessing steps were carried out for each subject. First, we performed skull-stripping with the Brain Extraction Tool [21] to remove regions such as the skull or the eyes. Second, a probabilistic vessel atlas built from multi-center MRA data sets [22] was co-registered to each patient's TOF-MRA using the Advanced Neuroimaging Tools (ANTS) [23]. Specifically, we first registered the

**Table 1.** Spatial distribution of aneurysms. MCA = Middle Cerebral Artery, ACOM = Anterior Communicating Artery, PCOM = Posterior Communicating Artery.

|                         | Count | %    |
|-------------------------|-------|------|
| MCA                     | 22    | 19.8 |
| ACOM                    | 20    | 18.0 |
| Intradural carotid other| 13    | 11.7 |
| Carotid extra           | 13    | 11.7 |
| MC other                | 8     | 7.2  |
| Carotid tip             | 8     | 7.2  |
| Pericallosal            | 8     | 7.2  |
| PCOM                    | 7     | 6.3  |
| Basilar tip             | 5     | 4.5  |
| Ophthalmic              | 4     | 3.6  |
| Post other              | 3     | 2.7  |

**Table 2.** MR acquisition parameters of TOF-MRA scans used for the study population.

| # scans | Vendor | Model | Field strength [T] | TR [ms] | TE [ms] | Pixel spacing [mm$^2$] | Slice thickness [mm] | Slice gap [mm] |
|---------|--------|-------|--------------------|---------|---------|------------------------|----------------------|----------------|
| 81 | Philips | Intera | 3.0 | 18.3 | 3.40 | 0.41 × 0.41 | 1.1 | 0.55 |
| 10 | Siemens healthineers | Aera | 1.5 | 24.0 | 7.0 | 0.35 × 0.35 | 0.5 | 0.09 |
| 21 | Siemens healthineers | Skyra | 3.0 | 21.0 | 3.43 | 0.27 × 0.27 | 0.5 | 0.08 |
| 35 | Siemens healthineers | Symphony | 1.5 | 39.0 | 5.02 | 0.39 × 0.39 | 1 | 0.25 |
| 28 | Siemens healthineers | TrioTim | 3.0 | 23.0 | 4.18 | 0.46 × 0.46 | 0.69 | 0.14 |
| 61 | Siemens healthineers | Verio | 3.0 | 22.0 | 3.95 | 0.46 × 0.46 | 0.70 | 0.13 |

probabilistic atlas to the T1-weighted anatomical scan of each patient through a symmetric diffeomorphic registration. Second, we registered the obtained warped volume to the TOF subject space through an affine registration. The registered atlas was used only to provide prior information about vessel locations for the patch sampling strategy (see Sect. 2.4 below). As for most of the previously mentioned studies, we adopt a patch-based approach for the classification of aneurysms: we use 3D TOF-MRA patches as input samples to our network, rather than the entire volumes.

## 2.3　An Anatomically-Informed 3D-CNN

The task of aneurysm classification is extremely spatially constrained, since not only aneurysms solely occur in arteries, but they also occur in precise locations of the vasculature that have higher probability than others. Inspired by previous works in neuroimaging [24, 25], we decided to include this strong anatomical prior into our model. This was achieved in two ways: first, we designed a two-channel CNN which analyzes patches of the input volume at different spatial scales, in order to provide anatomical context on the vascular tree surrounding the patch of interest. Second, we computed for each input sample a numerical vector $\mathbf{D}$ containing tailored spatial features which is integrated in the fully connected layers of the network; namely, the vector $\mathbf{D}$ includes the [x, y, z] coordinates of the center of the input patch in MNI space, and the Euclidean distances from this center to several coordinate and landmark points (also in MNI space). The coordinate points belong to a cubic (6 × 6 × 6), uniformly-sampled grid superimposed on the TOF-MRA volume. The landmark points correspond to 24 arterial locations where aneurysms are most recurrent; these were selected basing on the literature [26] and on our data. The final dimension of $\mathbf{D}$ is 243. A 3D visual representation of these distances and of the creation of $\mathbf{D}$ are provided in Fig. 1.

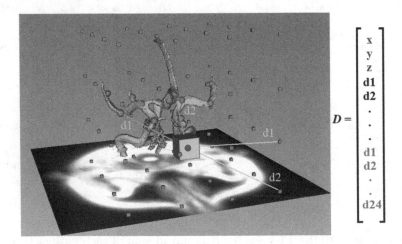

**Fig. 1.** Computation of spatial features: for each input patch, we extract a feature vector $\mathbf{D}$ which is composed of the [x, y, z] coordinates of the patch center (in purple), the distances from this center to the points of a uniform grid (light green) and the distances to some landmarks (red dots) recurrent for aneurysms (light blue). The main brain arteries are segmented from the vessel atlas and are depicted in yellow. (Color figure online)

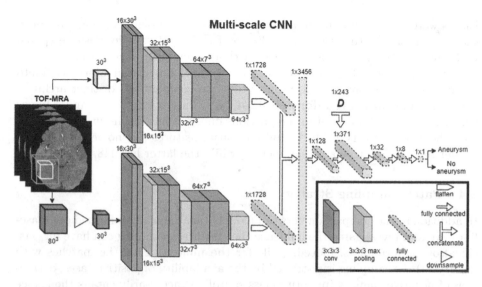

**Fig. 2.** CNN architecture: features are extracted in parallel from small-scale and large-scale TOF-MRA patches through a stack of convolutional layers. Then, they are merged into a single fully connected layer. Later, the spatial information vector **D** is concatenated to a fully-connected layer.

**Network Architecture -** We designed a custom CNN with building blocks inspired by the VGG-16 network [27]. Figure 2 illustrates in detail the structure of our CNN. As already proposed in [28,29], we performed late fusion of the features extracted from the input channels. Essentially, the same stack of convolutional layers is applied in parallel both to the small-scale and large-scale TOF-MRA patches. Then, feature vectors are merged, passed to a stack of fully connected layers, and further concatenated with vector **D**. The rationale behind the multi-scale approach is that the convolutions over the small-scale patches produce aneurysm-specific features, whereas the large-scale patches provide context/spatial descriptors. Since most of the aneurysms in our dataset (92%) had an equivalent diameter smaller than 30 voxels, we decided to fix the side of the small-scale input patches to 30. Instead, a side of 80 was set for the large-scale patches in order to include even the largest aneurysm (equivalent diameter = 58 voxels) and some context around it. All patches were standardized to have mean 0 and variance 1 before being fed to the CNN as suggested by [30]. The standardization was also performed to mitigate intensity differences which are inherently present across different patients and scanners [31]. A kernel size of 3 × 3 × 3 was used in all convolutional layers, with padding and a stride = 1 in all directions. We applied the Rectified Linear Unit (ReLU) activation function for all layers, except for the last fully connected layer which is followed by a sigmoid function. To fit the model, the Adam optimization algorithm [32] was applied with variable learning rate, together with the binary cross-entropy loss. Moreover, we used the Xavier initialization [33] for all the layers of the CNN.

Biases were initialized to 0 and a batch size of 4 was chosen. The final output of the CNN is simply the class probability $p$ of the input sample: positive (patch with aneurysm) if $p > 0.5$ or negative (without aneurysm) if $p < 0.5$.

To elucidate whether the injection of anatomical and spatial information into the model can improve classification results, we compare two distinct architectures: the **anatomically-informed 3D-CNN** illustrated in Fig. 2 and a **baseline** CNN which is identical to the previous one, but has one input channel (i.e. only the small-scale TOF-MRA) and no spatial features (i.e. no vector **D**). The former has 884,529 trainable parameters, while the latter has 448,417.

### 2.4   Patch Sampling Strategy

In addition to the comparison between models (anatomically-informed and baseline), we also investigated the influence that negative sampling can have on classification performances. Indeed, while for the minority class (i.e. patches with aneurysm) the sampling is restricted by the availability of positive cases, extraction of negative samples (majority-class sampling) necessarily entails the choice of one (or more) extraction criteria. Therefore, we chose two different sampling criteria for extracting negative patches:

**1) Random sampling:** negative samples were extracted randomly within the skull-stripped brain, without overlapping with the positive patches.

**2) Intensity-matched sampling:** we imposed intensity constraints for the extraction basing on the co-registered vessel atlas. More specifically, with an iterative search, we only extract the negative sample when the corresponding (i.e. same center coordinates) vessel patch has both a local (patch-wise) and global (volume-wise) brightness that are higher than some specific thresholds. These thresholds, in turn, were chosen empirically according to the local and global brightness of all positive patches in the vessel atlas. First, this sampling strategy avoids extracting patches that are too dark with respect to positive ones. Second, it allows us to extract patches which always include part of the vasculature. Needless to say, this sampling creates both more realistic and more difficult negative samples for the CNN.

Instead, positive patches were extracted around the aneurysms in a non-centered fashion, but ensuring that the aneurysm mask was always completely included in the small-scale patch. As last step, regardless of the sampling strategy, we combined the samples (negative and positive) of all subjects into a unique dataset that was fed as input to the CNN. We decided to extract 8 negative samples per subject. This led to a final dataset composed of 1808 negative and 111 positive samples (ratio $\simeq 1 : 16$). During training, a series of data augmentation techniques were applied on positive patches: namely, rotations ($90°, 180°, 270°$), horizontal flip, elastic deformation and contrast adjustment. Training and evaluation were performed with Tensorflow 2.0 and a GeForce RTX 2080TI GPU.

## 2.5 Evaluation Approach

We evaluated all different scenarios through a nested stratified Cross Validation (CV), with 5 external folds and 3 internal folds. This ensured that the patches in every test fold were always unseen samples with respect to the training set and to the chosen hyperparameters. The only hyperparameter that was tuned in the internal CV is the learning rate: 0.00001, 0.0001 and 0.001 were tested. All other hyperparameters were fixed, so as not to excessively lengthen training time. We set a dropout rate of 0.2, a sample weight factor of 3 to give more importance to the minority class and we trained the CNN for 50 epochs with an early stopping condition on the validation/test set. To statistically compare classification results, Wilcoxon signed-rank tests were performed [35]. For simplicity, the tests only accounted for the area under the PR (AUPR) curve of the classifiers, since this metric is particularly suited when working with imbalanced data sets [34]. A significance threshold level $\alpha = 0.05$ was set for comparing P values. First, we saved the best hyperparameters for each experiment. Then, we re-ran the training/test of the CNN 10 times. For each of the 10 realizations we always changed the patient order and ensured that the two models (baseline and anatomically-informed) were evaluated against the exact same samples.

**Table 3.** Classification results of baseline and anatomically-informed models both with random negative patches and with intensity-matched (IM) ones. Acc = accuracy, Sens = sensitivity, Spec = specificity, PPV = positive predictive value, NPV = negative predictive value, AUC = Area Under ROC Curve, AUPR = Area Under PR curve.

| Network | Negative samples | Acc (%) | Sens (%) | Spec (%) | PPV (%) | NPV (%) | AUC | AUPR |
|---|---|---|---|---|---|---|---|---|
| Baseline | **Random** | 95.4 | 84.7 | 96.2 | 59.7 | 99.0 | .961 | .779 |
| | IM | 93.2 | 77.5 | 94.1 | 45.8 | 98.6 | .949 | .608 |
| Anatomically Informed | **Random** | 97.3 | 91.9 | 97.7 | 72.6 | 99.5 | .979 | .875 |
| | IM | 94.7 | 77.5 | 95.7 | 53.6 | 98.6 | .946 | .714 |

# 3 Results

Overall, **4 experiments** were carried out: the two networks (anatomically-informed and baseline) were evaluated first against the dataset with random negative samples and then against the dataset with intensity-matched negative samples. Classification results of the four experiments are reported in Table 3. Training the model took about 2 h for the baseline model and 3 h for the anatomically-informed one. The most frequent learning rate across the external test folds was 0.0001. The Wilcoxon tests performed on the AUPRs distributions highlighted two main findings: first, both for the baseline and the anatomically-informed model, AUPRs were statistically higher when random negative sampling was used with respect to the intensity-matched sampling ($P = 0.01$). This proves how one task is evidently easier than the other. Second, when comparing the baseline model and the anatomically-informed model against the intensity-matched dataset (difficult scenario), AUPR distributions were again significantly different ($P = 0.01$), suggesting that the proposed anatomically-informed CNN indeed outperforms the baseline.

## 4   Discussion

This work presented an alternative approach for performing cerebral aneurysm detection when voxel-wise annotations are not available. To this end, we proposed a binary classification method, making use of weak labels enclosing the aneurysms of interest. In addition, we shed light over the recurrent problem of negative sampling in imbalanced and spatially-skewed data sets, showing how this step can dramatically alter final results. Lastly, we devised a tailored CNN able to mitigate the negative sampling problem, by incorporating spatial anatomical information. This CNN was able to outperform its baseline counterpart despite the small sample size and having about twice the number of parameters. We believe this general principle is applicable to several other brain diseases with sparse spatial extent.

Our work is limited by the relatively high number of false positive cases even for the anatomically-informed CNN (see low PPV in Table 3). In addition, a separate analysis should be performed to understand whether the added distances of vector $\mathbf{D}$ are indeed helpful: these might be redundant with respect to the [x, y, z] center coordinates of the patches, which could already be informative enough. Though the presented patch-wise analysis is useful to gain insights on the network performances, it cannot be easily exploited in a clinical scenario. Thus, future work will aim at shifting towards a patient-wise analysis. Lastly, we acknowledge that the dataset size is still limited and it should be increased.

## References

1. Rinkel, G.J.E., et al.: Prevalence and risk of rupture of intracranial aneurysms: a systematic review. Stroke **29**(1), 251–256 (1998)
2. Jaja, B.N.R., et al.: Clinical prediction models for aneurysmal subarachnoid hemorrhage: a systematic review. Neurocritical Care **18**(1), 143–153 (2013)
3. Frösen, J., et al.: Saccular intracranial aneurysm: pathology and mechanisms. Acta Neuropathol. **123**(6), 773–786 (2012)
4. Xu, Z., et al.: Intracranial aneurysms: pathology, genetics, and molecular mechanisms. Neuromolecular Med., 1–19 (2019)
5. Rao, B., et al.: Utility of artificial intelligence tool as a prospective radiology peer reviewer—detection of unreported intracranial hemorrhage. Acad. Radiol. (2020)
6. McDonald, R.J., et al.: The effects of changes in utilization and technological advancements of cross-sectional imaging on radiologist workload. Acad. Radiol. **22**(9), 1191–1198 (2015)

7. Nakao, T., et al.: Deep neural network-based computer-assisted detection of cerebral aneurysms in MR angiography. J. Magn. Reson. Imaging **47**(4), 948–953 (2018)

8. Chen, X., et al.: Meta-analysis of computed tomography angiography versus magnetic resonance angiography for intracranial aneurysm. Medicine **97**(20) (2018)

9. Syeda-Mahmood, T.: Role of big data and machine learning in diagnostic decision support in radiology. J. Am. Coll. Radiol. **15**(3), 569–576 (2018)

10. Shen, D., Wu, G., Suk, H.-I.: Deep learning in medical image analysis. Annu. Rev. Biomed. Eng. **19**, 221–248 (2017)

11. Razzak, M.I., Naz, S., Zaib, A.: Deep learning for medical image processing: overview, challenges and the future. In: Dey, N., Ashour, A.S., Borra, S. (eds.) Classification in BioApps. LNCVB, vol. 26, pp. 323–350. Springer, Cham (2018). https://doi.org/10.1007/978-3-319-65981-7_12

12. Ueda, D., et al.: Deep learning for MR angiography: automated detection of cerebral aneurysms. Radiology **290**(1), 187–194 (2019)

13. Stember, J.N., et al.: Convolutional neural networks for the detection and measurement of cerebral aneurysms on magnetic resonance angiography. J. Digit. Imaging **32**(5), 808–815 (2019)

14. Dai, X., et al.: Deep learning for automated cerebral aneurysm detection on computed tomography images. Int. J. Comput. Assist. Radiol. Surg., 1–9 (2020)

15. Sichtermann, T., et al.: Deep learning-based detection of intracranial aneurysms in 3D TOF-MRA. Am. J. Neuroradiol. **40**(1), 25–32 (2019)

16. Park, A., et al.: Deep learning-assisted diagnosis of cerebral aneurysms using the HeadXNet model. JAMA Netw. Open **2**(6), e195600–e195600 (2019)

17. Ke, R., et al.: A multi-task U-net for segmentation with lazy labels. arXiv preprint arXiv:1906.12177 (2019)

18. Ezhov, M., Zakirov, A., Gusarev, M.: Coarse-to-fine volumetric segmentation of teeth in Cone-Beam CT. In: 2019 IEEE 16th International Symposium on Biomedical Imaging (ISBI 2019). IEEE (2019)

19. Abousamra, S., et al.: Weakly-supervised deep stain decomposition for multiplex IHC images. In: 2020 IEEE 17th International Symposium on Biomedical Imaging (ISBI). IEEE (2020)

20. Gorgolewski, K.J., et al.: The brain imaging data structure, a format for organizing and describing outputs of neuroimaging experiments. Sci. Data **3**(1), 1–9 (2016)

21. Smith, S.M.: Fast robust automated brain extraction. Hum. Brain Mapp. **17**(3), 143–155 (2002)

22. Mouches, P., Forkert, N.D.: A statistical atlas of cerebral arteries generated using multi-center MRA datasets from healthy subjects. Sci. Data **6**(1), 1–8 (2019)

23. Avants, B.B., et al.: A reproducible evaluation of ANTs similarity metric performance in brain image registration. Neuroimage **54**(3), 2033–2044 (2011)

24. Ghafoorian, M., et al.: Location sensitive deep convolutional neural networks for segmentation of white matter hyperintensities. Sci. Rep. **7**(1), 1–12 (2017)

25. Ganaye, P.-A., Sdika, M., Benoit-Cattin, H.: Towards integrating spatial localization in convolutional neural networks for brain image segmentation. In: 2018 IEEE 15th International Symposium on Biomedical Imaging (ISBI 2018). IEEE (2018)

26. Brown Jr., R.D., Broderick, J.P.: Unruptured intracranial aneurysms: epidemiology, natural history, management options, and familial screening. Lancet Neurol. **13**(4), 393–404 (2014)

27. Simonyan, K., Zisserman, A.: Very deep convolutional networks for large-scale image recognition. arXiv preprint arXiv:1409.1556 (2014)

28. Huang, Y., et al.: Diagnosis of Alzheimer's disease via multi-modality 3D convolutional neural network. Front. Neurosci. **13**, 509 (2019)
29. Nie, D., et al.: Multi-channel 3D deep feature learning for survival time prediction of brain tumor patients using multi-modal neuroimages. Sci. Rep. **9**(1), 1–14 (2019)
30. Goodfellow, I., Bengio, Y., Courville, A.: Deep Learning. MIT Press, Cambridge (2016)
31. Zhuge, Y., Udupa, J.K.: Intensity standardization simplifies brain MR image segmentation. Comput. Vis. Image Underst. **113**(10), 1095–1103 (2009)
32. Kingma, D.P., Ba, J.: Adam: a method for stochastic optimization. arXiv preprint arXiv:1412.6980 (2014)
33. Glorot, X., Bengio, Y.: Understanding the difficulty of training deep feedforward neural networks. In: Proceedings of the Thirteenth International Conference on Artificial Intelligence and Statistics (2010)
34. Davis, J., Goadrich, M.: The relationship between Precision-Recall and ROC curves. In: Proceedings of the 23rd International Conference on Machine Learning (2006)
35. Wilcoxon, F.: Individual comparisons by ranking methods. In: Kotz, S., Johnson, N.L. (eds.) Breakthroughs in Statistics. SSS, pp. 196–202. Springer, New York (1992). https://doi.org/10.1007/978-1-4612-4380-9_16

# Ischemic Stroke Segmentation from CT Perfusion Scans Using Cluster-Representation Learning

Jianyuan Zhang[1,2], Feng Shi[2], Lei Chen[2], Zhong Xue[2], Lichi Zhang[3], and Dahong Qian[1(✉)]

[1] Institute of Medical Robotics, School of Biomedical Engineering, Shanghai Jiao Tong University, Shanghai, China
dahong.qian@sjtu.edu.cn
[2] Shanghai United Imaging Intelligence Co., Ltd., Shanghai, China
[3] Institute for Medical Imaging Technology, School of Biomedical Engineering, Shanghai Jiao Tong University, Shanghai, China
lichizhang@sjtu.edu.cn

**Abstract.** Computed Tomography Perfusion (CTP) images have drawn extensive attention in acute ischemic stroke assessment due to its imaging speed and ability to provide dynamic perfusion quantification. However, the cerebral ischemic infarcted core has high individual variability and low contrast, and multiple CTP parametric maps need to be referred for precise delineation of the core region. It has thus become a challenging task to develop automatic segmentation algorithms. The widely applied segmentation algorithms such as U-Net lack specific modeling for image subtype in the dataset, and thus the performance remains unsatisfactory. In this paper, we propose a novel cluster-representation learning approach to address these difficulties. Specifically, we first cluster the training samples based on their similarities of the segmentation difficulty. Each cluster represents a different subtype of training images and is then used to train its own cluster-representative model. The models will be capable of extracting cluster-representative features from training samples as clustering priors, which are further fused into an overall segmentation model (for all training samples). The fusion mechanism is able to adaptively select optimal subset(s) of clustering priors which can further guide the segmentation of each unseen testing image and reduce influences from high variability of CTP images. We have applied our method on 94 subjects of ISLES 2018 dataset. By comparing with the baseline U-Net, the experiments have shown an absolute increase of 8% in Dice score and a reduction of $10mm$ in Hausdorff Distance for ischemic infarcted core segmentation. This method can also be generalized to other U-Net-like architectures to further improve their representative capacity.

**Keywords:** Ischemic stroke segmentation · Cluster-representative priors · Multi-Clustering U-Net

---

L. Zhang and D. Qian—Equally Contributed.

S. M. Kia et al. (Eds.): MLCN 2020/RNO-AI 2020, LNCS 12449, pp. 67–76, 2020.
https://doi.org/10.1007/978-3-030-66843-3_7

# 1   Introduction

Precise segmentation of irreversibly damaged tissues (infarcted core) and distinguish between core and salvageable tissues (penumbra) are critical for making decision on implementing thrombolytic treatment and subsequent diagnosis process in acute ischemic stroke. Diffusion-Weighted Imaging (DWI) as one of Magnetic Resonance Imaging (MRI) is now commonly used for the diagnosis of acute ischemic stroke. But the speed of MR imaging has become one of its drawbacks due to the urgent onset and rapid progress of stroke, possibly miss the golden time window of thrombolytic treatment which is only 3 to 4.5h from the onset of stroke [1].

Recently, computed tomography perfusion (CTP) used for assessing the condition of stroke has drawn more attention due to its faster imaging speed compared to MRI. Several perfusion parametric maps analyzed from CTP raw images are used for recognizing the core and penumbra regions. Cerebral blood flow (CBF), cerebral blood volume (CBV), mean transit time (MTT) and time-to-peak (TTP or Tmax) are the four most commonly used maps. They describe the flow of blood in the brain from a hemodynamic perspective, which can be strong evidence for diagnosis of stroke ischemia. However, the accuracy of core segmentation using CTP maps is not as high as DWI [2,3], so deriving the core region from CTP maps is challenging but meaningful.

Convolutional neural network (CNN)-based segmentation algorithm U-Net [4] has been widely used in lesion segmentation, and has shown great segmentation performance. There are already many attempts based on U-Net for ischemic core segmentation. For example, based on the idea that DWI images contain more obvious region information of infarcted core, Song et al. [5] intended to generate DWI images from CTP images with generative adversarial networks (GAN), and used the synthesized DWI images for core segmentation. However, this method can not work when real DWI images are not accessible as the generation process needs to be supervised by DWI data. Dolz et al. [6] proposed to combine multi-parametric CTP maps to construct U-Net. Each modality was processed by the respective encoder of U-Net, which was fused in one common decoder. The framework also introduced hyperdense connections for every encoder path, which led to a significant increase in the number of parameters of the whole network and had a relatively higher computational cost.

There are some limitations in the U-Net algorithm which hamper its segmentation performance. The high variability of the sample distribution in the dataset may cause degradation of the segmentation performance with a single U-Net, which occurs in the segmentation of the infarcted core of brain images with ischemic stroke [6]. The size, shape and orientation of the core region vary greatly among the population, which has made the segmentation performance of the vanilla U-Net among different testing samples unstable. Our experiments also showed that the changes in training samples can result in significantly different performance when segmenting a given testing sample. Especially, such changes become decisive when there is none or limited training samples that have correlated information to the testing one.

In this work, we refer to the idea of guided bagging in the work of Lombaert *et al.* [7], which intended to group training samples that are representative of testing samples, and trained group-specific models. Herein, we advance this strategy further to develop a novel framework for ischemic stroke segmentation. Our main contribution is two-fold:

1. We propose a new method to cluster training samples into several subsets according to their similarities of the segmentation difficulty with each other, and then trained subset-specific segmentation models with corresponding training subsets. These specified models are capable of segmenting unseen testing samples while affiliating with cluster-representative training priors.
2. We develop a novel approach to adaptively fuse these cluster-representative training priors produced by corresponding subset-specific models to better guide the segmentation of unseen testing samples. For each unseen testing sample, we assume there exists at least one subset(s) of training samples that is representative to it and the corresponding subset-specific model is activated to guide the segmentation process of this unseen testing sample, which enhances its segmentation performance.

## 2   Method

The proposed method consists of two steps as shown in Fig. 1. 1) Sample clustering of the dataset into several clusters so the samples inside each cluster are with similar segmentation difficulty. Then the cluster-representative priors (CRPs) given by cluster-representative encoders (CREs) trained by each subset are produced to guide the segmentation of unseen testing samples. Details are in Sect. 2.1; 2) multi-clustering U-Net (MCU-Net) is proposed for cerebral infarcted core segmentation by the guidance of CRPs, which is detailed in Sect. 2.2.

The baseline U-Net here was proposed in [8], which is extended from the vanilla U-Net by introducing residual blocks [9] in the down-sampling path and deep supervision [10] so that the intermediate segmentation output of each scale in the up-sampling path can be integrated to the final segmentation.

### 2.1   Sample Clustering and Cluster-Representative Encoder

**Preparation for Sample Clustering: Affinity Matrix.** Refer to the idea of clustering from [11]. We first train the respective single-sample segmentation model for every sample in the training set with baseline U-Net, followed by cross-validation to capture the similarities of the segmentation difficulty between samples, which are reflected in the affinity matrix. The process can be seen in the dark red box of Fig. 2.

Specifically, we get $n$ (the size of the training set) segmentation models, each trained by one training sample, followed by using all samples to do cross-validation on every model in turn. We use the Dice score as the metric of segmentation performance. In this way, we get an $n \times n$ affinity matrix $P$, where

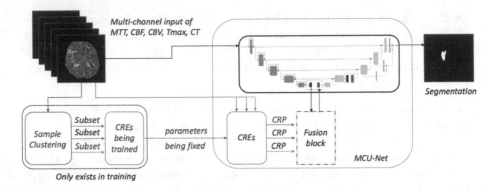

**Fig. 1.** The pipeline of the overall method. Sample clustering and cluster-representative encoders (CREs), which are encircled by the dark blue box, are detailed in Sect. 2.1 and multi-clustering U-Net (MCU-Net) is detailed in Sect. 2.2. (Color figure online)

$P._j$ is the $j^{th}$ column of $P$ and represents the Dice scores of all samples tested on the model trained with the $j^{th}$ training sample. $P_{ij}$ represents the Dice score of the $i^{th}$ training sample tested on the model trained with the $j^{th}$ training sample. The resulting $P$ is shown in Fig. 2. The redder the color the higher Dice score. The values on the diagonal of $P$ are all highly-activated, which is consistent with our perception.

**Sample Clustering.** We cluster the training set into several subsets according to the affinity matrix $P$ with the affinity propagation (AP) algorithm [12]. This makes each subset composed of the samples with similar capabilities in segmentation. It should be noted that the AP method can automatically determine the number of clusters according to the input of the affinity matrix without being prespecified. We finally cluster the training set into $m$ subsets.

**Cluster-Representative Encoder (CRE).** We then train $m$ subset-specific segmentation models based on the result of sample clustering. Specifically, we train the models with the samples from each subset and finally get $m$ segmentation models with cluster-representative information. Note that we then freeze all the parameters of these models after training in the subsequent process.

These U-shape models were all truncated in the *lowest / second lowest* (two settings of our experiments) level, as shown in Fig. 2. Then $m$ left half of the original models were actually $m$ encoders and acted as CREs being connected to multi-clustering U-Net, which is detailed in the next section.

## 2.2 Multi-Clustering U-Net (MCU-Net)

The MCU-Net is developed by inserting one fusion block into the baseline U-Net to fuse cluster-representative priors (CRPs) produced by CREs, which is

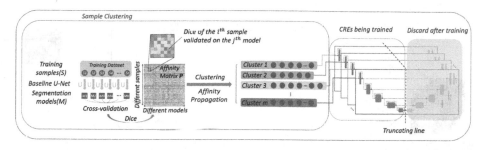

**Fig. 2.** Overview of sample clustering and cluster-representative encoder (CRE) modeling. This process only exists in the training stage to obtain CREs.

shown in Fig. 3. Inspired by [13], which introduced multi-view shape priors for segmentation of the left ventricular myocardium from short-axis MR images. Here we introduce CRPs into the main segmentation U-Net through a fusion block, which is a learnable residual block to adaptively fuse $m$ CRPs. Then, the fused information is used to guide the segmentation of unseen testing images.

Instead of multi-encoder-like U-Net which only combines clustering priors, we adopt the architecture which keeps the main segmentation U-Net while inserting a learnable fusion block. This can further introduce clustering priors while still preserving the coding from the main segmentation network. The key idea is to maintain the independence of the main segmentation structure, while CRPs are served as auxiliary guidance for segmentation. This is especially important to introduce high model variety which are specified CRPs while maintaining the independence of the main segmentation model.

The fusion block receives input as the concatenation of one coding from the encoder path of main segmentation U-Net and $m$ priors from CREs. It is a residual block consists of two $3 \times 3$ convolutional layers to fuse $(m + 1)$ codings. Then, the fused coding flows back to the main segmentation U-Net and goes through the rest of the model.

The main segmentation U-Net is trained jointly with the fusion block but with all parameters of CPEs frozen and only acting as encoders. For a given multi-channel image slice $S$, the MCU-Net can predict the segmentation $F = f_{MCU-Net}(S, e_1, e_2, e_3, ..., e_m; \theta)$, where $e_1$ - $e_m$ are $m$ CRPs and $\theta$ is the parameter of MCU-Net. MCU-Net is trained with two loss functions (two experimental settings), 1) Dice Loss; 2) BG Loss = **B**inary Cross Entropy − log (**G**eneralized *Dice*) [14].

## 3    Experiments

### 3.1    Dataset

We used the publicly released data from MICCAI ischemic stroke lesion segmentation (ISLES) challenge 2018[1], including a total of 94 CTP subjects.

---

[1] www.isles-challenge.org.

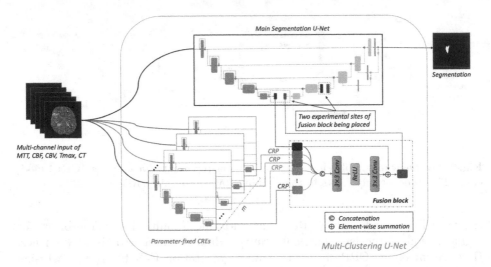

**Fig. 3.** Overview of MCU-Net. The architecture of U-Net is partially simplified for clarity of illustration. The two dotted boxes on the main segmentation U-Net are the two experimental settings for the position of fusion block can be inserted. Multi-channel input is sent to both main segmentation U-Net and $m$ CREs, while the segmentation output is given by the main segmentation U-Net.

Each subject has 4 parametric maps including CBF, CBV, MTT and Tmax, plus one plain CT image. The annotation was manually drawn on additional DWI trace images acquired in MRI scanners performed 3h after CTP scans although DWI images were not included in the dataset. The whole dataset was pre-processed to have the same *in-plane* size of $256 \times 256$ and spacing of $1mm \times 1mm$. The number of slices varies greatly in $z$-axis range from 2 to 18, and most cases have only 2 slices. Therefore, it is hard to capture 3D spatial context in this situation. We thus separated the images into 2D slices and used 2D segmentation models to do training. We stacked five maps as multi-channel input to our network. Each map was normalized respectively by subtracting the mean intensity and dividing by the standard deviation.

## 3.2 Experimental Settings

In our experiments, the dataset was randomly split into two subsets: a training set of 75 samples and a test set of 19 samples. The optimized configuration of the AP algorithm was used to obtain the optimal number of clusters for $m = 7$ clusters, as we observed the number of samples per cluster is relatively balanced in this condition. We also experimented on the case of $m = 4$ clusters.

To train single-sample segmentation models, we made several copies of every single sample so that they could be trained with regular batch-training strategy. We used the batch size of 4. The data augmentation included random rotations and mirroring. The model was trained using Adam optimizer. The initial learning

**Table 1.** Quantitative results of cerebral ischemic infarcted core segmentation with all experimental settings compared to baseline architecture. *L* or *SL* represent the fusion block is placed at the *lowest(L) or second-lowest(SL)* level of the main segmentation U-Net in MCU-Net, respectively. Meanwhile, *Dice Loss* and *BG Loss* are as two loss functions being experimented.

| Method | # Clusters | Dice(%) | HD($mm$) |
|---|---|---|---|
| Baseline U-Net [8] | —— | $48.04 \pm 22.85$ | $38.76 \pm 27.28$ |
| L w/ Dice | 7 | $53.72 \pm 22.20$ | $34.41 \pm 27.46$ |
| L w/ BG | | $52.64 \pm 20.30$ | $30.76 \pm 17.15$ |
| SL w/ Dice | | $56.30 \pm 21.83$ | $30.88 \pm 22.42$ |
| SL w/ BG | | $\mathbf{56.93 \pm 20.62}$ | $\mathbf{28.51 \pm 16.13}$ |
| L w/ Dice | 4 | $52.14 \pm 22.44$ | $34.58 \pm 21.49$ |
| L w/ BG | | $51.34 \pm 21.90$ | $34.63 \pm 18.19$ |
| SL w/ Dice | | $\mathbf{55.43 \pm 22.72}$ | $31.40 \pm 20.67$ |
| SL w/ BG | | $54.91 \pm 22.44$ | $\mathbf{30.81 \pm 17.63}$ |

rate was 5e-3 followed by the decay strategy introduced in [15]. The training epochs in single-sample training were 80, 200 for CREs and 300 for MCU-Net. All networks were trained on NVIDIA GeForce 2080 Ti. The proposed algorithm was implemented in TensorFlow.

### 3.3 Segmentation Results and Discussion

To evaluate the performance of segmentation, we used the Dice score and Hausdorff Distance (HD) as our metrics. The proposed method is compared to the baseline U-Net [8]. We conducted the configuration comparisons of different number of clusters, different locations of the fusion block being inserted in MCU-Net and two different loss functions. For fair comparison, the configuration study had the same number of filters at each level, and was trained with the same pre-processing and training strategy. We also adopt the 5-fold cross-validation scheme.

The quantitative results are shown in Table 1. It can be observed the performance of our MCU-Net is better than the baseline U-Net in all configurations. Our model has improved by up to 8% on average in absolute Dice score and reduction by up to $10mm$ in HD. These two metrics demonstrate the accuracy boosting of our method compared to the baseline model. Moreover, our method with BG loss has lower HD than that with Dice loss. Combination of pixel-wise classification (Binary Cross Entropy) and overlap measures (Generalized Dice) effectively constrain the segmentation process especially when the core region is extremely small and irregular [14].

Input CBV  Input CBF  Input MTT    Baseline   L w/ Dice    L w/ BG   SL w/ Dice   SL w/ BG     GT

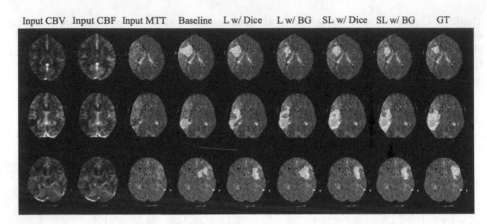

**Fig. 4.** Visualization results of all experimental settings with $m = 7$ clusters. For simplicity, we only show the CBV, CBF and MTT maps of multi-channel input. From $5^{th}$ to $8^{th}$ column: results for four combinations of experimental settings are shown.

For the number of clusters, we tried two settings of 7 clusters and 4 clusters. Our MCU-Net is equivalent to the baseline U-Net when the case of zero cluster occurs as there is no cluster-representative prior introduced to the segmentation model. The improvement of Dice and HD proves the effectiveness of the incorporation of cluster-representative information for ischemic stroke segmentation. As the number of clusters increases, the segmentation model has higher specificity which demonstrates a stronger ability to guide the segmentation of unseen testing samples.

Moreover, with fixed loss functions, a considerable improvement of segmentation performance is shown with the fusion block being placed at the second-lowest level compared to the lowest level of the main segmentation U-Net (see Fig. 3). This is because CRP from different CRE can be very abstract and different. One step of up-sampling by letting each of CRP maps to a higher resolution with their respective mapping layers in CRE, and then the mapped CRPs could be more concrete and similar which are then easier to be fused by the fusion block.

Visualization results of all settings with $m = 7$ clusters are shown in Fig. 4. Compared with the baseline U-Net, our method can provide more elaborate segmentation masks. This is very important in the segmentation of the core region, which is tightly surrounded by penumbra regions in the ischemic stroke. The possible errors of segmentation for the core region may overlap the area of penumbra, which will lead to serious misjudgment of subsequent diagnosis, and delay in treatment of acute patients.

## 4    Conclusion

We presented a new method to cluster training samples into subsets according to their similarities of the segmentation difficulty, and then trained subset-specific segmentation models which are capable of extracting cluster-representative information from each cluster. We further developed a novel fusion mechanism to adaptively fuse such cluster-representative information, which is then used to better guide the ischemic core segmentation of previously unseen images within the segmentation model. Our method outperforms the baseline U-Net and demonstrates a significant improvement in segmentation accuracy, and has the potential to be integrated into any other U-Net-like structures to further improve their representative capacity.

**Acknowledgements.** This work was supported in part by the National Key Research and Development Program of China under Grant 2018YFC0116402, and Department of Science and Technology of Zhejiang Province - Key Research and Development Program under Grant 2017C03029, and Shanghai Pujiang Program(19PJ1406800), and Interdisciplinary Program of Shanghai Jiao Tong University.

# References

1. Powers, W.J., et al.: Guidelines for the early management of patients with acute ischemic stroke: 2019 update to the 2018 guidelines for the early management of acute ischemic stroke: a guideline for healthcare professionals from the american heart association/american stroke association. Stroke **50**(12), e344–e418 (2019)
2. Bertels, J., Robben, D., Vandermeulen, D., Suetens, P.: Contra-lateral information CNN for core lesion segmentation based on native CTP in acute stroke. In: Crimi, A., Bakas, S., Kuijf, H., Keyvan, F., Reyes, M., van Walsum, T. (eds.) BrainLes 2018. LNCS, vol. 11383, pp. 263–270. Springer, Cham (2019). https://doi.org/10.1007/978-3-030-11723-8_26
3. Anand, V.K., Khened, M., Alex, V., Krishnamurthi, G.: Fully automatic segmentation for ischemic stroke using CT perfusion maps. In: Crimi, A., Bakas, S., Kuijf, H., Keyvan, F., Reyes, M., van Walsum, T. (eds.) BrainLes 2018. LNCS, vol. 11383, pp. 328–334. Springer, Cham (2019). https://doi.org/10.1007/978-3-030-11723-8_33
4. Ronneberger, O., Fischer, P., Brox, T.: U-Net: convolutional networks for biomedical image segmentation. In: Navab, N., Hornegger, J., Wells, W.M., Frangi, A.F. (eds.) MICCAI 2015. LNCS, vol. 9351, pp. 234–241. Springer, Cham (2015). https://doi.org/10.1007/978-3-319-24574-4_28
5. Song, T., Huang, N.: Integrated extractor, generator and segmentor for ischemic stroke lesion segmentation. In: Crimi, A., Bakas, S., Kuijf, H., Keyvan, F., Reyes, M., van Walsum, T. (eds.) BrainLes 2018. LNCS, vol. 11383, pp. 310–318. Springer, Cham (2019). https://doi.org/10.1007/978-3-030-11723-8_31
6. Dolz, J., Ben Ayed, I., Desrosiers, C.: Dense multi-path U-Net for ischemic stroke lesion segmentation in multiple image modalities. In: Crimi, A., Bakas, S., Kuijf, H., Keyvan, F., Reyes, M., van Walsum, T. (eds.) BrainLes 2018. LNCS, vol. 11383, pp. 271–282. Springer, Cham (2019). https://doi.org/10.1007/978-3-030-11723-8_27
7. Lombaert, H., Zikic, D., Criminisi, A., Ayache, N.: Laplacian forests: semantic image segmentation by guided bagging. In: Golland, P., Hata, N., Barillot, C., Hornegger, J., Howe, R. (eds.) MICCAI 2014. LNCS, vol. 8674, pp. 496–504. Springer, Cham (2014). https://doi.org/10.1007/978-3-319-10470-6_62

8. Isensee, F., Kickingereder, P., Wick, W., Bendszus, M., Maier-Hein, K.H.: Brain tumor segmentation and radiomics survival prediction: contribution to the BRATS 2017 challenge. In: Crimi, A., Bakas, S., Kuijf, H., Menze, B., Reyes, M. (eds.) BrainLes 2017. LNCS, vol. 10670, pp. 287–297. Springer, Cham (2018). https://doi.org/10.1007/978-3-319-75238-9_25

9. He, K., Zhang, X., Ren, S., Sun, J.: Identity mappings in deep residual networks. In: Leibe, B., Matas, J., Sebe, N., Welling, M. (eds.) ECCV 2016. LNCS, vol. 9908, pp. 630–645. Springer, Cham (2016). https://doi.org/10.1007/978-3-319-46493-0_38

10. Kayalibay, B., Jensen, G., van der Smagt, P.: CNN-based segmentation of medical imaging data. arXiv preprint arXiv:1701.03056 (2017)

11. Zhang, L., Wang, Q., Gao, Y., Guorong, W., Shen, D.: Automatic labeling of mr brain images by hierarchical learning of atlas forests. Med. Phys. **43**(3), 1175–1186 (2016)

12. Frey, B.J., Dueck, D.: Clustering by passing messages between data points. Science **315**(5814), 972–976 (2007)

13. Chen, C., Biffi, C., Tarroni, G., Petersen, S., Bai, W., Rueckert, D.: Learning shape priors for robust cardiac MR segmentation from multi-view images. In: Shen, D., Liu, T., Peters, T.M., Staib, L.H., Essert, C., Zhou, S., Yap, P.-T., Khan, A. (eds.) MICCAI 2019. LNCS, vol. 11765, pp. 523–531. Springer, Cham (2019). https://doi.org/10.1007/978-3-030-32245-8_58

14. Sudre, C.H., Li, W., Vercauteren, T., Ourselin, S., Jorge Cardoso, M.: Generalised dice overlap as a deep learning loss function for highly unbalanced segmentations. In: Cardoso, M.J., et al. (eds.) DLMIA/ML-CDS -2017. LNCS, vol. 10553, pp. 240–248. Springer, Cham (2017). https://doi.org/10.1007/978-3-319-67558-9_28

15. Tureckova, A., Rodríguez-Sánchez, A.J.: ISLES challenge: U-Shaped convolution neural network with dilated convolution for 3D stroke lesion segmentation. In: Crimi, A., Bakas, S., Kuijf, H., Keyvan, F., Reyes, M., van Walsum, T. (eds.) BrainLes 2018. LNCS, vol. 11383, pp. 319–327. Springer, Cham (2019). https://doi.org/10.1007/978-3-030-11723-8_32

# SeizureNet: Multi-Spectral Deep Feature Learning for Seizure Type Classification

Umar Asif[⊠], Subhrajit Roy, Jianbin Tang, and Stefan Harrer

IBM Research Australia, Southbank, Australia
umarasif@au1.ibm.com

**Abstract.** Automatic classification of epileptic seizure types in electroencephalograms (EEGs) data can enable more precise diagnosis and efficient management of the disease. This task is challenging due to factors such as low signal-to-noise ratios, signal artefacts, high variance in seizure semiology among epileptic patients, and limited availability of clinical data. To overcome these challenges, in this paper, we present SeizureNet, a deep learning framework which learns multi-spectral feature embeddings using an ensemble architecture for cross-patient seizure type classification. We used the recently released TUH EEG Seizure Corpus (V1.4.0 and V1.5.2) to evaluate the performance of SeizureNet. Experiments show that SeizureNet can reach a weighted $F1$ score of up to 0.95 for seizure-wise cross validation and 0.62 for patient-wise cross validation for scalp EEG based multi-class seizure type classification. We also show that the high-level feature embeddings learnt by SeizureNet considerably improve the accuracy of smaller networks through knowledge distillation for applications with low-memory constraints.

## 1 Introduction

Epilepsy is a neurological disorder which affects 1% of the world's population. It causes sudden and unforeseen seizures which can result in critical injury, or even death of the patient. One third of epileptic patients do not have appropriate medical treatments available. For the remaining two thirds of the patients, treatment options and quality vary because seizure semiology is different for every epileptic patient. An important technique to diagnose epilepsy is through visual inspection of electroencephalography (EEG) recordings by physicians to analyse abnormalities in brain activities. This task is time-consuming and subject to inter-observer variability. With the advancements in IoT-based data collection, machine learning based systems have been developed to capture abnormal patterns in the EEG data during seizures [5,6,12,25]. In this context, current systems have mostly focused on tasks such as seizure detection and seizure prediction [4,13,18,24,27,28], and the task of seizure type classification is largely undeveloped due to factors such as complex nature of the task and unavailability of clinical datasets with seizure type annotations. Nevertheless, the capability to

---

S. Roy now with Google.

© Springer Nature Switzerland AG 2020
S. M. Kia et al. (Eds.): MLCN 2020/RNO-AI 2020, LNCS 12449, pp. 77–87, 2020.
https://doi.org/10.1007/978-3-030-66843-3_8

discriminate between different seizure types (e.g., focal or generalized seizures) as they are detected has the potential to improve long-term patient care, enabling timely drug adjustments and remote monitoring in clinical trials [8]. Recently, Temple University released TUH EEG Seizure Corpus (TUH-EEGSC) [21] for epilepsy research making it the world's largest publicly available dataset for seizure type classification. The work of [19] presented baseline results on TUH-EEGSC [21] for seizure type classification by conducting a search space exploration of various standard machine learning algorithms. Other methods such as [20,23] used subsamples of data from selected seizure types for seizure analysis. Recently, the work of [2] presented a deep learning based framework consisting of a neural memory network with neural plasticity for seizure type classification. In this paper, we propose an ensemble learning approach and present new benchmarks for seizure type classification using seizure-wise and patient-wise cross-validation. The main contributions of this paper are as follows:

1. We present *SeizureNet*, a deep learning framework focused on diversifying individual classifiers of an ensemble by learning feature embeddings at different spatial and frequency resolutions of EEG data. Experiments show that our multi-spectral feature learning encourages diversity in the ensemble and reduces variance in the final predictions for seizure type classification.
2. We present *Saliency-encoded Spectrograms*, a visual representation which captures salient information contained in the frequency transform of the time-series EEG data. Experiments show that our saliency-encoded spectrograms produce improvements in seizure classification accuracy on TUH-EEGSC [21].
3. We evaluate the capability of our framework for transfering knowledge to smaller networks through knowledge distillation and present benchmark results for seizure type classification on TUH-EEGSC [21].

## 2   The Proposed Framework (SeizureNet)

Figure 1-A shows the overall architecture of our framework which transforms raw time-series EEG signals into the proposed saliency-encoded spectrograms, and uses an ensemble of deep CNN models to produce predictions for seizure type classification. In the following, we describe in detail the individual components of our framework.

### 2.1   Saliency-Encoded Spectrograms

Our saliency-encoded spectrograms are inspired from visual saliency detection [9], where we transform time-series EEG signals into a visual representation which captures multi-scale saliency information from the EEG data. Specifically, saliency-encoded spectrograms consist of three feature maps as shown in Fig. 1-D. **i)** a Fourier Transform map ($FT$) which encodes the *log* amplitude Fourier Transform of the EEG signals, **ii)** a spectral saliency map ($S_1$), which extracts saliency by computing the spectral residual of the $FT$ feature map, and

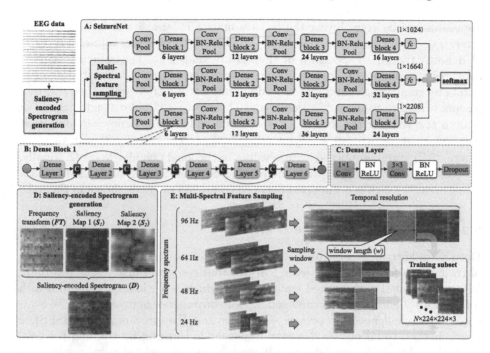

**Fig. 1.** The overall architecture of our framework. Input EEG data is first transformed into the proposed saliency-encoded spectrograms (D), which are then sampled at different frequency and spatial resolutions (E), and finally fed into an ensemble of deep CNN models. For illustrative purposes, we show the ensemble with only three sub-networks. The outputs of the sub-networks are combined through summation and fed into a Softmax operation for producing probabilistic distributions with respect to the target classes (A).

iii) a multi-scale saliency map ($S_2$), which captures spectral saliency at multiple scales using center-surround differences of the features of the $FT$ feature map [11,15]. Mathematically, given a time-series EEG sequence $X(c,t)$ from a channel $c$ parameterized by time $t$, we compute the Fast Fourier Transform ($\mathcal{F}$) of the sequence as: $\mathcal{F}(X) = \int_{\infty}^{-\infty} X(c,t)e^{-2\pi it}dt$. We compute $\mathcal{F}$ on data from selected 20 channels[1] and take the $log$ of the amplitude of the Fourier Transform. The output is reshaped into a $\mathbb{R}^{p \times 20}$–dimensional feature map ($FT$) where $p$ denotes the number of data points of the EEG sequence. Mathematically, $FT$ can be written as: $FT = log(Amplitude(\mathcal{F}(X)))$. Mathematically, $S_1$ can be written as: $S_1 = \mathcal{G} * \mathcal{F}^{-1}(\exp(FT - \mathcal{H} * FT) + \mathcal{P})^2$, where, $\mathcal{F}^{-1}$ denotes the Inverse Fourier Transform. The term $\mathcal{H}$ represents the average spectrum of $FT$

---

[1] The sclap EEG data was collected using 10–20 system [22], and TCP montage [14] was used to select 20 channels of the input. We used the following 20 channels: $FP1 - F7; F7 - T3; T3 - T5; T5 - O1; FP2 - F8; F8 - T4; T4 - T6; T6 - O2; T3 - C3; C3 - CZ; CZ - C4; C4 - T4; FP1 - F3; F3 - C3; C3 - P3; P3 - O1; FP2 - F4; F4 - C4; C4 - P4; P4 - O2.$

approximated by convoluting the feature map $FT$ by a $3 \times 3$ local averaging filter. The term $\mathcal{G}$ is a Gaussian kernel to smooth the feature values. The term $\mathcal{P}$ denotes the phase spectrum of the feature map $FT$. The saliency map $S_2$ captures saliency in the feature map $FT$ with respect to its surrounding data points by computing center-surround differences at multiple scales. Let $FT_i$ represents a feature value at location $i$, and $\Omega$ denotes a circular neighborhood of scale $\rho$ surrounding the location $i$. Mathematically, the saliency calculation at location $i$ can be written as: $S_2(i) = \sum_{\rho \in [2,3,4]} (FT_i - min([FT_{k,\rho}])), \forall k \in \Omega$, where, $[FT_{k,\rho}]$ represents the feature values in the local neighborhood $\Omega$. Finally, we concatenate the three feature maps $FT$, $S_1$, and $S_2$ into an RGB-like data structure ($\mathcal{D}$) which is normalized between 0 and 255 range as shown in Fig. 1-D.

## 2.2   Multi-Spectral Feature Learning

Deep neural networks are often over-parameterized and require sufficient amount of training data to effectively learn features that can generalize to the test data. When confronted with limited training data which is a common issue in health informatics [3], deep architectures suffer poor convergence or over-fitting. To overcome these challenges, we present *Multi-Spectral Feature Sampling* (MSFS), a novel method to encourage diversity in ensemble learning by training the sub-networks using data sampled from different frequency and temporal resolutions. Figure 1-E shows an overview of our MSFS method. Consider an $M-$dimensional training dataset $\boldsymbol{D} = \{(\mathcal{D}_i, y_i) | 0 \leq i \leq N_d\}$, which is composed of $N_d$ samples, where $\mathcal{D}_i$ is a training sample with the corresponding class label $y_i \in \mathcal{Y}$. During training, MSFS generates a feature subspace $\boldsymbol{D}^m = \{(\mathcal{D}_i^m, y_i) | 0 \leq i \leq N_d\}$ which contains spectrograms generated by a random selection of the sampling frequency $f \in F$ (Hz), a window length parameter $w \in \mathcal{W}$ (seconds), and a window step size parameter $o \in \mathcal{O}^2$. This process is repeated $N_e = 3$ times to obtain the combination of random subspace $\{\boldsymbol{D}_1^m, ..., \boldsymbol{D}_{N_e}^m\}$, where $N_e$ is the size of the ensemble.

## 2.3   The Proposed Ensemble Architecture (SeizureNet)

SeizureNet consists of $N_e$ deep Convolutional Neural Networks (DCNs). Figure 1-A shows the architecture of SeizureNet with three sub-networks. The basic building block of a DCN is a *Dense Block* which is composed of multiple bottleneck convolutions interconnected through dense connections [10]. Specifically, each DCN model starts with a $7 \times 7$ convolution followed by Batch Normalization (BN), a Rectified Linear Unit (ReLU), and a $3 \times 3$ average pooling operation. Next, there are four dense blocks, where each dense block consists of $N_l$ number of layers termed *Dense Layers* which share information from all the preceding layers connected to the current layer through fuse connections. Figure 1-B shows the structure of a dense block with $N_l = 6$ dense layers. Each dense layer consists of $1 \times 1$ and $3 \times 3$ convolutions followed by BN, a ReLU, and a dropout

---

² In this work, we used $F = [24, 48, 64, 96]$ Hz, $\mathcal{W} = [1]$ second, and $\mathcal{O} = [0.5, 1.0]$ seconds.

block as shown in Fig. 1-C. Mathematically, the output of the $l^{th}$ dense layer in a dense block can be written as: $\mathcal{X}_l = [\mathcal{X}_0, ..., \mathcal{X}_{l-1}]$, where $[\cdot \cdot \cdot]$ represents concatenation of the features produced by the layers $0, ..., l - 1$. The final dense block produces $Y_{dense} \in \mathbb{R}^{k \times R \times 7 \times 7}$−dimensional features which are squeezed to $k \times R$−dimensions through an averaging operation, and then fed to a linear layer $fc \in \mathbb{R}^K$ which learns probabilistic distributions of the input data with respect to $K$ target classes. To increase diversity among sub-networks of the ensemble, we vary the numbers of dense layers of Dense block 3 and Dense block 4 of the sub-networks.

**Table 1.** Statistics of TUH EEG Seizure Corp (v1.4.0 and v1.5.2) in terms of seizure types, number of patients and seizures count.

| Seizure type | Dataset v1.4.0 | | Dataset v1.5.2 | |
|---|---|---|---|---|
| | Patients | Seizures | Patients | Seizures |
| Focal Non-Specific (FN) | 109 | 992 | 150 | 1836 |
| Generalized Non-Specific (GN) | 44 | 415 | 81 | 583 |
| Simple Partial Seizure (SP) | 2 | 44 | 3 | 52 |
| Complex Partial Seizure (CP) | 34 | 342 | 41 | 367 |
| Absence Seizure (AB) | 13 | 99 | 12 | 99 |
| Tonic Seizure (TN) | 2 | 67 | 3 | 62 |
| Tonic Clonic Seizure (TC) | 11 | 50 | 14 | 48 |
| Myoclonic Seizure (MC) | 3 | 2 | 3 | 2 |

## 2.4   Training and Implementation

Consider a training dataset of spectrograms and labels $(D, y) \in (\mathbf{D}, \mathcal{Y})$, where each sample belongs to one of the $K$ classes ($\mathcal{Y} = 1, 2, ..., K$). The goal is to determine a function $f_s(D) : \mathbf{D} \rightarrow \mathcal{Y}$. To learn this mapping, we train SeizureNet parameterized by $f(D, \theta^*)$, where $\theta^*$ are the learned parameters obtained by minimizing a training objective function: $\theta^* = \arg \min_\theta \mathcal{L}_{CE}(y, f(D, \theta))$, where $\mathcal{L}_{CE}$ denotes a Cross-Entropy loss which is applied to the outputs of the ensemble with respect to the ground truth labels. Mathematically, $\mathcal{L}_{CE}$ can be written as: $\mathcal{L}_{CE} = \sum_{k=1}^K \mathbb{I}(k = y_i) \log \sigma(O_e, y_i)$, where $O_e = 1/N_e \sum_{e=1}^{N_e} O_k$ denotes the combined logits produced by the ensemble, $O_k$ denotes the logits produced by an individual sub-network, $\mathbb{I}$ is the indicator function, and $\sigma$ is the SoftMax operation. It is given by: $\sigma(z_i) = \exp z_i / \sum_{k=1}^K \exp z_k$. For training the networks, we initialized the weights of the networks from zero-mean Gaussian distributions. The standard deviations were set to 0.01, and biases were set to 0. We trained the networks for 200 epochs with a start learning rate of 0.01 (which was divided by 10 at 50% and 75% of the total number of epochs), and a parameter decay of 0.0005 (on the weights and biases). Our implementation is based on the auto-gradient computation framework of the Torch library [17]. Training was performed by ADAM optimizer with a batch size of 50.

## 3    Experiments and Results

We used TUH EEG Seizure Corpus (TUH-EEGSC) [21] which is the world's largest publicly available dataset of seizure recordings with type annotations. TUH-EEGSC v1.4.0 released in October 2018 contains 2012 whereas TUH-EEGSC v1.5.2 released in May 2020 contains 3050 seizures. Table 1 shows the statistics of TUH-EEGSC in terms of different seizure types and the number of patients. For experiments, we excluded Myoclonic (MC) seizures from our study because the number of seizures was too low for statistically meaningful analysis (only three seizures) as shown in Table 1. For evaluations, we conducted cross validation at patient-level and seizure-level. Specifically, for TUH-EEGSC v1.4.0, we considered seizure-wise cross validation. Since, TN and SP seizure types in TUH-EEGSC v1.4.0 contain data from only 2 patients, patient-wise cross validation will not yield statistically meaningful results. Hence previous studies on TUH-EEGSC v1.4.0 [2] considered 5-fold seizure-wise cross validation, in which the seizures from different seizure types were equally and randomly allocated to 5 folds. For a fair comparison with the existing work [2,19], we also performed experiments using 5-fold cross validation at the seizure-level to allow a direct performance comparison to these studies. For TUH-EEGSC v1.5.2, we considered patient-wise cross validation. Table 1 shows that the 7 selected seizure types in TUH-EEGSC v1.5.2 comprise data from at least 3 patients, allowing statistically meaningful 3-fold patient-wise cross validation. In this scenario, the data was split into train and test subsets, so that the seizures in train and test subsets

**Table 2.** Average weighted f1 of SeizureNet and other methods on TUH-EEGSC v1.5.2 for patient-wise seizure type classification.

| Methods | Weighted F1 |
|---|---|
| [19] Adaboost | 0.473 |
| [19] SGD | 0.432 |
| [19] XGBoost | 0.561 |
| [19] kNN | 0.467 |
| SeizureNet (this work) | **0.620** |

**Table 3.** Ablation study of SeizureNet in terms of architecture, model parameters (million), FLOPS (million), inference speed, and Knowledge Distillation (KD).

| Architecture | F1 | Param. | Flops | Time |
|---|---|---|---|---|
| SeizureNet | 0.950 | 45.94 | 14241 | 90 ms |
| ResNet | 0.718 | 0.08 | 12.75 | 2 ms |
| ResNet-KD | **0.788** | 0.08 | 12.75 | 2 ms |

**Table 4.** Average weighted f1 of SeizureNet and other methods on TUH-EEGSC v1.4.0 for seizure type classification at seizure-level.

| Methods | Weighted F1 |
|---|---|
| [19] Adaboost | 0.593 |
| SAE (based on [13]) | 0.675 |
| LSTM (based on [26]) | 0.701 |
| CNN (based on [1]) | 0.716 |
| [19] SGD | 0.724 |
| CNN-LSTM (using [25]) | 0.795 |
| CNN (based on [23]) | 0.802 |
| [2] CNN-LSTM | 0.824 |
| CNN (based on [16]) | 0.826 |
| CNN-LSTM (using [6]) | 0.831 |
| [19] XGBoost | 0.851 |
| [19] kNN | 0.898 |
| CNN (based on [7]) | 0.901 |
| [2] Plastic NMN | 0.945 |
| SeizureNet (this work) | **0.950** |

**Table 5.** Ablation study of SeizureNet in terms of the proposed Multi-Spectral Feature Sampling (MSFS) using different sizes of training data.

| Data | Weighted F1 scores (seizure-wise) | | Weighted F1 scores (subject-wise) | |
|---|---|---|---|---|
| Size | Without MSFS | With MSFS | Without MSFS | With MSFS |
| 10% | 0.429 | **0.561** | 0.456 | **0.475** |
| 50% | 0.645 | **0.753** | 0.457 | **0.464** |
| 100% | 0.939 | **0.950** | 0.584 | **0.615** |

were always from different patients. This approach makes it more challenging to improve model performance but has higher clinical relevance as it supports model generalisation across patients.

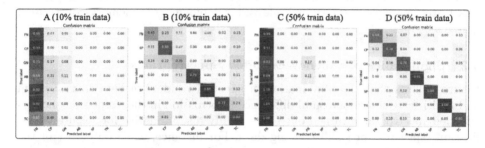

**Fig. 2.** Confusion matrices produced by SeizureNet using Fourier transform (A, C) and using the proposed saliency-encoded spectrograms (B, D), for different sizes of training data. The comparison shows that the confusions considerably decrease with the use of the proposed saliency-encoded spectrograms.

Table 2 shows that SeizureNet improved weighted f1 scores by around 6 points for patient-wise cross validation on TUH-EEGSC compared to the existing methods. These improvements are mainly attributed to the proposed multi-spectral feature learning which captures information from different frequency and spatial resolutions, and enables SeizureNet to learn more discriminative features compared to the other methods. Table 4 shows seizure-wise cross validation results on TUH-EEGSC. The results show that SeizureNet produced superior performance compared to the existing methods.

## 3.1 SeizureNet for Knowledge Distillation

Here, we evaluated the capability of SeizureNet in transfering knowledge to smaller networks for seizure classification. For this, we trained a student ResNet model with 3 residual layers in conjunction with SeizureNet acting as a teacher network using a knowledge distillation based training function. Our training function $\mathcal{L}_{KD}$ is a weighted combination of a CrossEntropy loss term $\mathcal{L}_{CE}$

and a distillation loss term $\mathcal{L}_{KL}$. Mathematically, $\mathcal{L}_{KD}$ can be written as: $\mathcal{L}_{KD} = \alpha \cdot \mathcal{L}_{CE}(P_t, y) + \beta \cdot \mathcal{L}_{CE}(P_s, y) + \gamma \cdot \mathcal{L}_{KL}$, where $P_t$ and $P_s$ represent the logits (the inputs to the SoftMax) of SeizureNet and the student model, respectively. The terms $\alpha \in [0, 0.5, 1]$, $\beta \in [0, 0.5, 1]$, and $\gamma \in [0, 0.5, 1]$ are the hyper-parameters which balance the individual loss terms. The distillation loss term $\mathcal{L}_{KL}$ is composed of Kullback-Leibler (KL) divergence function defined between log-probabilities computed from the outputs of SeizureNet and the student model. Mathematically, $\mathcal{L}_{KL}$ can be written as: $\mathcal{L}_{KL}(P_s, P_t) = \sigma(P_s) \cdot (\log(\sigma(P_s)) - \sigma(P_t)/T)$, where $\sigma$ represents the SoftMax operation and $T$ is a temperature hyper-parameter which controls the softening of the outputs SeizureNet. Table 3 shows that ResNet-KD produced improvement of around 7% in the mean f1 scores compared to the ResNet model without knowledge distillation. These results show that the feature embeddings learnt by SeizureNet can effectively be used to improve the accuracy of smaller networks (e.g., 3-layer ResNet having 45× less training parameters, 1100× less number of flops, and 45× faster inference as shown in Table 3), for deployment in memory-constrained systems.

## 3.2  Significance of Saliency-Encoded Spectrograms

Figure 2 shows that the combination of spectral residual of Fourier Transform and multi-scale center-surround difference information in the proposed saliency-encoded spectrograms turned out to be highly discriminative for seizure classification especially for small training data. For instance, when only 10% of the data was used for training, the model trained using saliency-encoded spectrograms produced considerable decrease in the confusions for all the target classes compared to the model that was trained using only Fourier Transform.

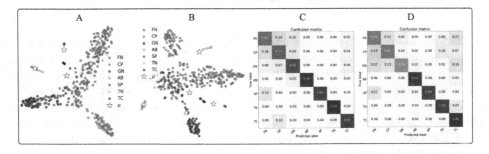

**Fig. 3.** TSNE visualizations and confusion matrices of the seizure type manifolds produced by SeizureNet using the proposed multi-spectral feature learning (A, C) and without using the proposed multi-spectral feature learning (B, D), respectively.

## 3.3  Significance of Multi-Spectral Feature Learning

Table 5 shows that the models trained using MSFS produced higher f1 scores compared to the frequency-specific models. For instance, when only 10%

training data was used, SeizureNet with MSFS produced improvements of around 9 points and 2 points in the seizure-wise and subject-wise f1 scores compared to the models trained without MSFS, respectively. These improvements show that information from different frequency bands compliment each other in better discriminating seizure classes especially for small data sizes compared to the features learnt at independent frequency bands. Furthermore, the combination of multiple DCN models with different layer configurations in the ensemble encourages diversity in feature learning thereby producing higher f1 scores compared to the independent models. Figure 3 shows a comparison of TSNE mappings produced by models trained with and without MSFS. The results show that the seizure manifolds produced with MSFS are better separated in the high-dimensional feature space (as shown in Fig. 3-A) compared to the seizure manifolds produced without MSFS (as shown in Fig. 3-B). This shows that increasing variation in the training information by combining data from different spatial and frequency bands is beneficial for learning discriminative features for seizure classification. Figure 3 also shows that models trained with MSFS produced considerably less confusions (as shown in Fig. 3-C) for almost all the seizure classes when 50% of training data was used to train the models, exhibiting the importance of combining data from different frequency and spatial resolutions.

## 4  Conclusion and Future Work

This paper presents a deep learning framework termed SeizureNet for EEG-based seizure type classification in patient-wise cross validation scenarios. The greatest challenge in a patient-wise validation approach is to learn robust features from limited training data which can effectively generalize to unseen test patient data. This is achieved through two novel contributions i) saliency-encoded spectrograms which encode multi-scale saliency information contained in the frequency transform of the EEG signals, and ii) multi-spectral feature learning within an ensemble architecture, where spectrograms generated at different frequency and spatial resolutions encourage diversity in the information flow through the networks, and ensembling reduces variance in the final predictions. Experiments on the world's largest publicly available epilepsy dataset show that our SeizureNet produces superior f1 scores for seizure type classification compared to the existing methods. Experiments also show that the feature embeddings learnt by SeizureNet considerably improve the accuracy of smaller networks through knowledge distillation. In future, we plan to investigate fusion of data from wearable sensors and videos for multi-modal seizure type classification in real-world epilepsy monitoring units. We also plan to release the source code of SeizureNet to promote research in this topic.

## References

1. Acharya, U.R., Oh, S.L., Hagiwara, Y., Tan, J.H., Adeli, H.: Deep convolutional neural network for the automated detection and diagnosis of seizure using EEG signals. Comput. Biol. Med. **100**, 270–278 (2018)

2. Ahmedt-Aristizabal, D., Fernando, T., Denman, S., Petersson, L., Aburn, M.J., Fookes, C.: Neural memory networks for robust classification of seizure type. arXiv preprint arXiv:1912.04968 (2019)
3. Alotaiby, T.N., Alshebeili, S.A., Alshawi, T., Ahmad, I., El-Samie, F.E.A.: EEG seizure detection and prediction algorithms: a survey. EURASIP J. Adv. Signal Process. **2014**(1), 183 (2014)
4. Antoniades, A., Spyrou, L., Took, C.C., Sanei, S.: Deep learning for epileptic intracranial EEG data. In: 2016 IEEE 26th International Workshop on Machine Learning for Signal Processing (MLSP), pp. 1–6. IEEE (2016)
5. Boubchir, L., Al-Maadeed, S., Bouridane, A.: On the use of time-frequency features for detecting and classifying epileptic seizure activities in non-stationary EEG signals. In: ICASSP, pp. 5889–5893. IEEE (2014)
6. Golmohammadi, M., et al.: Gated recurrent networks for seizure detection. In: 2017 IEEE Signal Processing in Medicine and Biology Symposium (SPMB), pp. 1–5. IEEE (2017)
7. Hao, Y., Khoo, H.M., von Ellenrieder, N., Zazubovits, N., Gotman, J.: DeepIED: an epileptic discharge detector for EEG-fMRI based on deep learning. NeuroImage Clinical **17**, 962–975 (2018)
8. Harrer, S., Shah, P., Antony, B., Hu, J.: Artificial intelligence for clinical trial design. Trends Pharmacol. Sci. **40**(8), 577–591 (2019)
9. Hou, X., Zhang, L.: Saliency detection: a spectral residual approach. In: CVPR, pp. 1–8 (2007)
10. Huang, G., Liu, Z., Weinberger, K.Q., van der Maaten, L.: Densely connected convolutional networks. In: CVPR (2017)
11. Itti, L., Koch, C., Niebur, E.: A model of saliency-based visual attention for rapid scene analysis. PAMI **11**, 1254–1259 (1998)
12. Längkvist, M., Karlsson, L., Loutfi, A.: A review of unsupervised feature learning and deep learning for time-series modeling. Pattern Recogn. Lett. **42**, 11–24 (2014)
13. Lin, Q., et al.: Classification of epileptic EEG signals with stacked sparse autoencoder based on deep learning. In: Huang, D.-S., Han, K., Hussain, A. (eds.) ICIC 2016. LNCS (LNAI), vol. 9773, pp. 802–810. Springer, Cham (2016). https://doi.org/10.1007/978-3-319-42297-8_74
14. Lopez, S., Gross, A., Yang, S., Golmohammadi, M., Obeid, I., Picone, J.: An analysis of two common reference points for EEGS. In: 2016 IEEE Signal Processing in Medicine and Biology Symposium (SPMB), pp. 1–5. IEEE (2016)
15. Montabone, S., Soto, A.: Human detection using a mobile platform and novel features derived from a visual saliency mechanism. Image Vis. Comput. **28**(3), 391–402 (2010)
16. O'Shea, A., Lightbody, G., Boylan, G., Temko, A.: Investigating the impact of CNN depth on neonatal seizure detection performance. In: 2018 40th Annual International Conference of the IEEE Engineering in Medicine and Biology Society (EMBC), pp. 5862–5865. IEEE (2018)
17. Paszke, A., et al.: Automatic differentiation in PyTorch (2017)
18. Pramod, S., Page, A., Mohsenin, T., Oates, T.: Detecting epileptic seizures from EEG data using neural networks. arXiv preprint arXiv:1412.6502 (2014)
19. Roy, S., Asif, U., Tang, J., Harrer, S.: Machine learning for seizure type classification: setting the benchmark. arXiv preprint arXiv:1902.01012 (2019)
20. Saputro, I.R.D., Maryati, N.D., Solihati, S.R., Wijayanto, I., Hadiyoso, S., Patmasari, R.: Seizure type classification on EEG signal using support vector machine. J. Phys. Conf. Ser. **1201**, 012065. IOP Publishing (2019)

21. Shah, V., et al.: The temple university hospital seizure detection corpus. Front. Neuroinformatics **12**, 83 (2018)
22. Silverman, D.: The rationale and history of the 10–20 system of the international federation. Am. J. EEG Technol. **3**(1), 17–22 (1963)
23. Sriraam, N., Temel, Y., Rao, S.V., Kubben, P.L., et al.: A convolutional neural network based framework for classification of seizure types. In: 2019 41st Annual International Conference of the IEEE Engineering in Medicine and Biology Society (EMBC), pp. 2547–2550. IEEE (2019)
24. Supratak, A., Li, L., Guo, Y.: Feature extraction with stacked autoencoders for epileptic seizure detection. In: EMBC, pp. 4184–4187. IEEE (2014)
25. Thodoroff, P., Pineau, J., Lim, A.: Learning robust features using deep learning for automatic seizure detection. In: Machine Learning for Healthcare Conference, pp. 178–190 (2016)
26. Tsiouris, K.M., Pezoulas, V.C., Zervakis, M., Konitsiotis, S., Koutsouris, D.D., Fotiadis, D.I.: A long short-term memory deep learning network for the prediction of epileptic seizures using EEG signals. Comput. Biol. Med. **99**, 24–37 (2018)
27. Turner, J., Page, A., Mohsenin, T., Oates, T.: Deep belief networks used on high resolution multichannel electroencephalography data for seizure detection. In: 2014 AAAI Spring Symposium Series (2014)
28. Vidyaratne, L., Glandon, A., Alam, M., Iftekharuddin, K.M.: Deep recurrent neural network for seizure detection. In: 2016 International Joint Conference on Neural Networks (IJCNN), pp. 1202–1207 (2016)

# Decoding Task States by Spotting Salient Patterns at Time Points and Brain Regions

Yi Hao Chan⬥, Sukrit Gupta⬥, L. L. Chamara Kasun,
and Jagath C. Rajapakse⁽⊠⁾⬥

School of Computer Science and Engineering, Nanyang Technological University,
Singapore, Singapore
{yihao001,sukrit001,chamarakasun,asjagath}@ntu.edu.sg

**Abstract.** During task performance, brain states change dynamically and can appear recurrently. Recently, recurrent neural networks (RNN) have been used for identifying functional signatures underlying such brain states from task functional Magnetic Resonance Imaging (fMRI) data. While RNNs only model temporal dependence between time points, brain task decoding needs to model temporal dependencies of the underlying *brain states*. Furthermore, as only a subset of brain regions are involved in task performance, it is important to consider subsets of brain regions for brain decoding. To address these issues, we present a customised neural network architecture, Salient Patterns Over Time and Space (SPOTS), which not only captures dependencies of brain states at different time points but also pays attention to key brain regions associated with the task. On language and motor task data gathered in the Human Connectome Project, SPOTS improves brain state prediction by 17% to 40% as compared to the baseline RNN model. By spotting salient spatio-temporal patterns, SPOTS is able to infer brain states even on small time windows of fMRI data, which the present state-of-the-art methods struggle with. This allows for quick identification of abnormal task-fMRI scans, leading to possible future applications in task-fMRI data quality assurance and disease detection. Code is available at https://github.com/SCSE-Biomedical-Computing-Group/SPOTS.

**Keywords:** Attention · Decoding brain activations · Embeddings · Recurrent neural networks · Task functional magnetic resonance imaging

## 1 Introduction

Deep neural network models have been recently used to decode brain states in functional Magnetic Resonance Imaging (fMRI) scans. For example, recurrent

**Electronic supplementary material** The online version of this chapter (https://doi.org/10.1007/978-3-030-66843-3_9) contains supplementary material, which is available to authorized users.

S. M. Kia et al. (Eds.): MLCN 2020/RNO-AI 2020, LNCS 12449, pp. 88–97, 2020.
https://doi.org/10.1007/978-3-030-66843-3_9

neural networks (RNN) were used to infer underlying task states from task-fMRI data [12,13] and feedforward neural networks were used to identify brain regions associated with disease states from resting-state fMRI data [9,10]. However, spatio-temporal variations that define dynamic brain states during task performance [15] have not been considered. This requires a decoding model that is able to pick out both spatial and temporal patterns associated with the task. In this paper, we improve the state-of-the-art for brain state classification of task-fMRI data by ameliorating issues that are present in previous approaches.

The first issue is the effect of task state repetition due to sub-tasks being performed repeatedly. During task-fMRI experiments, participants are often asked to perform different sub-tasks while their responses are recorded along with corresponding response times. In order to decode brain activations, dynamic brain state labels are assigned to time points for each sub-task. Although RNNs have been used to predict brain states dynamically from task-fMRI data [12,13], they do not deal with brain states (denoted by the sub-task label) appearing within the time window of the stimuli as they simply model the current state based on previous time points. This is insufficient as the present state may not just depend on previous time points, but on states occurring within the time window too. For example, when listening to a question based on a context described beforehand, the subject thinks about the answer that has to be selected after the question. Therefore, to determine the present state, we may have to give attention to time points (representing brain states that are important for the sub-task) within the entire stimulation window and not just to the previous time points.

The second issue is that they did not consider functional specialisation during task performance. In the human brain, specific regions perform specialized functions [11]. While there is a set of task-general regions that participate across all tasks, there is another set of task-specific regions that differentiates one task from another [17]. Thus, brain decoding needs to focus on specific brain regions associated with the task, instead of learning from all activations to the network.

We consider both issues and proposed a customised architecture, Salient Patterns Over Time and Space (SPOTS), that learns dependencies between brain states and handles spatial interactions, for the purpose of brain decoding. SPOTS uses spatial embedding to learn a subset of regions that can differentiate between the brain states. It also uses an RNN encoder-decoder to learn the dependencies between the states within the whole window of time points [21], so as to better model brain states. An attention mechanism [1] is implemented to focus on specific brain regions and time points that are associated with the task state.

The potential of the proposed SPOTS model is demonstrated on language and motor task-fMRI data obtained from the Human Connectome Project [6]. We showed that SPOTS performs significantly better than the existing state-of-the-art methods using RNN models for decoding brain states, and that such results are possible only with the combination of both spatial embedding and attention mechanism. Furthermore, we showed how SPOTS provides greater interpretability than baseline RNN models, in terms of studying spatio-temporal relationships. In sum, we have made the following three key contributions:

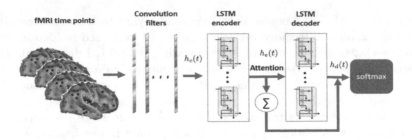

**Fig. 1.** The proposed architecture for SPOTS. Convolution filters are used to learn an embedding, reducing N brain regions into K dimensions. The spatially-compressed representation of the fMRI time series is then passed into an encoder-decoder network with an attention layer to identify salient time points.

- Proposed a customised architecture, SPOTS, that considers both spatial and temporal relationships in task-fMRI data for brain decoding;
- Performance of the proposed architecture is significantly better than the state-of-the art RNN models [13], especially for smaller window sizes; and
- Provided an interpretable method to study salient spatio-temporal patterns that are important considerations when predicting a brain state

## 2    Salient Patterns over Time and Space (SPOTS)

The SPOTS architecture (Fig. 1) is made up of 4 sub-modules: (1) an embedding layer consisting of 1-dimensional convolution filters; (2) an encoder consisting of one or more long short term memory (LSTM) layers; (3) a decoder consisting of one or more LSTM layers; and (4) an attention module consisting of an attention layer. These sub-modules are then followed by a softmax classification layer that outputs the predicted task state.

**Input.** SPOTS takes in fMRI time series in a time window of size $T$, from $N$ functionally relevant brain regions. Let the input time series be $x = (x(t))_{t=1}^{T}$ where $x(t) \in \mathbb{R}^{N}$ denotes the input features at time point $t$.

**Embedding Layer.** The embedding layer aims to learn a compact representation of task-specific brain regions using $K$ 1-dimensional spatial convolution operations. The use of such embeddings is motivated by the presence of functional specialisation in the brain whereby only a subset of regions are involved in task performance. Also, this has the benefit of shorter training time and a smaller model with fewer parameters (as compared to using time series from all $N$ region of interests). However, this is different from directly learning a $N \times K$ embedding - we use $K$ convolution filters that convolve across the $N$ regions for each time point in $T$. This is done because we want to predict labels for each time point in the window and not a single label for the whole window. Additionally, fMRI datasets are small (<1000) and directly learning a $N \times K$ embedding is unlikely to work well with limited data.

Let $w_k$ be the filter weights for $k$th filter and $h_c(t) = (h_{c,k}(t))_{k=1}^{K}$ be the convolution layer output where $h_{c,k}(t)$ is given by:

$$h_{c,k}(t) = x(t) \circledast w_k \tag{1}$$

where $\circledast$ denotes the convolution operation in spatial domain. Note that $w_k \in \mathbb{R}^N$ and output $h_c(t) \in \mathbb{R}^{1 \times K}$ where $K$ is the number of filters.

**Encoder.** In order to capture long term dependencies, we use a RNN encoder-decoder architecture to learn temporal relationships in fMRI data. The encoder of SPOTS consists of one or more LSTM layers. Considering one LSTM layer, the encoder output $h_e(t) \in \mathbb{R}^{E \times K}$, where $E$ is the number of hidden units of the encoder LSTM, is given by:

$$h_e(t) = \mathrm{lstm}(h_c(t), h_e(t-1)) \tag{2}$$

**Decoder.** The decoder consists of one or more LSTM layers. Instead of a traditional LSTM decoder, we use a random decoder that passes random values drawn from a normal distribution as inputs to the decoder [20]. For one LSTM layer, the decoder output $h_d(t) \in \mathbb{R}^{D \times K}$, where $D$ is the number of hidden units of the encoder LSTM, is given by:

$$h_d(t) = \mathrm{lstm}(h_e^*(t), h_d(t-1)) \tag{3}$$

$h_e^*(t)$ is obtained from drawing random samples Gaussianly from $h_e(t)$.

**Attention.** The attention layer aims to find the relevant time points in the task fMRI data that are useful to determine the brain state. Attention score output $s(t)$ is given by:

$$\alpha(t) = \mathrm{softmax}\big(V\tanh(Wh_d(t) + Uh_e(t))\big)$$
$$s(t) = \alpha(t) \cdot h_e(t) \tag{4}$$

where $U \in \mathbb{R}^{D \times E}, V \in \mathbb{R}^{1 \times E}, W \in \mathbb{R}^{E \times D}$ are weight matrices forming the attention module and the dot product ($\cdot$) is taken in the spatial domain.

**Softmax Layer.** The attention output $s(t)$ and the decoder output $h_d(t)$ are concatenated to obtain the input $h(t)$ to the output softmax layer:

$$h(t) = [h_d(t), s(t)] \tag{5}$$

where $h(t) \in \mathbb{R}^{D+E}$. The softmax layer output $\hat{y}(t)$ is given by:

$$\hat{y}(t) = \mathrm{softmax}(Zh(t) + b) \tag{6}$$

where $Z \in \mathbb{R}^{C \times (D+E)}$ and $b \in \mathbb{R}^C$ denote the weight matrix and bias vector of the softmax layer and $C$ denotes the number of brain states.

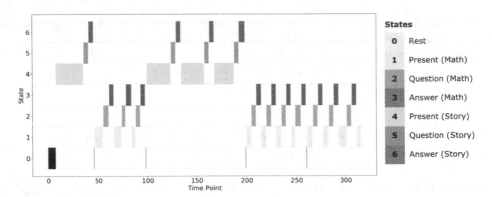

**Fig. 2.** Distribution of sub-tasks over time points (3 time points = 4 s) for the language task. Each block lasted for around 30 s. As math sub-tasks are shorter than story sub-tasks, more math sub-tasks were performed within a block.

**Learning of SPOTS.** Cross-entropy is used as the cost function $J$ as:

$$J = -E_x[y(t)\log(p(\hat{y}(t)))]  \tag{7}$$

where $E_x$ denotes the expectation over inputs $x(t)$ and $y(t)$ denotes the brain state label. The cross-entropy cost function is minimized using Adam optimiser.

## 3  Results

### 3.1  Dataset and Pre-processing

Data used in this paper were obtained from the S900 release of the Human Connectome Project (HCP) [2]. In total, 848 task-fMRI scans (each for right to left and left to right phase encoding) were obtained using a Siemens Skyra 3T scanner at the Washington University. The scans were pre-processed using the HCP pre-processing pipeline [7], which performs correction for gradient distortion, motion and echo-planar imaging distortion, as well as registration to the T1-weighted image. From the time series produced by the pipeline, the average time series of voxels found within a 2.5 mm radius for 264 regions of interests (ROI) derived from the Power atlas [17] were computed and used as the input.

Specifically, we used task-fMRI data from the language [3] and motor [4] tasks. The language task was chosen as it was made up of two sub-tasks of very different lengths: math sub-tasks and story sub-tasks. The math sub-tasks were much shorter than story sub-tasks. The motor task was made up of 5 sub-tasks involving feet (left and right), hand (left and right) and tongue movement. It was chosen as the length of its sub-tasks are relatively uniform (and are in between math and story sub-tasks), allowing us to study how the model performance changes depending on the mix of sub-tasks lengths present in the task. Furthermore, the two tasks engage different regions of the brain.

**Table 1.** Comparison of model accuracies from baseline LSTM (model adapted from Li et al. [13]), LSTM with embedding, LSTM with attention, and SPOTS across various window sizes and across language and motor tasks. Results for window sizes 10–50 are shown, Fig S4 shows the full results (window sizes 10–80).

| Window size | LSTM (Li et al. [13]) | LSTM (with embedding) | LSTM (with attention) | SPOTS |
|---|---|---|---|---|
| Language | | | | |
| 10 | 34.5% ± 0.8% | 47.3% ± 0.5% | 44.9% ± 0.6% | **08.0% ± 1.2%** |
| 20 | 43.8% ± 0.9% | 62.7% ± 1.0% | 45.7% ± 3.9% | **81.4% ± 0.4%** |
| 30 | 54.3% ± 0.7% | 72.7% ± 0.6% | 45.6% ± 5.9% | **84.8% ± 0.6%** |
| 40 | 60.1% ± 1.0% | 77.3% ± 0.5% | 46.0% ± 3.2% | **85.5% ± 2.4%** |
| 50 | 62.9% ± 0.9% | 78.4% ± 0.4% | 40.2% ± 0.6% | **85.6% ± 0.6%** |
| Motor | | | | |
| 10 | 30.3% ± 0.6% | 36.0% ± 0.5% | 36.2% ± 0.8% | **58.7% ± 1.0%** |
| 20 | 36.6% ± 1.2% | 66.9% ± 0.7% | 44.8% ± 1.0% | **88.3% ± 0.9%** |
| 30 | 51.4% ± 0.7% | 79.2% ± 0.5% | 72.2% ± 2.1% | **93.8% ± 2.0%** |
| 40 | 62.7% ± 0.8% | 86.0% ± 0.6% | 64.5% ± 2.8% | **94.7% ± 0.5%** |
| 50 | 78.6% ± 1.1% | 90.3% ± 0.6% | 72.2% ± 4.3% | **95.9% ± 1.2%** |
| Parameters | 1.6 million | 1.1 million | 3.2 million | 2.7 million |

The language task is made up of multiple interleaved activity blocks with each block comprising math (presentation of math question, math question, and answer to question) and story (presentation of story, question based on story, and answer to question) sub-tasks as seen in Fig. 2. The initial state was a 'rest' interval between each block. A similar illustration of the motor task can be found in figure S1 of the supplementary materials. All states were brought forward by 6s to account for the delay between stimulus and hemodynamic response [14] and were used as brain state labels for training the models.

## 3.2    Classifier Performance

SPOTS was implemented in Keras [5] with TensorFlow backend. Experiments were done on a server with 4 Nvidia P100 GPUs. As LSTMs are expensive to train, extensive hyperparameter tuning was infeasible. Thus, we determined the hyperparameters by referring to previous work done by [13]. They experimented with LSTMs ranging from 1 to 3 layers and number of hidden units ranging from 32 to 1024. We chose the model with 1 LSTM layer and 512 hidden units as it had the highest accuracy and was the least complex model with. We varied window size $T$ from 10 to 80. We used 85% of the samples[1] for training and the rest for testing. For each window size, we performed the experiment for 5 different seeds. The following hyperparameters were used: batch size = 32, early stopping with patience = 10, Adam optimizer with learning rate = 0.05, $\beta_1 = 0.9$ and $\beta_2 = 0.999$ with gradients clipped to a maximum norm of 1. Gaussian noise

---

[1] A sample refers to input data of length T. However, the model makes a prediction at every time point, thus accuracy is computed based on single time points.

with $\mu = 0.4$ and $\sigma = 0.2$ was used as inputs to the decoder. The same model architecture and hyperparameters were used for the two tasks.

Performance of SPOTS are shown in Table 1 in comparison with various RNN models that were implemented with LSTM. We experimented with only the LSTM layer (configuration is similar to [13]), LSTM with embedding, LSTM encoder-decoder with attention mechanism, and then SPOTS. We found that SPOTS gave the best classification performance across window sizes and tasks. These results were produced on the fMRI scans using the right to left phase encoding. We further validated them with the left to right phase encoding scans (for window size 10 to 50) and got similar performances, with SPOTS outperforming baseline RNNs (figure S3, supplementary materials). From these results, it can be inferred that the identification of both spatial and temporal patterns is needed to obtain the best model performance. Three key aspects are:

1. The advantage gained from finding spatio-temporal patterns increases with decreasing window sizes. With smaller window sizes, the amount of variation present in a time series window increases, which makes it harder for the LSTM to learn due to catastrophic forgetting [8]. For example, when the model is trained on windows containing math sub-tasks, the memory stored in LSTM units loses information about the story sub-tasks. Attention can overcome this by learning direct mappings between the time points [18].
2. However, when performed without spatial embedding, the LSTM encoder seems to struggle with the large dimensionality of the input and the attention mechanism isn't able to learn useful relationships. Interestingly, LSTM + Attention showed greater improvement (as time window increases) for the motor task than the language task. Thus, it can be inferred that attention (without embeddings) thrives in datasets where short sub-tasks are present.
3. For both tasks, using a more compressed representation obtained via the learnt embedding leads to an increase in model performance. While the use of embeddings results in huge performance gains by themselves, adding the attention mechanism further leads to improved performance and this increase is especially significant for small window sizes. One can see from Table 1 that LSTM + Attention has more parameters than LSTM but did not always perform better. On the contrary, SPOTS outperformed LSTM with attention despite being smaller. This shows the value of using spatial embeddings, and how the reduced dimensionality from the learnt embeddings helped the attention module to learn useful relationships.

### 3.3   Interpretation of Results

**Spatial Analysis.** Algorithms such as DeepLIFT [19] can be used to compute salience scores for each feature. However, they are difficult to be implemented on a customised model like SPOTS. As a proxy to evaluating salient regions, we looked into the filter weights of the convolution filters in the embedding layer. Using ROIs obtained from [11,17], we observed that rows which map to the ROIs in the auditory module have consistently greater weights despite having inputs

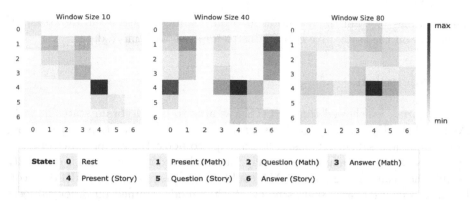

**Fig. 3.** Color-coded attention maps at various window sizes. Reading the attention map row by row shows which states (on the x-axis) are being focused on when predicting that the present state belongs to the current row.

that are well spread across the distribution of inputs (figure S3). Similarly, the learnt embeddings placed greater weight on motor-related ROIs for motor tasks (figure S3). These findings correspond to the expected task-based activations but they are not a guarantee of the saliency of these regions - they should be further reaffirmed with model interpretability approaches such as DeepSHAP [16].

**Temporal Analysis.** To study what states are important to discern between different states, we define the attention matrix $A = (a_{pq}) \in \mathbb{R}^{C \times C}$ where $a_{pq}$ denotes the sum of attention scores that task state $p$ (occurring at any time point) pays to task state $q$ for the sample. We computed the attention map for all time windows by adding attention matrices derived from all the test samples where at least half of the predictions for that window are correct. We produced a representative attention map for the language task (Fig. 3) and motor task (figure S2 in the supplementary materials). Although attention maps show mappings between time points only, studying the patterns produced on the maps allow us to make inferences about relationships between states.

For window size 10, not only was self-attention prominent but the story-based tasks and math-based tasks paid greater attention to their respective sub-tasks too. On the other hand, the motor task only had self-attention. This shows how the attention mechanism is able to pick up temporal dependencies of underlying brain states within the time window - not just previous time points.

For window size 40, maps from both tasks showed that the model started to pay attention on the other sub-tasks. Interestingly, self-attention is reduced more greatly in the motor task.

For window size 80, the attention map became more diffused for both tasks and the focus of the map is dominated by self-attention of the most prevalent class (state 4 for language and state 0 for motor). This could explain the reduced advantage of SPOTS as window size gets larger - larger windows means fewer data samples to train the attention map on, leading to less accurate attention weighting on the states. We expect this to improve with more data.

## 4   Conclusion

In this paper, we showed that SPOTS was able to decode brain states in task-fMRI better than existing methods such as those based on RNN. By spotting time points and salient regions, SPOTS helps to boost the performance of baseline RNNs by a large margin, especially for small window sizes. This is especially useful when considering how SPOTS could be used as part of the fMRI data collection process for large-scale studies. With a model trained on other subjects performing the same task, the model will be able to detect subtle differences in task performance and check if the subject is performing the task well. Being able to predict well with smaller window sizes, SPOTS makes early intervention possible, thus improving the quality of acquired data. Another avenue to explore is the use of SPOTS for disease diagnosis. After being trained on a dataset of healthy subjects, SPOTS could be used to identify patterns of activity that deviate from the norm. Requiring only a small window size will allow greater amount of training data to be generated, helping the model to learn better.

**Acknowledgement.** This work was partially supported by AcRF Tier 1 grant RG 116/19 of Ministry of Education, Singapore. Data were provided [in part] by the Human Connectome Project, WU-Minn Consortium (Principal Investigators: David Van Essen and Kamil Ugurbil; 1U54MH091657) funded by the 16 NIH Institutes and Centers that support the NIH Blueprint for Neuroscience Research; and by the McDonnell Center for Systems Neuroscience at Washington University.

## References

1. Bahdanau, D., Cho, K., Bengio, Y.: Neural machine translation by jointly learning to align and translate. In: ICLR (2015)
2. Barch, D.M., Burgess, G.C., Harms, M.P., Petersen, S.E., Schlaggar, B.L., Corbetta, M., Glasser, M.F., Curtiss, S., Dixit, S., Feldt, C., et al.: Function in the human connectome: task-fMRI and individual differences in behavior. Neuroimage **80**, 169–189 (2013)
3. Binder, J.R., et al.: Mapping anterior temporal lobe language areas with fMRI: a multi-center normative study. NeuroImage **54**(2), 1465 (2011)
4. Buckner, R.L., Krienen, F.M., Castellanos, A., Diaz, J.C., Yeo, B.T.: The organization of the human cerebellum estimated by intrinsic functional connectivity. J. Neurophysiol. **106**(5), 2322–2345 (2011). https://doi.org/10.1152/jn.00339.2011
5. Chollet, F.: Deep Learning with Python and Keras: The Practical Guide from the Developer of the Keras Library. MITP-Verlags GmbH & Co. KG, Bonn (2018)
6. Glasser, M.F., et al.: The human connectome project's neuroimaging approach. Nature Neurosci. **19**(9), 1175 (2016)
7. Glasser, M.F., et al.: The minimal preprocessing pipelines for the human connectome project. Neuroimage **80**, 105–124 (2013)

8. Goodfellow, I.J., Mirza, M., Xiao, D., Courville, A., Bengio, Y.: An empirical investigation of catastrophic forgetting in gradient-based neural networks. arXiv preprint arXiv:1312.6211 (2013)
9. Gupta, S., Chan, Y.H., Rajapakse, J.C.: Decoding brain functional connectivity implicated in AD and MCI. In: Shen, D., et al. (eds.) MICCAI 2019. Lecture Notes in Computer Science, vol. 11766, pp. 781–789. Springer, Cham (2019). https://doi.org/10.1007/978-3-030-32248-9_87
10. Gupta, S., Chan, Y.H., Rajapakse, J.C.: Obtaining leaner deep neural networks for decoding brain functional connectome in a single shot. Neurocomput. (2020). (in Press)
11. Gupta, S., Rajapakse, J.C.: Iterative consensus spectral clustering improves detection of subject and group level brain functional modules. Sci. Rep. **10**(1), 1–15 (2020)
12. Li, H., Fan, Y.: Brain decoding from functional MRI using long short-term memory recurrent neural networks. In: Frangi, A.F., Schnabel, J.A., Davatzikos, C., Alberola-López, C., Fichtinger, G. (eds.) MICCAI 2018. Lecture Notes in Computer Science, vol. 11072, pp. 320–328. Springer, Cham (2018). https://doi.org/10.1007/978-3-030-00931-1_37
13. Li, H., Fan, Y.: Interpretable, highly accurate brain decoding of subtly distinct brain states from functional MRI using intrinsic functional networks and long short-term memory recurrent neural networks. NeuroImage **202**, 116059 (2019)
14. Liao, C.H., Worsley, K.J., Poline, J.B., Aston, J.A., Duncan, G.H., Evans, A.C.: Estimating the delay of the fMRI response. NeuroImage **16**(3), 593–606 (2002)
15. Loula, J., Varoquaux, G., Thirion, B.: Decoding fMRI activity in the time domain improves classification performance. NeuroImage **180**, 203–210 (2018)
16. Lundberg, S.M., Lee, S.I.: A unified approach to interpreting model predictions. In: Advances in Neural Information Processing Systems, pp. 4765–4774 (2017)
17. Power, J.D., et al.: Functional network organization of the human brain. Neuron **72**(4), 665–678 (2011)
18. Serra, J., Suris, D., Miron, M., Karatzoglou, A.: Overcoming catastrophic forgetting with hard attention to the task. arXiv preprint arXiv:1801.01423 (2018)
19. Shrikumar, A., Greenside, P., Kundaje, A.: Learning important features through propagating activation differences. arXiv preprint arXiv:1704.02685 (2017)
20. Srivastava, N., Mansimov, E., Salakhutdinov, R.: Unsupervised learning of video representations using LSTMs. In: Proceedings of the 32nd International Conference on International Conference on Machine Learnings, vol. 37, pp. 843–852 (2015)
21. Sutskever, I., Vinyals, O., Le, Q.V.: Sequence to sequence learning with neural networks. In: NIPS (2014)

# Patch-Based Brain Age Estimation from MR Images

Kyriaki-Margarita Bintsi[1]([✉]), Vasileios Baltatzis[2], Arinbjörn Kolbeinsson[3],
Alexander Hammers[2], and Daniel Rueckert[1]

[1] BioMedIA, Department of Computing, Imperial College London, London, UK
m.bintsi19@imperial.ac.uk
[2] School of Biomedical Engineering and Imaging Sciences, King's College London,
London, UK
[3] Department of Epidemiology and Biostatistics, Imperial College London,
London, UK

**Abstract.** Brain age estimation from Magnetic Resonance Images
(MRI) derives the difference between a subject's biological brain age
and their chronological age. This is a potential biomarker for neurodegeneration, e.g. as part of Alzheimer's disease. Early detection of neurodegeneration manifesting as a higher brain age can potentially facilitate better medical care and planning for affected individuals. Many
studies have been proposed for the prediction of chronological age from
brain MRI using machine learning and specifically deep learning techniques. Contrary to most studies, which use the whole brain volume,
in this study, we develop a new deep learning approach that uses 3D
patches of the brain as well as convolutional neural networks (CNNs)
to develop a localised brain age estimator. In this way, we can obtain a
visualization of the regions that play the most important role for estimating brain age, leading to more anatomically driven and interpretable
results, and thus confirming relevant literature which suggests that the
ventricles and the hippocampus are the areas that are most informative.
In addition, we leverage this knowledge in order to improve the overall
performance on the task of age estimation by combining the results of
different patches using an ensemble method, such as averaging or linear
regression. The network is trained on the UK Biobank dataset and the
method achieves state-of-the-art results with a Mean Absolute Error of
2.46 years for purely regional estimates, and 2.13 years for an ensemble
of patches before bias correction, while 1.96 years after bias correction.

**Keywords:** Brain age estimation · Localization · Deep learning · MR
Images.

## 1 Introduction

Alzheimer's disease (AD) is a progressive neurodegenerative disease and the most
common cause of dementia [2]. It has been demonstrated that AD results in atrophy of the brain [30] as well as changes in the morphology of brain tissues. Specifically, atrophy firstly manifests itself in the hippocampus and it then expands

© Springer Nature Switzerland AG 2020
S. M. Kia et al. (Eds.): MLCN 2020/RNO-AI 2020, LNCS 12449, pp. 98–107, 2020.
https://doi.org/10.1007/978-3-030-66843-3_10

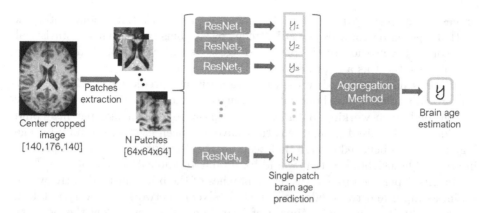

**Fig. 1.** Overview of the proposed method. $N$ 3D patches are being extracted from the center-cropped image. Every patch is used as input in a ResNet model that is trained to predict the subject's brain age, hence $N$ different age predictions $y_i$ are produced. The individual predictions are then combined using an ensemble method in order to achieve an improved estimation $y$.

through the cerebral cortex. Meanwhile, cerebrospinal fluid (CSF) spaces, i.e. the ventricles inside the brain and cisterns outside the brain, are enlarged. Biomarkers are an important diagnostic tool for detection of the early stages of AD [9]. A characteristic hallmark of neurodegenerative diseases such as AD is that they may result in accelerated aging of the human brain hence a promising biomarker that has been used in AD and other neuroimaging studies is brain age [6,10], which measures the difference between the biological brain age of a subject and their real (chronological) age.

Structural Magnetic Resonance (MR) images have been widely used for the measurement of brain changes related to age [12] and are often available in patients. For this reason, a considerable amount of work has been done on brain age estimation from MR images using machine learning (ML) techniques [3,11, 32]. The segmentation of the T1-weighted MR images into grey matter (GM), white matter (WM), and CSF regions, and region masks are usually used as input to a ML model [11,20], achieving a Mean Absolute Error (MAE) of as low as 4.3 years [25]. Recently, various CNN-based approaches which provide accurate brain age estimation using raw T1-weighted MR images with MAEs ranging from 3.3 to 4 years have been proposed [6,14,15]. In a recent competition on brain age estimation held last year (https://www.photon-ai.com/pac2019) the top performing submission achieved results with a MAE of less than 3 years. In [19], the authors implemented a 3D ResNet model enhanced by a randomized tensor regression layer, achieving state-of-the-art results, and a MAE of 2.6 years.

A common bias observed when estimating brain age, possibly because of regression dilution [23], is the overestimation in younger subjects and the underestimation in older subjects. The term bias correction used in age estimation should not be confused with the bias field correction that is used as a preprocessing step for MRI images [16]. There is a substantial amount of work [7,21,31] going on towards the adjustment of the bias by applying a statistical bias correction method to the predicted ages. Recent works [4,22] use the real age of the subject as a covariate to predict a bias-corrected age.

Patches have been widely used for brain disease prediction [24,26] as they can provide information about subtle changes at a local level that are probably disregarded when working globally. To our knowledge, although patches could provide more localised estimations, they have not been used successfully for age regression. It is believed though that accurate localized predictions could provide interpretable insights [28] that would be similar to clinical ones [3,5].

In this paper, we propose the use of patches of the brain, instead of the whole brain, as input and train independent 3D ResNet18 networks for every patch in order to obtain a regional estimate of brain age. Thus, we allow the network to focus on the specific patch without being affected by the rest of the brain. Furthermore, we evaluate which patches include important regions for the age regression and obtain a visualisation of these areas, thus making the results more interpretable and providing the first step for even more localised predictions. We, then, combine the results of the different patches to produce a more accurate brain age estimation for each subject, achieving state-of-the-art results with a MAE of 2.13 years before and 1.96 years after bias correction.

## 2 Materials and Methods

### 2.1 Dataset and Pre-processing

We use the UK Biobank (UKBB) dataset [1] for the task of age regression. It incorporates a large collection of MRI scans of vital organs, including brain MR images, acquired with many different protocols such us T1-weighted and T2-weighted. The dataset used in this study contains 3D T1-weighted brain images, acquired from nearly 15,000 healthy subjects (ages: 44–73 years, females: 52.3%). The images provided by the UKBB are sized $182 \times 218 \times 182$ and are already skull-striped and non-linearly registered to MNI152 standard space, allowing anatomically consistent voxels among the subjects. We also normalize each brain scan to zero mean and unit variance. From the 14,503 subjects provided by the UKBB, 753 did not provide their age and are removed from the study, thus leaving 13,750 3D brain images, 80% of which are used for the training set, 15% for the validation set and 5% for the test set.

### 2.2 Pipeline

An overview of the proposed method can be found in Fig. 1. We first describe a baseline model which was used for the evaluation of our method. We then present the pipeline which led to state-of-the-art and more localized predictions.

**Baseline Model.** As a baseline for the evaluation of our method, we implement a version of a ResNet model [13], which uses 3D convolutions instead of 2D, similar to the one used in [19].

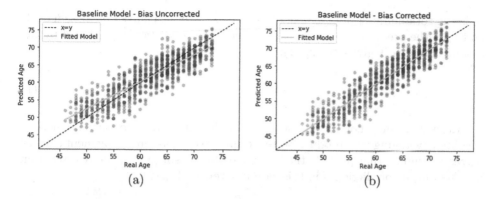

**Fig. 2.** The predicted over the real age of the subjects for the baseline model before (a), and after bias correction (b). The black dashed line shows the line of identity ($x = y$), while the orange solid one shows the fitted model.

**Table 1.** Comparison of the performance of the most important experiments in terms of Mean Absolute Error (MAE) and $R^2$ score.

| Experiment | MAE (years) | $R^2$ score |
|---|---|---|
| Baseline model (uncorrected) | 2.64 | 0.77 |
| Null model | 5.90 | 0.00 |
| Best single-patch network | 2.46 | 0.80 |
| Worst single-patch network | 4.19 | 0.14 |
| Averaging (selected patches) | 2.26 | 0.84 |
| Linear Regression (all patches, uncorrected) | **2.13** | **0.85** |
| Baseline model (corrected) | 2.43 | 0.80 |
| Linear Regression (all patches, corrected) | **1.96** | **0.87** |

**Patch-Based Prediction.** In brief, we utilize patches of the brain, instead of the whole brain scans, with the purpose of understanding the effect of different parts of the brain on the predictions, and hence acquiring more localised predictions. We center crop each brain scan from $182 \times 218 \times 182$ to $140 \times 176 \times 140$. Afterwards, we extract 3D patches sized $64 \times 64 \times 64$ with a stride of $38 \times 56 \times 38$ from each brain, which leads to 27 patches per brain scan. We then train 27 18-layer 3D ResNet models, similar to the baseline one described before. We train, validate, and test on the same patch, thus on a specific region of the brain. This allows the network to focus on the specific patch independently of the rest of the image.

**Ensemble Model.** We investigate whether the use of patches could lead to a more accurate brain age estimation. Therefore, we combine the 27 predictions of the single-patch networks with an ensemble model.

We experiment with two different ways for the fusion of the patch-based models. Firstly, we take the mean of the results of the multiple ResNets. So, if

$N$ is the total number of patch-based models, $P \leq N$ is a subset of these models and $y_i$ is the prediction of every one of them, the prediction $y$ produced by the ensemble model is given by Eq. (1):

$$y = \frac{1}{P} \sum_{i=1}^{P} y_i \tag{1}$$

Moreover, since not all patches are equally important for age prediction, weighted averaging may produce better results. We, therefore, implement a linear regression model that predicts the brain age of each subject on the test set from $y_i$. The output prediction $y$ in this case is given by Eq. (2):

$$y = w_0 + \sum_{i=1}^{P} w_i y_i \tag{2}$$

Here $w_0$ is the intercept term and $w_i$ are the learnable weights for each of the $P$ individual models, which are being learnt from the validation set.

In addition, based on the previous experiments, we make some conclusions on which patches contain important features for brain age and which not. For this reason, we choose the number of the selected patch-based models $P$ so that each individual $MAE < threshold$ on the validation set. We choose that threshold heuristically. We investigate both averaging the predictions and using a meta-regressor similar to the one described above.

**Bias Correction.** The bias correction technique adopted in this work is the one proposed by [4]. We fit the relationship of the brain age delta and the chronological age using Eq. (3):

$$\Delta = \alpha * Y_{chronological} + \beta \tag{3}$$

where $Y_{chronological}$ is the real age of the subject and $\Delta$ the brain age delta function. The $\alpha$ and $\beta$ represent the slope and intercept respectively and are then used for the estimation of the corrected predicted age from Eq. (4):

$$Y_{corrected} = Y_{predicted} - (\alpha * Y_{chronological} + \beta) \tag{4}$$

**Training.** We train the network using backpropagation [29], with batch size 8 for 40 epochs. We use a mean squared error loss for the age regression. Furthermore, we use the adaptive moment estimation (Adam) optimizer [18] with a learning rate lr = 0.0001. The experiments are implemented on an NVIDIA Titan RTX using Pytorch deep-learning library [27].

## 3   Results

Three different experiments are implemented. For the evaluation of the age regression task in every model, MAE and the $R^2$ coefficient are computed. The main results of the experiments can be found in Table 1.

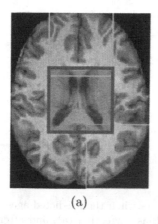
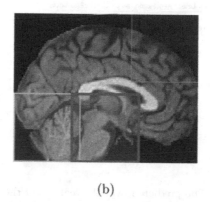

(a)                                           (b)

**Fig. 3.** Transverse (a) and mid-sagittal (b) slices of a brain MR image with three colored patches for each case. The colors of the patches indicate the performance of this single-patch model in terms of Mean Absolute Error (MAE). Specifically: red patches indicate a MAE of less than 3 years, orange patches between 3 and 3.5 years, green patches between 3.5 and 4 years, and blue patches greater than 4 years. The patches that perform best include the ventricles (a), and the hippocampus (b) (hippocampus further lateral than the plane shown).

**Baseline Model.** As depicted in Fig. 2, the network that uses the whole images as an input achieves a MAE of 2.64 years and an $R^2$ score of 0.77. Comparing to [19], our model performs better to their simple 3D ResNet, perhaps because we used a later release of the UKBB that includes around double the number of subjects. When bias correction is applied, the performance improves, with a MAE of 2.43 years and an $R^2$ score of 0.80 observed.

In addition, we create a model that predicts the average age of the population for every subject with the purpose of the comparison of the results of this null model with our results. The model achieves a MAE of 5.90 years.

**Patch-Based Predictions.** When we use a single patch as input, the results are highly dependent on the area of the brain where the patch is extracted from. We train 27 ResNets for 27 patches, achieving a MAE from around 2.5 to 4.2 years. The patches with the best performance are the ones that include the ventricles or the hippocampus, with MAEs of less than 2.5 and 2.7 years, respectively, and $R^2$ score of 0.80 and 0.76, respectively, as well as patches that include parts of these regions. On the contrary, patches that contain substantial amounts of background perform much worse with a MAE of 3.5–4.2 years and an $R^2$ score of 0.15–0.6. In Fig. 3, various patches, colored based on the performance of the corresponding models, are illustrated as part of a whole brain slice.

**Ensemble Model.** By combining the single-patch models, we achieve an improved performance. Concerning the aggregation of the individual models,

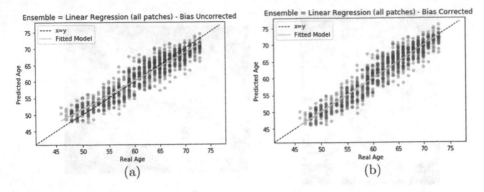

**Fig. 4.** The predicted over the real age of the subjects when the predicted ages result from a linear regression of all the patches before bias correction (a), and after bias correction (b). The black dashed line shows the line of identity ($x = y$), while the orange solid one shows the fitted model. (Color figure online)

apart from the average of all the patches, we also calculate the average of the 6 patches that achieve greater performance on the validation set ($MAE < 3$ years), hence the ones that include important information on brain aging. The MAE is 2.66 and 2.26 years, respectively, and the $R^2$ score 0.78 and 0.83, respectively.

The use of linear regression works better. Specifically, we achieve a MAE of 2.13 years when all the single-patch models are used. Furthermore, when we use only the models of the patches with the most important information for the age of the brain, we achieve a MAE of 2.16 years. Regarding $R^2$ score, it is 0.85 in both cases. In this case, bias correction is applied as well and we achieve a MAE of 1.96 years, and an $R^2$ score of 0.87. The scatter plots of the real over predicted ages, before and after bias correction is applied, are shown in Fig. 4.

## 4    Discussion

A plethora of deep learning methods based on CNNs which use whole brain images as input has been used for estimating brain age via regression, achieving good performance (MAE = 2.6 years) [19]. In this study, we have explored how patches of the brain can be used for this task, by training a network for each patch that tries to find robust but patch-specific features for the age estimation. Moreover, we combine the results of the different networks via an ensemble approach with the purpose of a more accurate estimation. The results of the main experiments can be found in Table 1.

Based on the results, we conclude that the patches that include parts of the ventricles and the hippocampus tend to predict the age of the subject more accurately with a MAE of less than 3 years, thus our results are consistent with the existing literature [30]. The MAE in some of these cases is lower than that for the baseline network which utilizes the volume of the whole brain, proving that not all parts of the brain are needed for an accurate prediction. Therefore, less computational effort is required for comparable results. On the other hand, patches that include part of the background do not perform as accurately. We observe that although the brain shrinks while age increases, the networks do not manage to capture the changes in the cerebral cortex as accurately. An explanation for this could be the way the images are registered, which reduces size differences between brains, or the relatively small range of existing ages in the dataset, especially of ages beyond 65 years when atrophy tends to accelerate [8]. Furthermore, the use of patches provides a visualization of the parts of the brain that are valuable for age prediction, leading to a more understandable prediction. Although the patches are big and do not provide detailed localization, this work is the first step towards an interpretable and localized brain age estimation. As our next step, we will use smaller patches (e.g. sized $32 \times 32 \times 32$ or $16 \times 16 \times 16$), either from the whole brain or from the best-performing patches. More localised detection of a deviation from normal trajectories may also be useful for the automatic detection of more focal pathologies such as ventricular enlargement in hydrocephalus or hippocampal atrophy in temporal lobe epilepsies [17].

We also improve the age prediction by combining the results of a few weak networks. Firstly, we do so by simply averaging the results of all the independent networks. However, this does not lead to any improvement on the predictions (MAE = 2.66 years). Thus, we then leverage the knowledge acquired from the previous experiment and average only the predictions from patches that seemed to include the most relevant information about brain age. There is a major boost in the regression performance (MAE = 2.26 years), showing that by combining results of weaker networks we can achieve a better prediction. Moreover, we aggregate the single-patch models by using a linear regression, as we believe that by giving appropriate weights to the results of every patch, better results could be achieved. Interestingly, in this case, using all the individual models performs similarly (MAE = 2.13 years) to when we use the selected ones (MAE = 2.16 years). The reason is, probably, that by learning the weights, the linear regression model can suppress the effect of the least accurately performing models, while promoting the best performing ones. This results in an age estimator which is more accurate than the baseline model as well as the existing literature. In future work, we intend to integrate the ensemble method with the training of the sub-networks in order to accommodate an end-to-end training.

After bias correction, we notice a considerable increase of the performance of the network (MAE = 1.96 years). Although using the chronological age as a covariate for the bias correction is not meaningful for a ML model, it could prove important clinically for giving insights for the subject's brain age, as demographics, including chronological age, are usually known.

## 5   Conclusion

In this work, we propose the use of patches of the brain, instead of the whole 3D brain scan, as input to separate 3D ResNets for brain age estimation. We combine the results of the networks with an ensemble method, such as linear regression. The method provides accurate results outperforming the state-of-the-art. In addition, we provide localized predictions by specifying the patches that perform better on the task. Precise age prediction in healthy participants, e.g. from UKBB as in this study, can now be used as a baseline to compare trajectories in different pathologies such as Alzheimer's [8].

**Acknowledgements.** KMB would like to acknowledge funding from the EPSRC Centre for Doctoral Training in Medical Imaging (EP/L015226/1).

# References

1. Alfaro-Almagro, F., et al.: Image processing and quality control for the first 10,000 brain imaging datasets from UK Biobank. Neuroimage **166**, 400–424 (2018)
2. Alzheimer's Association: 2019 Alzheimer's disease facts and figures includes a special report on Alzheimer's detection in the primary care setting: connecting patients and physicians. Technical report (2019). https://www.alz.org/media/Documents/alzheimers-facts-and-figures-2019-r.pdf
3. Becker, B.G., Klein, T., Wachinger, C., Initiative, A.D.N., et al.: Gaussian process uncertainty in age estimation as a measure of brain abnormality. Neuroimage **175**, 246–258 (2018)
4. Beheshti, I., Nugent, S., Potvin, O., Duchesne, S.: Bias-adjustment in neuroimaging-based brain age frameworks: a robust scheme. Neuroimage Clin. **24**, 102063 (2019)
5. Cole, J.H.: Multi-modality neuroimaging brain-age in UK Biobank: relationship to biomedical, lifestyle and cognitive factors. bioRxiv, p. 812982 (2019)
6. Cole, J.H., Franke, K.: Predicting age using neuroimaging: innovative brain ageing biomarkers. Trends Neurosci. **40**(12), 681–690 (2017)
7. Cole, J.H., et al.: Brain age predicts mortality. Mol. Psychiatry **23**(5), 1385–1392 (2018)
8. Coupé, P., Catheline, G., Lanuza, E., Manjón, J.V., Initiative, A.D.N.: Towards a unified analysis of brain maturation and aging across the entire lifespan: a MRI analysis. Hum. Brain Map. **38**(11), 5501–5518 (2017)
9. Davatzikos, C., Bhatt, P., Shaw, L.M., Batmanghelich, K.N., Trojanowski, J.Q.: Prediction of MCI to AD conversion, via MRI, CSF biomarkers, and pattern classification. Neurobiol. Aging **32**(12), 2322.e19–2322.e27 (2011)
10. Franke, K., Gaser, C.: Ten years of brainage as a neuroimaging biomarker of brain aging: what insights have we gained? Front. Neurol. **10**, 789 (2019)
11. Franke, K., Ziegler, G., Kloppel, S., Gaser, C., Initiative, A.D.N., et al.: Estimating the age of healthy subjects from T1-weighted MRI scans using kernel methods: exploring the influence of various parameters. Neuroimage **50**(3), 883–892 (2010)
12. Good, C.D., Johnsrude, I.S., Ashburner, J., Henson, R.N., Friston, K.J., Frackowiak, R.S.: A voxel-based morphometric study of ageing in 465 normal adult human brains. Neuroimage **14**(1), 21–36 (2001)
13. He, K., Zhang, X., Ren, S., Sun, J.: Deep residual learning for image recognition. In: Proceedings of the IEEE Conference on Computer Vision and Pattern Recognition, pp. 770–778 (2016)
14. Huang, T.W., et al.: Age estimation from brain MRI images using deep learning. In: 2017 IEEE 14th International Symposium on Biomedical Imaging (ISBI 2017), pp. 849–852. IEEE (2017)

15. Jonsson, B.A., Bjornsdottir, G., Thorgeirsson, T., Ellingsen, L.M., Walters, G.B., Gudbjartsson, D., Stefansson, H., Stefansson, K., Ulfarsson, M.: Brain age prediction using deep learning uncovers associated sequence variants. Nature Commun. **10**(1), 1–10 (2019)

16. Juntu, J., Sijbers, J., Van Dyck, D., Gielen, J.: Bias field correction for MRI images. In: Computer Recognition Systems, pp. 543–551. Springer. https://doi.org/10.1007/3-540-32390-2_64 (2005)

17. Keihaninejad, S., et al.: Classification and lateralization of temporal lobe epilepsies with and without hippocampal atrophy based on whole-brain automatic MRI segmentation. PLoS ONE **7**(4), e33096 (2012)

18. Kingma, D.P., Ba, J.: Adam: a method for stochastic optimization. arXiv preprint arXiv:1412.6980 (2014)

19. Kolbeinsson, A., et al.: Robust deep networks with randomized tensor regression layers. arXiv preprint arXiv:1902.10758 (2019)

20. Kondo, C., et al.: An age estimation method using brain local features for T1 weighted images. In: 2015 37th Annual International Conference of the IEEE Engineering in Medicine and Biology Society (EMBC), pp. 666–669. IEEE (2015)

21. de Lange, A.M.G., Cole, J.H.: Commentary: correction procedures in brain-age prediction. Neuroimage Clinical **26**, 102229 (2020)

22. de Lange, A.M.G., et al.: Population-based neuroimaging reveals traces of childbirth in the maternal brain. Proc. Natl. Acad. Sci. **116**(44), 22341–22346 (2019)

23. Le, T.T., et al.: A nonlinear simulation framework supports adjusting for age when analyzing brainage. Front. Aging Neurosci. **10**, 317 (2018)

24. Lian, C., Liu, M., Zhang, J., Shen, D.: Hierarchical fully convolutional network for joint atrophy localization and Alzheimer's disease diagnosis using structural MRI. IEEE Trans. Pattern Anal. Mach. Intell. **42**(4), 880–893 (2018)

25. Liem, F., et al.: Predicting brain-age from multimodal imaging data captures cognitive impairment. Neuroimage **148**, 179–188 (2017)

26. Liu, M., Zhang, J., Adeli, E., Shen, D.: Landmark-based deep multi-instance learning for brain disease diagnosis. Med. Image Anal. **43**, 157–168 (2018)

27. Paszke, A., et al.: PyTorch: an imperative style, high-performance deep learning library. In: Advances in Neural Information Processing Systems, pp. 8024–8035 (2019)

28. Pawlowski, N., Glocker, B.: Is texture predictive for age and sex in brain MRI? arXiv preprint arXiv:1907.10961 (2019)

29. Rumelhart, D.E., Hinton, G.E., Williams, R.J.: Learning internal representations by error propagation. Technical report California University San Diego La Jolla Inst for Cognitive Science (1985)

30. Savva, G.M., Wharton, S.B., Ince, P.G., Forster, G., Matthews, F.E., Brayne, C.: Age, neuropathology, and dementia. N. Engl. J. Med. **360**(22), 2302–2309 (2009)

31. Smith, S.M., Vidaurre, D., Alfaro-Almagro, F., Nichols, T.E., Miller, K.L.: Estimation of brain age delta from brain imaging. Neuroimage **200**, 528–539 (2019)

32. Tohka, J., Moradi, E., Huttunen, H., Initiative, A.D.N., et al.: Comparison of feature selection techniques in machine learning for anatomical brain MRI in dementia. Neuroinformatics **14**(3), 279–296 (2016)

# Large-Scale Unbiased Neuroimage Indexing via 3D GPU-SIFT Filtering and Keypoint Masking

Étienne Pepin[1], Jean-Baptiste Carluer[2], Laurent Chauvin[1], Matthew Toews[1(✉)] (iD), and Rola Harmouche[3]

[1] École de Techologie Supérieure, Montreal, Canada
etienne.pepin.1@ens.etsmtl.ca, matt.toews@gmail.com
[2] Université de Nantes, Nantes, France
[3] National Research Council Canada, Ottawa, Canada

**Abstract.** We propose a feature extraction method via a novel description and a scalable GPU implementation (the first to our knowledge) of the 3D scale-invariant feature transform (SIFT). The feature extraction is first represented as a shallow convolutional neural network with pre-computed filters, followed by a masked keypoint analysis. We use the implementation in order to investigate feature extraction for specific instance identification on natural non-skull-stripped magnetic resonance image (MRI) neuroimaging data. The proposed implementation is invariant to 3D similarity transforms and aims to improve robustness by reducing noise and bias for image processing convolution operations. We show interpretable feature visualizations, which help explain the obtained results. We demonstrate state-of-the-art results in large-scale neuroimage family indexing experiments on 3D data from the Human Connectome Project repository, and show significant speed gains compared to a CPU implementation. The results imply that using feature extraction using SIFT for neuroimaging analysis can lead to less noisy results without the need for hard masking during preprocessing. The resulting interpretable features can help understand brain similarities between family members, and can also be used on arbitrary image modalities and anatomical structures.

## 1 Introduction

Convolutional neural networks are considered state-of-the-art for medical image classification problems. Recent advances in computational power and parallel processing with GPUs have lead to quick and accurate classifiers, particularly in the presence of a large amount of training data and a small number of classes [10]. However, this does not hold when identifying image pairs in a large medical imaging cohort, where there is a large number of subjects and a limited number of samples per subject. In addition, CNNs introduce bias in their filters towards local object textures in contrast to global object shapes [19], whereas it has been shown that networks that learn shape-based representations can improve robustness, detection performance, and generalization [8]. Third, there is no standard

© Springer Nature Switzerland AG 2020
S. M. Kia et al. (Eds.): MLCN 2020/RNO-AI 2020, LNCS 12449, pp. 108–118, 2020.
https://doi.org/10.1007/978-3-030-66843-3_11

method for the interpretability of CNNs, resulting in a lack of trust in these systems from end users [9]. Finally, while segmentation masks are commonly used to extract structures of interest prior to processing, e.g. brain masking or 'skull-stripping' [5,6,15,21,22], hard masking produces an irregular and abrupt boundary in the image similar to zero-padding, which introduces artifacts such as ringing at mask borders [16]. An early study emphasized the need for reducing noise and bias for convolution operations in the context of image processing, and demonstrated the benefit of GPU implementations in that context [13]. Various GPU implementations of 2D SIFT have been proposed [2,20]. However, extending these to 3D medical image volumes is non-trivial and has not been done to date, particularly 3D keypoint description, and no work has described invariant keypoint descriptor correspondence as a massive scale convolution operation.

This paper addresses the limitations mentioned above by proposing an efficient GPU Gaussian scale-space feature extraction method for medical image analysis. A novel representation of 3D SIFT as a shallow convolutional neural network with pre-computed filters (SIFT-CNN) is shown for extracting visualizable and interpretable keypoints with powerful shallow information in image data. We show that the backbone of the SIFT algorithm is a single channel Gaussian CNN, i.e. the Gaussian scale-space generated via recursive Gaussian, and can be generated efficiently via separable filters. These features are designed to be rotation invariant [12] and thus are robust against rotation bias. We use these features in a keypoint masking process on neuroimaging data. Keypoints are first extracted on an entire image, and those outside the masks of the structures of interest are then discarded for future analysis. This helps avoid linear filtering artifacts due to sharp boundaries that would normally affect any linear filtering system including CNN or SIFT.

SIFT features [14] have shown to be efficient at image matching applications. Toews and Wells [23] developed a 3D-SIFT-Rank keypoint method and demonstrated its usefulness for model-to-image alignment on clinical images. Extracted image signatures using 3D keypoints require little memory usage and can thus be used on a large dataset. A recent study [4] used the 3D-SIFT-Rank keypoints in order to extract signatures of individuals and subsequently identify MRIs of siblings. This method was the first to detect subject duplication errors in the ADNI and OASIS cohorts. Keypoint extraction requires on the order of seconds per image, the keypoint data are approximately 100x smaller than the original image, and highly efficient nearest neighbor keypoint indexing may be computed in $O(logN)$ complexity in the number of keypoints $N$ via approximate nearest neighbor search [17].

Similarly to the work in [4], we demonstrate the effectiveness of our proposed keypoint masking algorithm in identifying similarities between brain MR image pairs, particularly due to family relationships, and show improvements when compared to previously obtained results on skull-stripped brain volumes. These extracted anatomically interpretable features, that would normally go unnoticed by a neurologist, can lead us to explore the nature of similarity in terms of familial relationships in the brain, and perhaps better understand pathology when such similarities are lacking. In order to allow for further speedups, the feature extraction is performed using a 3D graphics processing unit (GPU) SIFT implementation which results in an approximate 7× speedup compared to the CPU implementation. The contributions of our work can be summarized as follows:

- A robust method for Gaussian feature extraction in scale-space followed by keypoint masking via shallow CNN with precomputed filters
- A scalable GPU implementation of 3D SIFT which offers an approximate 7× speedup compared to the CPU implementation, which to our knowledge has not been done to date.
- Application of keypoint masking in order to classify all brain MRIs of the same family from a large dataset using with state of the art results for brain indexing.
- The first application keypoint transfer segmentation on brain MRI data.

## 2    Method

Methods here are two-fold. First, we present a solution to convolution filter bias and noise via an adaptation of Gaussian scale-space theory [12] to the GPU architecture widely used in deep CNN processing. Second, we propose an ROI analysis strategy, where neuroimage features are extracted from natural images without the limits of hard boundaries, followed by selection of feature points that lie within a ROI for further analysis.

### 2.1    Keypoint Extraction Using Gaussian Scale-Space Filtering on the GPU

Keypoint extraction seeks to represent an image as a list of salient keypoints located in space ($x$) and scale ($\sigma$), each with an associated descriptor ($f \in R^{64}$) encoding intensity gradients around the keypoint location. Let $x \in R^3$ represent a 3D coordinate system, and let $I_x : R^3 \to R^1$ represent a scalar image. Scale-space theory seeks to model the image in a manner independent of the image resolution, with defined continuous Gaussian convolutions: $I_{\sigma,x} : R^4 \to R^1 = I_x * G_\sigma$, where $G_\sigma$ is a Gaussian filter defined by pixel scale $\sigma$. The Gaussian filter is shown to be the only filter satisfying a number of axioms, including non-creation and non-enhancement of spurious local maxima and providing both an unbiased visual front end due rotational symmetry, and a means of computing scale-normalized derivative operators. In contrast, filters resulting from typical CNN training via stochastic backpropagation [11] are not invariant to image scaling or rotation and highly biased towards training data.

We propose integrating the Gaussian scale-space (GSS) directly into deep CNN filtering on the GPU, thereby limiting bias or image artifacts. Figure 1 shows our GPU implementation of the widely-used scale-invariant feature transform (SIFT) algorithm [14] based on 3D SIFT-Rank [23]. A detailed description is beyond the scope of this paper and is provided along with full source code[1]. Several notable details are as follows. The GSS is shown in Fig. 1 a), where scale is sampled in constant multiplicative increments $k : \sigma_{i+1} = k\sigma_i$ in order to remain invariant to scale change. Each sample $I_{\sigma,x}$ may be generated via a single convolution of the input $I_x$ (and thus remains a 'shallow' filtering operation), a more computationally efficient strategy is recursive filtering $I_{\sigma_{i+1},x} = I_{\sigma_i,x} * G_{\sigma'}$, in which case the GSS can be viewed as a 'deep' CNN with pre-defined filters, thus not requiring training.

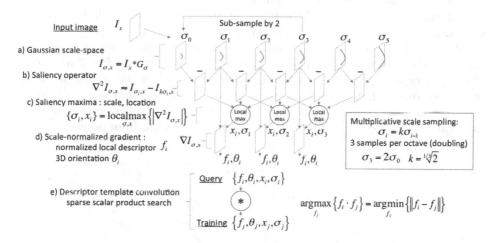

**Fig. 1.** The SIFT algorithm as a deep CNN. The Gaussian scale-space a) may be viewed as a deep CNN filtering process. Parallel networks approximate b) a Laplacian-of-Gaussian saliency operator as a difference-of-Gaussian (DoG) operation, where local saliency maxima $\{x_i, \sigma_i\}$ c) define the locations and scales of discrete scale-invariant keypoints representing informative, localizable image patches. Local scale-normalized image gradients d) are used to determine local keypoint orientation $\theta_i \in R^3$ and are sampled and normalized local keypoint descriptor templates $\{f_i\}$. Finally, e) peaks of convolution between the query image an a large bank of training descriptor templates $\{f_j\}$ can be efficiently detected via nearest neighbor search, as the Euclidean distance between normalised descriptors $\|f_j - f_j\|$ is a monotonically decreasing function of the scalar product $f_j \cdot f_i$. Scale space is sampled here at 3 equal multiplicative increments, similar to tones of an augmented triad in twelve-tone equal tempered musical scale.

Convolution via descriptor templates can be viewed as an evaluation of a scalar product evaluated at points on the geometrical lattice, for example the $\{x, \Theta, \sigma\} \in R^7$ coordinate space of 3D similarity transforms. Minimizing the distance between the normalized descriptors is equivalent to maximizing the convolution.

---

[1] https://github.com/CarluerJB/3D_SIFT_CUDA/ [3].

## 2.2   Masked Keypoint Analysis

Neuroimage datasets are often skull-stripped prior to processing, applying brain
ROI masks in order to restrict analysis to data arising from neuroanatomical
parenchyma as opposed to extraneous tissues such as skull, etc. Nevertheless,
segmentation algorithms may produce variable or noisy results along the segmentation boundary, even for different images of the same subject. These hard,
irregular boundaries generally exhibit unfavorable signal processing characteristics, e.g. Gibbs phenomenon, that may impact convolution responses, both in
the cases of shallow Gaussian filters and via deep CNN filters. Recent solutions
have investigated difference-of-Gaussian filtering to counter input bias [1], or
conditional random field regularization of output noise [26].

We thus propose a new approach to neuroimage processing, particularly
useful in the case of local keypoint analysis, as illustrated in Fig. 2 a) which
illustrates typical processing of skull-stripping pipeline, where image features
extracted from a skull-stripped neuroimage may represent spurious, noisy content. We propose instead extracting features in natural image space and then
use brain masks to separate keypoints present in the brain from others.

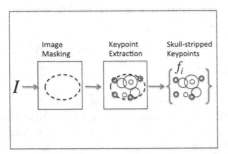
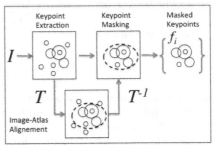

(a) Skull-stripped Keypoints        (b) Masked Keypoints (proposed method)

**Fig. 2.** Illustrating a) Skull-stripped keypoint analysis, where skull-masking prior to
filtering may lead to artifacts. b) Keypoint masking, where keypoints are extracted in
natural image data, then filtered according to a mask. Transform $T$ is a robust image-
to-atlas similarity transform determined via feature-based alignment [23], and $T^{-1}$ is
used to transform an existing atlas brain mask to image space in a manner equivalent
to keypoint transfer segmentation [25], except here the mask applied to filter keypoints
rather than to mask image intensity data.

# 3   Experiments

## 3.1   Data

The dataset used in this experiment is a subset of 1010 subjects from the Human
Connectome Project [24] Q4 release containing 439 unique families, including some unrelated subjects (see Table 1). T1-weighted MR images have been

acquired between 2012–2015 on a 3T MR scanner, at a 0.7 mm isotropic resolution. Through the Freesurfer pipeline [7], images have been registered to the MNI space, brain masks have been generated, and images have been resampled to a 1.25 mm isotropic resolution, as well as corrected for image artefacts such as eddy-currents and head-motion. Keypoints are extracted from individual images, numbers of keypoints per method is shown in Table 2.

**Table 1.** HCP demographic information

| Image number | 1010 |
|---|---|
| Age | $29 \pm 13$ |
| Male | 468 |
| Female | 542 |
| Full siblings (FS) | 607 |
| Dizygotic Twins (DZ) | 71 |
| Monozygotic Twins (MZ) | 134 |

**Table 2.** Average number of keypoints extracted and pairwise correspondence counts.

| Methods | | # keypoints | Corres. |
|---|---|---|---|
| 0.7 mm | Skull-stripped | $1468 \pm 189$ | 233.8 |
| | Masked | $1662 \pm 241$ | 264.8 |
| | Original | $2102 \pm 277$ | 335.4 |
| 1.25 mm | Skull-stripped | $180 \pm 34$ | 28.9 |
| | Masked | $253 \pm 54$ | 40.8 |
| | Original | $334 \pm 60$ | 53.8 |

### 3.2 Processing

We compare methods of keypoint extraction (see Fig. 1). Skull-stripped keypoints are generated by masking a brain volume with its mask, then extracting keypoints from the resulting image. Masked keypoints are generated by extracting keypoints from the original brain volume, then using a brain mask to filter non-brain keypoints outside of the mask. We hypothesize masked keypoints will result in improved performance in indexing experiments, as they are not subject to irregular segmentation boundaries.

Our evaluation replicates the methodology of Chauvin et al. [4], measuring the effectiveness of each method at classifying relationships between subject pairs. We will use 1010 subjects from the HCP dataset instead of the 7536 originally used. A pairwise comparison is done measuring the Jaccard overlap (Eq. 1) of each of the $\binom{N}{2} = N(N-1)/2$ image pairs. It is a measure of the proportion of the keypoint correspondences shared by an image pair [4]:

$$J(A, B) = \frac{|A \cap B|}{|A \cup B|} = \frac{|A \cap B|}{|A| + |B| - |A \cap B|} \tag{1}$$

where $|A \cap B|$ is a function of the euclidean distance between each keypoint in A and it's closest match in B, acting as a continuous intersection operator between keypoint sets A and B. Each class of relationships between pairs has a distinct Jaccard coefficient distribution that enables us to classify the relationship with a Jaccard coefficient threshold.

### 3.3  Keypoint Extraction Performance

Figure 3 a) shows a comparison of average computation times between a CPU and our GPU implementation for each processing step in the keypoint extraction process using a set of 1010 brain volumes. Overall, the GPU implementation results in an approximate 7× speedup. The biggest speedups observed were for the Gaussian scale-space (20×), saliency maxima (3×), sub-sampling (3×), and saliency operator (2×).

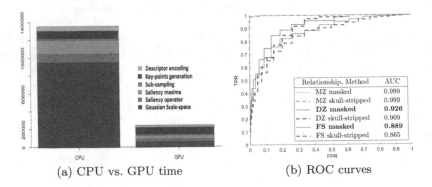

(a) CPU vs. GPU time                    (b) ROC curves

**Fig. 3.** Illustrating a) Comparison between average CPU and GPU processing times (in microseconds) for each processing step in the keypoint extraction process. b) ROC curves for relationship classification between pairs using a Jaccard score threshold (0.7mm resolution).

### 3.4  Keypoint Visualisation

Figure 4 shows a saggital brain MRI slice with original and skull-stripped keypoints. Matches between keypoints can be visualized and subsequently interpreted, and validated: Matches and non-matches between the keypoints are represented by different colored circles. Most matches between the two sets of keypoints are further inwards from the mask edge, and most unmatched keypoints are closer to the edge of the brain. There is significantly more keypoints on the non-skull-stripped image, most of which can be found on the cortex.

Across all images at 0.7mm resolution, 85% of the skull-stripped keypoints matched with the original keypoints of the same image, while at a 1.25 mm resolution, 75% of the skull-stripped keypoints matched with the original keypoints. To test our hypothesis that the percentage of matches scales with the volume of the mask, we modeled the brain as a sphere of keypoints, with it's volume being the total number of skull-stripped keypoints and the surface being the skull-stripped keypoints that did not match. Using this model, we predicted that 86% of the skull-stripped keypoints will match at 0.7mm resolution using the 1.25mm data. This is a simple model accurately representing our intuition that the border interference effect is dependent on the size of the mask.

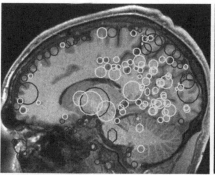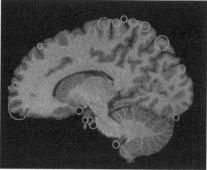

**Fig. 4.** Visualizing keypoints (circles) in original (left) and skull-stripped (right) images. Keypoints present in both images are shown as green (left), unique to original image as blue (left) and unique to skull-stripped image as red (right). Keypoint masking generally identifies additional keypoints located primarily on the cortex in regions affected by boundary artifacts.

## 3.5  HCP Family Relationship Classification

We performed experiments to measure the pairwise similarity between 1010 subjects from the HCP dataset using the Jaccard overlap score introduced in [4] following the same method. In the original article, skull-stripped keypoints at 0.7 mm resolution were used. We compared the ability to find relationships between subjects pairs using original, masked, and skull-stripped keypoints at both 0.7 mm and 1.25 mm resolutions. The Fig. 3 b) shows ROC curves for the masked and skull-stripped representations at 0.7 mm. Though the area under the curve (AUC) is similarly very high for MZ cases using masked and skull-stripped points, a higher AUC is observed in the case of FS and DZ using the masked points when compared to the skull-stripped points. Unlike previous work, the proposed masked method also leads to statistically significant differences between DZ and FS brain similarity at a 1.25 mm resolution. This may be because we have never been able to observe cortical morphology in this amount of detail, due to skull-stripping noise.

**Table 3.** AUC values for different keypoint representations and resolutions

| Keypoints | | FS | DZ | MZ |
|---|---|---|---|---|
| 0.7 mm | Skull-stripped | 0.865 | 0.909 | **0.999** |
| | Masked (ours) | **0.889** | **0.926** | **0.999** |
| | Original | 0.931 | 0.970 | **0.999** |
| 1.25 mm | Skull-stripped | 0.824 | 0.851 | 0.991 |
| | Masked (Ours) | **0.858** | **0.905** | **0.998** |
| | Original | 0.889 | 0.950 | **0.998** |

Table 3 compares relationship classification using original, masked, and skull-stripped keypoints at different resolutions. Using masked keypoints results in higher AUC than skull-stripped keypoints for any relationship at both resolutions. The increase in AUC is amplified at a lower resolution, because a higher fraction of the skull-stripped keypoints are affected by the brain mask.

## 4    Conclusion

We presented a fast GPU-based method for keypoint extraction based on a Gaussian scale space and ROI masking. The proposed method is the first GPU implementation of 3D SIFT, is invariant to 3D similarity transforms, offers a solution to convolution filter bias and circumvents limitations introduced by hard boundaries typically present in neuroimaging analysis, and is interpretable. Analysis using this method led to improvements to the current state-of-art for family indexing on a large cohort of 3D brain MRIs, which can be used to help better understand brain similarities in families, and has also led to significant speedups compared to a CPU implementation. This method can be used to detect similarities in addition to pathologies in medical images in studies which include a variety of image modalities and anatomical structures.

Our analysis opens various venues for future technological advancements. Keypoint networks can be trained for specific tasks [18,27] but a challenge will be coping with bias towards training data. While the majority of CNN implementations are limited to translation invariant convolution via brute force convolution over the 3-parameter space of 3D translations, we demonstrate that nearest neighbor correspondences between normalized descriptors achieve convolution peaks across 7-parameter 3D similarity transforms, thus offering a mechanism to achieve invariance to orientation and scaling within the CNN framework.

## References

1. Azad, R., Fayjie, A.R., Kauffman, C., Ayed, I.B., Pedersoli, M., Dolz, J.: On the texture bias for few-shot CNN segmentation (2020)
2. Björkman, M., Bergström, N., Kragic, D.: Detecting, segmenting and tracking unknown objects using multi-label MRF inference. Comput. Vis. Image Underst. **118**, 111–127 (2014)
3. Carluer, J.-B., Chauvin, L., Luo, J., Wells III, W.M., Machado, I., Toews, M.: GPU-based parallel optimisation of the 3D sift-rank algorithm and a novel brief-inspired 3d fast descriptor (2020, in preparation)
4. Chauvin, L., et al.: Neuroimage signature from salient keypoints is highly specific to individuals and shared by close relatives. NeuroImage (2019)
5. Doshi, J., Erus, G., Yangming, O., Gaonkar, B., Davatzikos, C.: Multi-atlas skull-stripping. Acad. Radiol. **20**(12), 1566–1576 (2013)
6. Eskildsen, S.F., et al.: BEaST: brain extraction based on nonlocal segmentation technique. NeuroImage **59**(3), 2362–2373 (2012)
7. Fischl, B.: FreeSurfer. Neuroimage **62**(2), 774–781 (2012)

8. Geirhos, R., Rubisch, P., Michaelis, C., Bethge, M., Wichmann, F.A., Brendel, W.: ImageNet-trained cnns are biased towards texture; increasing shape bias improves accuracy and robustness. In: 7th International Conference on Learning Representations, ICLR 2019, New Orleans, LA, USA, 6–9 May 2019. OpenReview.net (2019)
9. Gilpin, L.H., Bau, D., Yuan, B.Z., Bajwa, A., Specter, M., Kagal, L.: Explaining explanations: an overview of interpretability of machine learning. In: 2018 IEEE 5th International Conference on Data Science and Advanced Analytics (DSAA), pp. 80–89. IEEE (2018)
10. Krizhevsky, A., Sutskever, I., Hinton, G.E.: ImageNet classification with deep convolutional neural networks. In: Pereira, F., Burges, C.J.C., Bottou, L., Weinberger, K.Q. (eds.) Advances in Neural Information Processing Systems 25, pp. 1097–1105. Curran Associates Inc. (2012)
11. LeCun, Y., Bengio, Y., Hinton, G.: Deep learning. Nature $521(7553)$, 436–444 (2015)
12. Lindeberg, T.: Scale-space theory: a basic tool for analyzing structures at different scales. J. Appl. Stat. $21(1$–$2)$, 225–270 (1994)
13. Lindholm, S., Kronander, J.: Accounting for uncertainty in medical data: a CUDA implementation of normalized convolution. In: Proceedings of SIGRAD 2011. Evaluations of Graphics and Visualization-Efficiency; Usefulness; Accessibility; Usability, 17–18 November 2011, no. 065, pp. 35–42. KTH, Stockholm. Linköping University Electronic Press (2011)
14. Lowe, D.G.: Distinctive image features from scale-invariant keypoints. Int. J. Comput. Vis. $60(2)$, 91–110 (2004). https://doi.org/10.1023/B:VISI.0000029664.99615.94
15. Menze, B.H., et al.: The multimodal brain tumor image segmentation benchmark (brats). IEEE Trans. Med. Imaging $34(10)$, 1993–2024 (2014)
16. Mitchell, D.P., Netravali, A.N.: Reconstruction filters in computer-graphics. SIGGRAPH Comput. Graph. $22(4)$, 221–228 (1988)
17. Muja, M., Lowe, D.G.: Scalable nearest neighbor algorithms for high dimensional data. IEEE Trans. Pattern Anal. Mach. Intell. $36(11)$, 2227–2240 (2014)
18. Ono, Y., Trulls, E., Fua, P., Yi, K.M.: LF-Net: learning local features from images. In: Advances in Neural Information Processing Systems, pp. 6234–6244 (2018)
19. Ritter, S., Barrett, D.G.T., Santoro, A., Botvinick, M.M.: Cognitive psychology for deep neural networks: a shape bias case study. In: Precup, D., Teh, Y.W. (eds.) Proceedings of the 34th International Conference on Machine Learning, volume 70 of Proceedings of Machine Learning Research, pp. 2940–2949, 06–11 August 2017. International Convention Centre, Sydney. PMLR (2017)
20. Sinha, S.N., Frahm, J.-M., Pollefeys, M., Genc, Y.: GPU-based video feature tracking and matching. In: EDGE, Workshop on Edge Computing Using New Commodity Architectures, vol. 278, p. 4321 (2006)
21. Smith, S.M.: Fast robust automated brain extraction. Hum. Brain Mapp. $17(3)$, 143–155 (2002)
22. Ségonne, F., et al.: A hybrid approach to the skull stripping problem in MRI. NeuroImage $22(3)$, 1060–1075 (2004)
23. Toews, M., Wells III, W.M.: Efficient and robust model-to-image alignment using 3D scale-invariant features. Med Image Anal. $17(3)$, 271–82 (2013)
24. Van Essen, D.C., Smith, S.M., Barch, D.M., Behrens, T.E.J., Yacoub, E., Ugurbil, K., Wu-Minn HCP Consortium, et al.: The Wu-Minn human connectome project: an overview. Neuroimage $80$, 62–79 (2013)
25. Wachinger, C., Toews, M., Langs, G., Wells, W., Golland, P.: Keypoint transfer for fast whole-body segmentation. IEEE Trans. Med. Imaging $39(2)$, 273–282 (2020)

26. Wachinger, C., Reuter, M., Klein, T.: DeepNAT: deep convolutional neural network for segmenting neuroanatomy. NeuroImage **170**, 434–445 (2018)
27. Yi, K.M., Trulls, E., Lepetit, V., Fua, P.: LIFT: learned invariant feature transform. In: Leibe, B., Matas, J., Sebe, N., Welling, M. (eds.) ECCV 2016. LNCS, vol. 9910, pp. 467–483. Springer, Cham (2016). https://doi.org/10.1007/978-3-319-46466-4_28

# A Longitudinal Method for Simultaneous Whole-Brain and Lesion Segmentation in Multiple Sclerosis

Stefano Cerri[1](✉), Andrew Hoopes[2], Douglas N. Greve[2,3], Mark Mühlau[4], and Koen Van Leemput[1,2]

[1] Department of Health Technology, Technical University of Denmark, Lyngby, Denmark
stce@dtu.dk
[2] Athinoula A. Martinos Center for Biomedical Imaging, Massachusetts General Hospital, Harvard Medical School, Boston, USA
[3] Department of Radiology, Harvard Medical School, Boston, USA
[4] Department of Neurology and TUM-Neuroimaging Center, School of Medicine, Technical University of Munich, Munich, Germany

**Abstract.** In this paper we propose a novel method for the segmentation of longitudinal brain MRI scans of patients suffering from Multiple Sclerosis. The method builds upon an existing cross-sectional method for simultaneous whole-brain and lesion segmentation, introducing subject-specific latent variables to encourage temporal consistency between longitudinal scans. It is very generally applicable, as it does not make any prior assumptions on the scanner, the MRI protocol, or the number and timing of longitudinal follow-up scans. Preliminary experiments on three longitudinal datasets indicate that the proposed method produces more reliable segmentations and detects disease effects better than the cross-sectional method it is based upon.

## 1 Introduction

Multiple Sclerosis (MS) is an inflammatory autoimmune disorder of the central nervous system. It is characterized by the formation of lesions in the white matter, as well as marked brain atrophy primarily in deep gray matter structures [1,2]. The increased availability of longitudinal magnetic resonance imaging (MRI) scans opens up the prospect of tracking lesion evolution and atrophy trajectories over time, enabling a better assessment of disease progression and treatment efficacy [3].

Despite high potential clinical impact, work on computational methods for quantifying longitudinal changes in MS has remained fairly limited to date (cf. [4] for an overview). The methods that do exist suffer from one or more of the following limitations: They only assess changes in white matter lesions [5–8] or in aggregate measures of brain atrophy such as global brain or gray matter volume [9,10], but not in individual brain structures; they can only compare

© Springer Nature Switzerland AG 2020
S. M. Kia et al. (Eds.): MLCN 2020/RNO-AI 2020, LNCS 12449, pp. 119–128, 2020.
https://doi.org/10.1007/978-3-030-66843-3_12

between two consecutive time points [11–14] instead of characterizing entire temporal trajectories; or they are developed and tested in very specific settings only, with degraded performance when applied to data from different scanners and acquisition protocols [15] which limits their usefulness in practice.

In order to address these limitations, here we propose a dedicated model for simultaneously segmenting anatomical brain structures and white matter lesion from longitudinal multi-contrast MRI scans. The proposed method builds upon a contrast-adaptive method for simultaneous whole-brain and lesion segmentation that we previously developed and validated [16]. Here we extend this approach to the longitudinal setting by additionally modeling the expected temporal consistency between repeated scans of the same subject, using latent variables that introduce a statistical dependency between the time points. By segmenting both white matter lesions and anatomical brain structures across time, the resulting method enables tracking deep gray matter atrophy trajectories and lesion evolution simultaneously. The model is fully adaptive to different MRI contrasts and scanners, and does not put any constraints on the number or the timing of longitudinal follow-up scans. To the best of our knowledge, no other method with these capabilities currently exists.

We assessed the segmentation performance of the proposed method on three longitudinal datasets. Preliminary results indicate that it produces more reliable segmentations and detects disease effects better than the cross-sectional method. An example result produced by the longitudinal method is shown in Fig. 1.

## 2    Existing Cross-Sectional Method

We first summarize the existing cross-sectional method for simultaneous whole-brain and lesion segmentation [16] the proposed method builds upon.

Let $\mathbf{D} = (\mathbf{d}_1, \ldots, \mathbf{d}_I)$ be the image intensities of a multi contrast MRI scan with $I$ voxels, where the vector $\mathbf{d}_i = (d_i^1, \ldots, d_i^N)^T$ represents the log-transformed image intensity of voxel $i$ for all the available $N$ contrasts. Moreover, let $\mathbf{l} = (l_1, \ldots, l_I)^T$ be corresponding segmentation labels, where $l_i \in \{1, \ldots, K\}$ denotes one of the $K$ possible anatomical structures assigned to voxel $i$. In order for the model to be capable of segmenting white matter lesions, a binary lesion map $\mathbf{z} = (z_1, \ldots z_I)$ is introduced, where $z_i \in \{0, 1\}$ indicates the presence of lesion in voxel $i$. We use a generative model, illustrated in black in Fig. 2, to estimate a joint segmentation $\{\mathbf{l}, \mathbf{z}\}$ from MRI data $\mathbf{D}$. The model consists of a segmentation prior $p(\mathbf{l}, \mathbf{z}|\mathbf{h}, \mathbf{x})$ with parameters $\mathbf{h}$ and $\mathbf{x}$ that encode shape information, and a likelihood function $p(\mathbf{D}|\mathbf{l}, \mathbf{z}, \boldsymbol{\theta}, \boldsymbol{\theta}_z)$ with parameters $\boldsymbol{\theta}$ and $\boldsymbol{\theta}_z$ that govern intensity appearance. Below we briefly describe the segmentation prior and the likelihood function, as well as how the model is "inverted" to obtain automatic segmentations.

**Segmentation Prior:** The segmentation prior is composed of two components $p(\mathbf{l}|\mathbf{x})$ and $p(\mathbf{z}|\mathbf{h}, \mathbf{x})$ that encode spatial information regarding the neuroanatomical labels $\mathbf{l}$ and the lesion map $\mathbf{z}$ respectively: $p(\mathbf{l}, \mathbf{z}|\mathbf{h}, \mathbf{x}) = p(\mathbf{l}|\mathbf{x})p(\mathbf{z}|\mathbf{h}, \mathbf{x})$.

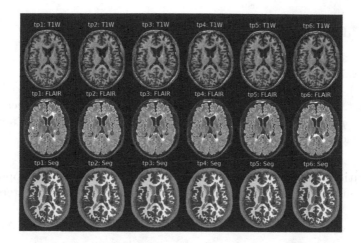

**Fig. 1.** Example segmentation produced by the proposed method on a longitudinal scan with T1w and FLAIR contrast.

The first component is a deformable probabilistic atlas, encoded as a tetrahedral mesh [17] with node positions $\mathbf{x}$ and with a deformation prior distribution defined as:

$$p(\mathbf{x}) \propto \exp\left[-K \sum_d U_d(\mathbf{x}, \mathbf{x}_{ref})\right].$$

Here $K$ controls the stiffness of the mesh deformations, $d$ loops over the tetrahedra in the mesh, and $U_d(\mathbf{x}, \mathbf{x}_{ref})$ is a cost [18] associated with deforming the $d^{th}$ tetrahedron from its shape in the atlas's reference position $\mathbf{x}_{ref}$. Letting $p(l_i = k|\mathbf{x})$ denote the probability of observing label $k$ at voxel $i$ for a given deformation, assuming conditional independence of the labels between voxels yields $p(\mathbf{l}|\mathbf{x}) = \prod_{i=1}^{I} p(l_i|\mathbf{x})$.

The second component of the segmentation prior is a model of the form: $p(\mathbf{z}|\mathbf{h}, \mathbf{x}) = \prod_{i=1}^{I} p(z_i|\mathbf{h}, \mathbf{x})$, $p(\mathbf{h}) = \mathcal{N}(\mathbf{h}|\mathbf{0}, \mathbf{I})$, where $p(z_i = 1||\mathbf{h}, \mathbf{x})$ is the probability that voxel $i$ is part of a lesion. This model takes into account both a voxel's spatial location within its neuroanatomical context (through $\mathbf{x}$), as well as lesion shape constraints through a variational autoencoder (VAE) [19] that "decodes" a low-dimensional latent code $\mathbf{h}$ using a convolutional neural network.

**Likelihood:** For the likelihood, which links segmentations $\{\mathbf{l}, \mathbf{z}\}$ to intensities $\mathbf{D}$, we use a multivariate Gaussian intensity model for each structure, and model the MRI bias field artifact as a linear combination of spatially smooth basis functions that is added to the local voxel intensities [20,21]. Letting $\boldsymbol{\theta}_z = \{\boldsymbol{\mu}_z, \boldsymbol{\Sigma}_z\}$ denote the mean and variance of lesion intensities, and $\boldsymbol{\theta}$ the collection of bias field parameters and intensity means and variances $\{\boldsymbol{\mu}_k, \boldsymbol{\Sigma}_k\}$ of all $K$ anatomical structures, the likelihood is defined as $p(\mathbf{D}|\mathbf{l}, \mathbf{z}, \boldsymbol{\theta}, \boldsymbol{\theta}_z) = \prod_{i=1}^{I} p(\mathbf{d}_i|l_i, z_i, \boldsymbol{\theta}, \boldsymbol{\theta}_z)$, where

$$p(\mathbf{d}_i | l_i = k, z_i, \boldsymbol{\theta}, \boldsymbol{\theta}_z) = \begin{cases} \mathcal{N}(\mathbf{d}_i | \boldsymbol{\mu}_z + \mathbf{C}^T \boldsymbol{\phi}_i, \boldsymbol{\Sigma}_z) & \text{if } z_i = 1, \\ \mathcal{N}(\mathbf{d}_i | \boldsymbol{\mu}_k + \mathbf{C}^T \boldsymbol{\phi}_i, \boldsymbol{\Sigma}_k) & \text{otherwise.} \end{cases}$$

Here $\boldsymbol{\phi}_i$ evaluates the bias field basis functions at the $i^{th}$ voxel, and $\mathbf{C} = (\mathbf{c}_1, \ldots, \mathbf{c}_N)$, where $\mathbf{c}_n$ denotes the parameters of the bias field model for the $n^{th}$ contrast. The model is completed by a flat prior on $\boldsymbol{\theta}$, and a weak conditional prior $p(\boldsymbol{\theta}_z | \boldsymbol{\theta})$ that ensures that the method can be robustly applied to scans with no or very small lesion loads [16].

**Segmentation:** Given an MRI scan $\mathbf{D}$, segmentation proceeds by approximating the segmentation posterior using point estimates of the parameters $\mathbf{x}$ and $\boldsymbol{\theta}$:

$$p(\mathbf{l}, \mathbf{z} | \mathbf{D}) \simeq p(\mathbf{l}, \mathbf{z} | \mathbf{D}, \hat{\boldsymbol{\theta}}, \hat{\mathbf{x}}), \tag{1}$$

and Markov chain Monte Carlo sampling to marginalize over the remaining, lesion-specific parameters $\boldsymbol{\theta}_z$ and $\mathbf{h}$. For the purpose of finding the point estimates $\hat{\mathbf{x}}$ and $\hat{\boldsymbol{\theta}}$, a simplified model is fitted to the data:

$$\hat{\boldsymbol{\Omega}} = \underset{\boldsymbol{\Omega}}{\arg\max} \, p(\boldsymbol{\Omega} | \mathbf{D}) \quad \text{with} \quad \boldsymbol{\Omega} = \{\mathbf{x}, \boldsymbol{\theta}, \boldsymbol{\theta}_z\}, \tag{2}$$

where the lesion-shape encoding VAE and its parameters $\mathbf{h}$ are temporarily removed to simplify the optimization process. More details can be found in [16].

## 3    Longitudinal Extension

In the longitudinal setting we are given $T$ scans with image intensities $\{\mathbf{D}_t\}_{t=1}^T$, and we wish to compute for each time point $t$ the corresponding segmentation $\{\mathbf{l}_t, \mathbf{z}_t\}$. In contrast to the cross-sectional setting where each image is treated independently, here we can exploit the fact that all images belong to the same subject to produce more consistent (and potentially more accurate) segmentations. Towards this end, we introduce subject-specific latent variables $\mathbf{x}_0$ and $\boldsymbol{\theta}_0$ in the segmentation prior and likelihood, respectively, imposing a statistical dependency between the time points that encourages the segmentations to be similar to one another. The augmented generative model is depicted in Fig. 2, where the parameters $\mathbf{x}_t, \mathbf{h}_t, \boldsymbol{\theta}_t$ and $\boldsymbol{\theta}_{t,z}$ denote the model parameters of time point $t$, and the blue parts indicate the additional components compared to the cross-sectional model.

**Segmentation Prior:** In order to obtain temporal consistency in the segmentation prior, we use the concept of a "subject-specific atlas" [22]: a deformation of the cross-sectional atlas to represent the average subject-specific anatomy across all time points. In particular,

$$p(\{\mathbf{x}_t\}_{t=1}^T | \mathbf{x}_0) = \prod_{t=1}^T p(\mathbf{x}_t | \mathbf{x}_0), \quad p(\mathbf{x}_t | \mathbf{x}_0) \propto \exp\left[-K_1 \sum_d U_d(\mathbf{x}_t, \mathbf{x}_0)\right],$$

where $\mathbf{x}_0$ are latent atlas node positions encoding subject-specific brain shape, with prior $p(\mathbf{x}_0) \propto \exp\left[-K_0 \sum_d U_d(\mathbf{x}_0, \mathbf{x}_{ref})\right]$. Here the mesh stiffnesses $K_0$ and $K_1$ are hyperparameters of the model; by choosing $K_0 = \infty$ and $K_1 = K$ the model devolves into the cross-sectional segmentation prior for each time point separately.

**Likelihood:** In a similar vein, we also introduce subject-specific latent variables to encourage temporal consistency in the Gaussian intensity models. For each anatomical structure, we condition the Gaussian parameters $\{\boldsymbol{\mu}_{t,k}, \boldsymbol{\Sigma}_{t,k}\}$ on latent variables $\{\boldsymbol{\mu}_{0,k}, \boldsymbol{\Sigma}_{0,k}\}$ using a normal-inverse-Wishart (NIW) distribution: $p(\{\boldsymbol{\theta}_t\}_{t=1}^T | \boldsymbol{\theta}_0) = \prod_{t=1}^T p(\boldsymbol{\theta}_t | \boldsymbol{\theta}_0)$ with

$$p(\boldsymbol{\theta}_t | \boldsymbol{\theta}_0) \propto \prod_{k=1}^K \mathcal{N}(\boldsymbol{\mu}_{t,k} | \boldsymbol{\mu}_{0,k}, P_{0,k} \boldsymbol{\Sigma}_{0,k}) \mathrm{IW}(\boldsymbol{\Sigma}_{t,k} | P_{0,k} \boldsymbol{\Sigma}_{0,k}, P_{0,k} - N - 2).$$

Here $\boldsymbol{\theta}_0 = \{\boldsymbol{\mu}_{0,k}, \boldsymbol{\Sigma}_{0,k}\}_{k=1}^K$ with prior $p(\boldsymbol{\theta}_0) \propto 1$, and $P_{0,k} \geq 0$ is a hyperparameter that governs the strength of the regularization across time for label $k$. Note that choosing $P_{0,k} = 0, \forall k$ yields the cross-sectional likelihood for each time point independently.

**Segmentation:** We follow the same overall segmentation strategy as in the cross-sectional setting: we first compute point estimates $\{\hat{\boldsymbol{\theta}}_t, \hat{\mathbf{x}}_t\}_{t=1}^T$ using a simplified model in which the lesion shape codes $\{\mathbf{h}_t\}_{t=1}^T$ are removed, and subsequently obtain segmentations as described in the cross-sectional setting, i.e., by using (1) for each time point separately. As in the cross-sectional case, we obtain the required point estimates by fitting the longitudinal model to the data:

$$\{\hat{\boldsymbol{\Omega}}_1, \ldots, \hat{\boldsymbol{\Omega}}_T, \hat{\boldsymbol{\theta}}_0, \hat{\mathbf{x}}_0\} = \underset{\{\boldsymbol{\Omega}_1, \ldots, \boldsymbol{\Omega}_T, \boldsymbol{\theta}_0, \mathbf{x}_0\}}{\operatorname{argmax}} p(\boldsymbol{\Omega}_1, \ldots, \boldsymbol{\Omega}_T, \boldsymbol{\theta}_0, \mathbf{x}_0 | \mathbf{D}_1, \ldots, \mathbf{D}_T), \quad (3)$$

where $\boldsymbol{\Omega}_t = \{\mathbf{x}_t, \boldsymbol{\theta}_t, \boldsymbol{\theta}_{t,z}\}$. For optimizing (3) we use coordinate ascent, updating one variable at a time in an iterative fashion. Because $p(\mathbf{x}_t | \mathbf{x}_0)$ is of the same form as the cross-sectional deformation prior, and the NIW distribution used in $p(\boldsymbol{\theta}_t | \boldsymbol{\theta}_0)$ is the conjugate prior for the mean and variance of a Gaussian distribution, estimating $\boldsymbol{\Omega}_t$ from $\mathbf{D}_t$ for given values of $\boldsymbol{\theta}_0$ and $\mathbf{x}_0$ simply involves performing an optimization of the form of (2) for each time point $t$ separately. Conversely, for given values $\{\boldsymbol{\Omega}_t\}_{t=1}^T$ the update for $\boldsymbol{\theta}_0$ is given in closed form:

$$\boldsymbol{\mu}_{0,k} \leftarrow \left(\sum_{t=1}^T \boldsymbol{\Sigma}_{t,k}^{-1}\right)^{-1} \sum_{t=1}^T \boldsymbol{\Sigma}_{t,k}^{-1} \boldsymbol{\mu}_{t,k}, \quad \boldsymbol{\Sigma}_{0,k}^{-1} \leftarrow \left(\frac{1}{T} \sum_{t=1}^T \boldsymbol{\Sigma}_{t,k}^{-1}\right) \frac{P_{0,k}}{P_{0,k} - N - 2},$$

whereas updating $\mathbf{x}_0$ involves the optimization (cf. [22])

$$\underset{\mathbf{x}_0}{\operatorname{argmin}} \sum_d \left[K_0 U_d(\mathbf{x}_0, \mathbf{x}_{ref}) + K_1 \sum_{t=1}^T U_d(\mathbf{x}_0, \mathbf{x}_t)\right],$$

which we solve numerically using a limited-memory BFGS algorithm.

**Implementation:** In order to avoid longitudinal processing biases resulting from not treated all time points in exactly the same way, we first compute an unbiased within-subject template using an inverse consistent registration method [23]. This template is a robust representation of the average subject anatomy over time, and we use it as an unbiased reference to register all time points to in a preprocessing step. We also use it to start the proposed iterative algorithm optimizing (3): we apply the cross-sectional method to the template, and use the estimated model parameters $\boldsymbol{\Omega}$ to initialize $\boldsymbol{\Omega}_t, t = 1, \ldots, T$. The proposed algorithm, which interleaves updating the latent variables $\boldsymbol{\theta}_0$ and $\mathbf{x}_0$ with updating the parameters $\{\boldsymbol{\Omega}_t\}_{t=1}^{T}$, is then run for five iterations, which we have found to be sufficient to reach convergence.

Based on initial pilot experiments on scans from the ADNI project[1] (distinct from the ones used in the experiments below), we set the method's hyperparameter values to $K_1 = 14K$ and $K_0 = K$, where $K$ is the mesh stiffness in the existing cross-sectional method, and $P_{0,k}$ to the number of voxels assigned to class $k$ in the segmentation of the within-subject template.

Our implementation builds upon the C++ and Python code of [16,24], and is publicly available from FreeSurfer[2]. Segmenting one subject takes approximately 15 min per time point on an Intel 12-core i7-8700K processor with a GeForce GTX 1060 graphics card.

## 4    Experiments and Results

In order to assess whether introducing subject-specific latent variables leads to better longitudinal performance, we compared the proposed method and the cross-sectional method on three different datasets:

- **Test-retest** [25]: This dataset consists of longitudinal T1-weighted (T1w) and FLuid Attenuation Inversion Recovery (FLAIR) scans of 2 MS subjects. For each subject 6 repeated scans were acquired from 3 different 3T scanners (Philips Achieva; Siemens Verio; GE Signa MR750) within 3 weeks.
- **Achieva**: This dataset consists of longitudinal T1w and FLAIR scans of 86 MS subjects. The subjects were scanned between 3 and 6 times (time between scans between 6 and 12 months) with a 3T Philips Achieva scanner at the Department of Neurology, School of Medicine, at the Technical University of Munich in the context of the in-house cohort study on MS named TUM-MS. All the subjects were diagnosed as relapsing-remitting MS.
- **ADNI**: This dataset consists of longitudinal T1w scans of 135 subjects randomly selected from the ADNI project. Scanners from multiple sites were used to acquired the scans, and subjects were scanned between 2 and 6 times, with 6 or 12 months between scans. The subjects were divided into 3 groups: cognitively normal (CN, n=45), mild cognitive impairment (MCI, n=54), and Alzheimer disease (AD, n=36).

---

[1] http://adni.loni.usc.edu/.
[2] http://freesurfer.net/.

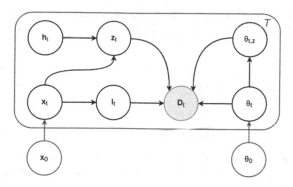

**Fig. 2.** Graphical representation of the proposed model. In black the existing cross-sectional method of [16] for each time point $t$; in blue the proposed additional latent variables for modeling temporal consistency between longitudinal scans with $T$ time points. (Color figure online)

We report results on the estimated volumes of the following 26 regions: left and right cerebral white matter, cerebellum white matter, cerebral cortex, cerebellum cortex, lateral ventricle, hippocampus, thalamus, putamen, pallidum, caudate, amygdala and nucleus accumbens, as well as brain stem and lesions. To avoid cluttering, results for left and right structures are averaged.

**Temporal Consistency:** We wished to assess whether the proposed method is able to reduce non-biological variations in longitudinal volume measurements, both within the short ($< 3$ weeks) and longer ($< 6$ years) time intervals of the test-retest and the Achieva datasets, respectively. For the test-retest dataset one can expect true biological changes to be minimal, and we therefore computed the coefficient of variation (ratio of the standard deviation to the mean) for each brain structure. The results, shown in Table 1, indicate that the longitudinal method indeed performs better in this respect than the cross-sectional one for almost all the structures.

For the Achieva dataset, one may assume that the true change in volume of a structure over the span of a few years is approximately linear, except for lesions whose temporal trajectory is affected by disease effects, with growing and shrinking lesions occurring at the same time. We therefore fitted, for each structure and for each subject, a linear regression model to the longitudinal volumes estimated by each method, and computed the ratio of the standard deviation of the residuals to the intersect (time of the first scan is taken as zero). The results are summarized in Table 2 and indicate that the proposed model indeed yields generally better results in this respect.

**Detecting Disease Effects:** In order to ensure that the proposed method is not simply over-regularizing, we also assessed whether it can capture known group differences in the temporal evolution of certain brain structures better

**Table 1.** Coefficients of variation in [%] on the test-retest dataset, both for the proposed longitudinal ("Long") and the cross-sectional ("Cross") method.

| Structure | Subject 1 | | | | | | Subject 2 | | | | | | Avg | |
|---|---|---|---|---|---|---|---|---|---|---|---|---|---|---|
| | GE | | Philips | | Siemens | | GE | | Philips | | Siemens | | | |
| | Cross | Long | Cross | Long | Cross | Long | Cross | Long | Cross | Long | Cross | Long | Cross | Long |
| Lesions | 3.79 | 3.90 | 4.78 | 3.79 | 6.27 | 3.39 | 2.84 | 4.04 | 2.57 | 1.95 | 2.35 | 1.22 | 3.77 | **3.05** |
| Cerebral white matter | 0.38 | 0.46 | 0.14 | 0.12 | 1.70 | 1.24 | 0.93 | 0.79 | 0.78 | 0.17 | 1.16 | 1.00 | 0.85 | **0.63** |
| Cerebellum white matter | 0.82 | 0.56 | 0.28 | 0.19 | 2.03 | 1.96 | 1.28 | 0.91 | 0.71 | 0.41 | 1.14 | 1.00 | 1.04 | **0.84** |
| Cerebral cortex | 0.53 | 0.50 | 0.50 | 0.44 | 1.50 | 1.84 | 0.60 | 1.08 | 0.30 | 0.40 | 0.74 | 1.10 | **0.70** | 0.89 |
| Cerebellum cortex | 0.38 | 0.34 | 0.31 | 0.36 | 1.13 | 1.25 | 0.61 | 0.63 | 0.42 | 0.36 | 0.86 | 0.57 | 0.62 | **0.58** |
| Lateral ventricles | 1.10 | 1.03 | 1.37 | 0.38 | 1.11 | 0.57 | 3.73 | 2.95 | 1.62 | 1.10 | 2.71 | 1.24 | 1.94 | **1.21** |
| Hippocampus | 1.03 | 0.67 | 0.55 | 0.43 | 0.84 | 1.46 | 1.88 | 1.39 | 0.55 | 0.57 | 1.37 | 0.91 | 1.04 | **0.90** |
| Thalamus | 0.44 | 0.44 | 0.52 | 0.31 | 1.21 | 0.54 | 0.92 | 0.79 | 0.50 | 0.35 | 1.02 | 0.36 | 0.77 | **0.46** |
| Putamen | 0.58 | 0.14 | 0.84 | 0.76 | 0.70 | 0.71 | 0.51 | 0.31 | 1.10 | 0.52 | 1.44 | 1.08 | 0.86 | **0.59** |
| Pallidum | 2.25 | 1.35 | 2.04 | 1.58 | 3.94 | 1.31 | 2.77 | 2.39 | 1.12 | 0.77 | 4.35 | 1.84 | 2.74 | **1.54** |
| Caudate | 0.80 | 1.09 | 0.96 | 0.90 | 1.00 | 0.84 | 1.79 | 1.04 | 0.92 | 0.54 | 0.61 | 0.41 | 1.01 | **0.80** |
| Amygdala | 1.51 | 0.47 | 0.42 | 0.20 | 1.85 | 1.04 | 1.17 | 0.64 | 1.05 | 0.41 | 0.60 | 0.42 | 1.10 | **0.53** |
| Accumbens | 1.84 | 1.27 | 1.77 | 1.40 | 1.80 | 1.39 | 1.96 | 0.69 | 0.80 | 0.80 | 1.73 | 0.80 | 1.65 | **1.06** |
| Brain stem | 0.70 | 0.53 | 0.32 | 0.19 | 1.10 | 0.93 | 0.78 | 0.59 | 0.54 | 0.34 | 0.61 | 0.63 | 0.67 | **0.53** |
| Intracranial volume | 0.30 | 0.06 | 0.13 | 0.18 | 0.53 | 0.56 | 0.46 | 0.06 | 0.22 | 0.08 | 0.52 | 0.36 | 0.36 | **0.22** |

**Table 2.** Average deviation from a linear trajectory in [%] for volumetric measurements in the Achieva dataset.

| Structure | Cross | Long | Structure | Cross | Long |
|---|---|---|---|---|---|
| Lesions | 9.41 | **9.27** | Cerebral white matter | 0.56 | **0.31** |
| Cerebellum white matter | 0.59 | **0.45** | Cerebral cortex | **0.54** | 0.59 |
| Cerebellum cortex | 0.45 | **0.42** | Lateral ventricles | 2.04 | **1.85** |
| Hippocampus | 0.69 | **0.55** | Thalamus | 0.51 | **0.49** |
| Putamen | 0.70 | **0.42** | Pallidum | 1.23 | **0.78** |
| Caudate | 1.01 | **0.80** | Amygdala | 0.70 | **0.40** |
| Accumbens | 1.39 | **0.82** | Brain stem | 0.62 | **0.46** |
| Intracranial volume | 0.28 | **0.08** | | | |

than the cross-sectional method. Towards this end, we compared the annualized percentage change (the slope of a linear regression model divided by its intersect) in the volume of the hippocampus between the CN, MCI and AD groups in the ADNI dataset. The results, shown in Fig. 3, indicate that the longitudinal method can indeed detect group differences better this way.

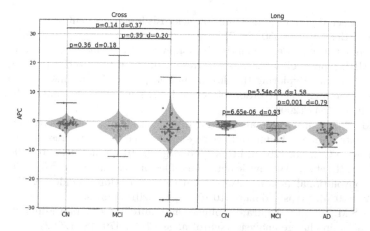

**Fig. 3.** Annualized percentage change (APC) in the volume of the hippocampus for the three groups of the ADNI dataset. Statistical significance was computed with a Welch's t-test and effect size with Cohen's d.

## 5  Discussion and Conclusion

In this paper we have proposed a novel method for the segmentation of longitudinal brain MRI scans of patients suffering from MS. The method is based on an existing cross-sectional method for simultaneous whole-brain and lesion segmentation, and leverages subject-specific latent variables to encourage segmentations across time points to be similar to each other. Preliminary results indicate that it is able to produce more consistent and reliable segmentations compared to the cross-sectional version, while being more sensitive to group differences. Future work will involve an extensive analysis of disease progression in different MS patient groups, as well as a more careful tuning of the hyperparameters of the model.

**Acknowledgments.** This project has received funding from the European Union's Horizon 2020 research and innovation program under the Marie Sklodowska-Curie project TRABIT agreement No 765148, the German Research Foundation No 428223038, and the NIH NINDS No R01NS112161.

## References

1. Barkhof, F., et al.: Imaging outcomes for neuroprotection and repair in multiple sclerosis trials. Nat. Rev. Neurol. **5**(5), 256–266 (2009)
2. Azevedo, C.J., et al.: Thalamic atrophy in multiple sclerosis: a magnetic resonance imaging marker of neurodegeneration throughout disease. Ann. Neurol. **83**(2), 223–234 (2018)
3. Thompson, A.J., et al.: Diagnosis of multiple sclerosis: 2017 revisions of the McDonald criteria. Lancet Neurol. **17**(2), 162–173 (2018)

4. Carass, A., et al.: Longitudinal multiple sclerosis lesion segmentation data resource. Data in Brief **12**, 346–350 (2017)
5. Guttmann, C.R.G., et al.: Quantitative follow-up of patients with multiple sclerosis using MRI: reproducibility. J. Magn. Reson. Imaging **9**(4), 509–518 (1999)
6. Gerig, G., et al.: Exploring the discrimination power of the time domain for segmentation and characterization of active lesions in serial MR data. Med. Image Anal. **4**(1), 31–42 (2000)
7. Schmidt, P., et al.: Automated segmentation of changes in FLAIR-hyperintense white matter lesions in multiple sclerosis on serial magnetic resonance imaging. NeuroImage Clin. **23** (2019). https://doi.org/10.1016/j.nicl.2019.101849
8. McKinley, R., et al.: Automatic detection of lesion load change in Multiple Sclerosis using convolutional neural networks with segmentation confidence. NeuroImage Clin. **25** (2020). https://doi.org/10.1016/j.nicl.2019.102104
9. Smith, S.M., et al.: Accurate, robust, and automated longitudinal and cross-sectional brain change analysis. NeuroImage **17**(1), 479–489 (2002)
10. Smeets, D., et al.: Reliable measurements of brain atrophy in individual patients with multiple sclerosis. Brain Behav. **6**(9), e00518 (2016)
11. Smith, S.M., et al.: Normalized accurate measurement of longitudinal brain change. J. Comput. Assist. Tomogr. **25**(3), 466–475 (2001)
12. Rey, D., et al.: Automatic detection and segmentation of evolving processes in 3D medical images: application to multiple sclerosis. Med. Image Anal. **6**(2), 163–179 (2002)
13. Battaglini, M., et al.: Automated identification of brain new lesions in multiple sclerosis using subtraction images. J. Magn. Reson. Imaging **39**(6), 1543–1549 (2014)
14. Jain, S., et al.: Two time point MS lesion segmentation in brain MRI: an expectation-maximization framework. Front. Neurosci. **10** (2016). https://doi.org/10.3389/fnins.2016.00576
15. García-Lorenzo, D., et al.: Review of automatic segmentation methods of multiple sclerosis white matter lesions on conventional magnetic resonance imaging. Med. Image Anal. **17**(1), 1–18 (2013)
16. Cerri, S., et al.: A contrast-adaptive method for simultaneous whole-brain and lesion segmentation in multiple sclerosis. NeuroImage **225**, 117471 (2021). https://doi.org/10.1016/j.neuroimage.2020.117471
17. Van Leemput, K.: Encoding probabilistic brain atlases using Bayesian inference. IEEE Trans. Med. Imaging **28**(6), 822–837 (2009)
18. Ashburner, J., et al.: Image registration using a symmetric prior - in three dimensions. Hum. Brain Mapp. **9**(4), 212–225 (2000)
19. Kingma, D.P., Welling, M.: Auto-encoding variational Bayes (2013)
20. Wells, W.M., et al.: Adaptive segmentation of MRI data. IEEE Trans. Med. Imaging **15**(4), 429–442 (1996)
21. Van Leemput, K., et al.: Automated model-based bias field correction of MR images of the brain. IEEE Trans. Med. Imaging **18**(10), 885–896 (1999)
22. Iglesias, J.E., et al.: Bayesian longitudinal segmentation of hippocampal substructures in brain MRI using subject-specific atlases. NeuroImage **141**, 542–555 (2016)
23. Reuter, M., et al.: Within-subject template estimation for unbiased longitudinal image analysis. NeuroImage **61**(4), 1402–1418 (2012)
24. Puonti, O., et al.: Fast and sequence-adaptive whole-brain segmentation using parametric Bayesian modeling. NeuroImage **143**, 235–249 (2016)
25. Biberacher, V., et al.: Intra- and interscanner variability of magnetic resonance imaging based volumetry in multiple sclerosis. NeuroImage **142**, 188–197 (2016)

# Towards MRI Progression Features for Glioblastoma Patients: From Automated Volumetry and Classical Radiomics to Deep Feature Learning

Yannick Suter[1,2]($\boxtimes$), Urspeter Knecht[2,3], Roland Wiest[4], Ekkehard Hewer[5], Philippe Schucht[6], and Mauricio Reyes[1,2]

[1] Insel Data Science Center, Inselspital, Bern University Hospital, Bern, Switzerland
yannick.suter@artorg.unibe.ch
[2] ARTORG Center for Biomedical Engineering Research, University of Bern, Bern, Switzerland
[3] Radiology Department, Spital Emmental, Burgdorf, Switzerland
[4] Support Center for Advanced Neuroimaging, Inselspital, Bern University Hospital, Bern, Switzerland
[5] Pathology Institute, University of Bern, Bern, Switzerland
[6] Department of Neurosurgery, Inselspital, Bern University Hospital, Bern, Switzerland

**Abstract.** Disease progression for Glioblastoma multiforme patients is currently assessed with manual bi-dimensional measurements of the active contrast-enhancing tumor on Magnetic Resonance Images (MRI). This method is known to be susceptible to error; in the lack of a data-driven approach, progression thresholds had been set rather arbitrarily considering measurement inaccuracies. We propose a data-driven methodology for disease progression assessment, building on tumor volumetry, classical radiomics, and deep learning based features. For each feature type, we infer progression thresholds by maximizing the correlation of the time-to-progression (TTP) and overall survival (OS). On a longitudinal study comprising over 500 data points, we observed considerable underestimation of the current volumetric disease progression threshold. We evaluate the data-driven disease progression thresholds based on expert ratings using the current clinical practice.

**Keywords:** Glioblastoma · Deep features · Disease progression · Radiomics

## 1 Introduction

Glioblastoma multiforme (GBM) ranks highest on the World Health Organization's malignancy scale. This most frequent primary brain tumor in humans

**Electronic supplementary material** The online version of this chapter (https://doi.org/10.1007/978-3-030-66843-3_13) contains supplementary material, which is available to authorized users.

grows very fast, and is hard to treat due to its highly infiltrative nature, leading to a median overall survival (OS) time of only 14 months [21]. There is currently no curative treatment available. The standard-of-care is maximum safe surgical resection, followed by chemo- and radiation therapy [18,21].

Due to the low OS time, disease progression is periodically evaluated on MRI follow-up scans within three month intervals. For clinical studies, treatment response is monitored using the *Response Assessment in Neuro Oncology (RANO)* criteria. At each follow-up, the neuroradiologist classifies the disease status according to the RANO protocol as *complete response, partial response, stable disease,* or *progressive disease.* To detect progression as early as possible, sensitive progression features ("biomarkers") are important. In the following, we describe how disease progression is currently assessed and which advanced imaging progression features are considered in our study.

### 1.1 Current Practice of Progression Assessment and Radiomics Research

Disease progression in GBM patients is currently detected by comparing the tumor burden to a reference point (*nadir*), where the tumor was smallest. Due to the prohibitively long time for manually segmenting tumors, a simpler two-dimensional metric is used. Tumor burden is measured by the longest contrast-enhancement diameter on axial post-contrast T1-weighted MRI slices, and the longest line perpendicular to this longest diameter. The sum of the product of these two diameters for each lesion is a surrogate metric for the current tumor burden. This measurement is error-prone, and, e.g., inconsistent head-placement in the MRI leads to large deviations [13]. The current RANO guidelines set the progression threshold at an increase by 25% of the bi-dimensional tumor size, and of 40% for the tumor volume [2]. However, the volume progression threshold is rarely used due to the unfeasibility of manual tumor segmentation in clinical practice. Overall, the two-dimensional metric and the associated thresholds are known to be rudimentary and rather arbitrarily set. The agreement between the two-dimensional and volumetric response threshold is highly dependent on the shape of the tumor [1,6]. Additionally, arising small non-measurable lesions and T2/FLAIR intensity changes are indications of progression according to the RANO guidelines.

Radiomics for GBM patients has largely focused on overall survival (OS) prediction from single-timepoint pre-treatment MRI, and was fueled by the yearly Brain Tumor Segmentation (BraTS) challenge [11], where an additional OS prediction competition was introduced. Successful methods for OS prediction mainly apply classical machine learning techniques using radiomic features extracted from tumor segmentation labels. Probably due to the scarcity and heterogeneity of publicly available data, end-to-end deep learning (DL) was consistently outperformed by classical machine learning regression approaches [19]. A notable exception is the use of pre-trained convolutional neural networks (CNNs), where the output of dense layers has been used as features to predict OS (e.g., [9]) To date, no studies have focused on investigating standard radiomics and deep learning based imaging biomarkers of GBM disease progression. We hypothesize that, contrary to the current 2D-based tumor size definition through longitudinal imaging-based biomarkers can provide a more accurate and robust description of tumor progression/response to therapy.

## 2    Proposed Data-Driven Approach

Our analyses build on the concept that an optimal disease progression biomarker has a high correlation between the time-to-progression (TTP) and OS. We follow the method conceptually proposed by Reardon et al. [12] to define an optimal progression biomarker threshold by maximizing this correlation. In this study, we chose the overall survival as clinical endpoint and Spearman's rank correlation ($\rho$) since we do not assume a linear relationship between the progression feature and OS [17].

Figure 1 depicts the general idea, where a feature is extracted from MRI longitudinally and compared to the previously lowest value (nadir). The TTP is calculated for different disease progression thresholds, and the threshold with the highest Spearman's rank correlation $\rho$ between the TTP and OS is chosen.

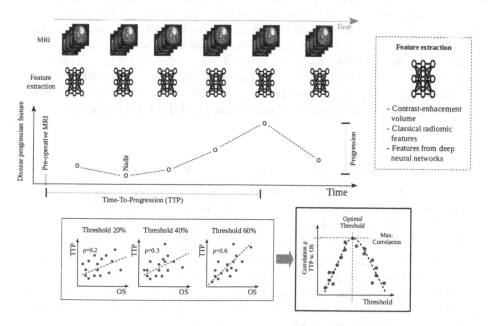

**Fig. 1.** Overview of the used progression feature assessment method. A potential disease progression feature is monitored longitudinally, and the time-to-progression is calculated for different disease progression thresholds. For each threshold, the correlation to the overall survival is calculated. An optimal biomarker threshold is set such that the correlation between time-to-progression and OS is maximized. Adapted from [12]. For each timepoint, tumor volume, classical radiomic features, and features from a dense layer of a CNN are extracted.

## 3    Materials and Methods

### 3.1    Data

There is currently only one public dataset containing both pre- and post-operative MRI of Glioblastoma patients [10], it only includes one post-surgery timepoint, and was therefore not usable for this study. We use single-center data from the University Hospital of Bern, Switzerland (Inselspital), since fully longitudinal data is needed for progression biomarker discovery. The records of 95 patients with pathologically confirmed primary GBM diagnosed between August 2008 and December 2013, and treated with resection and temozolomide-based chemoradiation, were reviewed retrospectively. Patients with available T1-weighted, T1-weighted with contrast agent, T2-weighted and T2-FLAIR MRIs for at least two post-operative follow-up scans were included. Only patients with known OS were considered, resulting in a population of 73 patients with 502 complete follow-ups. The ethics committee approved the study and waived informed consent.

Each timepoint was rated by an experienced neuroradiologist according to the RANO guidelines. Tumor burden was assessed with the aforementioned two-dimensional measurements. The expert TTP was calculated as the time between the first progression timepoint and the date of the pre-operative MRI acquisition. Pseudo-progression was handled according to the RANO guidelines, with only considering a timepoint as progression, if confirmed on the next follow-up.

The MRI images were bias-field corrected, resampled to $1\,mm^3$ isovoxels and registered to the MNI152 atlas to allow corresponding MRI slice selection across timepoints using `mri_robust_register` [14]. The contrast-enhancing tumor and T2-/FLAIR-abnormality was segmented using HD-GLIO-AUTO [4,5,7].

### 3.2    Experiments

We compare the following imaging-based progression feature types:

1. Automated tumor volumetry as "silver-standard" tumor burden surrogate, since manual segmentation is too labor-intensive in clinical practice.
2. Radiomics features extracted with PyRadiomics [3].
3. Features extracted from VGG-16-based deep neural networks [16]

We used three-fold stratified cross-validation for all experiments where training was necessary. The folds were composed such that the mean OS time was approximately the same. For each fold, two third of the full dataset was used for training, and the hold-out samples for prediction. With the stratification, predictions for the whole dataset were calculated.

**Automated Volumetry.** The current RANO guidelines define progression as a $\geq 40\%$ increase in tumor volume compared to the nadir. We tested how the TTP changes for a wide range of disease progression thresholds and where the correlation with the OS time was highest. This experiment tests the suitability of an automated segmentation tool for automated disease progression assessment.

**Classical Radiomic Features as Progression Biomarkers.** Radiomic features were extracted from the bias-field corrected MRI sequences using PyRadiomics, within the tumor labels from the HD-GLIO-AUTO segmentation output. The images were z-score normalized and intensity shifted to yield positive values. Scaling was applied to get 40 bins[1] for the full intensity range. The extracted features include first order statistics, shape, gray level cooccurrence matrix (GLCM), gray level run length matrix (GLRLM), gray level size zone matrix (GLSZM), neighbouring gray tone difference matrix (NGTDM), and gray level dependece matrix (GLDM) features. The TTP-OS correlation for these 107 features for a range of progression thresholds was plotted and inspected visually. Promising progression feature candidates were selected based on (a) maximum correlation of TTP and OS time, and (b) having a single peak.

**Deep Progression Feature Learning.** To leverage the successful use of deep features from pre-trained CNNs for survival prediction, we test the use of such features as progression biomarkers based on a VGG-16 network pre-trained on the ImageNet dataset [15]. Additionally, we tested multi-task network approaches, which have already been successfully used for other applications, e.g., [22]. We tested:

1. Unmodified VGG-16, average-pooled last dense layer input as a progression feature.
2. Multi-task networks, modifying the network to do regression for the presumably related tasks of contrast-enhancement tumor and edema burden regression, and regression of the residual survival time for each follow-up timepoint. Only the parameters of the dense layers were trained. The dimension of all dense layers was cut by half. The average-pooled last dense layer (1024 neurons) used as a progression feature. The network was trained for 50 epochs with a learning rate of $5 \cdot 10^{-5}$ and the Adam optimizer [8], all losses weighted equally. The stopping was set at 50 epochs, based on the observation that the networks started to over-fit to the training data at that point.

Axial slices of the T1c-, T1- and T2-weighted MRI volumes were used for the three VGG-16 input channels. The FLAIR image was omitted because of the low axial resolution due to the coronal acquisition. Since the CNN was pre-trained on ImageNet data, the images were normalized using the published mean and standard deviation for the z-score normalization. Only slices with a minimum edema or contrast-enhancement area of $90\,mm^2$ (slightly below the RANO measurability threshold), on any timepoint for a given patient were considered. For each timepoint, 30 slices were selected and the output features averaged, to emulate the volumetric features and to cover a larger tumor extent.

The code is available at https://github.com/ysuter/gbm-progressionfeatures.

---

[1] Following the recommendations for the number of bins in the PyRadiomics documentation.

# 4    Results

Table 1 gives an overview of the tested biomarker types and the derived progression thresholds. Figure 2 shows the correlation between TTP and OS for a range of threshold values. We note that for higher thresholds, a correlation increase can be observed for all feature types, since the TTP approaches the OS, giving a high correlation. This trivial case where the first detected progression occurs at the time of death should be avoided. The comparison between the expert TTP and the data-driven TTPs are shown in Fig. 3.

Since we want to detect disease progression early, we want to avoid longer TTPs than the expert-rated TTPs. The interquartile range of the difference between the data-driven TTP and expert TTP shows the variablity of the deviation from the expert TTP. Since we want a consistent progression detection, we aim for a low interquartile range with few outliers on both sides.

**Automated Volumetry.** Figure 2 shows the Spearman's rank correlation between the TPP and OS for the contrast-enhancing volume for different progression thresholds. The maximum correlation is reached on a wide plateau around 100% volume increase to nadir ($\rho = 0.32$), with the correlation slightly lower at the 40%-threshold of the RANO recommendation ($\rho = 0.31$). Both volumetric disease progression thresholds led to approximately 70 d earlier progression reading compared to the expert rating based on the two-dimensional measurement. On average, progression was detected earlier than the expert rating, but shows surprising variability. This might be due to the fact that automated segmentation methods have been designed to perform well on single-timepoints, but might still have difficulties to track individual lesions longitudinally. We note that the volumetric approach discards initial T2-progression and therefore an overestimation of the TTP is to be expected.

**Radiomics Features.** We identified two potential disease progression features based on the T1c image with the contrast-enhancement label: (i) GLCM autocorrelation, and (ii) the sphericity of the enhancing tumor. Disease progression was on average detected later than the expert has. The GLCM autocorrelation showed lower correlation between the TPP and OS ($\rho = 0.21$) compared to the tumor sphericity ($\rho = 0.35$), but the TTP derived from the autocorrelation features was closer to the expert rating.

**Deep Progression Feature Learning.** Using features from the pre-trained network achieved a lower correlation than the classical radiomic features, but when compared to the expert TTP, was more sensitive and progression on average could have been indicated 92 d earlier (i.e. approx. one follow-up visit earlier).

Extending the output of the pre-trained network to regress the contrast-enhancement and edema areas, as well as the residual survival time for every slice reduced the interquartile range of the difference to the expert TTP (146.5 for the multi-task features, 181 for the pre-trained model). The median TTP of the multi-task features is well-aligned with the expert TTP.

These results suggest, that we can learn disease progression features that are more sensitive than the classical radiomic features and the volumetric approach, but come at the cost of higher variability when compared to the expert TTP. Both deep feature types showed less outliers towards longer TTPs compared to the volume-based methods.

The results from further experiments including an ablation on the multi-task learning are reported in the supplementary material.

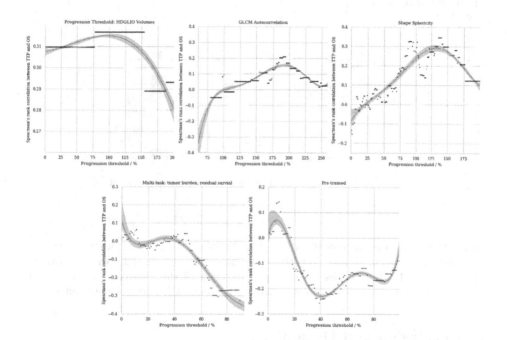

**Fig. 2.** Spearman's rank correlation of the time-to-progression and overall survival for potential disease progression features. Line: fitted polynomial with 95% confidence interval (shaded area).

**Table 1.** Deep and conventional progression features with threshold (Thresh.) at maximum Spearman's rank correlation $\rho$. IQR: Interquartile range

| Method | Thresh./% | Max. $\rho$ | Mean diff. to expert TTP/days $\pm$ std. dev. | IQR TTP - expert TTP/days |
|---|---|---|---|---|
| Volume - RANO | 40% | 0.31 | $-72.3 \pm 207.7$ | 110.0 |
| Volume - max. corr. | 100% | 0.32 | $-67.6 \pm 211.4$ | 110.0 |
| GLCM autocorrelation | 190% | 0.21 | $175.7 \pm 359.1$ | 327.5 |
| Shape sphericity | 137% | 0.35 | $284.0 \pm 294.9$ | 320.8 |
| Pre-trained | 8% | 0.14 | $-92.0 \pm 254.9$ | 181.0 |
| Multi-task: tumor burden and residual survival | 11% | 0.06 | $-82.2 \pm 263.0$ | 146.5 |

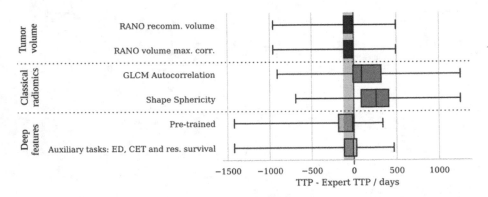

**Fig. 3.** Comparison of the calculated TTP to the expert rating TTP for the methods and thresholds listed in Table 1. Negative values indicate a smaller TTP than the expert rating. The shaded box marks the interquartile range of the difference to the expert TTP for the volume progression biomarkers. ED: edema, CET: contrast-enhancement

## 5    Conclusion and Outlook

We demonstrate the feasibility of MRI-based disease progression biomarkers for GBM patients, using a data-driven approach for disease progression threshold setting. Our experiments indicate that it is possible to extract MRI progression features with a higher sensitivity compared to the automated volumetry and two-dimensional measurement approaches. When the sensitivity of the disease progression assessment is important, imaging-based biomarkers e.g. from pre-trained deep neural networks and multi-task networks may be considered. Since high sensitivity can be accomplished by an arbitrarily low progression threshold, using an independent threshold optimization method is key, such as maximizing the correlation of the TTP with the OS.

The TTP based on automated tumor volumetry shows considerable variability when compared to the expert rating. Based on the presented data-driven approach and our dataset, a higher disease progression threshold around 100% should be investigated.

Of all tested progression feature candidates, the TTP derived from the contrast-enhacement feature *shape sphericity* had the highest Spearman's rank correlation with OS, but performed similarly as other classical features when the TTP was compared to the expert rating. The deep features studied managed to detect progression early, despite the lower correlation between the TTP and OS.

Hence, exploring other criteria apart from TTP-OS correlation is of great interest for future research. We expect the shape of the TTP-OS curve for different threshold settings to be an important factor regarding robustness. An additional challenge for future application is the lack of robustness of many MR radiomic features depending on the acquisition parameters (e.g., [20]).

**Acknowledgements.** We gladly acknowledge the funding received from the Swiss Cancer League (Krebsliga Schweiz), grant KFS-3979-08-2016 and the NVIDIA Corporation for donating a Titan Xp GPU. Computations were partly performed on Ubelix, the HCP cluster at the University of Bern.

# References

1. Chappell, R., Miranpuri, S.S., Mehta, M.P.: Dimension in defining tumor response. J. Clin. Oncol. **16**(3), 1234 (1998). https://doi.org/10.1200/JCO.1998.16.3.1234
2. Ellingson, B.M., Wen, P.Y., Cloughesy, T.F.: Modified criteria for radiographic response assessment in glioblastoma clinical trials. Neurotherapeutics **14**(2), 307–320 (2017). https://doi.org/10.1007/s13311-016-0507-6
3. van Griethuysen, J.J., et al.: Computational radiomics system to decode the radiographic phenotype. Cancer Res. **77**(21), e104–e107 (2017). https://doi.org/10.1158/0008-5472.CAN-17-0339
4. Isensee, F., Petersen, J., Kohl, S.A., Jäger, P.F., Maier-Hein, K.H.: nnU-Net: breaking the spell on successful medical image segmentation. arXiv preprint arXiv:1904.08128 vol. 1, pp. 1–8 (2019)
5. Isensee, F., et al.: Automated brain extraction of multisequence MRI using artificial neural networks. Hum. Brain Mapp. **40**(17), 4952–4964 (2019). https://doi.org/10.1002/hbm.24750
6. James, K., et al.: Measuring response in solid tumors: unidimensional versus bidimensional measurement. JNCI J. Nat. Cancer Inst. **91**(6), 523–528 (1999). https://doi.org/10.1093/jnci/91.6.523
7. Kickingereder, P., et al.: Automated quantitative tumour response assessment of MRI in neuro-oncology with artificial neural networks: a multicentre, retrospective study. Lancet Oncol. **20**(5), 728–740 (2019). https://doi.org/10.1016/S1470-2045(19)30098-1
8. Kingma, D.P., Ba, J.: Adam: a method for stochastic optimization (2014)
9. Lao, J., et al.: A deep learning-based radiomics model for prediction of survival in glioblastoma multiforme. Sci. Rep. **7**(1), 1–8 (2017). https://doi.org/10.1038/s41598-017-10649-8

10. Mamonov, A.B., Kalpathy-Cramer, J.: Data From QIN GBM Treatment Response. The Cancer Imaging Archive. https://doi.org/10.7937/K9/TCIA.2016.nQF4gpn2

11. Menze, B.H., Jakab, A., et al.: The multimodal brain tumor image segmentation benchmark (BRATS). IEEE Trans. Med. Imaging **34**(10), 1993–2024 (2015). https://doi.org/10.1109/TMI.2014.2377694

12. Reardon, D.A., Ballman, K.V., Buckner, J.C., Chang, S.M., Ellingson, B.M.: Impact of imaging measurements on response assessment in glioblastoma clinical trials. Neuro-Oncology **16**(August), v24-vii35 (2014). https://doi.org/10.1093/neuonc/nou286

13. Reuter, M., Gerstner, E.R., Rapalino, O., Batchelor, T.T., Rosen, B., Fischl, B.: Impact of MRI head placement on glioma response assessment. J. Neurooncol. **118**(1), 123–129 (2014). https://doi.org/10.1007/s11060-014-1403-8

14. Reuter, M., Rosas, H.D., Fischl, B.: Highly accurate inverse consistent registration: a robust approach. NeuroImage **53**(4), 1181–1196 (2010). https://doi.org/10.1016/J.NEUROIMAGE.2010.07.020

15. Russakovsky, O., et al.: ImageNet large scale visual recognition challenge. Int. J. Comput. Vision **115**(3), 211–252 (2015). https://doi.org/10.1007/s11263-015-0816-y

16. Simonyan, K., Zisserman, A.: Very deep convolutional networks for large-scale image recognition. In: 3rd International Conference on Learning Representations, ICLR 2015 - Conference Track Proceedings. International Conference on Learning Representations, ICLR, September 2015

17. Spearman, C.: The proof and measurement of association between two things. Am. J. Psychol. **15**(1), 72–101 (1904). https://doi.org/10.2307/1422689

18. Stupp, R., et al.: Radiotherapy plus concomitant and adjuvant temozolomide for glioblastoma. N. Engl. J. Med. **352**(10), 987–996 (2005). https://doi.org/10.1056/NEJMoa043330

19. Suter, Y., et al.: Deep learning versus classical regression for brain tumor patient survival prediction. In: Crimi, A., Bakas, S., Kuijf, H., Keyvan, F., Reyes, M., van Walsum, T. (eds.) BrainLes 2018. LNCS, vol. 11384, pp. 429–440. Springer, Cham (2019). https://doi.org/10.1007/978-3-030-11726-9_38

20. Suter, Y., et al.: Radiomics for glioblastoma survival analysis in pre-operative MRI: exploring feature robustness, class boundaries, and machine learning techniques. Cancer Imaging **20**(1), 1–13 (2020). https://doi.org/10.1186/s40644-020-00329-8

21. Weller, M., et al.: European Association for Neuro-Oncology (EANO) guideline on the diagnosis and treatment of adult astrocytic and oligodendroglial gliomas, June 2017. https://doi.org/10.1016/S1470-2045(17)30194-8

22. Xue, Z., Xin, B., Wang, D., Wang, X.: Radiomics-enhanced multi-task neural network for non-invasive glioma subtyping and segmentation. In: Mohy-ud-Din, H., Rathore, S. (eds.) RNO-AI 2019. LNCS, vol. 11991, pp. 81–90. Springer, Cham (2020). https://doi.org/10.1007/978-3-030-40124-5_9

# Generalizing MRI Subcortical Segmentation to Neurodegeneration

Hao Li[1], Huahong Zhang[1], Dewei Hu[1], Hans Johnson[2], Jeffrey D. Long[4,5], Jane S. Paulsen[3], and Ipek Oguz[1(✉)]

[1] Department of Electrical Engineering and Computer Science, Vanderbilt University, Nashville, TN, USA
ipek.oguz@vanderbilt.edu
[2] Department of Electrical and Computer Engineering, University of Iowa, Iowa City, IA, USA
[3] Department of Neurology, University of Wisconsin, Madison, WI, USA
[4] Department of Psychiatry, University of Iowa, Iowa City, IA, USA
[5] Department of Biostatistics, University of Iowa, Iowa City, IA, USA

**Abstract.** Many neurodegenerative diseases like Huntington's disease (HD) affect the subcortical structures of the brain, especially the caudate and the putamen. Automated segmentation of subcortical structures from MRI scans is thus important in HD studies. LiviaNET [2] is the state-of-the-art deep learning approach for subcortical segmentation. As all learning-based models, this approach requires appropriate training data. While annotated healthy control images are relatively easy to obtain, generating such annotations for each new disease population can be prohibitively expensive. In this work, we explore LiviaNET variants using well-known strategies for improving performance, to make it more generalizable to patients with substantial neurodegeneration. Specifically, we explored Res-blocks in our convolutional neural network, and we also explored manipulating the input to the network as well as random elastic deformations for data augmentation. We tested our method on images from the PREDICT-HD dataset, which includes control and HD subjects. We trained on control subjects and tested on both controls and HD patients. Compared to the original LiviaNET, we improved the accuracy of most structures, both for controls and for HD patients. The caudate has the most pronounced improvement in HD subjects with the proposed modifications to LiviaNET, which is noteworthy since caudate is known to be severely atrophied in HD. This suggests our extensions may improve the generalization ability of LiviaNET to cohorts where significant neurodegeneration is present, without needing to be retrained.

**Keywords:** MRI · Subcortical · Segmentation · Neurodegeneration

## 1 Introduction

Quantifying the atrophy to subcortical structures from MRI scans is key for many neurodegenerative diseases, such as Alzheimer's disease, Parkinson's

© Springer Nature Switzerland AG 2020
S. M. Kia et al. (Eds.): MLCN 2020/RNO-AI 2020, LNCS 12449, pp. 139–147, 2020.
https://doi.org/10.1007/978-3-030-66843-3_14

disease and Huntington's disease (HD) [1]. Automated segmentation of these structures has thus been an active field of research for many decades [9,12]. In recent years, learning-based methods have dominated this field due to their superior performance, not only in terms of the accuracy of the output, but also the computational efficiency of prediction on test datasets once a model has been trained. However, while the deep learning methods can be highly accurate, they tend to be dependent on the availability of appropriate training data that is tightly matched to the target test data. When such training data is unavailable, possible options include using poorly matched training data, or investing in creating a well-matched training dataset. Since neurodegenerative diseases typically affect the subcortical structures, a model trained on healthy controls can be inappropriate for use on a disease population. Generating new training data is typically time-consuming and requires expert manual annotations. Creating training data for each new disease population and acquisition protocol can thus be prohibitively expensive. It is thus desirable to improve the generalizability of deep learning models trained on healthy control datasets to disease populations.

In this paper, we explore various approaches to extend the popular LiviaNET model [2], which is the current state-of-the-art for this task, in an attempt to boost the generalizability of subcortical segmentation models trained on healthy controls for use on disease populations. Specifically, we explored using 9 convolution Res-blocks [3] with kernel size 3 in our convolutional neural network. We introduced the spatial coordinates of voxels as additional feature channels to improve the results by providing global context to the patch-based LiviaNET model. Finally, we explored random elastic deformations as a data augmentation strategy to mimic atrophied subcortical structures.

We apply our method on data from the PREDICT-HD dataset, where we trained on only healthy control subjects and tested on both control and HD subjects. Compared to the original LiviaNet, we find that our extensions improve the Dice score for all 8 considered subcortical structures (left-right pairs of thalamus, caudate, pallidum and putamen). It is well known that for the HD pathology, the caudate and putamen are the most severely atrophied subcortical structures [7,8,10]. Consistent with our hypothesis, our proposed extensions improve LiviaNET segmentation accuracy in HD patients especially for the caudate and the putamen. These findings suggest our approach may be more generalizable to cohorts where significant neurodegeneration is present, without needing to be retrained on disease-specific data.

## 2    Methods

### 2.1    Original LiviaNET

LiviaNET [2] is the current state-of-the-art method for subcortical segmentation. Building on Kamnitsas et al. [4], the LiviaNET uses multi-feature concatenation instead of multi-channel, which preserves the features at different scales. By using a small size kernel ($3 \times 3 \times 3$), LiviaNET goes deeper to perform better.

Axial      Sagittal     Coronal     3D

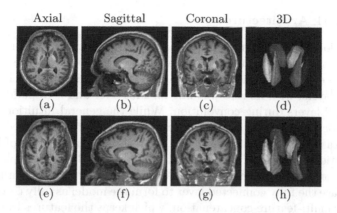

(a)        (b)        (c)        (d)

(e)        (f)        (g)        (h)

**Fig. 1.** Data augmentation with random elastic deformations. **(a–d)**, original image. **(e–h)** deformed image. We note that while the deformation is relatively exaggerated near the periphery of the brain, it is plausible near the subcortical structures.

## 2.2   Manipulating the Network Input

In the first LiviaNET variant we explore, we have used a 4-channel 3D patch as input. The 4 channels are the image patch itself and three spatial coordinate patches encoding the $x$, $y$ and $z$ coordinate of each voxel within the whole volume. Each channel has the fixed size, $37 \times 37 \times 37$, which was determined empirically to balance the trade-off between the amount of local context and the computational cost of a bigger input patch size. Patches are randomly sampled such that the foreground (8 subcortical structures) and the background (within skullstrip mask but outside the subcortical structures) are evenly represented.

## 2.3   Data Augmentation

In another LiviaNET variant, we use random elastic deformations to augment the data. Each training image and its corresponding label map are deformed along the same randomly generated deformation field. Our hypothesis is that the elastic deformation may be able to mimic the atrophy of subcortical structures in neurodegeneration, effectively augmenting the training dataset. We note that because subcortical structures are situated within close proximity of each other near the center of the brain, large amounts of global deformation are needed to create suitable atrophy in this region. The purpose of data augmentation is to increase the variance of model to better represent atrophied brains, even if the deformed images may be non-realistic. Figure 1 shows an example deformed image from our augmented dataset. While this image is a representative example, we note that other deformed images in our dataset have somewhat more pronounced deformations.

## 2.4  Network Architecture

We also explored a variation to the LiviaNET architecture. The proposed network architecture is shown in Fig. 2. We kept the backbone from the LiviaNet [2] and modified each convolution layer into a Res-block. The Res-block contains 3 convolution layers, with no zero-padding for first layer and zero-padding applied to following 2 layers during convolution. While the general intuition with deep learning models is, 'the deeper, the better', in practice, the increased number of layers may cause a degradation problem. With the skip connection of Res-block, the degradation problem is alleviated. Kernel size $3 \times 3 \times 3$ is employed on all convolution kernels in convolution blocks, and $1 \times 1 \times 1$ convolution kernels are used to replace the fully connected layer to form the model as fully convolutional. We kept the multi-feature concatenation, which keeps the features from previous block. Before the convolution operation, the batch normalization and non-linear activation function (PReLU) are applied to inputs to minimize effects of intensity and contrast variation. The output with size $9 \times 19 \times 19 \times 19$ is following the softmax layer, where the 9 channels represent each label (8 foreground + 1 background) in the resulting segmentation.

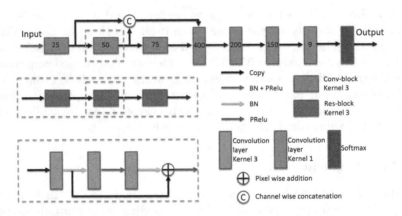

**Fig. 2.** The architecture of proposed LiviaNET variant. The network contains LiviaNet and Res-blocks. There are 3 convolution blocks in each convolution layer, and each block consists of 3 Res-blocks which are composed by 3 convolution layers with kernel size 3. The arrows denote different operations. The numbers on each block denote the number of channels. The dashed boxes are expanded for more detail in subsequent rows.

## 2.5  Post-processing

The segmentation result from the deep learning model often contains some disconnected islands that are considered noise. We note that the original LiviaNET [2] suffers from the same problem at a more pronounced level. We use a simple post-processing step to address this issue, namely, extracting the largest connected component for each label. 6-connectivity was used. This post-processing step was used for all the models presented in Sect. 3, including LiviaNET.

## 2.6   Experimental Setup

**Data.** We use a subset of the PREDICT-HD database. This subset consists of 37 control subjects, as well as 13 subjects with pre-manifest HD (prior to HD motor diagnosis based on the UHDRS Diagnostic Confidence Level), in each of the low-CAP, medium-CAP, high-CAP categories, as well as 13 HD subjects with clinical diagnosis. CAP is an HD progression marker based on age and CAG expansion at study entry [13]. For each subject, T1-w MPRAGE images from two different timepoints were used. Since PREDICT-HD is a multi-site study, the images were collected with a variety of 3.0T MRI scanners from different vendors (e.g., GE, Phillips, and Siemens), which means the intensity appearance is highly heterogeneous.

**Preprocessing.** The preprocessing has been conducted with the BRAINSAuto-Workup pipeline [5,11]. This pipeline consists of: (1) denoising with non-local means filter, (2) anterior/posterior commissure and intra-subject alignments with rigid transformation, (3) bias-field correction, and (4) subcortical segmentation with a multi-atlas method [6]. The multi-atlas segmentation results were visually quality controlled and used as the silver standard. All images were then intensity-normalized to the [0, 4096] range. Finally, skull-stripping was applied.

**Implementation Details.** We trained our models on NVIDIA RTX 2080 8GB GPU for a total of 600 epochs. Inside each epoch, we randomly sampled 500 patches whose centers are inside the skull, and we fed those patches into the model. The learning rate started from 0.0001, and was decayed by factor 0.5 every 30 epochs. We used an Adam optimizer with weight decay of 0.0001. The training loss function is an equally weighted combination of 3 different loss functions: cross entropy (CE) loss, L1 loss and L2 loss. With batch size 16, each training epoch takes approximately 1 min. Throughout the training process, the loss decreased in an exponential manner. After approximately 200 epochs, the loss had almost reached its minimum already, and the model was very close to the final model. However, for the following 400 epochs, the results continued to slightly improve. Therefore, all the models were trained for 600 epochs. All the training implementation was implemented in PyTorch.

**Training, Validation and Testing.** We used 20 of the control subjects as the training dataset, and 2 additional control subjects for validation. The testing dataset consists of the remaining (disjoint) set of 15 control subjects, as well as all 52 HD subjects: 13 subjects in each of low, medium and high CAP pre-manifest categories and 13 patients with clinical diagnosis. The two timepoints for each subject were either both in the training set or both in the test dataset.

# 3  Results and Discussion

The quantitative results of our experiments are presented in Table 1. We used the Dice similarity coefficient as our performance evaluation metric.

**Table 1.** Dice scores of segmentation results, presented as $\frac{mean}{std.\ dev.}$. We compare the original LiviaNET to variants with spatial coordinates, Res-blocks, elastic data augmentation and different loss function combination; statistically significant improvements over original LiviaNET are presented in **bold**, determined by two-tailed, paired t-test ($p < 0.05$). The loss function used in each model is L1+L2+CE, unless noted otherwise.

| | Control Subjects Dice Score (right/left) | | | |
|---|---|---|---|---|
| | Thalamus | Caudate | Putamen | Pallidum |
| Original LiviaNET | $\frac{0.965}{0.008}$ / $\frac{0.964}{0.006}$ | $\frac{0.951}{0.031}$ / $\frac{0.951}{0.019}$ | $\frac{0.962}{0.009}$ / $\frac{0.964}{0.009}$ | $\frac{0.938}{0.012}$ / $\frac{0.937}{0.011}$ |
| L+S | $\frac{0.969}{0.007}$ / $\frac{0.971}{0.005}$ | $\frac{0.961}{0.017}$ / $\frac{0.958}{0.017}$ | $\frac{0.972}{0.011}$ / $\frac{0.974}{0.008}$ | $\frac{0.950}{0.021}$ / $\frac{0.954}{0.014}$ |
| L+R | $\frac{0.971}{0.006}$ / $\frac{0.971}{0.005}$ | $\frac{0.956}{0.029}$ / $\frac{0.953}{0.028}$ | $\frac{0.972}{0.008}$ / $\frac{0.973}{0.008}$ | $\frac{0.953}{0.014}$ / $\frac{0.955}{0.012}$ |
| L+S+R | $\frac{0.970}{0.008}$ / $\frac{0.970}{0.006}$ | $\frac{0.962}{0.018}$ / $\frac{0.959}{0.016}$ | $\frac{0.972}{0.007}$ / $\frac{0.972}{0.007}$ | $\frac{0.951}{0.015}$ / $\frac{0.954}{0.012}$ |
| L+S+R+E | $\frac{0.972}{0.006}$ / $\frac{0.972}{0.005}$ | $\frac{0.961}{0.011}$ / $\frac{0.956}{0.020}$ | $\frac{0.970}{0.007}$ / $\frac{0.971}{0.007}$ | $\frac{0.952}{0.014}$ / $\frac{0.955}{0.010}$ |
| L+S+R+E (CE only) | $\frac{0.961}{0.025}$ / $\frac{0.962}{0.024}$ | $\frac{0.955}{0.009}$ / $\frac{0.948}{0.020}$ | $\frac{0.961}{0.019}$ / $\frac{0.960}{0.014}$ | $\frac{0.940}{0.016}$ / $\frac{0.930}{0.023}$ |
| | HD Diagnosed Subjects Dice Score (right/left) | | | |
| | Thalamus | Caudate | Putamen | Pallidum |
| Original LiviaNET | $\frac{0.955}{0.021}$ / $\frac{0.957}{0.013}$ | $\frac{0.820}{0.240}$ / $\frac{0.868}{0.149}$ | $\frac{0.924}{0.060}$ / $\frac{0.921}{0.067}$ | $\frac{0.855}{0.110}$ / $\frac{0.887}{0.056}$ |
| L+S | $\frac{0.957}{0.031}$ / $\frac{0.958}{0.023}$ | $\mathbf{\frac{0.859}{0.215}}$ / $\mathbf{\frac{0.888}{0.119}}$ | $\frac{0.911}{0.110}$ / $\frac{0.915}{0.082}$ | $\mathbf{\frac{0.818}{0.186}}$ / $\mathbf{\frac{0.857}{0.133}}$ |
| L+R | $\frac{0.958}{0.041}$ / $\frac{0.961}{0.014}$ | $\frac{0.856}{0.199}$ / $\frac{0.864}{0.194}$ | $\frac{0.930}{0.060}$ / $\frac{0.917}{0.095}$ | $\mathbf{\frac{0.882}{0.100}}$ / $\mathbf{\frac{0.906}{0.048}}$ |
| L+S+R | $\mathbf{\frac{0.963}{0.020}}$ / $\mathbf{\frac{0.963}{0.015}}$ | $\mathbf{\frac{0.875}{0.181}}$ / $\mathbf{\frac{0.894}{0.128}}$ | $\frac{0.931}{0.064}$ / $\mathbf{\frac{0.933}{0.055}}$ | $\mathbf{\frac{0.882}{0.123}}$ / $\mathbf{\frac{0.901}{0.058}}$ |
| L+S+R+E | $\mathbf{\frac{0.966}{0.016}}$ / $\mathbf{\frac{0.965}{0.011}}$ | $\mathbf{\frac{0.893}{0.135}}$ / $\mathbf{\frac{0.887}{0.167}}$ | $\mathbf{\frac{0.945}{0.039}}$ / $\mathbf{\frac{0.934}{0.058}}$ | $\mathbf{\frac{0.920}{0.043}}$ / $\mathbf{\frac{0.911}{0.055}}$ |
| L+S+R+E (CE only) | $\frac{0.959}{0.016}$ / $\frac{0.959}{0.010}$ | $\mathbf{\frac{0.883}{0.143}}$ / $\frac{0.872}{0.153}$ | $\frac{0.936}{0.030}$ / $\frac{0.921}{0.076}$ | $\mathbf{\frac{0.897}{0.032}}$ / $\frac{0.895}{0.040}$ |

**LiviaNET + Spatial coordinate** ($L + S$). In the results from Table 1, it can be seen that when using the spatial coordinates as additional input channels, the model is able to learn a 'prior' on the relative locations between subcortical structures, which compensates for the global context missing in the patch-based method. The impact seems most pronounced for the caudate in diagnosed subjects, which is worth noting since the caudate is known to be severely atrophied in HD populations.

**LiviaNET + Res-block** ($L + R$). With the increased number of layers, the model can learn deeper features than the original LiviaNET. The skip connection from Res-block can help handle the degradation problem. After post-processing, Table 1 shows this model also has better performance than the original LiviaNET, again most notable in the caudate of diagnosed subjects. However, this model seems more prone to overfitting, which means the raw segmentation result (without post-processing, data not shown) contains more spurious islands than the original LiviaNET.

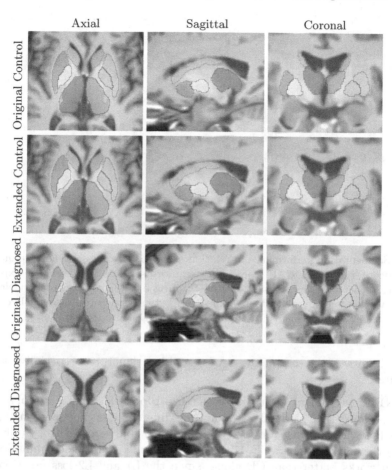

**Fig. 3.** Qualitative results from the original LiviaNET and the L+S+R variant. The model results are shown in solid colors, whereas the ground truth is shown as contrasting outline. We note the noisy thalamus segmentations in the original are improved in the L+S+R variant. The caudate of the control subject is undersegmented by the original method, improved by the L+S+R extension. Perhaps most importantly, we also note the tail of the caudate in the diagnosed subject is missed by original but is picked up by the L+S+R extension.

**LiviaNET + Spatial coordinate + Res-block ($L+S+R$).** As expected from (L+S) results, the spatial coordinate gave global information to the (L+S+R) model. This model has much less noise at the raw segmentation stage compared to the model without spatial coordinate as input (L+R). The improvement of this model over original LiviaNET is over 5 Dice points for the caudate in diagnosed patients. Qualitative results from this variant can be seen in Fig. 3, which shows that our caudate segmentation is visibly improved for both control and HD subjects. After post-processing, the pre-manifest HD detailed comparison with LiviaNET is shown in Fig. 4, where it can be clearly seen that the L+S+R

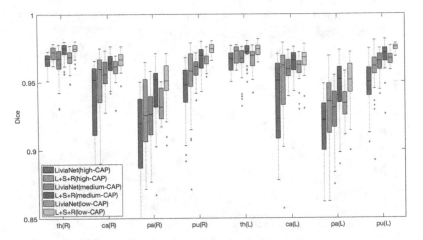

**Fig. 4.** Segmentation performance in relation to disease progression. For pre-manifest HD subjects, the higher CAP score indicates more severe atrophy can be expected, and thus harder to segment using healthy training data. Compared to LiviaNet, the L+S+R variant is more robust to atrophied subcortical structures, specifically caudate and putamen which are known to be impacted by HD neurodegeneration.

variant improves the segmentation of atrophied structures, especially caudate and putamen.

**LiviaNET + Spatial coordinate + Res-block + Elastic deformation** $(L + S + R + E)$**.** This model examines 2 different loss functions on training process (shown in the last two rows of Table 1): (1) only cross-entropy (CE) loss, and (2) the combination of CE, L1 and L2 loss functions. The combination loss function works better than CE alone, since the L1 and L2 loss functions can smoothly enhance the loss of false positive voxels, which produces the desired feedback to the model in back propagation. Moreover, with the combination loss function, the noise from raw segmentation is the least. While this model has the best Dice performance among the variants we explored, we have reservations about the stability of its use in practice, since the realism of the elastic data augmentation approach is somewhat questionable. A potential consequence of this instability can be observed in the putamens of HD subjects (Table 1, where the left putamen Dice is much lower than right; similar pattern can be observed even for the caudate of healthy controls). For these reasons, we focus on the more stable L+S+R model for Figs. 3 and 4. We nevertheless also report L+S+R+E as it may be preferable for certain applications.

## 4   Conclusion

In this work we explored different variants to the popular LiviaNET model for subcortical segmentation, with the goal of improving the generalization ability of the model to patients with neurodegeneration. Several of the modifications have

indeed significantly improved the segmentation accuracy of subcortical structures in diagnosed HD patients, most prominently in the caudate, one of the
most affected structures in HD. Exploring additional data augmentation strategies, such as GANs, remains as future work.

**Acknowledgements.** This work was supported, in part, by NIH grant R01-
NS094456. The PREDICT-HD study was funded by the NCATS, the NIH (NIH;
NS040068, NS105509, NS103475) and CHDI.org.

# References

1. Bates, G.P., et al.: Huntington disease. Nat. Rev. Dis. Prime. **1**(1), 1–21 (2015)
2. Dolz, J., Desrosiers, C., Ayed, I.B.: 3D fully convolutional networks for subcortical
   segmentation in MRI: a large-scale study. NeuroImage **170**, 456–470 (2018)
3. He, K., Zhang, X., Ren, S., Sun, J.: Deep residual learning for image recognition. In:
   Proceedings of the IEEE Conference on Computer Vision and Pattern Recognition,
   pp. 770–778 (2016)
4. Kamnitsas, K., et al.: Efficient multi-scale 3D CNN with fully connected CRF for
   accurate brain lesion segmentation. Med. Image Anal. **36**, 61–78 (2017)
5. Kim, E.Y., Johnson, H.: Robust multi-site mr data processing: iterative optimization of bias correction, tissue classification, and registration. Front. Neuroinform.
   **7**, 29 (2013)
6. Kim, E.Y., Lourens, S., Long, J., Paulsen, J., Johnson, H.: Preliminary analysis
   using multi-atlas labeling algorithms for tracing longitudinal change. Front. Neurosci. **9**, 242 (2015)
7. Long, J.D., Paulsen, J.S., Marder, K., Zhang, Y., Kim, J.I., Mills, J.A.: The
   Researchers of the PREDICT-HD Huntington's study group: tracking motor
   impairments in the progression of Huntington's disease. Mov. Disord. **29**(3), 311–
   319 (2013)
8. Long, J.D., Paulsen, J.S.: PREDICT-HD investigators and coordinators of the
   Huntington study group: multivariate prediction of motor diagnosis in Huntington's disease: 12 years of PREDICT-HD. Mov. Disord. **30**(12), 1664–1672 (2015)
9. Nugent, A.C., Luckenbaugh, D.A., Wood, S.E., Bogers, W., Zarate Jr., C.A.,
   Drevets, W.C.: Automated subcortical segmentation using first: test-retest reliability, interscanner reliability, and comparison to manual segmentation. Hum. Brain
   Mapping. **34**(9), 2313–2329 (2013)
10. Paulsen, J.S., et al.: PREDICT-HD investigators and coordinators of the Hunt-
    ington study group: prediction of manifest Huntington's disease with clinical and
    imaging measures: a prospective observational study. The Lancet Neurol. **13**(12),
    1193–1201 (2014)
11. Pierson, R., et al.: Fully automated analysis using BRAINS: AutoWorkup. Neu-
    roImage **54**(1), 328–336 (2011)
12. Wang, J., et al.: Multi-atlas segmentation of subcortical brain structures via the
    autoseg software pipeline. Front. Neuroinform. **8**, 7 (2014)
13. Zhang, Y., et al.: Indexing disease progression at study entry with individuals
    at-risk for Huntington disease. Am. J. Med. Genet. Part B Neuropsych. Genet.
    **156**(7), 751–763 (2011)

# Multiple Sclerosis Lesion Segmentation Using Longitudinal Normalization and Convolutional Recurrent Neural Networks

Sergio Tascon-Morales[1,2,3,4]([✉]), Stefan Hoffmann[1]([✉]), Martin Treiber[1]([✉]),
Daniel Mensing[1]([✉]), Arnau Oliver[2]([✉]), Matthias Guenther[1,5,6]([✉]),
and Johannes Gregori[1]([✉])

[1] mediri GmbH, Heidelberg, Germany
{s.tasconmorales,s.hoffmann,m.treiber,d.mensing,j.gregori}@mediri.com
[2] University of Girona, Girona, Spain
arnau.oliver@udg.edu
[3] University of Burgundy, Le Creusot, France
[4] University of Cassino and Southern Lazio, Cassino, Italy
[5] Fraunhofer MEVIS, Bremen, Germany
matthias.guenther@mevis.fraunhofer.de
[6] University of Bremen, Bremen, Germany

**Abstract.** Magnetic resonance imaging (MRI) is the primary clinical tool to examine inflammatory brain lesions in Multiple Sclerosis (MS). Disease progression and inflammatory activities are examined by longitudinal image analysis to support diagnosis and treatment decision. Automated lesion segmentation methods based on deep convolutional neural networks (CNN) have been proposed, but are not yet applied in the clinical setting. Typical CNNs working on cross-sectional single time-point data have several limitations: changes to the image characteristics between single examinations due to scanner and protocol variations have an impact on the segmentation output, while at the same time the additional temporal correlation using pre-examinations is disregarded.

In this work, we investigate approaches to overcome these limitations. Within a CNN architectural design, we propose convolutional Long Short-Term Memory (C-LSTM) networks to incorporate the temporal dimension. To reduce scanner- and protocol dependent variations between single MRI exams, we propose a histogram normalization technique as pre-processing step. The ISBI 2015 challenge data was used for network training and cross-validation.

We demonstrate that the combination of the longitudinal normalization and CNN architecture increases the performance and the inter-time-point stability of the lesion segmentation. In the combined solution, the dice coefficient was increased and made more consistent for each subject. The proposed methods can therefore be used to increase the performance and stability of fully automated lesion segmentation applications in the clinical routine or in clinical trials.

**Keywords:** Convolutional neural networks · Multiple sclerosis · Longitudinal normalization

© Springer Nature Switzerland AG 2020
S. M. Kia et al. (Eds.): MLCN 2020/RNO-AI 2020, LNCS 12449, pp. 148–158, 2020.
https://doi.org/10.1007/978-3-030-66843-3_15

# 1   Introduction

Multiple sclerosis (MS) is a chronic inflammatory disease of the central nervous system (CNS) that produces demyelination and axonal/neuronal damage [9]. The demyelinating process is associated with persistent inflammation throughout the CNS and, as a result, the demyelinated lesion, also known as plaque, is the main pathological feature of MS [1,10]. Due to its high sensitivity, magnetic resonance imaging (MRI) is extensively used for diagnosis and monitoring of MS [29]. However, manual segmentations by trained experts are tedious, time-consuming and often lack reproducibility [24]. For this reason, automated MS lesion segmentation techniques have been developed during the last years [29], and particularly convolutional neural networks (CNN) have gained popularity for this task, after proving their effectiveness in other neuroimaging tasks [26].

From the perspective of how the data is used to train a model, MS lesion segmentation algorithms can be classified as either longitudinal or cross-sectional. Longitudinal approaches make use of the time information provided by subsequent scans (known as time-points or visits) of the same patient. In cross-sectional approaches, all scans, even if belonging to the same patient, are treated as independent scans and no time information is considered. Only few CNN-based approaches can be found in the literature that tackle the problem of MS lesion segmentation in a longitudinal manner.

The first CNN-based longitudinal method found in the literature was proposed in [6]. Although the CNN is used only for classifying candidates extracted using intensity and atlas information, the method employs different time-points to perform the task. Another longitudinal method is described in [19], where the goal is to detect lesion load change using CNNs. To achieve this, a hybrid between the U-Net [23] and the Dense-Net [16] was used as basis. A special type of loss function generates probabilities that are used together with the segmentation masks for obtaining information about lesion change. Following this idea of detecting changes, a CNN is proposed in [27] for detecting new T2-weighted (T2-w) lesions. This architecture consists of a first block based on Voxelmorph [4] to learn deformation fields and register the baseline image to the follow-up images, and a second block to perform the segmentation of new lesions using the results of the first block.

One important issue when using longitudinal data is the normalization across time-points, or longitudinal normalization. The goal is to increase the similarity, in terms of image intensity regarding tissue classes, of the different time-points, without modifying the structures whose changes are due to pathological conditions. MS lesions are an example of those structures, as they can persist, change or disappear in time [25]. A statistical normalization method is proposed in [28], in which all histograms are centered using statistical measures obtained from the white matter voxels. Other methods based on histograms use landmarks to perform the normalization across different time-points [21]. Another longitudinal normalization method is presented in [25]. In this case voxel changes in time are modeled mathematically depending on temporal intensity variations and the lesion priors are used for keeping the lesion voxels unchanged.

Following the idea that including longitudinal information in CNNs can produce better segmentation results [6], this work proposes an effective pipeline based on the Chi-Square metric and convolutional long short-term memory (C-LSTM) [15] networks, for the exploitation of longitudinal MRI data for segmentation of MS lesions. To the best of our knowledge, this is the first MS lesion segmentation longitudinal method that combines traditional CNNs with convolutional recurrent neural networks (C-RNN).

## 2    Method

### 2.1    Longitudinal Normalization

A simple yet effective MRI longitudinal normalization based on the Chi-Square metric $\chi^2$ is proposed. The Chi-Square test is commonly used for analyzing the difference between observed and expected distributions [30], but in this case only the metric is used to measure and maximize the similarity between the histograms of volumes of the same modality for different patients and different time-points. Equation 1 shows the Chi-Metric as a means of comparison of two histograms $H_a$ and $H_b$, for voxel intensities $I$.

Let $s$, $t$ and $m$ represent subject, time-point and modality, respectively. For each modality $m$ a reference volume $V_{\hat{s}\hat{t}}^{(m)}$ is selected to normalize the other volumes $V_{st}^{(m)}$ of that modality, with $s \neq \hat{s}, t \neq \hat{t}$. For each $V_{st}^{(m)}$ an optimal scalar $\theta_{st}^{(m)}$ is found using Eq. 2, where $H_{\hat{s}\hat{t}}^{(m)}$ and $H_{st}^{(m)}$ are the histograms of the normal appearing white matter (NAWM) of $V_{\hat{s}\hat{t}}^{(m)}$ and $V_{st}^{(m)}$, respectively. The normalized images are the result of the product $\theta_{st}^{(m)} V_{st}^{(m)}$. To obtain the NAWM masks, the Computational Anatomy Toolbox (CAT12) [13] applied within the Statistical Parametric Mapping (SPM12) [22] toolkit was used.

$$dist_{\chi^2}(H_a, H_b) = \sum_I \frac{[H_a(I) - H_b(I)]^2}{H_a(I)} \tag{1}$$

$$\theta_{st}^{(m)} = \underset{\theta}{\mathrm{argmin}} \sum_I \frac{[H_{\hat{s}\hat{t}}^{(m)}(I) - H_{st}^{(m)}(\theta \cdot I)]^2}{H_{\hat{s}\hat{t}}^{(m)}(I)} \tag{2}$$

### 2.2    Network Architecture

In order to exploit time information, an extension of the architecture presented in [20] is proposed for the segmentation of MS lesions from longitudinal multimodal brain images. This architecture is a hybrid between the well known U-Net and the Convolutional Long Short-Term Memory (C-LSTM) network. Figure 1 shows the architecture. The input patches have size $(T, M, H, W, D)$, where $T$ and $M$ represent the number of selected time-points to process for each sample and the number of modalities, respectively. $H$, $W$ and $D$ represent the height, width and depth of the patches in each volume. The patches are extracted from the volumes that have been previously pre-processed. Just like in the U-Net architecture, there is an encoder for extracting hierarchical features, but these are extracted for each time-point separately. These features are then combined, at the deepest level and for all time-points, by a C-LSTM. After the features are processed by the first C-LSTM, a decoder upsamples them so that the input dimensions can be reached again. At the output of the decoder, a second C-LSTM combines again the features of the different time-points. Finally, the feature maps corresponding to a specific time-point (e.g. the one in the middle, if $T$ is odd) are selected and a last convolution takes place to reduce the number of maps to 2, one for each class, lesion or non-lesion.

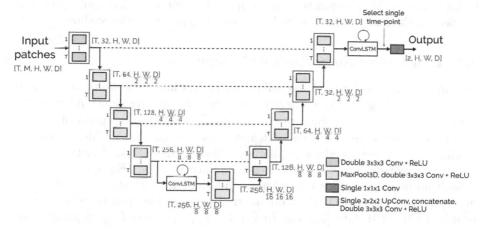

**Fig. 1.** U-Net ConvLSTM architecture. Patch dimensions are included in gray text, where $T$ and $M$ denote the number of selected time-points and number of modalities, respectively. $H$, $W$ and $D$ denote the spatial dimensions of the patches in the volumes. Dashed lines denote skip connections by copying and concatenation.

### 2.3 Post-processing

After a segmentation is produced, a post-processing step is performed to exclude potential false-positive (FP) detected lesions. This is achieved by imposing a minimal lesion size of 3 mm$^3$, as it has been found to improve the performance of MS lesion segmentation methods [12].

## 3 Experimental Setup

### 3.1 Dataset

One of the most popular datasets for MS lesion segmentation is the one provided by the longitudinal MS lesion segmentation challenge, which was part of the International Symposium on Biomedical Imaging (ISBI) in 2015 [17] and continues to be publicly available. The dataset, acquired with a 3T scanner, is subdivided into training (5 subjects) and testing (14 subjects) sets. Only the training set contains lesion segmentation masks generated by two different expert raters. Each subject contains between 4 and 6 time-points, each of which consists of T1-weighted (T1-w) magnetization prepared rapid gradient echo (MPRAGE), T2-weighted (T2-w) and Proton Density weighted (PDw) produced with double spin echo (DSE) and Fluid Attenuated Inversion Recovery (FLAIR) images. The average time between subsequent time-points is 1 year [8,17].

Both the original and the pre-processed images are available for use. For this work, the pre-processed images were used. The pre-processing steps are: first N4 correction, skull-stripping, dura stripping, second N4 correction and registration to an isotropic MNI template. The proposed longitudinal normalization was applied on the images that resulted from this pre-processing procedure.

## 3.2   Longitudinal Normalization Configuration

One important step for the longitudinal normalization is the white matter segmentation. The segmentation was performed on each volume using CAT with the default parameters. For finding the values of $\theta_{st}^{(m)}$, the first time-point of subject 01 was selected as reference for each modality and the Nelder–Mead Simplex method [11] was employed for the minimization of the distance function.

For comparison purposes, the min-max normalization (Eq. 3) was used as default normalization. This type of normalization, in which intensity values are mapped to the interval $[0, 1]$, is one of the methods that can be used as preprocessing in MRI data [5,7,14]. In Eq. 3 $I_{orig}$, $I_{min}$ and $I_{max}$ represent the original, minimum and maximum intensities of a volume, respectively, and $I_{norm}$ is the assigned intensity.

$$I_{norm} = \frac{I_{orig} - I_{min}}{I_{max} - I_{min}} \tag{3}$$

## 3.3   Training and Implementation Details

After having normalized the pre-processed images, a leave-one-out (subject-wise) cross-validation was performed on the training set. For each fold, from the 4 subjects not used for testing, one was used for validation and 3 for training. The model was trained using $32 \times 32 \times 32$ patches with step size $16 \times 16 \times 16$, and extracted only from the brain region using a brain mask generated by thresholding the pre-processed volumes. All four modalities were used ($M = 4$) and three time-points were taken for each training sample ($T = 3$). Sampling in time was performed using padding by repeating the first and last time-points. Training was performed using the Adam optimizer [18] for a maximum of 200 epochs with an early stopping condition of 20 epochs, and a batch size of 16.

To deal with the class imbalance (more normal tissue as compared to lesion tissue), the dice loss function was used. All models were trained with only one segmentation mask (mask1) of the two available, and the validation subjects were randomly chosen a first time obtaining the order 03, 03, 04, 05, 02, and then set to be the same for all experiments. No data augmentation was performed in order to increase the comparability between different experiments.

The proposed model was implemented in PyTorch, using a GPU NVIDIA Tesla T4.

### 3.4    Evaluation

Four experiments were carried out for determining the advantages of the normalization procedure and the longitudinal architecture: the cross-sectional version of the model (without ConvLSTM blocks and without considering the time dimension), which is a normal 3D U-Net, for both min-max and the proposed normalization; and the proposed model (Fig. 1) also for both types of normalization.

In order to evaluate the performance of the method, the Dice score (DSC), lesion-wise false positive rate (LFPR) and lesion-wise true positive rate (LTPR) were used. The DSC is computed according to Eq. 4, where TP, FP and FN denote number of true positive, false positive, and false negative voxels, respectively. The LFPR is the number of lesions in the produced segmentation that do not overlap with a lesion in the ground truth, divided by the total number of lesions in the produced segmentation. The LTPR is computed as the number of lesions in the ground truth that overlap with a lesion in the produced segmentation, divided by the total number of lesions in the ground truth [2].

$$DSC = \frac{2 \times TP}{2 \times TP + FP + FN} \tag{4}$$

## 4    Results

The results of the normalization process are presented in Fig. 2 for all preprocessed training subjects of the dataset.

Table 1 shows the mean values of the metrics for the four evaluated cases, computed for all time-points of all subjects. An increase is noticed in the DSC and LTPR, particularly, when the longitudinal approach is combined with the proposed normalization. Figure 3 shows an example of a segmentation result for which a higher DSC in the longitudinal approach denotes a better segmentation quality with respect to the cross-sectional (3D U-Net) version.

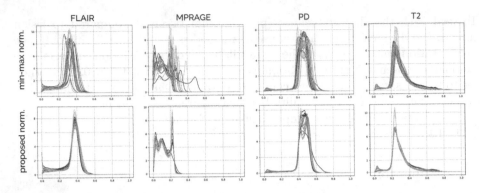

**Fig. 2.** Histograms of training cases for both considered normalization techniques. Only brain tissue is considered in the computation of the histograms.

**Table 1.** Cross-validation comparison of the proposed longitudinal normalization and architecture with the min-max normalization and U-Net architecture using "mask1" as ground truth. Standard deviations are presented in parenthesis.

| Case | Mean DSC | Mean LFPR | Mean LTPR |
|---|---|---|---|
| U-Net (min-max norm.) | 0.636 (0.194) | 0.396 (0.143) | 0.616 (0.189) |
| U-Net (proposed norm.) | 0.651 (0.148) | 0.453 (0.240) | 0.664 (0.198) |
| Proposed architecture (min-max norm.) | 0.652 (0.146) | 0.439 (0.213) | 0.638 (0.185) |
| Proposed architecture (proposed norm.) | 0.699 (0.090) | 0.462 (0.190) | 0.672 (0.174) |

## 5    Discussion and Conclusion

We have proposed a supervised longitudinal pipeline for MS lesion segmentation from MRI images. The approach combines a whole-volume longitudinal normalization scheme with a patch-based 3D CNN architecture that exploits time information. The method was evaluated on data from the ISBI 2015 challenge, obtaining an improvement in the DSC and LTPR with respect to a cross-sectional architecture and with respect to a simple normalization algorithm. Time padding allowed to reduce the impact of the reduction of samples that occurs when the time dimension is considered. Both intra- and inter-subject standard deviations were reduced in comparison to the cross-sectional approach for the DSC metric, which denotes more consistent segmentations in time. However, the LFPR increased for the proposed pipeline, which can be explained, to a certain extent, by the fact that in several cases (e.g. Fig. 3), the normalization and the C-RNN-based architecture allow to segment lesions that were not segmented for example in the cross-sectional case. These new lesions can represent a single lesion in the ground truth and therefore the LFPR is expected to increase. Ensembling several models could be used for reducing the amount of false positive lesions, while keeping high DSC and LTPR values. When compared to other approaches like for instance [7] in which the DSC for the same cross-validation was 0.684, or to [2] with a DSC of 0.698, our DSC (0.699) is

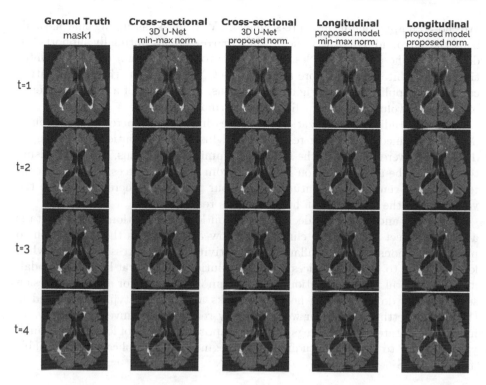

**Fig. 3.** Example of resulting segmentation masks from cross-validation experiment for patient 01, slice 89 from the ISBI training dataset for cross-sectional and longitudinal models. Masks are shown on FLAIR images and $t$ denotes time-point index. The standard cross-sectional approach (second column) leads to unsegmented lesions especially on $t = 2$. Both proposed techniques improve the segmentation when applied individually (third and fourth columns), while the combined method (last column) yields the best results as compared to the ground truth.

similar to these values, but it is lower than the best reported result, which is 0.765 [3]. Considering the absence of data augmentation in our experiments, our approach offers promising results.

The proposed CNN architecture requires a higher training time (about 1.5x the time of the cross-sectional approach), which can be seen as a limitation, but the improvement in both the time consistency and values of segmentation metrics justifies the increase in training time. The increase in training time also strongly depends on the implementation of the C-LSTM, which in our case has not yet been optimized for time efficiency.

In comparison to other normalization methods such as histogram matching, the proposed method allows to preserve the basic shape of the histograms, which prevents from loosing information about the lesions and other structures. The optimization of the similarity reduces problems that peak/landmark based methods can show when the histograms differ too much before normalization.

We chose an approach using a pre-segmented WM mask, assuming that normalizing the surrounding tissue value of white matter lesions optimally supports the detection of the pathological lesions. This approach relies on a rough segmentation of the white matter before applying the CNN. However, the normalization can also be applied on the original histograms, at the cost of a higher influence of the lesion volume in the quality of the normalization.

The longitudinal normalization pre-processing method increased the robustness of a trained network in respect to the histogram variations of the input data, which were present in the ISBI 2015 training data. Thus, it is a promising technique to be applied also on MRI data from various sources, e.g. in the context of multi-center trials. Future work of our group will therefore include the validation of the algorithm on heterogeneous real-life data.

Diagnosis and treatment decision based on lesion inspection on MRI data is a central aspect in MS. The clinical workflow also contains the comparison to pre-examinations to assess inflammatory activity. This process is tedious when looking at up to above 100 slices in high resolution imaging, at least four modalities and several pre-examinations. Still, common solutions for automated lesion segmentation do not rely on neural networks and are not typically applied in the clinical setting. Thus, our work is highly relevant as it investigates ways to improve the state-of-the art regarding the important aspect of longitudinal analysis, in order to make longitudinal lesion segmentation applicable and reliable in clinical MS neuroimaging.

**Acknowledgment.** Sergio Tascon-Morales was supported by the Education, Audiovisual and Culture Executive Agency (EACEA) as part of the Erasmus Mundus Joint Master degree in Medical Imaging and Applications (MAIA).

# References

1. Arnon, R., Miller, A.: Translational NeuroImmunology in Multiple Sclerosis, 1st edn. Academic Press Inc., London (2016)
2. Aslani, S., Dayan, M., Murino, V., Sona, D.: Deep 2D encoder-decoder convolutional neural network for multiple sclerosis lesion segmentation in brain MRI. In: Crimi, A., Bakas, S., Kuijf, H., Keyvan, F., Reyes, M., van Walsum, T. (eds.) BrainLes 2018. LNCS, vol. 11383, pp. 132–141. Springer, Cham (2019). https://doi.org/10.1007/978-3-030-11723-8_13
3. Aslani, S., et al.: Multi-branch convolutional neural network for multiple sclerosis lesion segmentation. NeuroImage **196**, 1–15 (2019). https://doi.org/10.1016/j.neuroimage.2019.03.068
4. Balakrishnan, G., Zhao, A., Sabuncu, M.R., Guttag, J., Dalca, A.V.: VoxelMorph: a learning framework for deformable medical image registration. IEEE Trans. Med. Imaging **38**(8), 1788–1800 (2019)
5. Baur, C., Wiestler, B., Albarqouni, S., Navab, N.: Deep autoencoding models for unsupervised anomaly segmentation in brain MR images. In: Crimi, A., Bakas, S., Kuijf, H., Keyvan, F., Reyes, M., van Walsum, T. (eds.) BrainLes 2018. LNCS, vol. 11383, pp. 161–169. Springer, Cham (2019). https://doi.org/10.1007/978-3-030-11723-8_16

6. Birenbaum, A., Greenspan, H.: Longitudinal multiple sclerosis lesion segmentation using multi-view convolutional neural networks **10008**, 58–67 (2016). https://doi.org/10.1007/978-3-319-46976-8_7

7. Brosch, T., Tang, L.Y., Yoo, Y., Li, D.K., Traboulsee, A., Tam, R.: Deep 3D convolutional encoder networks with shortcuts for multiscale feature integration applied to multiple sclerosis lesion segmentation. IEEE Trans. Med. Imaging **35**(5), 1229–1239 (2016). https://doi.org/10.1109/TMI.2016.2528821

8. Carass, A., et al.: Longitudinal multiple sclerosis lesion segmentation: resource and challenge. NeuroImage **148**, 77–102 (2017). https://doi.org/10.1016/j.neuroimage.2016.12.064

9. Cohen, J.A., Rae-Grant, A.: Handbook of Multiple Sclerosis, 1st edn. Springer Healthcare, London (2012). https://doi.org/10.1007/978-1-907673-50-4

10. Compston, A., et al.: McAlpine's Multiple Sclerosis, 4th edn. Churchill Livingstone. Elsevier Inc. (2005)

11. Dennis Jr., J.E., Woods, D.J.: Optimization on microcomputers. The Nelder-Mead simplex algorithm. Technical report (1985)

12. Fartaria, M.J., et al.: Partial volume-aware assessment of multiple sclerosis lesions. NeuroImage Clin. **18**, 245–253 (2018)

13. Gaser, C., Dahnke, R.: Cat-a computational anatomy toolbox for the analysis of structural MRI data. HBM **2016**, 336–348 (2016)

14. Ghafoorian, M., Bram, P.: Convolutional neural networks for MS lesion segmentation, method description of DIAG team. In: Proceedings of the 2015 Longitudinal Multiple Sclerosis Lesion Segmentation Challenge, pp. 1–2 (2015)

15. Hochreiter, S., Schmidhuber, J.: Long short-term memory. Neural Comput. **9**(8), 1735–1780 (1997)

16. Huang, G., Liu, Z., Van Der Maaten, L., Weinberger, K.Q.: Densely connected convolutional networks. In: Proceedings - 30th IEEE Conference on Computer Vision and Pattern Recognition, CVPR 2017 2017, vol. 2017 pp. 2261–2269 (2017). https://doi.org/10.1109/CVPR.2017.243

17. IACL: The 2015 longitudinal MS lesion segmentation challenge (2018). http://iacl.ece.jhu.edu/MSChallenge. Accessed 12 May 2020

18. Kingma, D.P., Ba, J.: Adam: a method for stochastic optimization. arXiv preprint arXiv:1412.6980 (2014)

19. McKinley, R., et al.: Automatic detection of lesion load change in Multiple Sclerosis using convolutional neural networks with segmentation confidence. NeuroImage Clin. **25**, 102104 (2020). https://doi.org/10.1016/j.nicl.2019.102104

20. Novikov, A.A., Major, D., Wimmer, M., Lenis, D., Buehler, K.: Deep sequential segmentation of organs in volumetric medical scans. IEEE Trans. Med. Imaging **38**(5), 1207–1215 (2018)

21. Nyul, L.G., Udupa, J.K., Zhang, X.: New variants of a method of MRI scale standardization. IEEE Trans. Med. Imaging **19**(2), 143–150 (2000)

22. Penny, W.D., Friston, K.J., Ashburner, J.T., Kiebel, S.J., Nichols, T.E.: Statistical Parametric Mapping: the Analysis of Functional Brain Images. Elsevier (2011)

23. Ronneberger, O., Fischer, P., Brox, T.: U-Net: convolutional networks for biomedical image segmentation. In: International Conference on Medical Image Computing and Computer Assisted Intervention, vol. 9351, pp. 234–241 (2015). https://doi.org/10.1007/978-3-319-24574-4_28

24. Roy, S., Butman, J.A., Reich, D.S., Calabresi, P.A., Pham, D.L.: Multiple sclerosis lesion segmentation from brain MRI via fully convolutional neural networks (2013) (2018). http://arxiv.org/abs/1803.09172

25. Roy, S., et al.: Longitudinal intensity normalization in the presence of multiple sclerosis lesions. In: 2013 IEEE 10th International Symposium on Biomedical Imaging, pp. 1384–1387. IEEE (2013)
26. Salem, M., et al.: Multiple sclerosis lesion synthesis in MRI using an encoder-decoder U-NET. IEEE Access **7**, 25171–25184 (2019). https://doi.org/10.1109/ACCESS.2019.2900198
27. Salem, M., et al.: A fully convolutional neural network for new T2-w lesion detection in multiple sclerosis. NeuroImage Clin. **25**, 102149 (2020). https://doi.org/10.1016/j.nicl.2019.102149
28. Shinohara, R.T., et al.: Statistical normalization techniques for magnetic resonance imaging. NeuroImage Clin. **6**, 9–19 (2014)
29. Valverde, S., et al.: Improving automated multiple sclerosis lesion segmentation with a cascaded 3D convolutional neural network approach. NeuroImage **155**, 159–168 (2017). https://doi.org/10.1016/j.neuroimage.2017.04.034
30. Weaver, K.F., Morales, V.C., Dunn, S.L., Godde, K., Weaver, P.F.: An Introduction to Statistical Analysis in Research: with Applications in the Biological and Life Sciences. Wiley, Hoboken (2017)

# Deep Voxel-Guided Morphometry (VGM): Learning Regional Brain Changes in Serial MRI

Alena-Kathrin Schnurr[1]([✉]) [iD], Philipp Eisele[2,5], Christina Rossmanith[2],
Stefan Hoffmann[3], Johannes Gregori[3], Andreas Dabringhaus[4],
Matthias Kraemer[4], Raimar Kern[6], Achim Gass[2], and Frank G. Zöllner[1] [iD]

[1] Computer Assisted Clinical Medicine, Mannheim Institute for Intelligent Systems in Medicine, Medical Faculty Mannheim, Heidelberg University, Mannheim, Germany
{alena-kathrin.schnurr,frank.zoellner}@medma.uni-heidelberg.de

[2] Department of Neurology, University Medical Center Mannheim, Medical Faculty Mannheim, Heidelberg University, Mannheim, Germany
{philipp.eisele,christina.rossmanith,achim.gass}@medma.uni-heidelberg.de

[3] mediri GmbH, Heidelberg, Germany
{s.hoffmann,j.gregori}@mediri.com

[4] Brainalyze GbR, Cologne, Germany
{andreas.dabringhaus,matthias.kraemer}@brainalyze-dk.de

[5] Mannheim Center for Translational Neurosciences, Heidelberg University, Mannheim, Germany

[6] MedicalSyn GmbH, Stuttgart, Germany
raimar.kern@medicalsyn.com

**Abstract.** Change detection and progression assessment in multiple sclerosis (MS) by serial magnetic resonance imaging (MRI) are important, yet challenging tasks. Analysis algorithms such as Voxel-Guided Morphometry (VGM) enable detection and quantification of even minor changes of the brain at different time points. To shorten computation times and ameliorate clinical applicability, we developed a convolutional neural network based VGM (Deep VGM) providing a fast solution for intra-individual serial volume change analysis in MS.

We developed a residual architecture based on the 3D U-Net and investigated several loss functions to predict VGM maps from a base line and a follow up brain MRI. We train and test our approach in 71 MS patients. The Deep VGM maps are compared to the respective VGM maps via several image metrics and rated by an experienced neurologist.

Deep VGM configured with the Mean Absolute Error and Gradient loss outperformed all other tested loss functions. Deep VGM maps showed high similarity to the original VGM maps (SSIM = 0.9521 ± 0.0236). This was additionally confirmed by a neurologist analysing the MS lesions. Deep VGM resulted in a 3% lesion error rate compared to the original VGM approach. Computation time of Deep VGM was 99.62% shorter than VGM. Our experiments demonstrate that Deep VGM can approximate the complex VGM mapping at high quality while saving computation time.

© Springer Nature Switzerland AG 2020
S. M. Kia et al. (Eds.): MLCN 2020/RNO-AI 2020, LNCS 12449, pp. 159–168, 2020.
https://doi.org/10.1007/978-3-030-66843-3_16

**Keywords:** Convolutional neural networks · Change detection · Magnetic resonance imaging · Multiple sclerosis · Longitudinal analysis · Voxel-guided morphometry

# 1   Introduction

Magnetic Resonance Imaging (MRI) has become a fundamental part of the routine clinical management of individual patients with Multiple Sclerosis (MS) [6]. Analysis of subtle changes between examinations is important for the assessment of disease activity and development over time. This includes the analysis of white matter lesions, CSF-compartment enlargement, but also of grey matter atrophy [4].

While the progression of MS can be monitored via segmentation of lesions [10], this approach neglects the impact on the surrounding tissue and requires (manual) lesion segmentation. The automatic computation of complete maps which quantify the structural change of the brain tissue offers clinicians more detailed information concerning global and regional morphological changes including appearance of new lesions and information about lesion activity. Change analysis generally requires the images to be registered to the same geometry. They can then be analyzed e.g. via subtraction [12], feature comparison [17], or a high-dimensional deformation field [15], also called Voxel-Guided Morphometry (VGM). The latter allows for the analysis of large spatial deformations, simultaneously achieving sub-voxel accuracy.

Deep learning approaches have become the state of the art solution in many medical image processing tasks. They have been applied to MRI acquisition, segmentation and disease prediction [11]. Convolutional neural networks (CNNs) have been successfully used to predict the progression of multiple sclerosis [20] and to detect new and enlarging lesions in longitudinal brain MRIs [18].

We present a novel CNN approach combined with an optimized loss function called Deep VGM to analyze brain changes between MRI examinations. We investigate whether Deep VGM can sufficiently approximate VGM for fast clinical usage.

# 2   Materials and Methods

## 2.1   Image Data

In this retrospective study 71 patients with MS were included according to the 2010 diagnostic criteria [13]. The study was approved by the local ethics committee. Each patient underwent two MRI exams, one baseline imaging and a follow-up after 12 months. Imaging was performed using a 3T scanner (Magnetom Skyra, Siemens Healthineers, Erlangen, Germany) and a 3D T1-weighted Magnetization Prepared Rapid Gradient Echo (MPRAGE) sequence with parameters TE = 2.49 ms, TR = 1900 ms, TI = 900 ms, field-of-view $240 \times 240 \, \text{mm}^2$, and spatial resolution = $0.94 \times 0.94 \times 2.00 \, \text{mm}^3$. The data set includes a total number of 444 lesions with an average number of 6.25 lesions per subject.

## 2.2    Voxel-Guided Morphometry

VGM is a 3D-image alignment method generating maps which show global and regional brain changes between two 3D-MRI data sets from different time points. Usually, T1-weighted data sets are used for alignment, as these have the most accurate morphological resolution. The algorithm needs high quality brain masks as a prerequisite, which can be obtained using the freesurfer software package [16]. It then proceeds with the following four steps: (i) an affine transformation is determined, which maximizes the overlap of the brain masks (coarse linear alignment). (ii) An inhomogeneity correction to eliminate low frequency bias is performed by comparison of the coarsely aligned images [9]. (iii) A cross-correlation-based technique is then applied to the bias-corrected images for fine linear alignment. (iv) Finally, the applied high-dimensional multiresolution full multigrid method determines the nonlinear deformations, thereby achieving a complete exploitation of information and effective processing [15]. Typical computation times on a recent CPU are 4 min for step (i)–(iii) and 7 min for step (iv).

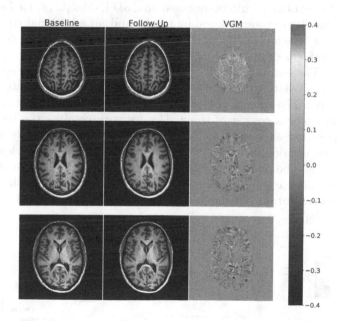

**Fig. 1.** Example Data - Three slices from a patient scan. Left column: baseline image; middle column: follow-up image; right column: according VGM map. Two MS lesions which decreased in volume are visible in the middle slice.

The method determines a grey-value-guided movement of each voxel from source to target. In the final step volume alterations for each voxel are extracted from the high-dimensional deformation field. The final output is a map with a quantified value for each voxel, which indicates how much this area increased or decreased in volume. An example case consisting of baseline image, follow-up image and VGM map is given in Fig. 1. While VGM has initially been applied to stroke data [8,15], its benefit to MS has recently been shown [4,7]. Its clinical application is currently hindered by the high computation time of 11 min per case.

## 2.3   Preprocessing

VGM maps were computed for all 71 patients. We truncated the VGM maps at $[-5, 5]$ and set values in $[-0.01, 0.01]$ to zero. For Deep VGM the input images were skull-stripped, bias-corrected, and rigidly registered as they were for VGM. The intensities were normalized to the interval $[-1, 1]$. We performed 5-fold-cross-validation. Each fold uses 55 training cases, 2 validation cases and 14 test cases.

## 2.4   Deep VGM: Architecture

We developed a residual architecture based on a 3D U-Net [2,14] for Deep VGM. The network has four en- and decoding blocks and an additional convolutional block in between. Each convolutional block is extended by residual connections. Encoding is performed via max-pooling, while decoding is performed using a deconvolution. The encoder and the decoder are connected via skip connections, which pass intermediate features from the encoder to be concatenated with the decoding features. The two upper blocks of both sides consist of two convolutions, while the lower blocks consist of three. The network receives the baseline and the follow-up image as a two channel input. The top level blocks have eight channels, which are doubled with every encoding block, until the lowest block has 128 channels. The final output is produced by a $1 \times 1 \times 1$ convolution. All other convolutions use $3 \times 3 \times 3$ kernels. We apply zero-padding, therefore, the size of the network output is equal to the input size. The Deep VGM architecture is depicted in Fig. 2.

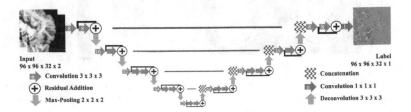

**Fig. 2.** Scheme of the Deep VGM architecture. The network is based on a 3D U-Net. All operations are given in the legend. The number of resulting channels is marked by the number on each operation symbol.

## 2.5   Deep VGM: Training and Loss Functions

We compare different loss functions $\mathcal{L}$ between the predictions $\hat{Y}$ and the labels $Y$. The number of voxels in a batch is denoted by $N$, while the predictions and labels of the individual voxels are denoted by $\hat{y}_i$ and $y_i$ respectively. The voxel index in the image is denoted as $i$. We initially train the networks using the averaged voxel-wise Mean Squared Error (MSE, Eq. 1) and the Mean Absolute Error (MAE, Eq. 2).

$$\mathcal{L}_{MSE}\left(Y,\hat{Y}\right) = \frac{1}{N}\sum_{i=1}^{N}(\hat{y} - y)^2 \tag{1}$$

$$\mathcal{L}_{MAE}\left(Y,\hat{Y}\right) = \frac{1}{N}\sum_{i=1}^{N}|\hat{y} - y| \tag{2}$$

Recent studies in image regression have shown that more sophisticated loss function can significantly improve the predictions results [1]. Therefore, we additionally test weighted error loss functions (Eq. 3), which put more emphasis on the high value regions. High change areas (VGM > 0.5) are weighted with one while low change areas are weighted with a step function in the interval [0.4, 0.1].

$$\mathcal{L}_{\text{WME}}\left(Y,\hat{Y}\right) = \frac{1}{N}\sum_{i=1}^{N} w_i \cdot E\left(\hat{y}_i, y_i\right) \tag{3}$$

We also combine the error losses with a 3D gradient loss (cf. Eq. 4).

$$\begin{aligned}
\mathcal{L}_{ME+Grad}\left(Y,\hat{Y}\right) = &\frac{1}{N}\sum_{i=1}^{N} E\left(\hat{y}_i, y_i\right) \\
&+ \lambda \cdot \sum_{i,j,k} \left(|y_{i,j,k} - y_{i-1,j,k}| - |\hat{y}_{i,j,k} - \hat{y}_{i-1,j,k}|\right)^2 \\
&+ \left(|y_{i,j,k} - y_{i,j-1,k}| - |\hat{y}_{i,j,k} - \hat{y}_{i,j-1,k}|\right)^2 \\
&+ \left(|y_{i,j,k} - y_{i,j,k-1}| - |\hat{y}_{i,j,k} - \hat{y}_{i,j,k-1}|\right)^2
\end{aligned} \tag{4}$$

For training we apply L2 regularization on the network weights. The regularization term is weighted with $10^{-7}$. Training is performed using the Adam optimizer with a learning rate of lr $= 10^{-3}$. We use $96 \times 96 \times 32$ voxel patches for training with a batch size of eight. Training patch selection is distributed slice-wise along the cranio-caudal axis. Patches are sampled randomly with the constraint that patch centers have to be inside the brain mask. Each network is trained for 200 epochs. The number of epochs is based on an initial set of experiments.

## 2.6   Evaluation

To evaluate the similarity between the original VGM maps and the Deep VGM maps we employ three metrics. Firstly, the Structural Similarity Index (SSIM) [21] which expresses a combined similarity value for luminance, contrast, and structure between two images is used. Secondly, we compute the MAE for all voxels inside the brain mask. Lastly, we test whether the non-change regions inside the brain mask are the same for VGM and Deep VGM. This is verified by computing the overlap of $|VGM| < 0.01$ and $|Deep\ VGM| < 0.01$ using the Dice Sørensen Coefficient (DSC) [3,19].

For 12 patients, the maps from the best performing network were additionally compared to the original VGM maps by an experienced neurologist. For the quantitative evaluation individual lesions were first identified on the T1-weighted images. Based on the VGM maps each lesion was then classified by the neurologist as "chronic-active" (either chronic enlarging or chronic shrinking) or "chronic-stable". This process was repeated using the Deep VGM maps and the results were compared.

## 2.7   Implementation

All networks were implemented using TensorFlow 2.0 and Python 3.5. For the evaluation and image processing we used SimpleITK. Training and testing were performed on an NVIDIA GTX 1050 graphics card. The training time for each network was 26 h.

## 3   Results

### 3.1   Quantitative Evaluation

The prediction of each Deep VGM map took 2.5 s. This equals a reduction of 99.62% in comparison to VGM. Combined with the computation time for the preprocessing, Deep VGM takes 4.04 min to compute one map. Evaluation results for the three metrics are listed in Table 1. Of the two simple error loss functions, the $\mathcal{L}_{MAE}$ loss performed better for all evaluation metrics (SSIM, MAE, and DSC) than the $\mathcal{L}_{MSE}$ loss.

Weighting the loss functions decreased the quality of the predicted maps. Adding the gradient loss function improved the predictions only in combination with $\mathcal{L}_{MAE}$. Here, SSIM and MAE showed a significant improvement, i.e. increase in the values for SSIM and decrease in MAE, respectively. The DSC did increase, but not significantly. Predictions from all networks and difference maps are shown in Fig. 3.

### 3.2   Qualitative Evaluation

Based on the aforementioned results, we selected the network trained with the $\mathcal{L}_{MAE+Grad}$ loss function for Deep VGM. 94 chronic MS lesions (69 stable; 17

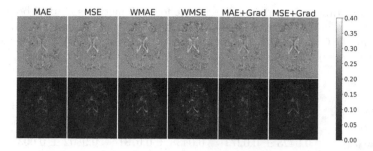

**Fig. 3.** Results - Top row shows the predicted Deep VGM maps from of the networks trained with different loss functions. Bottom row shows the respective absolute difference maps in comparison to the original VGM.

shrinking; 8 enlarging) in the test images were examined. Using the Deep VGM maps all 17 shrinking lesions were correctly identified. Only one enlarging lesion was not detected. Out of the 69 stable lesions Deep VGM falsely showed two lesions as "chronic-active" (one enlarging, one shrinking). Deep VGM therefore, has a 3% lesion error rate in reference to the original VGM maps. Figure 4 shows two correct cases and the two falsely classified stable lesions.

## 4 Discussion

Predicting VGM maps by our convolutional neural network combined with the $\mathcal{L}_{MAE+Grad}$ loss function (Deep VGM) is feasible. It produces VGM maps similar to the original approach. As depicted in Fig. 3 high errors only occur in the brain periphery, close to the borders of the brain mask. In these regions registration errors have the highest influence. We also see high differences in some cases for the outer rim of the lateral ventricle. For white matter, Deep VGM maps are estimated with high accuracy.

However, there is a slight systematic under estimation of exceptionally high VGM values. Since the majority of cases in our study don't have VGM values >3 and thus, these values are rare in the training data and therefore, the networks do not predict them in the test cases. Weighting the high change values stronger in the loss functions did reduce this problem, but lead to a systematic overestimation instead. Another weighting scheme could potentially achieve better results, those investigated here did not improve the result. However, the addition of the gradient loss significantly improved the overall performance and seems to be a better solution to this problem.

Our initial experiments only included data from MS patients. In future, we plan to include more diverse training data to be able to apply Deep VGM to other brain diseases such as stroke.

**Table 1.** Quantitative Evaluation - best value for each metric is marked bold. Significantly better values ($p < 0.01$, paired t-test) are additionally underlined. High values for SSIM and DSC represent better results (depicted by up arrow) and low values for MAE (down arrow), respectively.

| | SSIM ↑ | MAE ↓ | DSC ↑ |
|---|---|---|---|
| $\mathcal{L}_{MAE}$ | $0.9504 \pm 0.0242$ | $0.0385 \pm 0.0120$ | $0.9806 \pm 0.0033$ |
| $\mathcal{L}_{MSE}$ | $0.9452 \pm 0.0265$ | $0.0417 \pm 0.0131$ | $0.9799 \pm 0.0031$ |
| $\mathcal{L}_{WMAE}$ | $0.9425 \pm 0.0273$ | $0.0438 \pm 0.0131$ | $0.9802 \pm 0.0038$ |
| $\mathcal{L}_{WMSE}$ | $0.9425 \pm 0.0332$ | $0.0500 \pm 0.0142$ | $0.9788 \pm 0.0037$ |
| $\mathcal{L}_{MAE+Grad}$ | $\underline{\mathbf{0.9521 \pm 0.0236}}$ | $\underline{\mathbf{0.0377 \pm 0.0116}}$ | $\mathbf{0.9807 \pm 0.0034}$ |
| $\mathcal{L}_{MSE+Grad}$ | $0.9450 \pm 0.0265$ | $0.0412 \pm 0.0123$ | $0.9800 \pm 0.0033$ |

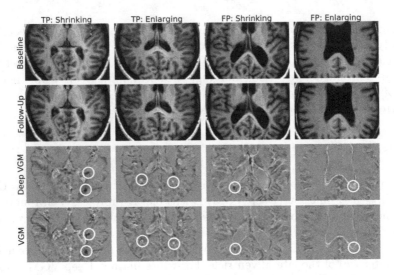

**Fig. 4.** Results - Examples of examined lesions with respective T1w baseline MRI and follow-up, VGM and Deep VGM map. Each lesion is marked with a white circle. First column shows true positive (TP) shrinking lesions which have been correctly identified by Deep VGM. The second column shows TP enlarging lesions. The third and fourth column show the two false positive (FP) lesions.

## 5   Conclusion

Our novel Deep VGM can produce quantified VGM maps at high quality while saving computational time compared to the original VGM approach. This opens the possibility to further translate this approach towards clinical routine. To facilitate the use of VGM analysis for clinical users, Deep VGM was already integrated into the clinical image analysis software mTRIAL [5], an integrated solution for use in clinical trials and diagnostics. Eventually, automated, objective and therefore, personalized diagnostics of disease evolution in patients with MS might become possible.

**Acknowledgments.** This research project is funded by the Ministry of Economic Affairs Baden Württemberg within the framework "KI für KMU".

# References

1. Bauer, D.F., et al.: Synthesis of CT images using CycleGANs: enhancement of anatomical accuracy. In: International Conference on Medical Imaging with Deep Learning, London, United Kingdom, July 2019
2. Çiçek, Ö., Abdulkadir, A., Lienkamp, S.S., Brox, T., Ronneberger, O.: 3D U-Net: learning dense volumetric segmentation from sparse annotation. In: Ourselin, S., Joskowicz, L., Sabuncu, M.R., Unal, G., Wells, W. (eds.) MICCAI 2016. LNCS, vol. 9901, pp. 424–432. Springer, Cham (2016). https://doi.org/10.1007/978-3-319-46723-8_49
3. Dice, L.R.: Measures of the amount of ecologic association between species. Ecology **26**(3), 297–302 (1945). https://doi.org/10.2307/1932409
4. Fox, J., et al.: Individual assessment of brain tissue changes in MS and the effect of focal lesions on short-term focal atrophy development in MS: a voxel-guided morphometry study. Int. J. Mol. Sci. **17**(4), 489 (2016). https://doi.org/10.3390/ijms17040489
5. Gregori, J., et al.: Feasibility of fully automated atrophy measurement of the upper cervical spinal cord for group analyses and patient-individual diagnosis support in MS. In: Congress of the European Committee for Treatment and Research in Multiple Sclerosis, Berlin, Germany, p. P1120, October 2018
6. Kaunzner, U.W., Gauthier, S.A.: MRI in the assessment and monitoring of multiple sclerosis: an update on best practice. Ther. Adv. Neurol. Disord. **10**(6), 247–261 (2017). https://doi.org/10.1177/1756285617708911
7. Kraemer, M., et al.: Individual assessment of chronic brain tissue changes in MRI-the role of focal lesions for brain atrophy development. A voxel-guided morphometry study. Klin. Neurophysiol. **39**(01), A178 (2008). https://doi.org/10.1055/s-2008-1072980
8. Kraemer, M., Schormann, T., Hagemann, G., Qi, B., Witte, O.W., Seitz, R.J.: Delayed shrinkage of the brain after ischemic stroke: preliminary observations with voxel-guided morphometry. J. Neuroimaging **14**(3), 265–272 (2004)
9. Lewis, E.B., Fox, N.C.: Correction of differential intensity inhomogeneity in longitudinal MR images. Neuroimage **23**(1), 75–83 (2004). https://doi.org/10.1016/j.neuroimage.2004.04.030
10. Lladó, X., et al.: Automated detection of multiple sclerosis lesions in serial brain MRI. Neuroradiology **54**(8), 787–807 (2012). https://doi.org/10.1007/s00234-011-0992-6
11. Lundervold, A.S., Lundervold, A.: An overview of deep learning in medical imaging focusing on MRI. Zeitschrift für Medizinische Physik **29**(2), 102–127 (2019). https://doi.org/10.1016/j.zemedi.2018.11.002
12. Patel, N., et al.: Detection of focal longitudinal changes in the brain by subtraction of MR images. Am. J. Neuroradiol. **38**(5), 923–927 (2017). https://doi.org/10.3174/ajnr.A5165

13. Polman, C., et al.: Diagnostic criteria for multiple sclerosis: 2010 revisions to the McDonald criteria. Ann. Neurol. **69**(2), 292–302 (2011). https://doi.org/10.1002/ana.22366
14. Ronneberger, O., Fischer, P., Brox, T.: U-Net: convolutional networks for biomedical image segmentation. In: Navab, N., Hornegger, J., Wells, W.M., Frangi, A.F. (eds.) MICCAI 2015. LNCS, vol. 9351, pp. 234–241. Springer, Cham (2015). https://doi.org/10.1007/978-3-319-24574-4_28
15. Schormann, T., Kraemer, M.: Voxel-guided morphometry ("VGM") and application to stroke. IEEE Trans. Med. Imaging **22**(1), 62–74 (2003)
16. Segonne, F., et al.: A hybrid approach to the skull stripping problem in MRI. Neuroimage **22**, 1060–1075 (2004). https://doi.org/10.1016/j.neuroimage.2004.03.032
17. Seo, H.J., Milanfar, P.: A non-parametric approach to automatic change detection in MRI images of the brain. In: IEEE International Symposium on Biomedical Imaging, Boston, MA, USA, pp. 245–248, June 2009. https://doi.org/10.1109/ISBI.2009.5193029
18. Sepahvand, N.M., Arnold, D.L., Arbel, T.: CNN detection of new and enlarging multiple sclerosis lesions from longitudinal MRI using subtraction images. In: IEEE International Symposium on Biomedical Imaging, Iowa City, IA, USA, pp. 127–130, April 2020. https://doi.org/10.1109/ISBI45749.2020.9098554
19. Sørensen, T.J.: A method of establishing groups of equal amplitude in plant sociology based on similarity of species content and its application to analyses of the vegetation on Danish commons. I kommission hos E. Munksgaard (1948)
20. Tousignant, A., Lemaître, P., Precup, D., Arnold, D.L., Arbel, T.: Prediction of disease progression in multiple sclerosis patients using deep learning analysis of MRI data. In: International Conference on Medical Imaging with Deep Learning, PMLR, vol. 102, London, United Kingdom, pp. 483–492, July 2019
21. Wang, Z., Bovik, A.C., Sheikh, H.R., Simoncelli, E.P.: Image quality assessment: from error visibility to structural similarity. IEEE Trans. Image Process. **13**(4), 600–612 (2004)

# A Deep Transfer Learning Framework for 3D Brain Imaging Based on Optimal Mass Transport

Ling-Li Zeng[1,2(✉)], Christopher R. K. Ching[2], Zvart Abaryan[2],
Sophia I. Thomopoulos[2], Kai Gao[1], Alyssa H. Zhu[2], Anjanibhargavi Ragothaman[2],
Faisal Rashid[2], Marc Harrison[2], Lauren E. Salminen[2], Brandalyn C. Riedel[2],
Neda Jahanshad[2], Dewen Hu[1], and Paul M. Thompson[2]

[1] College of Intelligence Science and Technology, National University of Defense Technology,
Changsha, Hunan, China
{zengphd,dwhu}@nudt.edu.cn

[2] Imaging Genetics Center, Stevens Neuroimaging & Informatics Institute, Keck School of
Medicine of USC, University of Southern California, Marina del Rey, CA, USA
pthomp@usc.edu

**Abstract.** Deep learning has attracted increasing attention in brain imaging, but many neuroimaging data samples are small and fail to meet the training data requirements to optimize performance. In this study, we propose a deep transfer learning network based on Optimal Mass Transport (OMTNet) for 3D brain image classification using MRI scans from the UK Biobank. The major contributions of the OMTNet method include: a way to map 3D surface-based vertex-wise brain shape metrics, including cortical thickness, surface area, curvature, sulcal depth, and subcortical radial distance and surface Jacobian determinant metrics, onto 2D planar images for each MRI scan based on area-preserving mapping. Such that some popular 2D convolution neural networks pretrained on the ImageNet database, such as ResNet152 and DenseNet201, can be used for transfer learning of brain shape metrics. We used a score-fusion strategy to fuse all shape metrics and generate an ensemble classification. We tested the approach in a classification task conducted on 26k participants from the UK Biobank, using body mass index (BMI) thresholds as classification labels (normal vs. obese BMI). Ensemble classification accuracies of $72.8 \pm 1.2\%$ and $73.9 \pm 2.3\%$ were obtained for ResNet152 and DenseNet201 networks that used transfer learning, with 5.4–12.3% and 6.1–13.0% improvements relative to classifications based on single shape metrics, respectively. Transfer learning always outperformed direct learning and conventional linear support vector machines with 3.4–8.7% and 4.9–6.0% improvements in ensemble classification accuracies, respectively. Our proposed OMTNet method may offer a powerful transfer learning framework that can be extended to other vertex-wise brain structural/functional imaging measures.

**Keywords:** Transfer learning · Brain shape · Optimal Mass Transport · Magnetic resonance imaging · Body Mass Index · UK Biobank

S. M. Kia et al. (Eds.): MLCN 2020/RNO-AI 2020, LNCS 12449, pp. 169–176, 2020.
https://doi.org/10.1007/978-3-030-66843-3_17

# 1  Introduction

Deep learning is attracting increasing attention in brain imaging studies, but there are many challenges to using deep learning in studies of brain health and disease that limit its use as an impactful discovery tool in the health sciences. In particular, small sample sizes of training datasets are typical for brain imaging studies and have hindered the identification of more generalized features and improved performance [1, 2]. There is currently no method to boost brain imaging samples to those typically used in computer vision and visual image recognition studies, and there is an urgent need to address this methodological limitation in brain imaging.

Transfer learning offers a promising approach for deep learning in brain imaging applications [3]. Typical brain imaging scans are three- or four-dimensional data, such as 3D structural MRI scans. To date, there have been few sophisticated deep learning models for 3D volume objects. Furthermore, 3D deep neural networks have a large number of parameters and take a long convergence time. FreeSurfer is a well-known toolkit that can generate 3D surface-based brain shape metrics, including cortical thickness, surface area, curvature, and sulcal depth [4, 5]. If 3D surface meshes can be projected onto 2D canonical planar images, then powerful 2D convolutional neural networks (CNN), such as ResNet and DenseNet, can be transferred to perform pattern classification on parameterized 3D surfaces derived from brain scans [6, 7]. Fortunately, efficient optimal mass transport (OMT) mapping methods have been developed for brain surface mapping [8, 9]. In this study, we propose an OMT mapping-based deep transfer learning Network (OTMNet) for pattern classification applied to 3D brain images, by combining efficient OMT mapping and sophisticated 2D CNN models.

# 2  Methods

## 2.1  Overview

Area-preserving mappings can outperform angle-preserving mappings (e.g., quasi-conformal mappings) in complexity, simplicity, and efficiency. In morphometric applications, they induce lower area distortions. Here we used an area preserving mapping method proposed by Su et al. [9] for the OMT mapping of 3D brain surface meshes. After projecting 3D brain surface meshes onto 2D planar meshes, vertex-wise brain shape metrics, including cortical thickness, surface area, curvature, sulcal depth, and subcortical radial distance (RD) and surface Jacobian determinant metrics [10, 11], can be mapped into 2D planar images for each MRI scan. Some popular 2D CNN networks pretrained on the ImageNet database were fine-tuned for the purpose of brain image classification. In this study, we tested these surface-based CNNs on a classification task, using the 3D surface mesh data from over 26,000 participants from the UK Biobank – a large prospective study of aging epidemiology [12]. As a simple test of the method, with a reliable ground truth classification, we used body mass index (BMI) as a categorical label, after binarizing participants into obese versus normal BMI categories using published cutpoints (https://www.cdc.gov/healthyweight/assessing/bmi/index.html). Our major contributions in this study include: a way to map 3D surface-based vertex-wise brain shape metrics onto 2D planar images for each MRI scan based on OMT theory. Such that 2D CNNs pretrained on the ImageNet database can be used for transfer learning of 3D brain imaging, overcoming the sample size limitations.

## 2.2 Datasets

T1-weighted structural brain MRI images from 26,194 individuals (16,909 neurologically healthy) were analyzed from the UK Biobank dataset, (https://www.ukbiobank. ac.uk/). BMI status was used as categorical label, and was defined by: 1) normal weight, if $18.5 \leq BMI < 25$, and 2) obese, if $BMI \geq 30$ (https://www.cdc.gov/healthyweight/ assessing/bmi/index.html). Out of the neurologically healthy subjects, 2,563 individuals were defined as obese, and 6,909 were defined as normal. To balance the sample sizes between the two groups, we selected 2,563 subjects with normal BMI to ensure that sex, age, and education were matched between the two groups (Table 1). To classify normal versus overweight, we compared 6,909 subjects with $BMI < 25$ and 6,911 subjects with $BMI \geq 25$.

**Table 1.** Demographic information for the selected sample from the UK Biobank.

| Variable | Normal | Obese | $p$-value |
|---|---|---|---|
| Subject# | 2,563 | 2,563 | |
| Sex (F/M) | 1,256/1,307 | 1,264/1,299 | 0.82 |
| Age (years) | $62.45 \pm 7.37$ | $62.27 \pm 7.36$ | 0.37 |
| Education (years) | $16.44 \pm 3.94$ | $16.39 \pm 3.99$ | 0.64 |

## 2.3 Image Acquisition and Preprocessing

T1-weighted brain images using a 3D magnetization-prepared rapid gradient-echo sequence at 1-mm isotropic resolution were processed using FreeSurfer and the ENIGMA-Shape Pipeline to derive vertex-wise cortical thickness (Thickness), surface area (Area), curvature (Curv), and sulcal depth (Sulc), and vertex-wise subcortical radial distance and surface Jacobian determinant metrics (14 subcortical structures). In this study, we focus on the spatial patterns of cortical and subcortical shape metrics, so we registered and downsampled the individual cortical shape metrics to the FreeSurfer fsaverage6 template (~40 k vertices per hemisphere).

## 2.4 Area Preserving Mapping of Brain Shape Metrics

Area-preserving mapping is based on OMT theory, while the OMT problem is formulated from the transportation cost for moving a pile of dirt from one spot to the other: Let 在此处键入公式。other: Let $\Omega_k \subset \mathbb{R}^k$, with positive density functions $\mu_k$, then

$\int_{\Omega_0} \mu_0 dx = \int_{\Omega_1} \mu_1 dx$; Considering a diffeomorphism $f: \Omega_0 \to \Omega_1$, the mass preservation is: $\mu_0 = |J_f| \mu_1 \circ f$, where $J_f$ is the Jacobian of the mapping $f$; The mass transport cost is $C(f) := \int_{\Omega_0} |x - f(x)|^2 \mu_0(x) dx$. If an optimal mass transport map exists, it can be computed based on Monge-Brenier theory and achieve area preserving [8, 9]. The Monge-Brenier theory shows that there is a convex function $\mu : \Omega_0 \to \mathbb{R}$, its gradient map $\nabla \mu$ gives the optimal mass transport map and preserves the mass: $\mu_0 = \det|H(\mu)| \mu_1 \circ \nabla \mu$, where $H$ is Hessian matrix. More details about the algorithm for area-preserving mapping can be seen in [8, 9], and the codes can be download from Github (https://github.com/cfwen/optimal-mass-transport).

As one open boundary needs to be defined for a triangle surface mesh before mapping, we cut a hole around the unlabeled medial walls on the FreeSurfer fsaverage6 template for each hemisphere [13]. Area preserving mapping was conducted to compute an OMT map between the fsaverage6 cortical surface and a unit square. We parceled the unit square into a $224 \times 224$ matrix with regular intervals. Finally, we computed the average of each cortical shape measure for each bin of the matrix. For those bins including no vertices, the morphological values were filled with the average of the eight neighbor bins. Thus, we obtained eight $224 \times 224$ cortical shape matrices (lArea, lCurv, lSulc, lThickness, rArea, rCurv, rSulc, and rThickness) for the whole cerebral cortex in total.

For subcortical surface meshes, we cut a small hole into each structure to provide an open boundary, thus making its topology consistent with a square. We computed an OMT map between each subcortical surface and a unit square. We parceled the unit square into a $32 \times 32$ matrix with regular intervals – a sparser sampling due to the limited number of vertices and smaller size of the subcortical structures. Finally, we computed the average of each brain shape measure for each bin. For bins with no vertices, the morphological values were filled with the average of 8 neighboring bins, resulting in two $32 \times 32$ shape matrices for each subcortical structure (radial distance, and surface Jacobian determinant metrics). We stitched all 28 subcortical shape matrices together, and obtained a $128 \times 224$ subcortical shape matrix for each subject, and then expanded it to $224 \times 224$ by filling in zeros.

To meet the input requirements of the ImageNet-based pretrained CNN networks, all 2D brain shape matrices were converted into 2D planar shape images, in which all three channels were filled with the same shape matrices.

## 2.5  Transfer Learning Based on Pretrained ImageNet CNN Networks

Due to the limited sample size, we used transfer learning for brain image classification. Two 2D CNN networks pretrained on the ImageNet database, i.e., ResNet152 and DenseNet201 [6, 7], were used in this study. Although these databases are not brain images, it is important to know whether features learned in these contexts can assist classification tasks on the maps used in this study (we later compare this with direct learning, where features are re-learned from the brain data). All convolutional layers were frozen with loaded pretrained weights and transferred into a new network as fixed feature extractors, while the final, fully connected layers and softmax layers were recreated and retrained from a random initialization for the classification of our groups. Figure 1 provides a schematic of the transfer learning approach applied to area-preserving maps of

3D brain shape metrics. As we had eight cortical shape images and one subcortical shape image for each subject, we trained both the ResNet152 and DenseNet201 networks on each input image, i.e., we trained nine different ResNet152 networks and nine different DenseNet201 networks totally. Furthermore, we averaged the output scores of all nine shape images for each network to generate an ensemble classification.

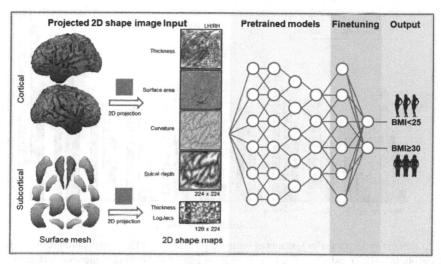

**Fig. 1.** A flowchart showing the transfer learning approach, applied to maps of 3D surface morphometric features that are embedded in 2D planar domains using optimal mass transport.

The 2D CNN models were trained on an Ubuntu 18.04.3 computer with two Intel Xeon CPUs, using four NVIDIA Tesla V100 GPUs for training and testing (Pytorch V1.3.1 and CUDA V10.1.243). Training of layers was performed by stochastic gradient descent with a batch size of 16 and a learning rate of 0.001. The number of epochs was set to 50, while the learning rate was allowed to decay by a factor of 0.1 every 15 epochs. We used 10-fold cross-validation (90% of the sample for training, and the remaining 10% for testing). The average accuracies and AUCs across the ten folds were considered as the final classification performance, which was kept for testing. For comparison, we conducted direct learning, in which all convolutional layers were retrained without loaded pre-trained weights. In addition, we used conventional linear support vector machine classifiers as a baseline comparison method, in which principal component analysis was used to reduce over-fitting and speed up model training, and the number of principal components were set to N-1 (N denotes the sample size).

## 3   Results

The accuracies of the classification between individuals with a normal versus obese BMI are provided in Fig. 2. The results show that transfer learning always outperformed direct learning for single shape images, with 5.0–15.5% and 1.8–7.3% improvements in classification accuracies for ResNet152 and DenseNet201, respectively. Surface area and cortical thickness, especially for the left hemisphere, exhibited high discriminative power (highest accuracies) in the classification, together with subcortical shape metrics.

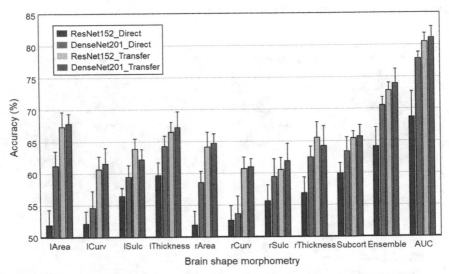

**Fig. 2.** Results of deep transfer learning of brain shape metrics for the classification between normal and obese BMI. Transfer learning tends to be associated with better classification performance, for this task, than direct learning.

When averaging the output scores of all nine shape images and generating an ensemble classification, accuracies of 72.8 ± 1.2% and 73.9 ± 2.3% were obtained for the ResNet152 and DenseNet201 networks using transfer learning, and the corresponding AUCs were 0.80 ± 0.01 and 0.81 ± 0.02, respectively (Fig. 2). The ensemble classification outperformed single shape metrics classifications with 5.5–12.3% and 6.1–13.0% improvements in accuracies for the two networks, respectively. In contrast, accuracies of 64.1 ± 3.0% and 70.5 ± 1.3% were obtained for the ResNet152 and DenseNet201 networks using direct learning (AUCs: 0.69 ± 0.04 and 0.78 ± 0.01), respectively, and conventional linear support vector machine classifiers with principal component analysis showed ensemble classification accuracies of 67.9 ± 6.3%, with AUCs of 0.74 ± 0.07.

In the ensemble classification with a BMI cut-off at 25, accuracies of 64.1 ± 1.4% and 63.8 ± 0.9% were obtained for the ResNet152 and DenseNet201 networks that used transfer learning (AUCs: 0.69 ± 0.01 and 0.69 ± 0.01), respectively. Surface area, cortical thickness, and subcortical shape metrics, exhibited the highest accuracies - in line with the classification of normal versus obese BMI.

## 4   Discussion

In this study, we proposed an OMTNet framework for 3D brain image classification. The advantages of this framework were demonstrated on a classification task of individuals with normal versus obese BMI based on vertex-wise brain shape metrics extracted from structural MRI scans from the UK Biobank. Although the task of predicting BMI is somewhat artificial, BMI measures have high reliability in brain imaging studies making it more certain that the ground truth labels do not themselves have a high associated error. Our major contributions in this study include: a way to map 3D surface-based vertex-wise brain shape metrics onto 2D planar images for each MRI scan based on area-preserving mapping. Such that 2D CNNs pretrained on the ImageNet database can be used for transfer learning of 3D brain imaging, overcoming the sample size limitations. Our results demonstrate feasibility for using the network to make diagnostic or prognostic predictions from 3D brain scans, with the appropriate labeled training data.

Deep learning is a powerful approach in computer vision and pattern recognition, but it has had limited utility for 3D brain imaging tasks due to the generally small available sample sizes, high data dimensionality, subtle population differences that are often clinically significant, and large inter-site heterogeneity [1]. In this study, our proposed OMTNet method addresses several of these limitations. First, we used area-preserving maps to project 3D brain surface meshes into 2D planar images, so that 2D CNN models can be used for end-to-end learning and classification for surfaces derived from 3D brain images. Second, we used several popular networks pretrained on the ImageNet database for transfer learning of vertex-wise brain shape metrics, overcoming the sample size limitations, and showing significant improvements in classification performance. Furthermore, we used a score-fusion strategy to generate an ensemble classification based on all shape images, which outperformed all single shape image classifications with significant improvements in accuracy. In addition to brain shape metrics, any other brain structural and functional measures that may be mapped onto surface meshes could be used to generate 2D planar images for transfer learning. Therefore, our proposed OMT-Net method may provide a powerful transfer learning framework for other structural and functional neuroimaging features.

In this study, we created categorical labels of normal weight and obesity based on BMI. Previous studies have shown that BMI has subtle effects on brain structure [14, 15], making BMI prediction from engineered brain features a difficult problem to test new methods. However, our proposed OMTNet method can reach ensemble accuracies of ~74%, and accuracies of ~64% could be obtained in the classification between normal weight and overweight, even though the brain shape differences are quite subtle between groups. Moreover, surface area and cortical thickness, especially in the left hemisphere, consistently achieved the highest classification accuracies, together with subcortical shape metrics, suggesting asymmetric effects of BMI on surface area, cortical thickness, and subcortical shape. In future studies, we plan to use deep model visualization methods to examine localized brain regions affected by BMI, and locations of features used in the classifications.

The current study has several limitations. First, the influence of sample size on the classification results remains unclear to some extent. Further studies are now possible with larger and larger data releases by the UK Biobank. Second, we used an area-preserving mapping for 2D mapping of 3D brain surface meshes in the current study, and other mapping methods will be compared to this (e.g., quasi-conformal, or holomorphic 1-form maps) in the future. Third, we only tested ResNet152 and DenseNet201 networks in this study, and other CNN models will be tested in the future. Fourth, it may be possible to obtain better performance by optimizing the hyperparameters of the tested models. Lastly, future studies will incorporate other raw and engineered brain structural and functional measures to potentially improve BMI classification and adapt the network to other diagnostic and prognostic tasks.

**Funding.** LLZ was supported in part by the National Natural Science Foundation of China Grant 61722313, Fok Ying Tung Education Foundation Grant 161057, and Science & Technology Innovation Program of Hunan Province Grant 2018RS3080; CRKC, PMT, and SIT were supported in part by NIH Grant U54 EB020403, R01 MH116147, R56 AG058854, P41 EB015922, and R01MH111671; CRKC was supported by NIA T32AG058507. CRKC, NJ, and PMT received partial research support from Biogen, Inc. (Boston, USA). DWH was supported by the National Key Research and Development Program of China Grant 2018YFB1305101.

# References

1. Rashid, B., Calhoun, V.: Towards a brain-based predictome of mental illness. Hum. Brain Mapp. **41**, 3468–3535 (2020)
2. Vieira, S., Pinaya, W.H.L., Mechelli, A.: Using deep learning to investigate the neuroimaging correlates of psychiatric and neurological disorders: Methods and applications. Neurosci. Biobehav. Rev. **74**, 58–75 (2017)
3. Pan, S.J., Yang, Q.A.: A survey on transfer learning. IEEE Trans. Knowl. Data Eng. **22**, 1345–1359 (2010)
4. Dale, A.M., Fischl, B., Sereno, M.I.: Cortical surface-based analysis - I. Segmentation and surface reconstruction. NeuroImage **9**, 179–194 (1999)
5. Fischl, B., Sereno, M.I., Dale, A.M.: Cortical surface-based analysis - II: inflation, flattening, and a surface-based coordinate system. NeuroImage **9**, 195–207 (1999)
6. He, K., Zhang, X., Ren, S., Sun, J.: Deep residual learning for image recognition. In: IEEE Conference on Computer Vision and Pattern Recognition (CVPR). IEEE, Las Vegas (2016)
7. Huang, G., Liu, Z., Maaten, L.v.d., Weinberger, K.Q.: Densely connected convolutional networks. In: IEEE Conference on Computer Vision and Pattern Recognition (CVPR), Honolulu, HI, USA. IEEE (2017)
8. Gu, X., Yau, S.-T.: Computing conformal structures of surfaces. Commun. Inf. Syst. **2**, 121–146 (2002)
9. Su, Z., Zeng, W., Shi, R., Wang, Y., Sun, J., Gu, X.: Area preserving brain mapping. In: IEEE Conference on Computer Vision and Pattern Recognition, Portland, OR, USA. IEEE (2013)
10. Gutman, B.A., Wang, Y., Rajagopalan, P., Toga, A.W., Thompson, P.M.: Shape matching with medial curves and 1-D group-wise registration. In: IEEE International Symposium on Biomedical Imaging (ISBI), pp. 716–719, Barcelona, Spain (2012)
11. Gutman, B.A., et al.: Medial demons registration localizes the degree of genetic influence over subcortical shape variability: An N = 1480 meta-analysis. In: IEEE International Symposium on Biomedical Imaging (ISBI), pp. 1402–1406, New York, NY, USA (2015)
12. Miller, K.L., et al.: Multimodal population brain imaging in the UK Biobank prospective epidemiological study. Nat. Neurosci. **19**, 1523–1536 (2016)
13. Yeo, B.T.T., et al.: The organization of the human cerebral cortex estimated by intrinsic functional connectivity. J. Neurophysiol. **106**, 1125–1165 (2011)
14. Raji, C.A., et al.: Brain structure and obesity. Hum. Brain Mapp. **31**, 353–364 (2010)
15. Ho, A.J., et al.: The effects of physical activity, education, and body mass index on the aging brain. Hum. Brain Mapp. **32**, 1371–1382 (2011)

# Communicative Reinforcement Learning Agents for Landmark Detection in Brain Images

Guy Leroy, Daniel Rueckert, and Amir Alansary[(✉)]

Imperial College London, London, UK
a.alansary14@imperial.ac.uk

**Abstract.** Accurate detection of anatomical landmarks is an essential step in several medical imaging tasks. We propose a novel communicative multi-agent reinforcement learning (C-MARL) system to automatically detect landmarks in 3D medical scans. C-MARL enables the agents to learn explicit communication channels, as well as implicit communication signals by sharing certain weights of the architecture among all the agents. The proposed approach is evaluated on two brain imaging datasets from adult magnetic resonance imaging (MRI) and fetal ultrasound scans. Our experiments show that involving multiple cooperating agents by learning their communication with each other outperforms previous approaches using single agents.

## 1 Introduction

Robust and fast landmark localization is an essential step in medical imaging analysis applications including biometric measurements of anatomical structures [13], registration of 3D volumes [9] and extraction of 2D clinical standard planes [8]. Manual labeling of such landmarks is often a time-consuming and tedious task, which is also error-prone and requires human experts. Developing accurate and automatic detection methods will help reduce the human error and speed the diagnosis process. Recent advances in reinforcement learning (RL) have shown a significant contribution to clinical applications such as automated medical diagnosis, object localization, and landmark detection [21]. RL enables learning from reward signals that guide the agent towards the target solution in sequential steps during training. It learns to perform a non-exhaustive search without using the full 3D image as an input. RL can be data efficient by using the same 3D image for training with different starting points and states. RL has proven to achieve the best performance for landmark detection outperforming supervised methods [2,6,7].

**Related Work:** Previous works detecting anatomical landmarks have examined approaches including statistical shape priors, regression forests [5,12], Hough voting [3], supervised convolutional neural network (CNN) [8] and attention-based autoencoder [22]. With the recent advances of deep RL, Ghesu et al. [6]

© Springer Nature Switzerland AG 2020
S. M. Kia et al. (Eds.): MLCN 2020/RNO-AI 2020, LNCS 12449, pp. 177–186, 2020.
https://doi.org/10.1007/978-3-030-66843-3_18

introduced the application of RL to detect anatomical landmarks by learning sequential actions towards the target landmark, while outperforming supervised methods. Alansary et al. [2] then evaluated multiple deep Q-network (DQN) variants for the detection task, namely DQN [10], double DQN [16], dueling DQN [19], and double dueling DQN. They also incorporated hierarchical steps with the multi-scale search strategy, which significantly decreased the search time. Multi-scale agents have proven to outperform fixed-scale agents for detecting the majority of landmarks [2,7]. Vlontzos et al. [17] proposed the first multi-agent system for landmark detection, where the agents communicate efficiently by sharing the convolutional weights of the CNN model. Furthermore, RL has been utilized in various medical applications such as the detection of standardized view planes in MRI scans [1], organ localization in CT scans [11], and re-identifying the location of brain landmarks in pre- and post-operative images [18].

**Contributions:** (I) We propose a novel communicative multi-agent reinforcement learning for multiple landmarks detection. (II) Experiments are evaluated on two different brain imaging datasets from adult MRI and fetal ultrasound, outperforming previously published RL state-of-the-art results. (III) The implementation of the code is publicly available.

## 2   Background

Reinforcement learning (RL) is a sub-field of machine learning (ML), which lies under the bigger umbrella of artificial intelligence (AI). Inspired from behavioral psychology and neuroscience [15], an RL agent takes actions within an environment and receives updated states with associated rewards during training. These reward signals guide the agent to take correct actions towards the target solution, and penalize otherwise. Thus, the agent learns a policy $\pi$ directly from high-dimensional inputs. In most modern applications, including ours, agents will not have total knowledge of all environment's states. This is referred to as a partially observable Markov decision process (MDP). RL offers an efficient solution to deal with the MDP by learning a policy that maximizes the total rewards. For instance, Q-learning [20] seeks to find a q-value that measures the quality of taking an action $a$ given a current state $s$ by learning a policy $\pi$ that maximizes the total reward during training. Mnih et al. [10] proposed to approximate these q-values using a deep neural network ($\theta$), named DQN. The $Q$-function is based on the Bellman equation [4], and defined as the expected discounted cumulative rewards:

$$Q^\pi(s_t, a_t) = E_\pi[\sum_{k=0}^{\infty} \gamma^k r_{t+k+1}|s_t, a_t], \tag{1}$$

where $s_t$ and $a_t$ represent the state and action at step $t$. $\gamma^k$ is the discount factor at $k$-th future state. DQN introduces another target network $\hat{Q}$ that stabilizes the training, and reduce the overestimation of the maximum Q-value [10]. Whereas at every predefined interval during training, the weights $\theta$ of the Q-network are copied to the target network $\hat{\theta}$. The DQN loss function is defined as:

$$L_i(\theta_i) = E_{s,a,r,s'} \left[ \left( r + \gamma \max_{a'} \hat{Q}(s', a'; \hat{\theta}_i) - Q(s, a; \theta_i) \right)^2 \right], \tag{2}$$

where $s'$ and $a'$ are the next state and action. Van Hasselt et al. [16] introduced a modification to the DQN loss function to decouple the selected action from the target network, known as double DQN. This changes the loss function to,

$$L_i(\theta_i) = E_{s,a,r,s'} \left[ \left( r + \gamma \hat{Q}(s', \operatorname*{argmax}_{a'} Q(s', a'; \theta); \hat{\theta}_i) - Q(s, a; \theta_i) \right)^2 \right]. \tag{3}$$

The dueling network [19] uses the hypothesis that Q-values are only important in key states. It has two sequences of fully connected layers to separately estimate state-values and the advantages for each action as scalars.

Alansary et al. [2] have shown that the optimal DQN architecture depends on each landmark, where there was no overall best architecture for all landmarks. Thus, we use the double DQN as a baseline architecture.

## 3   Methods

In this work, we propose a communicative DQN-based RL agents for the detection of anatomical landmarks in brain images. These agents are designed to learn by communication during their search for different landmarks in 3D medical scans. This is motivated by the fact that anatomical landmarks are usually spatially correlated in the brain. Figure 1 demonstrates a schematic visualization of these navigating agents in a 3D scan or environment $E$.

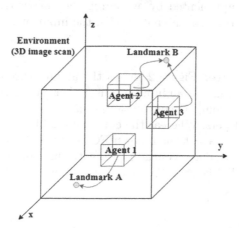

**Fig. 1.** A schematic diagram of the proposed multi-agents interacting with the 3D image environment $E$. At each step, each agent takes an action towards a target landmark. The learned policy is formed by the path between the starting points and the target landmarks after taking the sequential actions.

**States:** Each state $s$ is defined as a region of interest (ROI) of size $45 \times 45 \times 45$ voxels, and centered around each agent. To improve the network's stability and convergence, it takes as an input a history of the last 4 states [10]. Each agent starts at a random location within the 80% of the inner region of the image at the beginning of each episode. An agent terminates navigating when it finds the target landmark. During inference the terminal state is triggered when the agent oscillates around a target point.

**Action Space:** It is defined based on the six directions in the 3D Cartesian coordinates, namely left, right, up, down, forward or backward. Similar to [2], we adopt a multi-scale search strategy with hierarchical steps by reducing the step and ROI size when the agent oscillates around a target point. We use three levels of scales $\{3, 2, 1\}$ mm. The episode is terminated when all agents reach their terminal states at the 1mm scale.

**Rewards:** First, we calculate the Euclidean distance between the current point of interest and target landmark $d_t$, and between the point of interest of the previous step and the target landmark $d_{t-1}$. The reward signal is then calculated using the difference between $d_{t-1}$ and $dt$, and clipped between $-1$ and $1$. This ensures that positive rewards are given, if the movements of the agent are towards the target solution.

**Communicative Agents:** We leverage two types of communications between the agents. Implicit communication is learned by sharing the convolutional layers of the model among all the agents [17]. Besides, communication signals are learned explicitly by sharing communication channels in the fully connected (FC) layers [14]. This is implemented by averaging the output of each FC layer for each agent, which is then concatenated with the input of the next FC layer, as seen in Fig. 2.

**Network Architecture:** Figure 2 shows the architecture of the proposed C-MARL model, which takes as an input a tensor of size `number_agents` $\times 4 \times 45 \times 45 \times 45$. It consists of four 3D convolutional and three 3D max pooling layers, followed by four FC layers. Whereas the convolutional layers are shared between all the agents, and each agent has its own FC layer. The output of all FC layers of each agent are averaged and concatenated with the input of the next FC layer. The size of the last FC layer is the same size of the action space. Finally, the model is trained using Eq. 3.

## 4    Experiments

The performance of the proposed C-MARL agents for anatomical landmark detection is tested on two brain imaging datasets, and evaluated against a single RL agent [2] and multi-agents that share only their convolutional layers

(Collab-DQN) [17]. Clinical experts manually annotated all selected landmarks using three orthogonal views. We have randomly split both datasets into train (70%), validation (15%) and test (15%) subsets. Best model is selected during training based on the best accuracy on the validation subset. The Euclidean distance error between the detected and target landmarks is used to measure the reported accuracy. The agents follow an $\epsilon$-greedy policy, where each agent can take a random action step uniformly sampled from the action space with an initial probability of $\epsilon = 1$ to $\epsilon = 0.1$, instead of selecting the step with the highest Q-value. During testing, agents follow a full greedy policy with $\epsilon = 0$. The episode ends when all agents oscillate at the smallest scale, or after a predefined maximum number of 200 steps. Figure 3 shows C-MARL performing with five agents to detect five different landmarks from a brain MRI scan.

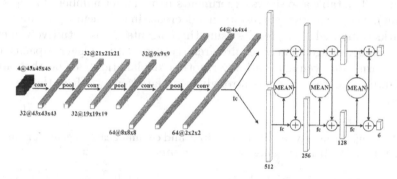

**Fig. 2.** The proposed C-MARL architecture for anatomical landmark detection. Here is an example of two agents sharing the same convolutional layers. They learn to communicate by averaging the output of the FC layer of each agent, which is then concatenated to the input of the next FC layer.

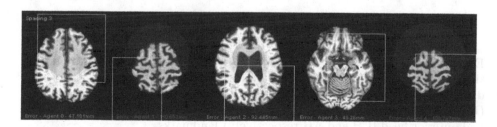

**Fig. 3.** An example of our proposed C-MARL system consisting of 5 agents. These agents are looking for 5 different landmarks in a brain MRI scan. Each agent's ROI is represented by a yellow box and centered around a blue point, while the red point is the target landmark. ROI is sampled with 3 mm spacing at the beginning of every episode. The length of the circumference of red disks denotes the distance between the current and target landmarks in $z$-axis. (Color figure online)

## 4.1   Results

**Experiment (I):** We use 832 T1-weighted 1.5T MRI brain scans from the Alzheimer's disease neuroimaging initiative (ADNI)[1]. All brain images are skull-stripped, and have an isotropic $1\,mm^3$ voxel size. The selected subjects include patients with cognitively normal (CN), mild cognitive impairment (MCI), and early Alzheimer's disease (AD). We select 8 landmarks, namely the anterior commissure (AC), the posterior commissure (PC), the outer aspect, the inferior tip and inner aspect of the splenium of the corpus callosum (SCC), the outer and inner aspect of the Genu of corpus callosum (GCC), and the superior aspect of pons.

Table 1 demonstrates the performance of the different approaches, whereas C-MARL with three agents achieves the best accuracy for all the three selected landmarks. The table also shows experiments using larger number of agents (five and eight). These experiments results in a decrease in the accuracy in most of the landmarks compared to the results using three agents. Thus, intuitively, increasing the number of agents may require architectures with a bigger capacity to be able to learn more communications. Another explanation can be that adding more landmarks, that are not strongly correlated, may affect the detection accuracy.

**Table 1.** Comparison between single, multiple, and communicative agents for landmark detection in brain MRIs. Distance errors are in *mm*.

| | Single agent [2] | Collab-DQN [17] | | | C-MARL | | |
|---|---|---|---|---|---|---|---|
| Landmark | | 3 agents | 5 agents | 8 agents | 3 agents | 5 agents | 8 agents |
| AC | $1.14 \pm 0.53$ | $1.16 \pm 0.59$ | $1.13 \pm 0.64$ | $1.21 \pm 0.92$ | $\mathbf{1.04 \pm 0.58}$ | $1.12 \pm 0.65$ | $1.84 \pm 0.91$ |
| PC | $1.18 \pm 0.55$ | $1.25 \pm 0.57$ | $1.19 \pm 0.61$ | $1.22 \pm 0.93$ | $\mathbf{1.13 \pm 0.66}$ | $1.25 \pm 0.55$ | $1.38 \pm 0.64$ |
| Outer SCC | $1.47 \pm 0.64$ | $1.38 \pm 0.75$ | $1.51 \pm 0.77$ | $1.46 \pm 0.90$ | $\mathbf{1.35 \pm 0.66}$ | $1.62 \pm 0.79$ | $5.20 \pm 13.49$ |
| Inferior SCC | $2.40 \pm 1.13$ | – | $\mathbf{1.39 \pm 0.85}$ | $1.53 \pm 0.87$ | – | $1.50 \pm 0.89$ | $1.87 \pm 1.28$ |
| Inner SCC | $1.46 \pm 0.73$ | – | $1.53 \pm 0.97$ | $2.09 \pm 3.65$ | – | $\mathbf{1.53 \pm 0.76}$ | $3.56 \pm 9.42$ |

**Experiment (II):** We use 72 subjects of 3D fetal head ultrasound scans from the iFIND project[2]. All images are resampled to isotropic voxel size with average dimensions of $324 \times 207 \times 279$ voxels. We select the right and left cerebellum (RC and LC respectively), the cavum septum pellucidum (CSP) and the center and anterior head (CH and AH respectively) landmarks.

Table 2 shows multiple agents have a lower distance error across all fetal landmarks, while C-MARL significantly outperforms the other methods for detecting the CSP and CH. Similar to the previous experiment, increasing the number of agents did not necessarily improve the detection accuracy. However, the AH landmark has significantly benefited from increasing the number of agents. In this

---

[1] http://adni.loni.usc.edu.
[2] http://www.ifindproject.com.

experiment, results show that multi-agent system is superior in all landmarks, but rather suggest the best architecture depends on the landmark.

**Table 2.** Comparison between single, multiple, and communicative agents for landmark detection in fetal head ultrasound. Distance errors are in $mm$.

| Landmark | Single agent [2] | Collab-DQN [17] | | | C-MARL | | |
|---|---|---|---|---|---|---|---|
| | | 3 agents | 5 agents | 8 agents | 3 agents | 5 agents | 8 agents |
| RC | 7.23 ± 3.54 | **2.73 ± 1.71** | 4.20 ± 3.76 | 3.39 ± 2.36 | 6.53 ± 4.21 | 4.06 ± 2.95 | 4.75 ± 3.28 |
| LC | 4.37 ± 1.45 | **4.20 ± 2.87** | 5.98 ± 8.58 | 5.42 ± 4.50 | 5.10 ± 3.66 | 4.43 ± 32.26 | 4.64 ± 3.16 |
| CSP | 9.90 ± 3.13 | 5.18 ± 2.05 | 8.02 ± 5.34 | 5.74 ± 5.07 | 5.78 ± 3.04 | **5.13 ± 3.51** | 7.08 ± 4.13 |
| CH | 29.43 ± 17.83 | – | 14.45 ± 5.25 | 16.83 ± 12.54 | – | **13.00 ± 4.97** | 16.29 ± 8.94 |
| AH | 5.73 ± 2.88 | – | 8.11 ± 5.22 | **4.10 ± 2.26** | – | 4.33 ± 2.96 | 8.89 ± 4.91 |

**Experiment (III):** The previous experiments are conducted in the scenario of using a single agent for the detection of one landmark. In this experiment, we proceed to evaluate the performance of using multi-agents for detecting the same single landmark. The final location of the agents are averaged at the end of an episode. To give a baseline, we include a column for five single agents looking for the same landmark in parallel. We report the results on a selected landmark from each dataset used in the previous two experiments, namely AC and CSP. Table 3 shows C-MARL's results are much better than in any of the previous methods. Parallel single agents are not significantly better than the results with only one agent.

**Table 3.** Results from using five agents looking for the same landmark. Distance error are in $mm$.

| Landmarks | Single agents [2] | Collab-DQN [17] | C-MARL |
|---|---|---|---|
| AC | 0.97 ± 0.40 | 0.81 ± 0.36 | **0.75 ± 0.34** |
| CSP | 10.43 ± 4.28 | 6.66 ± 4.19 | **5.10 ± 4.25** |

**Experiment (IV):** We further evaluate using multi agents for detecting multiple landmarks, where each single landmark have multiple agents. In this experiment, we train four agents to detect the AC and PC landmarks, where each landmark has two dedicated agents. Similar to the previous experiment, to give a baseline, we compare with four non communicating agents as a baseline. Table 4 shows that C-MARL agents perform better than the baseline, but worse than using five agents for a single landmark from Experiment (III). Finally, these experiments show that multiple cooperative agents trained to detect one single landmark can outperform the same number of agents detecting different landmarks.

**Table 4.** Results from using two pairs of agent looking for two landmarks (four agents in total). Distance error are in *mm*.

| Landmarks | Single agents [2] | C-MARL |
|-----------|-------------------|--------|
| AC | $1.17 \pm 0.61$ | $\mathbf{0.95 \pm 0.43}$ |
| PC | $1.12 \pm 0.55$ | $\mathbf{0.97 \pm 0.46}$ |

**Implementation:** We run each experiment for four days, but each would converge usually after one or two days. We used Nvidia Tesla or Nvidia GeForce GTX Titan Xp with 12 GB RAM, using CUDA v10.0.130 and Torch v1.4. A 24-core/48 thread Intel Xeon CPU was used with 256 GB RAM. In four days, collab-DQN ran 30k episodes while our proposed method only ran 20k episodes. The memory space during training is mostly driven up by the memory buffer, which we set to $\frac{100,000}{\#agents}$ episodes. As for the model's size, more agents take up more space and communication channels are added on the collab-DQN's architecture. More precisely, our model size is $5,504,759$ and $8,144,365$ bytes for three and five agent respectively, while for collab-DQN it is $3,529,451$ and $4,852,185$ bytes. For comparison, three single agents working independently have model size $2,206,723 \times 3 = 6,620,169$ bytes and for five single agents it is $2,206,723 \times 5 = 11,033,615$ bytes. This shows multi-agent models greatly reduce the models' trainable parameters. For the testing speed, our method takes around 2.5 and 4.9 s per episode for three and five agents respectively and those figures are 2.2 and 4.2 s for collab-DQN. The code is publicly available on Github, https://github.com/gml16/rl-medical.

## 5    Conclusion

We introduced a communicative multi-agent reinforcement learning (C-MARL) system for detecting multiple anatomical landmarks from brain medical images. Multi-agents share the weights of the convolutional layers to learn implicit communications. They also learn explicit communication channels calculated from the output of their fully connect layers, which are then shared among them by concatenating to the input of the following fully connected layers. C-MARL was evaluated on adult brain MRI and fetal head ultrasound, outperforming single- and multi-agents approaches.

**Future Work:** The optimal number of agents and combination of landmarks will be further investigated. It will be also interesting to research weighted communication channels based on nearby agents to reduce noise from distant landmarks. We will incorporate more complex communication channels, e.g. skip connections and temporal units. Another direction is to investigate competitive approaches for communication instead of collaboration between the agents.

# References

1. Alansary, A., et al.: Automatic view planning with multi-scale deep reinforcement learning agents. In: Frangi, A.F., Schnabel, J.A., Davatzikos, C., Alberola-López, C., Fichtinger, G. (eds.) MICCAI 2018. LNCS, vol. 11070, pp. 277–285. Springer, Cham (2018). https://doi.org/10.1007/978-3-030-00928-1_32
2. Alansary, A., et al.: Evaluating reinforcement learning agents for anatomical landmark detection. Med. Image Anal. **53**, 156–164 (2019)
3. Basher, A., et al.: Hippocampus localization using a two-stage ensemble Hough convolutional neural network. IEEE Access **7**, 73436–73447 (2019)
4. Bellman, R.: Dynamic programming. Science **153**(3731), 34–37 (1966)
5. Gauriau, R., Cuingnet, R., Lesage, D., Bloch, I.: Multi-organ localization with cascaded global-to-local regression and shape prior. Med. Image Anal. **23**(1), 70–83 (2015)
6. Ghesu, F.C., Georgescu, B., Mansi, T., Neumann, D., Hornegger, J., Comaniciu, D.: An artificial agent for anatomical landmark detection in medical images. In: Ourselin, S., Joskowicz, L., Sabuncu, M.R., Unal, G., Wells, W. (eds.) MICCAI 2016. LNCS, vol. 9902, pp. 229–237. Springer, Cham (2016). https://doi.org/10.1007/978-3-319-46726-9_27
7. Ghesu, F.C., et al.: Multi-scale deep reinforcement learning for real-time 3D-landmark detection in CT scans. IEEE Trans. Pattern Anal. Mach. Intell. **41**(1), 176–189 (2017)
8. Li, Y., et al.: Fast multiple landmark localisation using a patch-based iterative network. In: Frangi, A.F., Schnabel, J.A., Davatzikos, C., Alberola-López, C., Fichtinger, G. (eds.) MICCAI 2018. LNCS, vol. 11070, pp. 563–571. Springer, Cham (2018). https://doi.org/10.1007/978-3-030-00928-1_64
9. Lian, C., Liu, M., Zhang, J., Shen, D.: Hierarchical fully convolutional network for joint atrophy localization and Alzheimer's disease diagnosis using structural MRI. IEEE Trans. Pattern Anal. Mach. Intell. **42**, 880–893 (2018)
10. Mnih, V., et al.: Human-level control through deep reinforcement learning. Nature **518**(7540), 529–533 (2015)
11. Navarro, F., Sekuboyina, A., Waldmannstetter, D., Peeken, J.C., Combs, S.E., Menze, B.H.: Deep reinforcement learning for organ localization in CT. arXiv preprint arXiv:2005.04974 (2020)
12. Oktay, O., et al.: Stratified decision forests for accurate anatomical landmark localization in cardiac images. IEEE Trans. Med. Imaging **36**(1), 332–342 (2016)
13. Payer, C., Štern, D., Bischof, H., Urschler, M.: Regressing heatmaps for multiple landmark localization using CNNs. In: Ourselin, S., Joskowicz, L., Sabuncu, M.R., Unal, G., Wells, W. (eds.) MICCAI 2016. LNCS, vol. 9901, pp. 230–238. Springer, Cham (2016). https://doi.org/10.1007/978-3-319-46723-8_27
14. Sukhbaatar, S., Fergus, R., et al.: Learning multiagent communication with backpropagation. In: Advances in Neural Information Processing Systems, pp. 2244–2252 (2016)

15. Sutton, R.S., Barto, A.G.: Reinforcement Learning: An Introduction. MIT Press, Cambridge (2018)
16. Van Hasselt, H., Guez, A., Silver, D.: Deep reinforcement learning with double q-learning. In: Thirtieth AAAI Conference on Artificial Intelligence (2016)
17. Vlontzos, A., Alansary, A., Kamnitsas, K., Rueckert, D., Kainz, B.: Multiple landmark detection using multi-agent reinforcement learning. In: Shen, D., et al. (eds.) MICCAI 2019. LNCS, vol. 11767, pp. 262–270. Springer, Cham (2019). https://doi.org/10.1007/978-3-030-32251-9_29
18. Waldmannstetter, D., et al.: Reinforced redetection of landmark in pre- and postoperative brain scan using anatomical guidance for image alignment. In: Špiclin, Ž., McClelland, J., Kybic, J., Goksel, O. (eds.) WBIR 2020. LNCS, vol. 12120, pp. 81–90. Springer, Cham (2020). https://doi.org/10.1007/978-3-030-50120-4_8
19. Wang, Z., Schaul, T., Hessel, M., Hasselt, H., Lanctot, M., Freitas, N.: Dueling network architectures for deep reinforcement learning. In: International Conference on Machine Learning, pp. 1995–2003 (2016)
20. Watkins, C.J., Dayan, P.: Q-learning. Mach. Learn. 8(3–4), 279–292 (1992)
21. Yu, C., Liu, J., Nemati, S.: Reinforcement learning in healthcare: a survey. arXiv preprint arXiv:1908.08796 (2019)
22. Zhong, Z., Li, J., Zhang, Z., Jiao, Z., Gao, X.: An attention-guided deep regression model for landmark detection in cephalograms. In: Shen, D., et al. (eds.) MICCAI 2019. LNCS, vol. 11769, pp. 540–548. Springer, Cham (2019). https://doi.org/10.1007/978-3-030-32226-7_60

**RNO-AI 2020**

# State-of-the-Art in Brain Tumor Segmentation and Current Challenges

Sobia Yousaf[1], Harish RaviPrakash[2], Syed Muhammad Anwar[1(✉)],
Nosheen Sohail[1], and Ulas Bagci[2]

[1] Department of Software Engineering, UET Taxila, Taxila, Pakistan
s.anwar@uettaxila.edu.pk
[2] CRCV, University of Central Florida, Orlando, FL, USA

**Abstract.** Brain tumors are the third most common type of cancer among young adults and an accurate diagnosis and treatment demands strict delineation of the tumor effected tissue. Brain tumor segmentation involves segmenting different tumor tissues, particularly, the enhancing tumor regions, non-enhancing tumor and necrotic regions, and edema. With increasing computational power and data sharing, computer vision algorithms, particularly deep learning approaches, have begun to dominate the field of medical image segmentation. Accurate tumor segmentation will help in surgery planning as well as monitor the progress in longitudinal studies enabling a better understanding of the factors effecting malignant growth. The objective of this paper is to provide an overview of the current state-of-the-art in brain tumor segmentation approaches, an idea of the available resources, and highlight the most promising research directions moving forward. We also intend to highlight the challenges that exist in this field, in particular towards the successful adoption of such methods to clinical practice.

## 1 Introduction

Brain tumor, a type of primary central nervous system tumor, is the growth of abnormal cells in the human brain. An average survival rate for 36% of patients diagnosed with brain tumor is just 5 years [2]. Brain tumors can be broadly divided into two categories: primary and secondary/metastatic tumors. Primary tumors tend to originate in the brain, while metastatic tumors spread to the brain from an origin elsewhere in the body. Among these, metastatic brain tumors are more common and effect one in four cancer patients [1]. While primary brain tumors can be benign or malignant, metastatic cancer tends to be cancerous. Specific causes for brain tumor are not fully understood, however most tumors are caused by changes to DNA cells. Based on symptoms and clinical history of a patient, the diagnosis of brain tumor can be performed using various imaging techniques such as computed tomography (CT), angiograms, and magnetic resonance imaging (MRI) [28]. In the imaging domain, analysis primarily involves segmentation that enables delineation of the tumor regions for tumor localization, volume estimation, and surgery planning tasks. In practice, CT and MRI scans are used for identifying, segmenting, and evaluating various abnormalities.

© Springer Nature Switzerland AG 2020
S. M. Kia et al. (Eds.): MLCN 2020/RNO-AI 2020, LNCS 12449, pp. 189–198, 2020.
https://doi.org/10.1007/978-3-030-66843-3_19

Over the past few years, a significant utilization of deep learning (DL) methods has emerged in medical image analysis domain [6]. Similarly various techniques have been proposed for brain tumor segmentation, for the purpose of diagnosis and prognosis [5,16,17]. We have seen a lot of research coming out in this line of research and datasets are curated to create baselines for tumor segmentation. A comprehensive comparison of DL methods for the prediction of tumor abnormality can reflect upon the advances in this area. Some of the challenges that exist include prognosis, diagnostic decision systems, and survival prediction. In this paper, we provide a broad review of the most recent machine learning (ML) and DL approaches applied to brain tumor segmentation and prognosis tasks and look into the direction that the field is currently headed. The organization of the paper is as follows: In Sect. 2 we highlight the datasets that have been used and are publicly available for future research followed by a review of the most recent advances in brain tumor image analysis. We then provide a glimpse into the potential of DL-based approaches for providing meaningful results before concluding with a summary and a look at the future directions in this field.

## 2    Benchmark Datasets

Based on brain MRI, there are a number of datasets being used for developing automated tumor detection systems. The cancer imaging archive (TCIA) is a large repository consisting of a wide collection of clinical images[1] [11]. For instance, a large-scale publicly available brain tumor data including high- and low-grade gliomas, is included in the QIN-BRAIN-DSC-MRI repository [24]. This repository comprises of data acquired from 49 patients of different age groups. Harvard dataset is an online repository based on whole brain MRI atlas [29]. The data includes more than 13000 MRI brain images collected from healthy subjects as well as cases representing brain lesions such as ischemic infarct, Alzheimer's disease (AD), gliomas, and other infectious diseases.

In 2015, MICCAI organized the ischemic stroke lesion segmentation (ISLES) challenge targeted towards the development of robust methods to locate and perform segmentation of brain lesions [21]. All expert segmentation were contributed by experienced raters. In subsequent years (2016 and 2017) the data were modified to predict lesion segmentation based on acute MRI. The four modalities included in data are: T1-weighted, diffusion-weighted imaging (DWI), FLAIR, and T2-weighted images. The brain tumor and segmentation (BraTS) challenge has been organized under MICCAI for the last 9 years. Various recently developed methods are evaluated on this data and is now considered as a benchmark [7]. The dataset contains multi-institutional pre-operative MRI scans of low- and high-grade tumors. The data also includes ground-truth annotations corresponding to the segmentation of the different tumor types - enhancing, necrotic and non-enhancing, and edema. While the initial editions of the challenge focused

---

[1] https://www.cancerimagingarchive.net.

more on the segmentation task, the recent editions focus equally on both segmentation and survival prognosis. Survival information for subjects with high-grade gliomas is included in the dataset [8]. A brief summary of BRATS data as it has evolved over the years is presented in Table 1.

**Table 1.** A summary of BRATS challenge data used over the years in terms of data instances and tasks.

| Year | No of subjects | Training data | Test and validation data | Task |
|------|----------------|---------------|--------------------------|------|
| 2012 | 50 | 35 | 15 | Segmentation |
| 2013 | 60 | 35 | 25 | Segmentation |
| 2014 | 238 | 200 | 38 | Tumor segmentation growth |
| 2015 | 253 | 200 | 53 | Tumor segmentation growth |
| 2016 | 391 | 200 | 191 | Tumor segmentation growth |
| 2017 | 477 | 285 | 192 | Segmentation, survival prediction |
| 2018 | 542 | 285 | 257 | Segmentation, survival prediction |
| 2019 | 461 | 334 | 127 | Segmentation, survival prediction |

## 3    Brain Tumor Segmentation and Diagnosis

Primary brain tumors that originate in the glial cells are generally called gliomas, which vary based on their aggressiveness. Slow-growing gliomas, low-grade gliomas (LGG) are possibly curable while the more aggressive fast-growing tumors- high-grade gliomas (HGG)-are difficult to cure. The World Health Organization (WHO) have graded brain tumors on a scale of 1 to 4 with grades 1 and 2 falling under LGG and grades 3 and 4, under HGG. HGG tumors tend to recur even after treatment and is part of the reason that patients with HGG have a far worse prognosis than patients with LGG. Brain tumors are commonly screened with MRI scanners which provide more detailed images of the soft tissues, to detect sub-brain tumorous regions. Additionally, MRI scans are utilized by physicians for pre-surgical procedures. Therefore, an accurate, time efficient, and coherent segmentation of cancerous brain tissues in MRI scans has become indispensable in today's medical practice for physicians. Identification of the cancer type is integral for prognosis, however, with the true cause for brain tumor not being fully understood, accurate survival prediction from purely imaging data remains an open challenge.

To correctly segment different sub-regions of gliomas in multi-modal MRI scans is crucial. However, segmentation of the sub-regions is challenging due to the highly multifarious nature and shape of these tumors. In this complex scenario, DL-based approaches have been shown to be most effective for the segmentation task. The standard pipeline towards deep-learning segmentation includes pre-processing of the image, followed by architecture design which influences how the data is used. Image pre-processing is integral to ensure cleaner images that can enable better comparisons between the same group and different groups of images. The network architecture determines how the image data is processed - patch-based systems require 2D/3D image patches, slice-based architectures read in the data slice by slice, while 3D architectures use the whole 3D image volumes which may or may not be cropped for background reduction. The network training is supervised using different tumor class labels for each pixel/voxel. For the survival prognosis task, the pipeline remains similar with the difference being the supervision labels.

In terms of survival, patients are generally categorized into long- (survival duration larger than 15 months), mid- (10 to 15 months), and short-term (less than 10 months) survival. The overall survival (OS) can be predicted using deep features from trained segmentation models, radiomic features, age, gender, etc. In general for OS prediction, the proposed frameworks includes high-level feature extraction from the learned parameters, appropriate fitting of the proposed model, and determining an output by voting all radiomics-based feature classification results [12].

### 3.1   Machine Learning Approaches for Brain Tumor Segmentation

Although DL-based methods have become pervasive in various computer vision applications like object segmentation and recognition, yet its implementation in biological image segmentation has been relatively slow owing to the shortage of large scale annotated datasets. Lately, these methods have shown great performance on a variety of publicly available datasets that are mainly focused on the segmentation of a large pathology such as tumor [14]. While various neurological diseases like multiple sclerosis have lesions that are very small in size, their segmentation on MRI scans plays a key role in the disease severity assessment as well as in the assessment of the treatment efficacy during clinical trials. In particular, DL-based methods such as convolutional neural networks (CNN) have outperformed conventional approaches in brain lesion segmentation problems [19]. In [36], a novel technique was proposed for brain tumor segmentation by incorporating fully connected neural network with conditional random fields. The method was evaluated on BRATS data and achieved improved performance as compared to other DL methods. The average dice score achieved from this network was 86% for complete tumor, 76% for enhancing tumor and 83% for tumor core. In [32], a deep interactive brain lesion segmentation technique was proposed. The framework was based on two stages: first a P-Net was used to perform automatic segmentation, where user interaction was used to identify mis-segmentation. Secondly, an R-Net was used to improve the initial segmentation result by taking the original image input and user interaction.

In place of the more common multi-network approach where each network is trained separately to segment a tumor sub-type, in [37], a one-pass multi-task approach was proposed treating each class as a different task within the same network. The architecture involved incorporating a cascaded spatial attention to influence the output of different tasks and a staggered training strategy was employed to learn each individual task. Biophysical tumor growth modelling was used to perform longitudinal brain tumor segmentation with better longitudinal tumor prediction [23]. Cirillo et al. proposed a generative adversarial network

(GAN) to generate segmentation from multi-channel 3D MRI images [10]. The benefit of utilizing GAN was to penalize unrealistic segmentation that were generated in the early phases of training.

## 3.2  Diagnosis and Prediction

Diagnosis of tumors typically involves detection and classification in to different tumor types. Early approaches involved using simple transfer-learning and fine-tuning of VGG19 networks for classifying different types of gliomas with accuracy as high as 94% [26]. A more tailored network architecture using the recently proposed capsule networks was used to improve the performance over conventional CNN based approaches [3]. A separate study examined the diagnostic accuracy of grading glioma tumors by assessing the heterogeneity and texture analysis based on preoperative MRI data from 95 patients having high and low grade gliomas (HGG & LGG). The low and high grades were discriminated best with a sensitivity metric of 93% and specificity metric of 81%. This study concluded that assessing the diversification of gliomas based on MRI modality has improved the accuracy of grading tumor thereby providing a rapid treatment decision [27]. Huang et al proposed the use of context aware GAN for MRI data synthesis to improve glioma grading and achieved an accuracy of 89% on the heterogeneous BraTS dataset [15]. Another study conducted in 2019, reports that a multivariate ML model, i.e., resting-state functional connectivity (rsFC) predicted the severity of aphasia in 126 patients with left-sided low- or high-grade gliomas, affecting the brain's speech centers. These findings advanced the knowledge regarding large-scale language network reorganization in patients with gliomas, and shed light on why resection of the areas critical to language processing, may not necessarily induce aphasia [35].

## 4  Generalization and Explainable Models

Computer aided diagnostic (CAD) systems provide radiologists a second opinion in addition to accelerating the diagnosis process. By using artificial intelligence, CAD offers an effective way to make the process of diagnosis more efficient and reliable. DL is one of the leading state of the art approach that uses artificial intelligence to solve a variety of problems in the domain of computer vision and medical imaging analysis. It has been extensively used for medical imaging task like live cancer detection, classification of Alzheimer, skin cancer diagnosis and retinal disease detection etc. Although CAD systems, that are AI based, give remarkable results in medical applications but still they are not significantly deployed in the clinics. This is because the DL methods have a black-box nature with limited capability to explain the knowledge of the task performed by them along with the high computational cost problem. DL algorithms learn to abstract features automatically, unlike traditional ML algorithms that use hand-crafted features that define the domain. Adding an explainable aspect to DL models will enable human interpretation in addition to high accuracy that can lead to identifying potential bio-markers. Explainable DL is a more recent direction in the AI field and there has been limited work towards its application in the medical imaging domain. Some of the more recent works in explainable DL in brain imaging have been on subjectively large datasets problems such as Intracranial haemorrhage (ICH) [20], Alzheimer's [22], etc. For the detection of ICH, Lee et al. proposed the use of attention maps on the classification of CT images to understand the contributing regions of the image [20]. Towards explaining Alzheimer's diagnosis, Nigri et al. proposed to use a swap test wherein patches of a reference image were replaced with patches of the test image to generate a prediction probability [22]. This enabled the generation of a heat map based on the prediction probability of the patches enabling an understanding of the true contributing parts of an image. Similarly, limited work has been done towards explainable models for brain tumor datasets. Afshar et al. proposed to use recently developed capsule architecture based models to differentiate between the different tumor types [4]. Windisch et al. proposed to differentiate between MRI slices containing either a vestibular schwannoma, a glioblastoma, or no tumor and combined this with the popular GradCAM approaches to observe the region of attention for this task [33].

Traditional DL models provide a single class label for the task. This tends to be insufficient particularly in cases which lie on the border of the classifier. These cases may require that the clinician take another look at the scan. Hence to enable a clinician to make rationale decisions, including uncertainty in the model predictions is essential. By providing the radiologist with a confidence in the prediction, the radiologist can spend more time and attention on the uncertain cases. Some of the recent work incorporating uncertainty in brain tumor data lies in the task of segmentation. Wang et al. estimated the uncertainty of whole tumor segmentation both in the data (*aleatoric uncertainty*) and in the model parameters (*epistemic uncertainty*) by using test-time augmentation strategies and monte-carlo dropout approaches respectively [30]. In an extension to this work, the authors used a triple cascaded convolutional network to perform segmentation and combined this with a monte-carlo sampling for test-time augmentation to estimate the uncertainty in the segmentation of the tumor substructures [31]. More recently, Jungo et al. found that models tend to have better dataset level predictions but poor subject-level predictions and this was attributed to the averaging out of over-confidence and under-confidence in subject level predictions at the dataset level [18]. This suggests the need to focus more on subject level models and to better curate the dataset.

To be successful, CAD systems should be understandable, transparent, generalizable and explainable. Ideally the system should be intelligent enough to explain the logic of decisions and let human experts like physicians to review the decisions and use their verdicts. Hence explainability has a vital role in safety, trustworthiness, rational use of AI technology, and hence their deployment in real world applications. The concept of interpretability and explainabilty are interchangeable. In explainabilty the domain of features that contributed in the decision making of the model is described, while interpretability maps towards a better understanding of the output class. There are two broad categories of the methods that are used to explain deep neural networks results in the medical imaging domain: attribution based and domain specific approaches. Majority of the work in medical imaging has used the attribution based methods for explaining deep networks. Those methods are considered more convenient because of having plug and play nature with open source implementations. Therefore, a recent focus in the DL community is to design optimal, generalizable, and explainable models for better understanding of the decision making process in CAD.

## 5  Discussion and Conclusion

Despite recent advances, automatic brain tumor image analysis remains a challenging task. The small size of the datasets as well as the heterogeneity therein can lead to over-confidence and under-confidence in subject level predictions. A potential approach for improving the segmentation accuracy in such small datasets is via the use of active learning wherein the model is initially trained on a small dataset and then new samples that are dissimilar to the available data are used to improve the performance [25]. This approach can help better capture the diversity in the tumor types. Another potential strategy is the use of federated learning [34]. In federated learning, an algorithm is trained across multiple decentralized servers/locations. This enables training of the model on datasets that are not publicly available thus potentially providing a more generalized model. There exist several other challenges to the clinical deployment of the trained models. First, no standardized evaluation metric has been proposed to evaluate and compare model performance. More importantly, model explainability is still in its infancy and unexplained results make it almost impossible for clinical usage in high-risk tasks such as tumor risk assessment. Identification of genotypes is important for determining treatment for gliomas. Combining the genome information such as the IDH mutations in the training of MRI based models can help improve the understanding of the trained models. Recently, Fukuma et al. proposed an approach to identify the tumor genotype in a non-invasive manner using MRIs [13]. Choi et al. proposed the identification of IDH genotype using dynamic susceptibility contrast perfusion MRI images and recurrent neural networks [9]. The time-series from each tumor sub-type was used to train the network and an attention mechanism was used to identify the contributing time-points. Combining genotype identification with segmentation tasks is a potential direction to interpreting the features learned by the network. There has been a significant contribution in the development of generalizable and explainable deep network models for medical diagnosis. Recently, the publicly available datasets, particularly the BRATS benchmark data has provided a common platform where different DL models can be evaluated and improved.

In summary, we present a review of the state-of-the-art deep network models proposed for brain tumor segmentation. We conclude that although DL-based methods are found to be well suited for glioma segmentation owing to their ability to learn complex features from the input data, the learned features and models are not explainable. A model designer could analyze significant features (in a black-box manner) and perform decision making which meets certain performance requirements. Whereas, explainable models can be beneficial for the success of DL in clinical practice in the neuro-imaging domain. This would enable deep learning practitioners to design better models based on understanding the deep features, while end users (clinical experts) can make decisions based on a well-defined reasoning for the model decision. This would develop trust and confidence on the AI-based model decisions. Future modifications and improvement in deep network's architecture, feature understanding and additional information from imaging modalities can help experts in developing clinically acceptable segmentation techniques for better diagnosis of brain tumors and their treatment strategies.

# References

1. American association of neurological surgeons. https://www.aans.org/Patients/Neurosurgical-Conditions-and-Treatments/Brain-Tumors, Accessed 07 Dec 2020
2. Cancer.net. https://www.cancer.net/cancer-types/brain-tumor/statistics, Accessed 07 Jan 2019
3. Afshar, P., Mohammadi, A., Plataniotis, K.N.: Brain tumor type classification via capsule networks. In: 2018 25th IEEE International Conference on Image Processing (ICIP), pp. 3129–3133. IEEE (2018)
4. Afshar, P., Plataniotis, K.N., Mohammadi, A.: Capsule networks' interpretability for brain tumor classification via radiomics analyses. In: 2019 IEEE International Conference on Image Processing (ICIP), pp. 3816–3820. IEEE (2019)
5. Anwar, S.M., Altaf, T., Rafique, K., RaviPrakash, H., Mohy-ud-Din, H., Bagci, U.: A survey on recent advancements for AI enabled radiomics in neuro-oncology. In: Mohy-ud-Din, H., Rathore, S. (eds.) RNO-AI 2019. LNCS, vol. 11991, pp. 24–35. Springer, Cham (2020). https://doi.org/10.1007/978-3-030-40124-5_3
6. Anwar, S.M., Majid, M., Qayyum, A., Awais, M., Alnowami, M., Khan, M.K.: Medical image analysis using convolutional neural networks: a review. J. Med. Syst. 42(11), 226 (2018)
7. Bakas, S., et al.: Advancing the cancer genome atlas glioma MRI collections with expert segmentation labels and radiomic features. Sci. Data 4, 170117 (2017)
8. Bakas, S., et al.: Identifying the best machine learning algorithms for brain tumor segmentation, progression assessment, and overall survival prediction in the brats challenge. arXiv preprint arXiv:1811.02629 (2018)
9. Choi, K.S., Choi, S.H., Jeong, B.: Prediction of IDH genotype in gliomas with dynamic susceptibility contrast perfusion MR imaging using an explainable recurrent neural network. Neuro-oncology 21(9), 1197–1209 (2019)
10. Cirillo, M.D., Abramian, D., Eklund, A.: Vox2Vox: 3D-GAN for brain tumour segmentation. arXiv preprint arXiv:2003.13653 (2020)
11. Clark, K., et al.: The cancer imaging archive (TCIA): maintaining and operating a public information repository. J. Digital Imaging 26(6), 1045–1057 (2013)
12. Feng, X., Tustison, N.J., Patel, S.H., Meyer, C.H.: Brain tumor segmentation using an ensemble of 3D U-nets and overall survival prediction using radiomic features. Front. Comput. Neurosci. 14, 25 (2020)

13. Fukuma, R., et al.: Prediction of IDH and TERT promoter mutations in low-grade glioma from magnetic resonance images using a convolutional neural network. Sci. Rep. **9**(1), 1–8 (2019)
14. Havaei, M., et al.: Brain tumor segmentation with deep neural networks. Med. Image Anal. **35**, 18–31 (2017)
15. Huang, P., et al.: CoCa-GAN: common-feature-learning-based context-aware generative adversarial network for glioma grading. In: Shen, D., Liu, T., Peters, T.M., Staib, L.H., Essert, C., Zhou, S., Yap, P.-T., Khan, A. (eds.) MICCAI 2019. LNCS, vol. 11766, pp. 155–163. Springer, Cham (2019). https://doi.org/10.1007/978-3-030-32248-9_18
16. Hussain, S., Anwar, S.M., Majid, M.: Brain tumor segmentation using cascaded deep convolutional neural network. In: 2017 39th Annual International Conference of the IEEE Engineering in Medicine and Biology Society (EMBC), pp. 1998–2001. IEEE (2017)
17. Hussain, S., Anwar, S.M., Majid, M.: Segmentation of glioma tumors in brain using deep convolutional neural network. Neurocomputing **282**, 248–261 (2018)
18. Jungo, A., Balsiger, F., Reyes, M.: Analyzing the quality and challenges of uncertainty estimations for brain tumor segmentation. Front. Neurosci. **14**, 282 (2020)
19. Kamnitsas, K., et al.: Efficient multi-scale 3D CNN with fully connected CRF for accurate brain lesion segmentation. Med. Image Anal. **36**, 61–78 (2017)
20. Lee, H., et al.: An explainable deep-learning algorithm for the detection of acute intracranial haemorrhage from small datasets. Nat. Biomed. Eng. **3**(3), 173 (2019)
21. Maier, O., et al.: Isles 2015-a public evaluation benchmark for ischemic stroke lesion segmentation from multispectral mri. Med. Image Anal. **35**, 250–269 (2017)
22. Nigri, E., Ziviani, N., Cappabianco, F., Antunes, A., Veloso, A.: Explainable deep CNNs for MRI-based diagnosis of alzheimer's disease. arXiv preprint arXiv:2004.12204 (2020)
23. Pei, L., Bakas, S., Vossough, A., Reza, S.M., Davatzikos, C., Iftekharuddin, K.M.: Longitudinal brain tumor segmentation prediction in MRI using feature and label fusion. Biomed. Signal Process. Control **55**, 101648 (2020)
24. Schmainda, K., Prah, M., Connelly, J., Rand, S.: Glioma DSC-MRI perfusion data with standard imaging and rois. The Cancer Imaging Archive (2016). https://doi.org/10.7937/K9/TCIA.2016.5DI84Js8
25. Sharma, D., Shanis, Z., Reddy, C.K., Gerber, S., Enquobahrie, A.: Active learning technique for multimodal brain tumor segmentation using limited labeled images. In: Wang, Q., et al. (eds.) DART/MIL3ID -2019. LNCS, vol. 11795, pp. 148–156. Springer, Cham (2019). https://doi.org/10.1007/978-3-030-33391-1_17
26. Swati, Z.N.K., et al.: Brain tumor classification for MR images using transfer learning and fine-tuning. Comput. Med. Imaging Graph. **75**, 34–46 (2019)
27. Szychot, E., et al.: Predicting outcome in childhood diffuse midline gliomas using magnetic resonance imaging based texture analysis. J. Neuroradiol. (2020)
28. Tiwari, A., Srivastava, S., Pant, M.: Brain tumor segmentation and classification from magnetic resonance images: review of selected methods from 2014 to 2019. Pattern Recogn. Lett. **131**, 244–260 (2020)
29. Vidoni, E.D.: The whole brain atlas: www.med.harvard.edu/aanlib. J. Neurologic Phys. Therapy **36**(2), 108 (2012)
30. Wang, G., Li, W., Aertsen, M., Deprest, J., Ourselin, S., Vercauteren, T.: Aleatoric uncertainty estimation with test-time augmentation for medical image segmentation with convolutional neural networks. Neurocomputing **338**, 34–45 (2019)

31. Wang, G., Li, W., Vercauteren, T., Ourselin, S.: Automatic brain tumor segmentation based on cascaded convolutional neural networks with uncertainty estimation. Front. Comput. Neurosci. **13**, 56 (2019)
32. Wang, G., et al.: Deepigeos: a deep interactive geodesic framework for medical image segmentation. IEEE Trans. Pattern Anal. Mach. Intell. **41**(7), 1559–1572 (2018)
33. Windisch, P., et al.: Implementation of model explainability for a basic brain tumor detection using convolutional neural networks on MRI slices. Neuroradiology **62**, 1515–1518 (2020)
34. Yang, Q., Liu, Y., Chen, T., Tong, Y.: Federated machine learning: concept and applications. ACM Trans. Intell. Syst. Technol. (TIST) **10**(2), 1–19 (2019)
35. Yuan, B., Zhang, N., Yan, J., Cheng, J., Lu, J., Wu, J.: Tumor grade-related language and control network reorganization in patients with left cerebral glioma. Cortex (2020)
36. Zhao, X., Wu, Y., Song, G., Li, Z., Zhang, Y., Fan, Y.: A deep learning model integrating FCNNs and CRFs for brain tumor segmentation. Med. Image Anal. **43**, 98–111 (2018)
37. Zhou, C., Ding, C., Wang, X., Lu, Z., Tao, D.: One-pass multi-task networks with cross-task guided attention for brain tumor segmentation. IEEE Trans. Image Process. **29**, 4516–4529 (2020)

# Radiomics and Radiogenomics with Deep Learning in Neuro-oncology

Jay Patel[1,2], Mishka Gidwani[1], Ken Chang[1,2],
and Jayashree Kalpathy-Cramer[1(✉)]

[1] Athinoula A. Martinos Center for Biomedical Imaging, Department of Radiology,
Massachusetts General Hospital, Boston, MA, USA
jkalpathy-cramer@mgh.harvard.edu
[2] Massachusetts Institute of Technology, Cambridge, MA, USA
https://qtim-lab.github.io/

**Abstract.** The clinical utility of predictive and/or prognostic machine learning models using routinely acquired imaging has resulted in a surge of radiomics and radiogenomics research. Using these methods, large numbers of quantitative imaging features can be extracted in a high-throughput manner, with subsequent feature selection strategies used to systematically find a subset with high predictive power toward a specific task (e.g. survival prediction). While these approaches have traditionally relied upon the use of handcrafted imaging features, automatic feature learning via convolutional neural networks has become increasingly common due to the recent success of deep learning based methods in image-related tasks. In this review, we first present an overview of both the traditional and newer deep learning based radiomics methodologies. Further, we highlight some recent applications of these methods to neuro-oncology.

**Keywords:** Radiomics · Deep learning · Neuro-oncology

## 1 Introduction

Gliomas are the most common type of primary brain malignancy in adults, and cause varying rates of morbidity and mortality depending on the tumor anatomic location, histology, and molecular characteristics [13]. The current standard for glioma nomenclature and classification comes from the 2016 World Health Organization (WHO) grading scale, which stratifies tumors based on both histopathological characteristics and molecular profiles [42]. Briefly, histologic grading is done by assessing four main morphologic criteria: cellular atypia, mitotic activity, microvascular proliferation, and presence of necrosis. Based on qualitative evaluation of this criterion, tumors are denoted a grade between I and IV, with grades I and II loosely referred to as low grade gliomas (LGG) and grades III and IV referred to as high grade gliomas (HGG). From a clinical standpoint, LGG are associated with long-term survival (mean survival of approximately 7 years post diagnosis), as these tumors tend to be slow growing

© Springer Nature Switzerland AG 2020
S. M. Kia et al. (Eds.): MLCN 2020/RNO-AI 2020, LNCS 12449, pp. 199–211, 2020.
https://doi.org/10.1007/978-3-030-66843-3_20

and non-malignant [20]. Conversely, the highly aggressive nature of HGG is associated with far worse prognosis, with mean survival time of between 1 to 5 years [50]. This large range of prognoses for tumors with similar histologic characteristics has been attributed to differences in the genotypic makeup of those tumors, with an increasing number of studies showing strong links between molecular markers and clinical outcome. For instance, 1p19q codeletion, MGMT promoter methylation, and mutations in IDH1/IDH2 have all been shown to confer more favorable patient outcomes [23,28,61].

In addition to histologic and molecular characterization of gliomas, examination of multi-modal magnetic resonance (MR) imaging is integral in the standard-of-care, enabling radiologists to make informed decisions with regards to surgical planning, treatment response assessment, and guidance of patient management [9]. Common anatomical MR sequences include gadolinium enhanced T1-weighted (T1Gd), which is used to identify areas of high cell replication and neo-angiogenesis [2], and T2 weighted (T2) and T2w-Fluid attenuation recovery (FLAIR), which is used to identify the extent of peritumoral edema [22]. While these imaging modalities do not directly detect the presence of tumor cells, abnormalities at the cellular and molecular level are subtly reflected at the radiographic level.

Under the hypothesis that tumor physiology [30] and treatment mediated changes [3,16] are reflected on clinical imaging, it stands to reason that one can extract a large set of high-dimensional, quantitative descriptors from raw MR (or other imaging modalities such as computed tomography, x-ray, etc.) such that specifically chosen subsets of these features are indicative/predicative of prognosis, treatment evaluation, and clinical outcome. This methodology, known as *radiomics* [35], has been widely adopted by the neuroimaging community, with publications in tasks such as the prediction of overall survival [7,44,52], differentiation between tumor recurrence and radiation necrosis [40,56,59], classification of glioma subtypes [43,53,63], and treatment response [10,32]. More recently, enthusiasm has been growing over using this same baseline methodology to discover imaging features correlated to a tumor's molecular/genetic profile, a field known as *radiogenomics*.

## 2    Methodological Approach of Radiomics

Formally, the radiomics pipeline for neuroimaging is comprised of four main steps: 1) preprocessing, 2) segmentation, 3) feature extraction, and 4) classification/regression. This general workflow is shown in Fig. 1.

*1) Preprocessing*: There is a general lack of standardization between image acquisition and reconstruction protocols across medical imaging centers, making robust quantitative analysis from heterogeneous, multi-institutional data challenging. To account for these variations, typical preprocessing of brain MR involves 1) resampling all images to the same resolution, 2) co-registration to the same anatomical space, 3) N4 bias correction to reduce the effects of field inhomogeneity [58], 4) brain extraction, and 5) intensity normalization.

*2) Segmentation*: Before performing feature extraction, accurate delineations of the region of interest (ROI) must be generated. For gliomas, this involves dividing the tumor into three distinct sub-regions: enhancing tumor (ET), tumor core (TC), and whole tumor (WT). Manual delineation of these sub-region boundaries is inherently challenging due to the heterogeneity of glioma phenotypes, and further compounded by the milieu of the brain. When coupled with artifacts that degrade image quality such as motion and acquisition errors, this leads to significant amounts of intra- and inter-rater variability [46]. To mitigate these issues, fully automatic deep learning based segmentation methods can be used to generate reproducible annotations, thereby reducing the variability of downstream extracted features.

*3) Feature Extraction*: In a traditional radiomics pipeline, a set of diverse algorithms is chosen manually based on expert knowledge in order to extract quantitative features in a high-throughput manner. These *handcrafted* features can broadly be categorized as either semantic or agnostic [19]. Generally speaking, semantic features are any descriptors that a radiologist may use to describe an ROI. Examples of semantic features include shape, size, and location of a tumor, among others. Conversely, any mathematical descriptor not used in current clinical practice is known as agnostic. These features attempt to quantify nuanced morphological and textural attributes of the ROI using first, second, and higher order statistics. First-order features characterize the distribution of image intensities within the ROI without conditioning on spatial relationships. Examples include simple histogram-based statistics such as mean, entropy, kurtosis, etc. Second-order features (usually referred to as texture features) capture complex interactions between intensity and spatial structure. While many such features exist, commonly extracted features include gray-level co-ocurrence matrices (GLCM) [21], gabor filter banks [26], and histogram of oriented gradients (HOG) [12]. Finally, higher-order features involve applying a non-trivial transformation, such as the wavelet transform [45], to an image prior to feature extraction, which can enable detection of patterns or details that were not initially perceivable [65].

In contrast to handcrafted features, *learned* features are automatically generated and refined during the training of a deep learning model on some pre-defined task, an approach that has numerous advantages over that of standard handcrafted feature extraction. First, one may choose to use the deep network (DN) simply as a feature extractor (e.g. by training the DN in an unsupervised fashion and passing learned features to a secondary classifier) or one may couple the feature extraction and downstream classification steps (e.g. by directly training the DN to predict the task of interest). For unsupervised learning, a common approach is to train an autoencoder to reconstruct the input imaging, where features from the end of the bottleneck layer of the network can be harvested for downstream classification tasks [41]. With supervised learning, a variety of DNs exist that can learn highly task-specific features, enabling researchers to directly optimize performance metrics on the task of interest. Another benefit of using a DN is that stronger feature representations can be learned when more training data is available, something that is especially important now that large, multi-institutional datasets are becoming more accessible to researchers.

*4) Classification/Regression*: Often times, many thousands of hand-crafted and/or learned features are extracted with the intent of fitting a machine learning model such as a support vector machine (SVM) or random forest (RF) [6] with only hundreds of data points. Without proper dimensionality reduction of the feature space, the risk of overfitting on the training set is high [51]. Fortunately, simple methods to remove redundant and non-relevant features can greatly reduce this risk, and in turn, enable the creation of more robust and generalizable models. In the scenario where a researcher is using a DN to perform coupled feature extraction and classification/regression, no explicit feature reduction stage is necessary; instead the researcher should take care to properly regularize the network and stop model training when validation accuracy has plateaued, as the network is itself capable of assigning relative importance to the learned features.

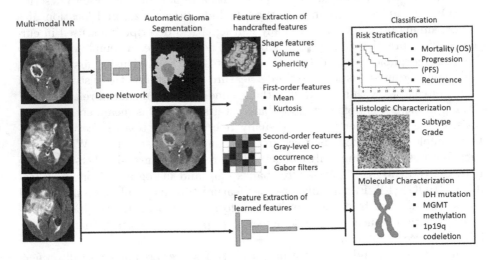

**Fig. 1.** Schematic showing workflow for traditional and deep learning based radiomics in neuro-oncology.

## 3 Segmentation via Deep Learning

While deep learning based feature extractors can be applied to raw MR images without explicitly defining an ROI, the extraction of robust handcrafted imaging features is reliant upon accurate annotations of ET, TC, and WT. Presently, all state-of-the-art automatic segmentation models are variations of 3D U-Nets [54] and other convolutional networks, with specific emphasis on the network design and optimization strategy. The development of these deep learning methods has been expedited by the availability of open-source code and packages [4,18,24].

The following reviewed approaches are top performers in the 2018 and 2019 Multimodal Brain Tumor Segmentation Challenge (BraTS) [48] competitions, with validation set segmentation performance for each approach shown in Table 1. Isensee et al. [25] showed that a standard U-Net architecture with only minor modifications could achieve highly competitive performance when using meticulously chosen hyperparameter settings and training procedures. Moreover, the authors examine the effect of training dataset size on segmentation performance, showing more than a 1% increase in validation set dice score when training with additional data on top of the official 2018 BraTS dataset. Meanwhile, Zhao et al. [64] designed a U-Net with dense blocks in place of the standard convolutional layers. They trained their network using a multitude of optimization strategies (called "tricks" in their paper), including variable patch/batch size training, heuristic sampling, and semi-supervised learning. Myronenko [49] utilized an asymmetrical U-Net with pre-activated residual blocks, wherein most of the trainable parameters of the model resided in the encoder. Furthermore, the author appended an additional branch off the end of the encoder which was used to reconstruct the input image. This autoencoding branch, which was only used during the training of the network, helped regularize the encoder, and led him to win the BraTS competition in 2018. Inspired by this, Jiang et al. [29] placed first the following year in 2019 using a two-stage cascaded asymmetrical residual U-Net, where the second stage of their cascade was used to refine the coarse segmentation maps generated by the first stage.

**Table 1.** Dice scores on BraTS validation data.

|  | Validation set dice | | |
|---|---|---|---|
|  | ET | WT | TC |
| Isensee et al. [25] (2018) | 0.809 | 0.913 | 0.863 |
| Myronenko [49] (2018) | 0.823 | 0.910 | 0.867 |
| Zhao et al. [64] (2019) | 0.754 | 0.908 | 0.823 |
| Jiang et al. [29] (2019) | 0.802 | 0.909 | 0.865 |

We note that countless other glioma segmentation methods exist (indeed, upwards of 70 to 100 teams participate in BraTS every year). While each approach has its own unique twist, some components are shared across all state-of-the-art methods. First, as high-memory GPUs become increasingly available, researchers are no longer computationally restricted. Thus, to ensure that the network learns enough anatomic context, large input patch sizes of at least 128x128x128 voxels have become the standard for training 3D networks. Next, there is extensive utilization of regularization techniques, which mitigate overfitting when training multi-million parameter networks on datasets of hundreds of images. These techniques include, but are not limited to, weight decay [34], dropout [17,55,57], and data augmentation. Finally, as the variability of an individual model can be quite high, it is often recommended to ensemble the predictions of multiple models trained via a K-fold cross-validation.

## 4  Radiomics Using Handcrafted Features

Radiomic phenotypes are vastly heterogeneous depending on their purpose. When developing a radiomic signature for risk prediction, there are a number of factors to consider. First, what is the endpoint of interest? While overall survival (OS) is the outcome of interest in many studies, risk stratification at intermediate endpoints, such as progression free survival (PFS), presence of adverse events, or radiologic or clinical response to treatment, is recommended due to the poor prognosis for most glioma and brain metastases patients. To that end, Liu et al. [39] developed a radiomic signature from T2 MR, with the goal of predicting PFS for LGG patients. Using a multivariable Cox regression, the authors found a significant association between their radiomics signature and PFS ($p < 0.045$, C-index $= 0.823$) on a validation set consisting of 84 patients. Second, the method of feature reduction may be correlated with the endpoint of interest. For instance, supervised principal component analysis (PCA), a generalization of standard PCA that estimates the sequence of principal components that have maximal dependence on the response variable, has been used by Kickingereder et al. [32] for prediction of recurrent glioblastoma response to bevacizumab. Their resultant radiomic predictor proved to be significant for OS (AUC $= 0.792$) and PFS (AUC $= 0.678$), outperforming clinical (age, KPS score) and radiologic (contrast-enhancing tumor volume, edema volume) variables. Finally, which imaging modalities inform the outcome of interest? In their study, McGarry et al. [47] compile T1, ADC, T1C, and FLAIR MRI series into a unique voxel-wise radiomic profile (RP) based on the degree of enhancement in each series. Their study found a hazard ratio of 1.44 with $p < 0.001$) for overall survival with increasing RP severity.

## 5  Radiomics Using Learned Features

Similar to when using handcrafted features, the outcome of interest should be carefully selected when using deep learning for risk prediction. Survival networks typically perform a classification task based on a binary (censored) outcome, such as mortality. These networks utilize nearest log likelihood loss, which approximates the Cox proportional hazards model by treating each input/output pair as a hazard and rewarding the network for correctly assessing the relative order of survival [31]. Fu et al. [15] aimed to compare the predictive power of Cox regression models trained using handcrafted features vs. learned features. For extraction of learned features, the authors pass multi-modal MR through an ImageNet pre-trained VGG19, harvesting feature representations at various layers along the network. Using a training set of 122 glioblastoma (GMB) patients, the authors find that the Cox model created using learned features outperformed the model created using handcrafted features. Furthermore, using a test set of 41 patients, they note that only the model using learned features was able to stratify patients into two risk groups with statistical significance ($p < 0.01$), indicating that learned features are perhaps more generalizable than handcrafted features. Also working on predicting OS, Lao et al. [36] utilized a similar methodology for extraction of learned features from multi-modal MR. When these were combined with handcrafted features and traditional risk factors (e.g. ages, Karnofsky Performance Score), their model was capable of stratifying patients into high and low risk groups of OS with hazard ratio (HR) = 4.608 (95% CI = (1.884,11.270), $p < 0.001$).

Moreover, deep learning models offer added flexibility in the types of data input when making predictions. Jang et al. [27] utilized a recurrent neural network (RNN) structure to consider multiple MR axial slices in order to parse true progression from pseudoprogression in GBM. When combined with clinical (age, gender), genetic (IDH status, MGMT methylation), and therapeutic (radiation dose, fraction, and duration) variables, this model achieved 0.83 AUC. In certain cases, it can be more prudent to predict a clinical variable that is a canonical assay of survival risk (such as tumor grade), in that it has application beyond survival and often a more readily-accessible ground-truth label. Using digitized histopathology slides, Ertosen et al. [14] developed a multi-stage convolutional neural network approach to first differentiate LGG from GBM, and second, perform grading of the tumor if it was predicted to be an LGG. On an independent test set of 10 slides, their method achieved 96% and 71% accuracy for these two tasks, respectively. Using conventional MR instead of histology for glioma grading, Yang et al. [62] examined the effects of ImageNet pre-training on final performance. Using a GoogLeNet architecture, they found that pre-training resulted in a 3.6% increase in test set accuracy over the baseline, indicating that pre-training on non-medical imaging can still be beneficial when limited data is available for the target task.

# 6   Radiogenomics Using Handcrafted Features

The majority of radiogenomic analyses have focused on linking quantitative imaging features to either pre-defined gene groups or specific somatic mutations already extensively validated as clinical biomarkers.

In order to discover correlations between multi-modal MR and tumor hypoxia, Beig et al. [5] curated a dataset of 115 GBM patients, stratifying patients based on OS and extent of hypoxia (as determined by 21 key hypoxia-associated genes). In the first stage of their study, they identified 8 handcrafted features strongly associated with tumor hypoxia. In the second stage, they used those same 8 features to predict OS via a RF model, noting significant separation between short- and long-term survivors ($p = 0.0032$) on a validation set of 30 patients. Meanwhile, Xi et al. [60] aimed to predict MGMT promoter methylation status of 98 GBM patients. A total of 1665 handcrafted features were extracted, and with subsequent feature selection using least absolute shrinkage and selection operator (LASSO) regularization. Interestingly, model performance was highly dependent on MR modality, with features coming from non contrast-enhanced T1 only reaching an accuracy of 67.5% while features from T1Gd reaching 82%. These results were shown to be robust, with an accuracy of 80% produced on an independent validation cohort of 20 patients. Prediction of IDH1 mutation status from imaging has seen even more success. Li et al. [38] extracted 1614 features from each of the glioma sub-regions, and created both single-region and multi-region radiomic models. The authors show that single-region models reached AUCs of between 0.80 to 0.88 on the independent validation cohort of 107 patients, whereas a multi-region model that pooled features from across the tumor sub-regions reached an AUC of 0.90. Moreover, the incorporation of known clinical factors such as age, sex, and Karnofsky performance status into the radiomics model increased performance 0.96 AUC.

## 7    Radiogenomics Using Learned Features

When large quantities of imaging are available, deep learning based approaches can significantly outperform models built with handcrafted features.

Endeavouring to show that a DN could predict MGMT methylation status from imaging without the need of explicitly providing a tumor segmentation ROI, Korfiatis et al. [33] trained three deep residual neural networks of varying size on a training dataset of 110 patients with T2 imaging. This dataset was artificially increased in size by splitting all 3D imaging into 2D axial slices, resulting in 7856 total training images. After extensive experiments, the authors find that deeper, more parametrized networks produce better results, with their ResNet50 model achieving an accuracy of 94.9% on the test set (45 patients with 2612 slices). Meanwhile, Chang et al. [8] used a similar methodology for prediction of IDH status, choosing to utilize a residual neural network with 2D inputs. However, their network was trained on cropped tumor images only, thus necessitating a predefined ROI. The authors performed exceptional multi-institutional validation, acquiring data from three different sites and reporting a final accuracy and AUC of 87.6% and 0.95, respectively, on the their testing set of 147 patients. Also aiming to predict IDH status, Li et al. directly compare model performance when using learned vs. handcrafted features [37]. These authors decoupled the feature extraction and classification steps, to which end they designed a six layer convolutional neural network tasked to segment gliomas. After the network was fully trained, 16,384 learned features were extracted from the last convolutional layer. For comparison, they additionally extract 671 handcrafted features directly from the segmented images. After rigorous feature reduction was applied, they found that an SVM trained with learned features achieved an AUC of 0.95, whereas an SVM trained with handcrafted features scored only 0.86 AUC, demonstrating the greater predictive power of learned features. Akkus et al. [1] focus on prediction of 1p19q codeletion, a highly prognostic molecular marker associated with longer survival in LGG patients. With much less data than the previous studies (only 387 slices in the training data), the authors note extreme overfitting, initially seeing perfect training sensitivity, specificity, and accuracy. To mitigate this issue, they make use of data augmentation techniques such as random translations, rotations, and flips, which increased final test set accuracy from 63.3% to 87.7%. Finally, Chang et al. [11] aim to integrate prediction of MGMT methylation status, IDH mutation status, and 1p19q codeletion into a single residual network. After five-fold cross-validation of their dataset of 259 patients (5259 slices), they achieve mean accuracy of 83%, 94% and 92%, respectively, on the three tasks.

# 8 Conclusion

Significant progress in the development of predictive and/or prognostic machine learning models has been made in the past few years, in part due to greater accessibility of large-scale multi-institutional datasets and better computational resources. These two factors in tandem have enabled the wide-spread use of deep learning based methods, which has produced state-of-the-art results in many neuro-oncology related tasks, including tumor segmentation, risk stratification, and non-invasive evaluation of genetic and molecular biomarkers. Our review has outlined the rapid development of machine learning in neuro-oncology, starting from the use of handcrafted features with manually delineated segmentations to state-of-the-art fully automated deep learning based methods for coupled feature extraction and classification. In recent years, authors have integrated increasingly complex neural network architectures with multiple imaging modalities in order to capture maximally relevant imaging information. As models begin to approach the upper bound for performance, the next hurdle to overcome will be the efficient deployment and utilization of these models in the clinical setting.

# References

1. Akkus, Z., et al.: Predicting deletion of chromosomal arms 1p/19q in low-grade gliomas from MR images using machine intelligence. J. Digit. Imaging **30**(4), 469–476 (2017). https://doi.org/10.1007/s10278-017-9984-3. https://pubmed.nc bi.nlm.nih.gov/28600641, https://www.ncbi.nlm.nih.gov/pmc/articles/PMC553 7096/
2. Arevalo, O.D., et al.: Assessment of glioblastoma response in the era of bevacizumab: longstanding and emergent challenges in the imaging evaluation of pseudoresponse. Frontiers Neurol. **10**, 460 (2019). https://doi.org/10.3389/fneur.2019. 00460. https://www.frontiersin.org/article/10.3389/fneur.2019.00460
3. Batchelor, T.T., et al.: Improved tumor oxygenation and survival in glioblastoma patients who show increased blood perfusion after cediranib and chemoradiation. Proc. Nat. Acad. Sci. **110**(47), 19059–19064 (2013)
4. Beers, A., et al.: DeepNeuro: an open-source deep learning toolbox for neuroimaging. Neuroinformatics, 1–14 (2020). https://doi.org/10.1007/s12021-020-09477-5
5. Beig, N., et al.: Radiogenomic analysis of hypoxia pathway is predictive of overall survival in Glioblastoma. Sci. Rep. **8**(1), 7 (2018). https://doi.org/10.1038/s41598-017-18310-0
6. Breiman, L.: Random forests. Mach. Learn. **45**(1), 5–32 (2001). https://doi.org/10.1023/A:1010933404324

7. Chaddad, A., Sabri, S., Niazi, T., Abdulkarim, B.: Prediction of survival with multi-scale radiomic analysis in glioblastoma patients. Med. Biol. Eng. Comput. **56**(12), 2287–2300 (2018). https://doi.org/10.1007/s11517-018-1858-4
8. Chang, K., et al.: Residual convolutional neural network for the determination of IDH status in low- and high-grade gliomas from MR imaging. Clin. Cancer Res. **24**(5), 1073–1081 (2018). https://doi.org/10.1158/1078-0432.CCR-17-2236. https://clincancerres.aacrjournals.org/content/24/5/1073
9. Chang, K., et al.: Automatic assessment of glioma burden: a deep learning algorithm for fully automated volumetric and bidimensional measurement. Neuro-oncology **21**(11), 1412–1422 (2019). https://doi.org/10.1093/neuonc/noz106
10. Chang, K., et al.: Multimodal imaging patterns predict survival in recurrent glioblastoma patients treated with bevacizumab. Neuro-oncology **18**(12), 1680–1687 (2016)
11. Chang, P., et al.: Deep-learning convolutional neural networks accurately classify genetic mutations in gliomas. Am. J. Neuroradiol. (2018). https://doi.org/10.3174/ajnr.A5667, http://www.ajnr.org/content/early/2018/05/10/ajnr.A5667
12. Dalal, N., Triggs, B.: Histograms of oriented gradients for human detection. In: 2005 IEEE Computer Society Conference on Computer Vision and Pattern Recognition (CVPR'05), vol. 1, pp. 886–893 (2005)
13. Eckel-Passow, J.E., et al.: Glioma groups based on 1p/19q, IDH, and TERT promoter mutations in tumors. N. Engl. J. Med. **372**(26), 2499–2508 (2015). https://doi.org/10.1056/NEJMoa1407279. pMID: 26061753
14. Ertosun, M.G., Rubin, D.L.: Automated grading of gliomas using deep learning in digital pathology images: a modular approach with ensemble of convolutional neural networks. In: AMIA ... Annual Symposium proceedings. AMIA Symposium 2015, pp. 1899–1908 (2015). https://www.ncbi.nlm.nih.gov/pubmed/26958289, https://www.ncbi.nlm.nih.gov/pmc/PMC4765616/
15. Fu, J., et al.: An automatic deep learning-based workflow for glioblastoma survival prediction using pre-operative multimodal MR images (2020)
16. Gerstner, E.R., et al.: Bevacizumab reduces permeability and concurrent temozolomide delivery in a subset of patients with recurrent glioblastoma. Clin. Cancer Res. **26**(1), 206–212 (2020)
17. Ghiasi, G., Lin, T.Y., Le, Q.V.: DropBlock: a regularization method for convolutional networks (2018)
18. Gibson, E., et al.: NiftyNet: a deep-learning platform for medical imaging. Comput. Methods Programs Biomed. **158**, 113–122 (2018)
19. Gillies, R.J., Kinahan, P.E., Hricak, H.: Radiomics: images are more than pictures, they are data. Radiology **278**(2), 563–577 (2016). https://doi.org/10.1148/radiol.2015151169. pMID: 26579733
20. Gupta, A., Dwivedi, T.: A simplified overview of world health organization classification update of central nervous system tumors 2016. J. Neurosci. Rural Pract. **8**(4), 629–641 (2017). https://doi.org/10.4103/jnrp.jnrp_168_17
21. Haralick, R.M., Shanmugam, K., Dinstein, I.: Textural features for image classification. IEEE Trans. Syst. Man Cybern. SMC **3**(6), 610–621 (1973)
22. Hawkins-Daarud, A., Rockne, R.C., Anderson, A.R.A., Swanson, K.R.: Modeling tumor-associated edema in gliomas during anti-angiogenic therapy and its impact on imageable tumor. Frontiers Oncol. **3**, 66 (2013). https://doi.org/10.3389/fonc.2013.00066
23. Houillier, C., Wang, X., Kaloshi, G., Mokhtari, K., Guillevin, R., Laffaire, J.: IDH1 or IDH2 mutations predict longer survival and response to temozolomide in low-grade gliomas (2010)

24. Isensee, F., Jäger, P.F., Kohl, S.A., Petersen, J., Maier-Hein, K.H.: Automated design of deep learning methods for biomedical image segmentation. arXiv preprint arXiv:1904.08128 (2019)
25. Isensee, F., Kickingereder, P., Wick, W., Bendszus, M., Maier-Hein, K.H.: No new-net. CoRR abs/1809.10483 (2018). http://arxiv.org/abs/1809.10483
26. Jain, A.K., Farrokhnia, F.: Unsupervised texture segmentation using Gabor filters. Pattern Recogn. **24**(12), 1167–1186 (1991). https://doi.org/10.1016/0031-3203(91)90143-S. http://www.sciencedirect.com/science/article/pii/0031320391 90143S
27. Jang, B.S., Jeon, S.H., Kim, I.H., Kim, I.A.: Prediction of pseudoprogression versus progression using machine learning algorithm in glioblastoma. Sci. Rep. **8**(1), 12516 (2018). https://doi.org/10.1038/s41598-018-31007-2
28. Jenkins, R., Blair, H., Ballman, K., Giannini, C., Arusell, R., Law, M.: A t(1;19)(q10;p10) mediates the combined deletions of 1p and 19q and predicts a better prognosis of patients with oligodendroglioma (2006)
29. Jiang, Z., Ding, C., Liu, M., Tao, D.: Two-stage cascaded U-Net: 1st place solution to BraTS challenge 2019 segmentation task. In: Crimi, A., Bakas, S. (eds.) BrainLes 2019. LNCS, vol. 11992, pp. 231–241. Springer, Cham (2020). https://doi.org/10. 1007/978-3-030-46640-4_22
30. Kalpathy-Cramer, J., Gerstner, E.R., Emblem, K.E., Andronesi, O.C., Rosen, B.: Advanced magnetic resonance imaging of the physical processes in human glioblastoma. Cancer Res. **74**(17), 4622–4637 (2014)
31. Katzman, J.L., Shaham, U., Cloninger, A., Bates, J., Jiang, T., Kluger, Y.: Deep-Surv: personalized treatment recommender system using a Cox proportional hazards deep neural network. BMC Med. Res. Methodol. **18**(1), 24 (2018). https:// doi.org/10.1186/s12874-018-0482-1
32. Kickingereder, P., et al.: Large-scale radiomic profiling of recurrent glioblastoma identifies an imaging predictor for stratifying anti-angiogenic treatment response. Clin. Cancer Res. Off. J. Am. Assoc. Cancer Res. **22**(23), 5765–5771 (2016). https://doi.org/10.1158/1078-0432.CCR-16-0702
33. Korfiatis, P., Kline, T.L., Lachance, D.H., Parney, I.F., Buckner, J.C., Erickson, B.J.: Residual deep convolutional neural network predicts MGMT methylation status. J. Digit. Imaging **30**(5), 622–628 (2017). https://doi.org/10.1007/s10278-017-0009-z
34. Krogh, A., Hertz, J.A.: A simple weight decay can improve generalization. NIPS'91, pp. 950–957. Morgan Kaufmann Publishers Inc., San Francisco (1991)
35. Lambin, P., et al.: Radiomics: extracting more information from medical images using advanced feature analysis. Eur. J. Cancer (Oxford, England : 1990) **48**(4), 441–446 (2012). https://doi.org/10.1016/j.ejca.2011.11.036
36. Lao, J., et al.: A deep learning-based radiomics model for prediction of survival in glioblastoma multiforme. Sci. Rep. **7**(1), 10353 (2017). https://doi.org/10.1038/ s41598-017-10649-8
37. Li, Z., Wang, Y., Yu, J., Guo, Y., Cao, W.: Deep learning based radiomics (DLR) and its usage in noninvasive IDH1 prediction for low grade glioma. Sci. Rep. **7**(1), 5467 (2017). https://doi.org/10.1038/s41598-017-05848-2
38. Li, Z.C., et al.: Multiregional radiomics profiling from multiparametric MRI: identifying an imaging predictor of IDH1 mutation status in glioblastoma. Cancer Med. **7**(12), 5999–6009 (2018). https://doi.org/10.1002/cam4.1863. https://pubmed. ncbi.nlm.nih.gov/30426720PMC63, https://www.ncbi.nlm.nih.gov/pmc/articles/ 08047/

39. Liu, X., et al.: A radiomic signature as a non-invasive predictor of progression-free survival in patients with lower-grade gliomas. NeuroImage. Clin. **20**, 1070–1077 (2018). https://doi.org/10.1016/j.nicl.2018.10.014. https://pubmed.ncbi.nlm.nih.gov/30366279, https://www.ncbi.nlm.nih.gov/pmc/articles/PMC6202688/

40. Lohmann, P., et al.: Combined FET PET/MRI radiomics differentiates radiation injury from recurrent brain metastasis. NeuroImage: Clin. **20**, 537–542 (2018). https://doi.org/10.1016/j.nicl.2018.08.024. http://www.sciencedirect.com/science/article/pii/S2213158218302651

41. Lou, B., et al.: An image-based deep learning framework for individualising radiotherapy dose: a retrospective analysis of outcome prediction. Lancet Digi. Health **1**(3), e136–e147 (2019)

42. Louis, D.N., et al.: The 2016 world health organization classification of tumors of the central nervous system: a summary. Acta Neuropathol. **131**(6), 803–820 (2016). https://doi.org/10.1007/s00401-016-1545-1

43. Lu, C.F., et al.: Machine learning-based radiomics for molecular subtyping of gliomas. Clin. Cancer Res. Off. J. Am. Assoc. Cancer Res. **24**(18), 4429–4436 (2018). https://doi.org/10.1158/1078-0432.CCR-17-3445

44. Macyszyn, L., et al.: Imaging patterns predict patient survival and molecular subtype in glioblastoma via machine learning techniques. Neuro-oncology **18**(3), 417–425 (2016). https://doi.org/10.1093/neuonc/nov127

45. Mallat, S.G.: A theory for multiresolution signal decomposition: the wavelet representation. IEEE Trans. Pattern Anal. Mach. Intell. **11**(7), 674–693 (1989)

46. Mazzara, G.P., Velthuizen, R.P., Pearlman, J.L., Greenberg, H.M., Wagner, H.: Brain tumor target volume determination for radiation treatment planning through automated MRI segmentation. Int. J. Radiat. Oncol. Biol. Phys. **59**(1), 300–312 (2004). https://doi.org/10.1016/j.ijrobp.2004.01.026

47. McGarry, S.D., et al.: Magnetic resonance imaging-based radiomic profiles predict patient prognosis in newly diagnosed glioblastoma before therapy. Tomography (Ann Arbor, Mich.) **2**(3), 223–228 (2016). https://doi.org/10.18383/j.tom.2016.00250. https://pubmed.ncbi.nlm.nih.gov/27774518

48. Menze, B.H., et al.: The multimodal brain tumor image segmentation benchmark (BRATS). IEEE Trans. Med. Imaging **34**(10), 1993–2024 (2015). https://doi.org/10.1109/TMI.2014.2377694

49. Myronenko, A.: 3D MRI brain tumor segmentation using autoencoder regularization. In: Crimi, A., Bakas, S., Kuijf, H., Keyvan, F., Reyes, M., van Walsum, T. (eds.) BrainLes 2018. LNCS, vol. 11384, pp. 311–320. Springer, Cham (2019). https://doi.org/10.1007/978-3-030-11726-9_28

50. Ostrom, Q.T., et al.: CBTRUS statistical report: primary brain and central nervous system tumors diagnosed in the United States in 2008–2012. Neuro-oncology **17**(Suppl4), iv1–iv62 (2015). https://doi.org/10.1093/neuonc/nov189

51. Parmar, C., Grossmann, P., Bussink, J., Lambin, P., Aerts, H.J.: Machine learning methods for quantitative radiomic biomarkers. Sci. Rep. **5**, 13087 (2015)

52. Prasanna, P., Patel, J., Partovi, S., Madabhushi, A., Tiwari, P.: Radiomic features from the peritumoral brain parenchyma on treatment-naïve multi-parametric MR imaging predict long versus short-term survival in glioblastoma multiforme: preliminary findings. Eur. Radiol. **27**(10), 4188–4197 (2017). https://doi.org/10.1007/s00330-016-4637-3

53. Rathore, S., et al.: Radiomic MRI signature reveals three distinct subtypes of glioblastoma with different clinical and molecular characteristics, offering prognostic value beyond IDH1. Sci. Rep. **8**(1), 5087 (2018). https://doi.org/10.1038/s41598-018-22739-2

54. Ronneberger, O., Fischer, P., Brox, T.: U-Net: Convolutional Networks for Biomedical Image Segmentation. CoRR abs/1505.0 (2015). http://arxiv.org/abs/1505.04597

55. Srivastava, N., Hinton, G., Krizhevsky, A., Sutskever, I., Salakhutdinov, R.: Dropout: a simple way to prevent neural networks from overfitting. J. Mach. Learn. Res. **15**, 1929–1958 (2014). http://jmlr.org/papers/v15/srivastava14a.html

56. Tiwari, P., et al.: Computer-extracted texture features to distinguish cerebral radionecrosis from recurrent brain tumors on multiparametric MRI: a feasibility study. AJNR. Am. J. Neuroradiol. **37**(12), 2231–2236 (2016). https://doi.org/10.3174/ajnr.A4931

57. Tompson, J., Goroshin, R., Jain, A., LeCun, Y., Bregler, C.: Efficient object localization using convolutional networks. CoRR abs/1411.4280 (2014). http://arxiv.org/abs/1411.4280

58. Tustison, N.J., et al.: N4ITK: improved N3 bias correction. IEEE Trans. Med. Imaging **29**(6), 1310–1320 (2010). https://doi.org/10.1109/TMI.2010.2046908. https://www.ncbi.nlm.nih.gov/pubmed/20378467

59. Wang, K., et al.: Individualized discrimination of tumor recurrence from radiation necrosis in glioma patients using an integrated radiomics-based model. Eur. J. Nucl. Med. Mol. Imag. **47**(6), 1400–1411 (2020). https://doi.org/10.1007/s00259-019-04604-0

60. Xi, Y.B., et al.: Radiomics signature: a potential biomarker for the prediction of MGMT promoter methylation in glioblastoma. J. Magn. Reson. Imaging JMRI **47**(5), 1380–1387 (2018). https://doi.org/10.1002/jmri.25860

61. Yan, H., et al.: IDH1 and IDH2 mutations in gliomas. N. Engl. J. Med. **360**(8), 765–773 (2009). https://doi.org/10.1056/NEJMoa0808710. pMID: 19228619

62. Yang, Y., et al.: Glioma grading on conventional MR images: a deep learning study with transfer learning. Frontiers Neurosci. **12**, 804 (2018). https://doi.org/10.3389/fnins.2018.00804. https://pubmed.ncbi.nlm.nih.gov/30498429, https://www.ncbi.nlm.nih.gov/pmc/articles/PMC6250094/

63. Zhang, B., et al.: Multimodal MRI features predict isocitrate dehydrogenase genotype in high-grade gliomas. Neuro-oncology **19**(1), 109–117 (2017)

64. Zhao, Y.-X., Zhang, Y.-M., Liu, C.-L.: Bag of tricks for 3D MRI brain tumor segmentation. In: Crimi, A., Bakas, S. (eds.) BrainLes 2019, Part I. LNCS, vol. 11992, pp. 210–220. Springer, Cham (2020). https://doi.org/10.1007/978-3-030-46640-4_20

65. Zhou, M., et al.: Radiomics in brain tumor: image assessment, quantitative feature descriptors, and machine-learning approaches. Am. J. Neuroradiol. **39**(2), 208–216 (2018)

# Machine Learning and Glioblastoma: Treatment Response Monitoring Biomarkers in 2021

Thomas C. Booth[1,2](✉) (iD), Bernice Akpinar[1], Andrei Roman[3,4], Haris Shuaib[5,6], Aysha Luis[1,7], Alysha Chelliah[1], Ayisha Al Busaidi[2], Ayesha Mirchandani[8], Burcu Alparslan[2,9], Nina Mansoor[10], Keyoumars Ashkan[11], Sebastien Ourselin[1], and Marc Modat[1]

[1] School of Biomedical Engineering and Imaging Sciences, King's College London, St. Thomas' Hospital, London SE1 7EH, UK
tombooth@doctors.org.uk
[2] Department of Neuroradiology, King's College Hospital NHS Foundation Trust, London SE5 9RS, UK
[3] Department of Radiology, Guy's and St. Thomas' NHS Foundation Trust, London SE1 7EH, UK
[4] The Oncology Institute "Prof. Dr. Ion Chiricuţă" Cluj-Napoca, Strada Republicii 34-36, 400015 Cluj-Napoca, Romania
[5] Department of Medical Physics, Guy's and St. Thomas' NHS Foundation Trust, London SE1 7EH, UK
[6] Institute of Psychiatry, Psychology and Neuroscience, King's College London, London SE5 8AF, UK
[7] Lysholm Department of Neuroradiology, National Hospital for Neurology and Neurosurgery, Queen Square, London, UK
[8] Cambridge University Hospitals NHS Foundation Trust, Hills Road, Cambridge CB2 0QQ, UK
[9] Department of Radiology, Kocaeli University, İzmit, Kocaeli, Turkey
[10] Department of Radiology, King's College Hospital NHS Foundation Trust, London SE5 9RS, UK
[11] Department of Neurosurgery, King's College Hospital NHS Foundation Trust, London SE5 9RS, UK

**Abstract.** The aim of the systematic review was to assess recently published studies on diagnostic test accuracy of glioblastoma treatment response monitoring biomarkers in adults, developed through machine learning (ML). Articles published 09/2018–09/2020 were searched for using MEDLINE, EMBASE, and the Cochrane Register. Included study participants were adult patients with high grade glioma who had undergone standard treatment (maximal resection, radiotherapy with concomitant and adjuvant temozolomide) and subsequently underwent follow-up imaging to determine treatment response status (specifically, distinguishing progression/recurrence from progression/recurrence mimics - the target condition). Risk of bias and applicability was assessed with QUADAS 2 methodology. Contingency tables were created for hold-out test sets and recall, specificity, precision, F1-score, balanced accuracy calculated. Fifteen studies were included with 1038 patients in training sets and 233 in test sets. To determine whether there was progression or a mimic, the reference standard combination of

© Springer Nature Switzerland AG 2020
S. M. Kia et al. (Eds.): MLCN 2020/RNO-AI 2020, LNCS 12449, pp. 212–228, 2020.
https://doi.org/10.1007/978-3-030-66843-3_21

follow-up imaging and histopathology at re-operation was applied in 67% (10/15) of studies. External hold-out test sets were used in 27% (4/15) to give ranges of diagnostic accuracy measures: recall = 0.70–1.00; specificity = 0.67–0.90; precision = 0.78–0.88; F1 score = 0.74–0.94; balanced accuracy = 0.74–0.83; AUC = 0.80–0.85. The small numbers of patient included in studies, the high risk of bias and concerns of applicability in the study designs (particularly in relation to the reference standard and patient selection due to confounding), and the low level of evidence, suggest that limited conclusions can be drawn from the data. There is likely good diagnostic performance of machine learning models that use MRI features to distinguish between progression and mimics. The diagnostic performance of ML using implicit features did not appear to be superior to ML using explicit features. There are a range of ML-based solutions poised to become treatment response monitoring biomarkers for glioblastoma. To achieve this, the development and validation of ML models require large, well-annotated datasets where the potential for confounding in the study design has been carefully considered. Therefore, multidisciplinary efforts and multicentre collaborations are necessary.

**Keywords:** Neuro-oncology · Machine learning · Diagnostic monitoring · Biomarkers

# 1   Introduction

Glioblastoma, the commonest primary malignant brain tumour has a median overall survival of 14.6 months despite standard of care treatment which consists of maximal debulking surgery and radiotherapy, with concomitant and adjuvant temozolomide [1]. After treatment, monitoring biomarkers are required to detect any change in the extent of disease or provide evidence of treatment response [2]. Magnetic resonance imaging (MRI) is particularly useful as it is non-invasive and captures the entire tumour volume and adjacent tissues and has been incorporated into recommendations for determining treatment response in trials [3, 4]. However, false-positive progressive disease (pseudoprogression) may occur within 6 months of chemoradiotherapy, typically determined by changes in contrast enhancement on $T_1$-weighted MRI images, representing non-specific blood brain barrier disruption [5, 6]. Because true progression is associated with worse clinical outcomes, a monitoring biomarker that reliably differentiates pseudoprogression and true progression would allow an early change in treatment strategy with termination of ineffective treatment and the option of implementing second-line therapies [7]. Because pseudoprogression is common occurring in approximately 10–30% of cases [8, 9], the neuro-oncologist is commonly presented with the difficult decision as to whether to continue adjuvant temozolomide or not. Distinguishing pseudoprogression and true progression has been an area of research with significant potential clinical impact for more than a decade.

Pseudoprogression is an early-delayed treatment effect, in contrast to the late-delayed radiation effect (or radiation necrosis) [10]. Whereas pseudoprogression occurs during or within 6 months of chemoradiotherapy, radiation necrosis occurs after this period, but with an incidence that is an order of magnitude less than the earlier pseudoprogression [11]. Nonetheless, in the same way that it would be beneficial to have a monitoring biomarker that discriminates true progression from pseudoprogression, an imaging technique that discriminates true progression from radiation necrosis would also be beneficial to allow the neuro-oncologist to know whether to implement second-line therapies or not.

Multiple studies have attempted to develop monitoring biomarkers to determine treatment response. Many incorporate machine learning (ML) as a central pillar of the process. A review of studies up to 2018 showed that those taking advantage of enhanced computational processing power to build neuro-oncology monitoring biomarker models, for example using convolutional neural networks (CNNs), have yet to show benefit compared to ML techniques using explicit feature engineering and less computationally expensive classifiers, for example using multivariate logistic regression [11]. It is also notable that studies applying ML to build neuro-oncology monitoring biomarker models have yet to show overall advantage over those using traditional statistical methods. The discipline of applying radiomic studies to neuro-oncology is expanding and evolving rapidly thereby motivating the need to appraise the latest evidence as the findings from 2018 may have been superseded.

Building on previous work [11, 12], the aim of the study is to systematically review recently published studies on diagnostic accuracy of treatment response monitoring biomarkers developed through ML for patients with glioblastoma.

## 2  Methods

This systematic review was prepared according to the Preferred Reporting Items for Systematic Reviews and Meta-Analysis: Diagnostic Test Accuracy (PRISMA-DTA) [13] and informed by Cochrane review methodology with emphasis on developing criteria for including studies [14], searching for studies [15], and assessing methodological quality [16].

### 2.1  Search Strategy and Selection Criteria

MEDLINE, EMBASE and the Cochrane Register were searched using a wide variety of search terms, both text words and database subject headings to describe each concept for original research articles published between September 2018 and September 2020 (Supplementary Table S1). The search was not limited by language. A search for pre-prints and other non-peer reviewed material was not carried out. Included study participants were adult patients with high grade glioma who had undergone standard treatment (maximal resection, radiotherapy with concomitant temozolomide and adjuvant temozolomide) and subsequently underwent follow up imaging in order to determine treatment response status (specifically, distinguishing progression/recurrence from progression/recurrence mimics - the target condition).

Studies were excluded if they were focused on paediatrics, pseudoresponse (bevacuzimab-related response mimic), had no ML algorithm used in feature extraction, selection, or classification/regression. The treatment response outcome for the index test was determined by the ML model. The treatment response outcome for the reference standard was determined either by subsequent follow-up imaging or histopathology at re-operation or a combination of both. The reference list of each acquired article for relevant studies was checked manually.

## 2.2  Data Extraction and Risk of Bias Assessment

Risk of bias and concerns regarding applicability for each study were assessed using QUADAS 2 methodology [17] and modified proformas. Data was extracted to determine whether the gliomas analysed were glioblastomas, anaplastic astrocytomas, anaplastic oligodendrogliomas or a combination of all (high-grade glioma); the ML technique used for the index test including cross validation techniques; information on training and hold-out test sets; the reference standard employed; MRI sequence type and non-imaging features used for analysis.

Reference standard follow-up imaging protocols were extracted and assessed for appropriateness. One assessment was the handling of confounding factors of second-line drug therapy, discontinuation of temozolomide and steroid use. The appropriateness of the treatment response term (target condition) used in the published study was also assessed. Evidence shows that contrast enhancing lesions enlarging for the first time due to pseudoprogression typically occur 0–6 months after chemoradiation and that contrast enhancing lesions enlarging for the first time due to radiation necrosis typically occur beyond 6 months after chemoradiation. If "post treatment related effects" (PTRE) was used as a treatment response term this incorporates both pseudoprogression and radiation necrosis [18, 19]. Any deviation in the use of the three terms defined here was recorded. Information on the duration of follow-up imaging after contrast enhancing lesions enlarged was also extracted and assessed. Optimal strategies to determine any PTRE or progression/recurrence included assigning the baseline scan after chemoradiation, excluding $T_2$-w image enlargement [20] and allowing 6-month follow up from the time of contrast enhancement with two follow up scans to mitigate capturing the upslope of PTRE again over a short interval [21, 22].

## 2.3  Data Synthesis and Statistical Analysis

Using the published study data, 2 × 2 contingency tables were created for hold-out test sets and the principal diagnostic accuracy measures of recall (sensitivity), specificity, precision (positive predictive value), F1-score and balanced accuracy calculated. Reported area under the receiver operating characteristic curve (AUC) values and confidence intervals from the published study were collated. In studies where principal diagnostic accuracy measures and the available published study raw data did not match, the discrepancy was highlighted - a calculation was made for all diagnostic accuracy measures based on those diagnostic accuracy measures that had been published, rather than available raw data. If there were both internal and external hold-out test sets, only the external test set principal diagnostic accuracy measures were calculated. In cases where there was no hold-out test set, "no test set" was recorded and a brief summary of the training set principal diagnostic accuracy measures was recorded. The unit of assessment was per-patient.

### 2.4 Subgroup Analysis: Prognostic Biomarkers to Predict Subsequent Treatment Response

Prognostic imaging biomarkers applied to glioblastoma typically predict overall survival from baseline images. However, we included a subgroup of studies whose method was to apply ML models to baseline images to serve as prognostic biomarkers to predict subsequent treatment response. The studies were analysed using the same methodology.

## 3 Results

### 3.1 Characteristics of Included Studies and Bias Assessment

Figure 1 shows that overall, 2017 citations met the search criteria, and the full text of 43 potentially eligible articles was scrutinized. Fifteen studies, of which 13 were retrospective, from September 2018 to September 2020 (including online first article publication prior to September 2018) were included. The total number of patients in training sets was 1038 and in test sets 233. The characteristics of 12 studies are shown in Table 1 and the characteristics of 3 studies applying ML models to baseline images (or genomic alterations) to serve as prognostic biomarkers to predict subsequent treatment response are shown in Table 2.

The risk of bias assessment was performed for each study and summarised (Supplementary Figure S1). All or most of the studies were in the highest category for risk of bias relating to the reference standard (15/15, 100%) and patient selection (13/15, 87%). A third to a quarter of studies relating to the index test (5/15, 33%) and flow and timing (4/15, 27%) were in the highest category for risk of bias or the risk was unclear, respectively. In terms of concerns regarding applicability, the results largely mirrored the risk of bias.

### 3.2 Treatment Response

Table 1 shows a variety of treatment response target conditions that individual studies were designed to predict. Approximately a quarter of studies assigned only the first 12 weeks after treatment as the time interval when pseudoprogression occurs - the full 6-month interval when there might be pseudoprogression was not incorporated (4/15, 27%). Approximately a quarter of studies predicted PTRE as a target condition (4/15, 27%). No study predicted radiation necrosis alone. Some studies analysed high grade glioma whereas the majority analysed only glioblastoma (13/15, 87%).

### 3.3 Follow-up Imaging and Histopathology at Re-Operation

Most studies used a combination of follow-up imaging and histopathology at re-operation to determine whether there was progression or a mimic (10/15, 67%). Some used one reference standard for one decision (progression) and another for the alternative decision (mimic) – this and other idiosyncratic rules caused a high risk of bias in some studies in terms of the reference standard and patient selection.

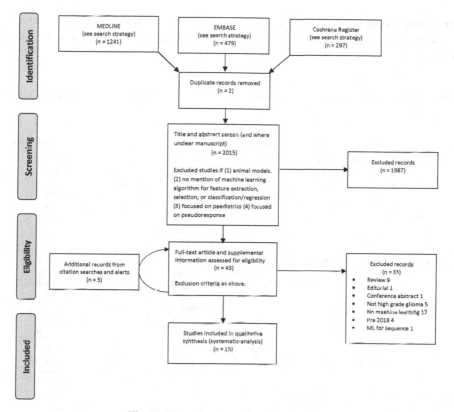

**Fig. 1.** Flow diagram of search strategy.

### 3.4 Features

Most studies only analysed imaging features alone (13/15, 87%). Three studies used implicit feature engineering based on convolutional neural networks (3/15, 20%).

### 3.5 Test Sets

One third of studies did not use hold-out test sets (5/15, 33%) with a high risk of bias for index test methodology. Four studies used external hold-out test sets (4/15, 27%). In these four studies the ranges of diagnostic accuracy measures were: recall = 0.70–1.00; specificity = 0.67–0.90; precision = 0.78–0.88; F1 score = 0.74–0.94; balanced accuracy = 0.74–0.83; AUC = 0.80–0.85.

### 3.6 Subgroup Analysis: Prognostic Biomarkers to Predict Subsequent Treatment Response

Two studies were prospective and both had a small samples size (both n = 10). One study used genomic alterations alone as features to predict the MRI treatment response. Diagnostic accuracy measures could not be determined because of study design. The unit of assessment in one study was per-lesion; another per-voxel; and another used a prognostic metric of 1-year progression free survival for the predicted treatment response groups. The studies are best considered as proof of concept.

**Table 1.** Studies applying machine learning to the development of high-grade glioma monitoring biomarkers

| Author(s) | Prediction | Reference | Dataset | Method | Features selected | Test set performance |
|---|---|---|---|---|---|---|
| [a]Kim JY et al. 2019 [27] | Early True progression vs. early pseudoprogression | Mixture of histopathology & imaging follow-up | Training = 61 Testing = 34 $T_1$, FLAIR, DWI, DSC | Retrospective 2 centres: 1 train & 1 external test set LASSO feature selection with 10-fold CV Linear generalized model | First-order, (volume/ shape), Second-order (texture), wavelet ADC & CBV parameters included | Recall 0.71 Specificity 0.90 Precision 0.83 F1 0.77 BA 0.81 AUC 0.85 (CI 0.71–0.99) |
| Kim JY et al. 2019 [28] | Early True progression vs. early pseudoprogression | Mixture of histopathology & imaging follow-up | Training = 59 Testing = 24 $T_1$ C, FLAIR, DTI, DSC | Retrospective 1 centre LASSO feature selection with 10-fold CV Linear generalized model | First-order, Second-order (texture), wavelet FA & CBV parameters included | Recall 0.80 Specificity 0.63 Precision 0.36 F1 0.50 BA 0.72 AUC 0.67 (0.40–0.94) |
| Bacchi S et al. 2019 [29] | True progression vs. PTRE (HGG) | Histopathology for progression & imaging follow-up for pseudoprogression | Training = 44 Testing = 11 $T_1$ C, FLAIR, DWI | Retrospective 1 centre 3D CNN & 5-fold CV | CNN FLAIR & DWI parameters | Recall 1.00 Specificity 0.60 Precision 0.75 F1 0.86 BA 0.80 AUC 0.80 |
| Elshafeey N et al. 2019 [30] | True progression vs. PTRE[b] | Histopathology | Training = 98 Testing = 7 DSC, DCE | Retrospective 3 centres MRMR feature selection. 1 test (i) decision tree algorithm C5.0 (ii) SVM including LOO & 10-fold CV | $K_{trans}$ & CBV parameters | Insufficient published data to determine diagnostic performance (CV training results available recall 0.91; specificity 0.88) |
| Verma G et al. 2019[x] [31] | True progression vs. Pseudoprogression | Mixture of histopathology & imaging follow-up | Training = 27 3D-EPSI | Retrospective 1 centre Multivariate logistic regression LOOCV | Cho/NAA & Cho/Cr | No test set (CV training results available recall 0.94; specificity 0.87) |
| Ismail M et al. 2018 [32] | True progression vs. Pseudoprogression | Mixture of histopathology & imaging follow-up | Training = 59 Testing = 46 $T_1$ C, $T_2$/ FLAIR | Retrospective 2 centres: 1 train & 1 external test set. SVM & 4-fold CV | Global & curvature shape | Recall 1.00 Spectficity 0.67 Precision 0.88 F1 0.94 BA 0.83 |

*(continued)*

## Table 1. *(continued)*

| Author(s) | Prediction | Reference | Dataset | Method | Features selected | Test set performance |
|---|---|---|---|---|---|---|
| [a] Bani-Sadr A et al. 2019 [33] | True progression vs. Pseudoprogression | Mixture of histopathology & imaging follow-up | Training = 52 Testing = 24 $T_1$ C, FLAIR MGMT promoter status | Retrospective 1 centre Random Forest. | Second-order features +/- MGMT promoter status | Recall 0.94 (0.71–1.00) Specificity 0.38 (0.09–0.76) Precision 0.36 F1 0.84 BA 0.66 AUC 0.77 |
| | | | | | | + non-MRI: Recall 0.80 (0.56–0.94) Specificity 0.75 (0.19–0.99) Precision 0.86 F1 0.83 BA 0.74 AUC 0.85 |
| Gao XY et al. 2020 [34] | True progression vs PTRE | Mixture of histopathology & imaging follow-up $T_1$ C, FLAIR | Training = 34 Testing = 15 $T_1$ C, FLAIR | Retrospective 2 centres SVM & 5-fold CV | $T_1$ C, FLAIR subtraction map parameters | Recall 1.00 Specificity 0.90 Precision 0.83 F1 0.91 BA 0.95 AUC 0.94 (0.78–1.00) |
| Jang B-S et al. 2018 [35] | True progression vs. Pseudoprogression | Mixture of histopathology & imaging follow-up | Training = 59 & testing = 19 $T_1$ C & clinical features & IDH/ MGMT Promoter status | Retrospective 2 centres 1 train & 1 external test set CNN LSTM & 10-fold CV (compared to Random Forest) | CNN $T_1$ C parameters +/– Age, Gender, MGMT status, IDH mutation, radiotherapy dose & fractions, follow up interval | Recall 0.64 Specificity 0.50 Precision 0.64 F1 0.63 BA 0.57 AUC 0.69 |
| | | | | | | + non-MRI: Recall 0.72 Specificity 0.75 Precision 0.80 F1 0.76 BA 0.74 AUC 0.83 |
| Li M et al. 2020 [36] | True progression vs PTRE[b] | Imaging follow-up | Training = 84 DTI | Retrospective 1 centre DCGAN & AlexNet CNN with SVM including 5 & 10 & 20-fold CV (compared to DCGAN, VGG, ResNet, and DenseNet) | CNN DTI | No test set (CV training results available recall 0.98; specificity 0.88; AUC 0.95) |

*(continued)*

**Table 1.** (*continued*)

| Author(s) | Prediction | Reference | Dataset | Method | Features selected | Test set performance |
|---|---|---|---|---|---|---|
| Akbari H et al. 2020 [37] | True progression vs. Pseudoprogression | Histopathology | Training = 40 Testing = 23 Testing = 20 $T_1$ C, $T_2$/ FLAIR, DTI, DSC, DCE | Retrospective 2 centres. 1 train & test. 1 external test set imagenet_vgg_f CNN SVM & LOOCV | First-order, second-order (texture). CBV, PH, TR, $T_1$ C, $T_2$/FLAIR parameters included | Recall 0.70 Specificity 0.80 Precision 0.78 F1 0.74 BA 0.75 AUC 0.80 |
| Li X et al. 2018 [38] | Early True progression vs. early pseudoprogression (HGG) | Mixture of histopathology & imaging follow-up | Training = 362 $T_1$ C, $T_2$, multi-voxel & single voxel 1H-MRS, ASL | Gabor dictionary & sparse representation classifier (SRC) | sparse representations | No test set (CV training results available recall 0.97; specificity 0.83) |

PTRE = post treatment related effects

HGG = high grade glioma

Magnetic resonance imaging sequences: $T_1$ C = post contrast $T_1$-weighted; $T_2 = T_2$-weighted; FLAIR = fluid-attenuated inversion recovery; DWI = diffusion-weighted imaging; DCE = dynamic contrast-enhanced; DSC = dynamic susceptibility-weighted; DTI = diffusor tensor imaging; ASL = arterial spin labelling.

Magnetic resonance imaging parameters: CBV = cerebral blood volume; PH = peak height; ADC = apparent diffusion coefficient; FA = fractional anisotropy; TR = trace (DTI); $K_{trans}$ = volume transfer constant.

1H-MRS = 1H-magnetic resonance spectroscopy; 3D-EPSI = 3D echo planar spectroscopic imaging.

Magnetic resonance spectroscopy parameters: Cho = choline; NAA = N-acetyl aspartate; Cr = creatine.

Molecular markers: MGMT = O6-methylguanine-DNA methyltransferase; IDH = isocitrate dehydrogenase.

Machine learning techniques: CNN = convolutional neural network; SVM = support vector machine; LASSO = least absolute shrinkage and selection operator; mRMR = minimum redundancy and maximum relevance; CV = cross validation; LOOCV = leave-one-out cross validation; LSTM = long short-term memory; DCGAN = deep convolutional generative adversarial network; DC-AL GAN = DCGAN with AlexNet; VGG = Visual Geometry Group (algorithm).

Statistical measures: AUC = area under the receiver operator characteristic curve; BA = balanced accuracy; CI = confidence intervals.

[a] some data appears mathematically discrepant within publication

[b] unclear or discrepant information (e.g. time after chemoradiotherapy)

# 4 Discussion

## 4.1 Summary of Findings

There is only low level evidence [23] available to determine the diagnostic accuracy of glioblastoma treatment response monitoring biomarkers in adults developed through ML. The available evidence is at high risk of bias and there are concerns regarding applicability, particularly in determining treatment response status using the reference standards of histopathology at re-operation or follow-up imaging. There are similar and

**Table 2.** Studies applying machine learning models to baseline images (or genomic alterations) to serve as prognostic biomarkers to predict subsequent treatment response

| Author(s) | Prediction | Reference | Dataset | Method | Features selected | Test set performance |
|---|---|---|---|---|---|---|
| Wang S et al. 2019 [39] | True progression vs. Pseudoprogression (immunotherapy for EGFRvIII mutation) Baseline prediction | Histopathology | Model testing set = 10 DTI, DSC & 3D-EPSI | Prospective 1 centre Multivariate logistic regression | CL, CBV, FA parameters | Insufficient published data to determine diagnostic performance (per lesion results available recall = 0.86 specificity = 0.60) |
| Yang K et al. 2019 [40] | True progression vs. not (stable disease, partial & complete response & pseudoprogression) Baseline prediction | Imaging follow-up | Training = 49 Genomic alterations | 1 centre Analysis including Gene Set Enrichment Analysis (GSEA) | Genomic alterations including CDKN2A & EGFR mutations | No test set (Insufficient published data to determine diagnostic performance from training dataset 1-year PFS for responder 45% & non-responder 0%) |
| Lundemann M et al. 2019 [41] | Early recurrence vs. not (voxel-wise) Baseline prediction | Mixture of histopathology & imaging follow-up | Training = 10 18F-FET PET/CT 18F-FDG PET/MRI $T_1$ C, $T_2$/FLAIR, DTI, DCE | Prospective 1 centre Multivariate logistic regression LOOCV | FET, FDG, MD, FA, F, Vb, Ve, Ki, & MTT parameters | No test set (Insufficient published data to determine diagnostic performance from training dataset. Voxel-wise recurrence probability AUC 0.77) |

EGFR = Epidermal growth factor receptor; EGFRvIII = EGFR variant III; CDKN2A = cyclin-dependent kinase Inhibitor 2A.

Magnetic resonance imaging sequences: $T_1$ C = post contrast $T_1$-weighted; $T_2$ = $T_2$-weighted; FLAIR = fluid-attenuated inversion recovery; DSC = dynamic susceptibility-weighted; DTI = diffusor tensor imaging; DCE = dynamic contrast-enhanced.

Additional imaging techniques: 3D-EPSI = 3D echo planar spectroscopic imaging; 18F-FET = [18F]-fluoroethyl-L-tyrosine; 18F-FDG = [18F]-fluorodeoxyglucose; PET/CT = positron emission tomography and computed tomography; PET/MRI = positron emission tomography and magnetic resonance imaging.

Magnetic resonance imaging parameters: CBV = cerebral blood volume; FA = fractional anisotropy; MD = mean diffusivity; F = blood flow; Vb = vascular blood volume; Ve = extra-vascular, extra-cellular blood volume; Ki = vascular permeability; MTT = mean transit time; CL = linear anisotropy.

LOOCV = leave-one-out cross validation.

AUC = area under the receiver operator characteristic curve.

PFS = progression free survival.

related concerns regarding study patient selection. One third of studies did not use hold-out test sets. Most studies used classic ML approaches with radiomic features; less than a quarter of studies used deep learning methodology.

## 4.2 Limitations

### 4.2.1 Studies Assessed

The reference standards used led to a high risk of bias and concerns regarding applicability in all studies. Other than in the subgroup of prognostic biomarker studies, all studies were retrospective which increases the risk of confounding. Confounding factors, related to histopathological and imaging follow up reference standards, were second-line drug therapy and discontinuation of temozolomide– all of which were rarely accounted for. Similarly, steroid use was rarely accounted for and is a confounding factor for the imaging follow up reference standard. Some authors stated they followed RANO guidelines [4] which would overcome some of these limitations such as the use of steroids which is carefully integrated with the imaging assessment. However, a limitation in using RANO guidelines is that in some scenarios the upslope of any PTRE may be observed for second time over a short interval confounding assessment [21, 22].

Patient selection was also problematic and is related to confounding – for example patients on second-line drug therapy should have been excluded from imaging follow-up response assessment.

One third of studies did not use hold-out test sets which are expected in ML studies for diagnostic accuracy assessment. Four studies, however, used external hold-out tests which is optimal practice.

### 4.2.2 Review Process

Publication bias might have influenced the diagnostic accuracy of the monitoring biomarkers included in this review. Another limitation is that imaging reference standards such as RANO trial guidelines [4], and subsequent developments thereof [20], are themselves confounded and, when used, are rarely applied correctly [24]. In addition to the example described above regarding the upslope of PTRE [21, 22], another limitation is not acknowledging that pseudoprogression occurs over a 6 month interval rather than a 3 month interval (although it is acknowledged that even 6 months is an arbitrary cut-off) [21]. For the purposes of the systematic review, study design would require imaging follow up of sufficient duration to take these issues into account. A limitation of this or other systematic reviews is therefore that it is highly challenging for studies to be designed with sufficient nuance to be at low risk of bias in relation to the reference standard. A further limitation of this review is that whilst histopathology at re-operation is not an entirely reliable reference standard [25], it was pragmatically chosen as acceptable in the absence of more reliable available reference standards at re-operation.

### 4.3  Interpretation of the Results in the Context of Other Evidence

There is good diagnostic performance of machine learning models that use MRI features to distinguish between progressive disease and mimics. As in the previous review, the diagnostic performance of ML using implicit features was not superior to ML using explicit features. However, the small numbers of patient included in studies, the high risk of bias and concerns of applicability in the study designs, and the low level of evidence given that the monitoring biomarker studies are retrospective, suggest that limited conclusions can be drawn from the data.

### 4.4  Implications for Future Research and Clinical Practice

The results show that glioblastoma treatment response monitoring biomarkers developed through ML are promising but are at an early phase of development and are not ready to be incorporated into clinical practice. All studies would benefit from improvements in the methodology highlighted above. Future studies would benefit from analytical validation using external hold-out tests as exemplified by several studies in the current review. Future studies would also benefit from larger datasets to reduce overfitting.

## 5  Conclusion

There are a range of ML-based solutions poised to become treatment response monitoring biomarkers for glioblastoma suitable for the clinic. To achieve this, the development and validation of ML models require large, well-annotated datasets where the potential for confounding in the study design has been carefully considered. Therefore, multidisciplinary efforts and multicentre collaborations are necessary [26].

**Acknowledgements.** This work was supported by the Wellcome/EPSRC Centre for Medical Engineering [WT 203148/Z/16/Z], The Royal College of Radiologists and King's College Hospital Research and Innovation.

# Appendix

**Supplementary Table S1.** MEDLINE, EMBASE and Cochrane Register search strategies. Recommendations for a sensitive search with low precision; with subject headings with exploded terms; and with no language restrictions, were followed [15].

MEDLINE (OVID). PubMed was included.
The search strategy for Title/Abstract terms used a combination of subject headings (MeSH terms) and keywords:
Database: Ovid MEDLINE(R) ALL <1946 to September 11, 2020>
Search Strategy:
--------------------------------------------------------------------------------

1 exp Glioblastoma/ (25451)
2 high grade glioma.mp. (2986)
3 pseudoprogression.mp. (633)
4 radiomics.mp. (2262)
5 exp Artificial Intelligence/ or exp Machine Learning/ or exp Neural Networks, Computer/ (99521)
6 exp Deep Learning/ (2761)
7 monitoring biomarker.mp. (71)
8 treatment response.mp. (29303)
9 imaging.mp. (2039219)
10 exp Magnetic Resonance Imaging/ or MRI.mp. (544944)
11 pet.mp. (103253)
12 exp Positron-Emission Tomography/ (61544)
13 9 or 10 or 11 or 12 (2117006)
14 1 or 2 or 3 (28462)
15 4 or 5 or 6 or 7 or 8 (130625)
16 13 and 14 and 15 (321)
17 limit 16 to last 2 years (130)
18 13 and 14 (6464)
19 limit 18 to last 2 years (1241)
***************************
strategy 17 was insensitive so strategy 19 was employed for final search

(*continued*)

(*continued*)

EMBASE (OVID).
Subject headings and keywords:
Database: Embase <1974 to 2020 Week 37>
Search Strategy:

--------------------------------------------------------------------------

1 exp glioblastoma/ (68063)
2 high grade glioma.mp. (5411)
3 pseudoprogression.mp. (1225)
4 exp radiomics/ (1271)
5 exp machine learning/ or exp artificial intelligence/ (227658)
6 exp deep learning/ (9382)
7 monitoring biomarker.mp. (108)
8 exp treatment response/ (265476)
9 exp multiparametric magnetic resonance imaging/ or exp imaging/ or exp nuclear magnetic resonance imaging/ (1112723)
10 magnetic resonance imaging.mp. (925155)
11 MRI.mp. (445714)
12 PET.mp. or exp positron emission tomography/ (249021)
13 1 or 2 or 3 (72158)
14 4 or 5 or 6 or 7 or 8 (492158)
15 9 or 10 or 11 or 12 (1331815)
16 13 and 15 (14315)
17 limit 16 to last 2 years (3209)
**18 limit 17 to exclude medline journals (479)**
*****************************

strategy 18 was employed for final search to prevent duplication from MEDLINE

Cochrane Register.
Epistemonikos review database included, protocols included, CENTRAL (Cochrane central register of controlled trials included which includes https://www.ebscohost.com/nursing/products/cinahl-databases, https://clinicaltrials.gov, https://www.who.int/ictrp/en/).
Subject headings and keywords:
Date Run: 13/09/2020 15:52:52
ID Search Hits
#1 MeSH descriptor: [Glioblastoma] explode all trees 628
#2 high grade glioma 524
#3 pseudoprogression 69
#4 imaging68926
#5 MeSH descriptor: [Magnetic Resonance Imaging] explode all trees 7660
#6 MRI 23753
#7 PET 6912
#8 MeSH descriptor: [Positron-Emission Tomography] explode all trees 988
#9 {OR #1-#3}1167
#10 {OR #4-#8} 79474
**#11 {AND #9-#10} 297**
strategy 11 was employed for final search

(*continued*)

(*continued*)

Health Technology Assessment. https://database.inahta.org/
Subject headings and keywords:
(("Glioblastoma"[mh]) OR (high grade glioma) OR (pseudoprogression))

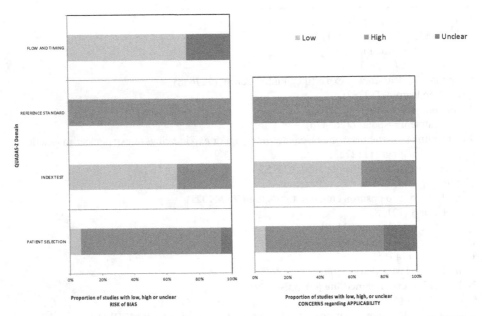

**Supplementary Figure S1.** Bar chart showing risk of bias and concerns of applicability assessment

# References

1. Stupp, R., et al.: Radiotherapy plus concomitant and adjuvant temozolomide for glioblastoma. N. Engl. J. Med. **352**, 987–996 (2005). https://doi.org/10.1056/NEJMoa043330
2. FDA-NIH Biomarker Working Group: BEST (Biomarkers, EndpointS, and other Tools) Resource. Food and Drug Administration (US), Silver Spring. Co-published by National Institutes of Health (US), Bethesda (2016)
3. MacDonald, D., Cascino, T.L., Schold, S.C., Cairncross, J.G.: Response criteria for phase II studies of supratentorial malignant glioma. J. Clin. Oncol. **8**, 1277–1280 (2010). https://doi.org/10.1200/jco.1990.8.7.1277
4. Wen, P.Y., Macdonald, D.R., Reardon, D.A., Cloughesy, T.F., Sorensen, A.G., Galanis, E.: Updated response assessment criteria for high-grade gliomas: response assessment in neuro-oncology working group. J. Clin. Oncol. **28**, 1963–1972 (2010). https://doi.org/10.1200/JCO.2009.26.3541
5. Booth, T.C., et al.: Neuro-oncology single-photon emission CT: a current overview. Neurographics **01**, 108–120 (2011)
6. Chamberlain, M.C., Glantz, M.J., Chalmers, L., Van Horn, A., Sloan, A.E.: Early necrosis following concurrent Temodar and radiotherapy in patients with glioblastoma. J. Neurooncol. **82**, 81–83 (2007). https://doi.org/10.1007/s11060-006-9241-y

7. Dhermain, F.G., et al.: Advanced MRI and PET imaging for assessment of treatment response in patients with gliomas. Lancet Neurol. **9**, 906–920 (2010). https://doi.org/10.1016/S1474-4422(10)70181-2

8. Brandsma, D., et al.: Clinical features, mechanisms, and management of pseudoprogression in malignant gliomas. Lancet Oncol. **9**, 453–461 (2008)

9. Radbruch, A., et al.: Pseudoprogression in patients with glioblastoma: clinical relevance despite low incidence. Neuro Oncol. **17**, 151–159 (2015)

10. Verma, N., et al.: Differentiating tumor recurrence from treatment necrosis: a review of neuro-oncologic imaging strategies. Neuro Oncol. **15**, 515–534 (2013)

11. Booth, T.C., Williams, M., Luis, A., Cardoso, J., Ashkan, K., Shuaib, H.: Machine learning and glioma imaging biomarkers. Clin. Radiol. **75**, 20–32 (2020). https://doi.org/10.1016/j.crad.2019.07.001

12. Booth, T.C.: An update on machine learning in neuro-oncology diagnostics. In: Crimi, A., Bakas, S., Kuijf, H., Keyvan, F., Reyes, M., van Walsum, T. (eds.) BrainLes 2018. LNCS, vol. 11383, pp. 37–44. Springer, Cham (2019). https://doi.org/10.1007/978-3-030-11723-8_4

13. McInnes, M.D.F., Moher, D., Thombs, B.D., McGrath, T.A., Bossuyt, P.M., The PRISMA-DTA Group: Preferred reporting items for a systematic review and meta-analysis of diagnostic test accuracy studies: the PRISMA-DTA statement. JAMA **319**, 388–396 (2018). https://doi.org/10.1001/jama.2017.19163

14. Bossuyt, P.M., Leeflang, M.M.: Chapter 6: Developing criteria for including studies. In: Cochrane Handbook for Systematic Reviews of Diagnostic Test Accuracy Version 0.4. The Cochrane Collaboration (2008)

15. de Vet, H.C.W., Eisinga, A., Riphagen, I.I., Aertgeerts, B., Pewsner, D.: Chapter 7: Searching for studies. In: Cochrane Handbook for Systematic Reviews of Diagnostic Test Accuracy Version 0.4. The Cochrane Collaboration (2008)

16. Reitsma, J.B., Rutjes, A.W.S., Whiting, P., Vlassov, V.V., Leeflang, M.M.G., Deeks, J.J.: Chapter 9: Assessing methodological quality. In: Deeks, J.J., Bossuyt, P.M., Gatsonis, C. (eds.) Cochrane Handbook for Systematic Reviews of Diagnostic Test Accuracy Version 1.0.0. The Cochrane Collaboration (2009). http://srdta.cochrane/org/

17. Whiting, P.F., et al.: QUADAS-2: a revised tool for the quality assessment of diagnostic accuracy studies. Ann. Intern. Med. **155**, 529–536 (2011)

18. Booth, T.C., et al.: Re: "Tumour progression or pseudoprogression? A review of post-treatment radiological appearances of glioblastoma". Clin. Radiol. **5**, 495–496 (2016)

19. Booth, T.C., et al.: Comment on "The role of imaging in the management of progressive glioblastoma. A systematic review and evidence-based clinical practice guideline". J. Neurooncol. **121**, 423–424 (2015)

20. Ellingson, B.M., Wen, P.Y., Cloughesy, T.F.: Modified criteria for radiographic response assessment in glioblastoma clinical trials. Neurotherapeutics **14**(2), 307–320 (2017). https://doi.org/10.1007/s13311-016-0507-6

21. Booth, T.C., et al.: Analysis of heterogeneity in T2-weighted MR images can differentiate pseudoprogression from progression in glioblastoma. PLoS ONE **12**, 0176528 (2017). https://doi.org/10.1371/journal.pone.0176528

22. Gahramanov, S., et al.: Pseudoprogression of glioblastoma after chemo- and radiation therapy: diagnosis by using dynamic susceptibility-weighted contrast-enhanced perfusion MR imaging with ferumoxytol versus gadoteridol and correlation with survival. Radiology **266**, 842–852 (2013)

23. Howick, J., et al.: The Oxford 2011 levels of evidence. Oxford Centre for Evidence-Based Medicine, Oxford (2016). http://www.cebm.net/index.aspx?o=5653

24. Buwanabala, J., et al.: The (mis)use of imaging criteria in the assessment of glioblastoma treatment response. American Society of Neuroradiology, Boston. Scientific Poster 2616 (2019)

25. Holdhoff, M., et al.: The consistency of neuropathological diagnoses in patients undergoing surgery for suspected recurrence of glioblastoma. J. Neurooncol. **141**(2), 347–354 (2018). https://doi.org/10.1007/s11060-018-03037-3. pmid:30414096

26. Davatzikos, C., et al.: AI-based prognostic imaging biomarkers for precision neurooncology: the ReSPOND consortium. Neuro Oncol. **22**, 886–888 (2020). https://doi.org/10.1093/neuonc/noaa045

27. Kim, J.Y., et al.: Incorporating diffusion- and perfusion-weighted MRI into a radiomics model improves diagnostic performance for pseudoprogression in glioblastoma patients. Neuro-oncology **21**, 404–414 (2019)

28. Kim, J.Y., Yoon, M.J., Park, J.E., Choi, E.J., Lee, J., Kim, H.S.: Radiomics in peritumoral non-enhancing regions: fractional anisotropy and cerebral blood volume improve prediction of local progression and overall survival in patients with glioblastoma. Neuroradiology **61**(11), 1261–1272 (2019). https://doi.org/10.1007/s00234-019-02255-4

29. Bacchi, S., et al.: Deep learning in the detection of high-grade glioma recurrence using multiple MRI sequences: a pilot study. J. Clin. Neurosci. **70**, 11–13 (2019)

30. Elshafeey, N., et al.: Multicenter study demonstrates radiomic features derived from magnetic resonance perfusion images identify pseudoprogression in glioblastoma. Nat. Commun. **10**, 3170 (2019)

31. Verma, G., et al.: Three-dimensional echo planar spectroscopic imaging for differentiation of true progression from pseudoprogression in patients with glioblastoma. NMR Biomed. **32**, 4042 (2019)

32. Ismail, M., et al.: Shape features of the lesion habitat to differentiate brain tumor progression from pseudoprogression on routine multiparametric MRI: a multisite study. AJNR Am. J. Neuroradiol. **39**, 2187–2193 (2018)

33. Bani-Sadr, A., et al.: Conventional MRI radiomics in patients with suspected early- or pseudo-progression. Neurooncol. Adv. **1**, 1–9 (2019)

34. Gao, X.Y., et al.: Differentiation of treatment-related effects from glioma recurrence using machine learning classifiers based upon pre-and post-contrast T1WI and T2 FLAIR subtraction features: a two-center study. Cancer Manag. Res. **12**, 3191–3201 (2020)

35. Jang, B.S., Jeon, S.H., Kim, I.H., Kim, I.A.: Prediction of pseudoprogression versus progression using machine learning algorithm in glioblastoma. Sci. Rep. **8**, 12516 (2018)

36. Li, M., Tang, H., Chan, M.D., Zhou, X., Qian, X.: DC-AL GAN: pseudoprogression and true tumor progression of glioblastoma multiform image classification based on DCGAN and AlexNet. Med. Phys. **47**, 1139–1150 (2020)

37. Akbari, H., et al.: Histopathology- validated machine learning radiographic biomarker for noninvasive discrimination between true progression and pseudo-progression in glioblastoma. Cancer **0**, 1–12 (2020). https://doi.org/10.1002/cncr.32790

38. Li, X., Xu, G., Cao, Q., Zou, W., Xu, Y., Cong, P.: Identification of glioma pseudoprogression based on gabor dictionary and sparse representation model. NeuroQuantology **16**, 43–51 (2018). https://doi.org/10.14704/nq.2018.16.1.1178

39. Wang, S., et al.: Multiparametric magnetic resonance imaging in the assessment of anti-EGFRvIII chimeric antigen receptor T cell therapy in patients with recurrent glioblastoma. Br. J. Cancer **120**, 54–56 (2019)

40. Yang, K., et al.: Cancer genetic markers according to radiotherapeutic response in patients with primary glioblastoma - radiogenomic approach for precision medicine. Radiother. Oncol. **131**, 66–74 (2019)

41. Lundemann, M., et al.: Feasibility of multi-parametric PET and MRI for prediction of tumour recurrence in patients with glioblastoma. Eur. J. Nucl. Med. Mol. Imaging **46**(3), 603–613 (2018). https://doi.org/10.1007/s00259-018-4180-3

# Radiogenomics of Glioblastoma: Identification of Radiomics Associated with Molecular Subtypes

Navodini Wijethilake[1]([✉]), Mobarakol Islam[2], Dulani Meedeniya[1], Charith Chitraranjan[1], Indika Perera[1], and Hongliang Ren[2]

[1] Department of Computer Science Engineering, University of Moratuwa, Moratuwa, Sri Lanka
`navodiniw@cse.mrt.ac.lk`
[2] Department of Biomedical Engineering, National University of Singapore, Seremban, Singapore

**Abstract.** Glioblastoma is the most malignant type of central nervous system tumor with GBM subtypes cleaved based on molecular level gene alterations. These alterations are also happened to affect the histology. Thus, it can cause visible changes in images, such as enhancement and edema development. In this study, we extract intensity, volume, and texture features from the tumor subregions to identify the correlations with gene expression features and overall survival. Consequently, we utilize the radiomics to find associations with the subtypes of glioblastoma. Accordingly, the fractal dimensions of the whole tumor, tumor core, and necrosis regions show a significant difference between the Proneural, Classical and Mesenchymal subtypes. Additionally, the subtypes of GBM are predicted with an average accuracy of 79% utilizing radiomics and accuracy over 90% utilizing gene expression profiles.

**Keywords:** Glioblastoma · Gene expression · Survival · Subtype

## 1 Introduction

Glioblastoma (GBM) is a common malignant tumor that occurs mostly in adults, >50 years of age and accounts for 14.7% of primary brain and central nervous system tumors. GBM has the highest incidence rate of 3.21 per 100000 population, concerning other malignant tumors. Despite the treatment followed by the diagnosis, GBM patients have poor survival, with a median survival of one year and a five-year survival rate of 5% according to a study done from 2010 to 2015 [14]. This aggressive behavior of GBM is mainly due to the molecular level heterogeneity and complexity. Thus, identifying the prognostic genetic biomarkers is essential to decide the appropriate therapies and the treatment required for each GBM patient.

Accordingly, many research groups have focused on identifying genetic biomarkers through gene expression profiling, copy number alterations, mutation

© Springer Nature Switzerland AG 2020
S. M. Kia et al. (Eds.): MLCN 2020/RNO-AI 2020, LNCS 12449, pp. 229–239, 2020.
https://doi.org/10.1007/978-3-030-66843-3_22

studies. Thus, gene mutations such as Tumor Protein p53 (TP53), Retinoblastoma protein (RB1), Neurofibromin (NF1), and Telomerase Reverse Transcriptase (TERT) have shown associations with GBM [20]. Moreover, Isocitrate dehydrogenase 1 (IDH1) mutations are common in secondary GBM, developing from a low-grade glioma. Other than that, overexpression of Epidermal growth factor receptor (EGFR), Phosphatase and Tensin homolog (PTEN), Platelet-derived growth factor receptors (PDGFR) genes found to have had an impact on GBM prognosis [3]. Consequently, Verhaak et al. [20] have identified 4 GBM subtypes, named Proneural, Neural, Mesenchymal, and Classical, based on gene expression profiles and other genetic alterations.

A classical subtype can be recognized with the overexpression of EGFR and the loss of chromosome 10. In contrast, Mesenchymal subtype is mostly related to the expression of the NF1 gene and PTEN deletions. The patterns in these two subtypes are commonly seen in astrocytes. The proneural subtype is recognizable with the alterations of PDGFR, IDH1, and TP53 in oligodendrocytes, whereas the expressions in neurons characterize the Neural subtype. Nevertheless, the Proneural subtype has a better prognosis for the other subtypes [2,3]. The Neural subtype existence has been revisited and removed as it has emerged through contamination with the non-tumor cells [18,21]. The specific treatments are given for each subtype by the clinicians, and therefore, it is important to identify the subtypes at first. However, due to the costs and the invasive approach, gene expression profiling analysis is not routinely performed on GBM patients and is an existing challenge.

Alternatively, Magnetic Resonance Imaging (MRI) is a widely used noninvasive imaging tool to identify gliomas. With different types of MRI modalities, such as T1, T1 Contrast, T2, and Flair (T2 fluid-attenuated inversion recovery), underlying tissues of gliomas can be visualized for diagnosis [3]. With the advancements in the field of artificial intelligence, deep learning-based tools have been developed for segmenting the gliomas using MRI. This further has extended the area of radiomics through extracting features for diagnosing, predicting survival, etc [9]. Moreover, the field of radiogenomics was emerged by analyzing the associations between genetic biomarkers and radiomics. Nonetheless, to address the current limitations in identifying the subtypes, imaging biomarkers can be in-cooperated. As we mentioned above, there are limitations exploiting gene expression profiling routinely, due to invasive behavior and the cost. Therefore, this motivated our study to predict the subtype, with noninvasive biomarkers obtained from MRI imaging, commonly used clinical practice.

In several studies related to various cancer types, imaging features are utilized to determine the underlying molecular subtype [12,19]. Nonetheless, different statistical analyses are performed to identify imaging biomarkers related to each subtype of GBM patients separately [13]. Prior studies have also focused on predicting the subtypes as a 4 class classification [11]. The novelty of our research is, despite imaging biomarkers related to a single subtype, we identify imaging biomarkers that are different between the three main GBM subtypes. Additionally, we classify existing subtypes, Proneural, Mesenchymal, and Classical, separately as a binary classification task with accuracy over 80%, since the Neural subtype does not exist anymore.

In this work, we use the TCGA-GBM dataset with both MRI and gene expression data for analyzing the associations with the survival of each feature. The main contribution of our study is to identify radiomic features that are significantly different between the subtypes of GBM patients. Moreover, we utilize those features to predict the existing subtypes, Proneural, Mesenchymal, and Classical separately. We perform cross-validation to verify our results.

## 2 Methods

### 2.1 Dataset

The radiogenomic analysis is performed on The Cancer Genome Atlas (TCGA)[1] GBM dataset. We have obtained 202 cases used in the study [20] with the subtype of each instance, including the gene expression profiles. Out of 202, 59 cases have the corresponding MRI data, with T1 contrast and flair modalities. MRI images are skull stripped initially with Matlab. Then, registered to $155 \times 155 \times 240$ 3D image volume with the origin at $(0, -239, 0)$, making the metadata similar to BraTS 2019 dataset, with open-source 3D slicer software [15].

The gene expression profiles of 59 patients consist of 1740 genes for each patient. Moreover, for these patients, subtypes class (Classical, Mesenchymal, Proneural, or Neural) and the overall survival from the diagnosis are also filtered.

For the fully automated segmentation with Deep Learning, Brats 2019 dataset is used for training the segmentation model using T1 Contrast and Flair modalities. The segmentation includes three sub-regions, necrosis, enhancing tumor region and edema region, annotated manually in the BraTS dataset.

### 2.2 Segmentation

We utilize the 3D UNet architecture [10], with 3D attention module [17], that we proposed for BraTS challenge 2019. The 3D spatial and channel squeeze and excitation modules learn more important and meaningful feature maps through spatial and channel re-calibration. In this module, the channel wise dependencies are captured through $1 \times 1 \times C$ convolution of the feature map (with the dimensions of $H \times W \times C$), and the spatial feature correlation are captured through max-pooling the feature map. This boosts the quality of segmentation prediction, minimally changing the model complexity.

$155 \times 155 \times 240$ 3D MRI volume is given as the input of the segmentation model, to obtain the segmentation feature map. The model is trained with the BraTS manually annotated feature maps. The segmentation of the TCGA dataset is achieved with the trained model giving the FLAIR and T1 Contrast modalities as input.

---

[1] https://www.cancer.gov/tcga.

## 2.3    Feature Extraction

The segmentation of the GBM is followed by the imaging feature extraction from the tumor's relevant sub-regions. Intensity, Geometric and volume features are extracted from the segmented sub-regions of the tumor.

The intensity and texture-based features, kurtosis, the histogram of oriented gradients, entropy, mean intensity, are extracted for the necrosis, enhancement, tumor core (necrosis + enhancement region), whole tumor (tumor core + edema) regions. These histogram features are extracted from both T1 contrast and Flair images, since both of them, magnify different sub-regions of the tumor. For example, T1 contrast provides a clear picture of the enhancement region.

The extracted geometric features include the major axis length, minor axis length, centroid coordinates, Inertia tensor, Eigenvalues of the inertia tensor. Moreover, the volume features are extracted with the bounding box and with the factual dimensions. These features are extracted for the necrosis, tumor core, and the whole tumor regions. Totally 122 imaging features are extracted from the MRI images.

## 2.4    Statistical Analysis

Our initial experiments are to find the associations between genomics and radiomics. Thus, we have utilized the Pearson's correlation to find the association among imaging features and the gene expression levels of GBM patients. Further, we use both feature types, radiomics and genomics, separately to find the correlation with the overall survival of glioma patients. For that also, Pearson's correlation is used. Nevertheless, univariate and multivariate cox proportional hazard analysis is performed to identify the radiogenomic features associated with survival.

Next, we have focused on identifying the imaging biomarkers associated with the molecular subtypes of GBM. First, to clarify the normality of the radiomic features, the Kolmogorov-Smirnov test [13] is utilized, and the features with $p <$ 0.05 are identified as features with a normal distribution. Accordingly, we have performed Kruskal Wallis non-parametric test [13] to identify the significantly different imaging biomarkers between the four subtypes, with the features that are not normally distributed. Additionally, to identify the subtype pairs that are significantly different Wilcoxon test [5] is applied between each pair. The Bonferroni correction is performed on the multiple comparison tests to avoid the familywise error rate. For visualization of the significance and the feature distribution, GraphPad prism software is used.

## 2.5    Subtype Predictive Model

We have used the significantly different features between subtypes to predict the subtype using Machine Learning algorithms. All the features are standard normalized before training the learning algorithm. Linear Kernel function of Support Vector Machine (linear-SVM), radial basis kernel function of Support

Vector Machine (r-SVM), polynomial kernel function of Support Vector Machine (p-SVM), Random Forest Classification (RFC), Decision Tree (DT) and Logistic Regression (LR) are utilized for predicting Classical, Mesenchymal and Proneural subtypes separately with the imaging biomarkers. The parameters used in the above learning models are given in the Table 1. This is performed as a 2 class classification (subtype/non-subtype).

Nevertheless, linear-SVM, r-SVM, p-SVM, DT and RFC are used to predict the subtypes with the differentially expressed genes between the subtypes. This is performed as a 4 class classification (Mesenchymal, Proneural, Neural, and Classical).

Further, four-fold cross-validation is performed to validate the performance of all the subtype predictions. All the experiments are performed with e1071 R package [4] and WEKA software [8].

**Table 1.** Parameters of the subtype prediction learning models

| ML tool | Parameters |
|---------|-----------|
| l-SVM | Linear kernel function |
| r-SVM | Radial basis function |
| p-SVM | Polynomial kernel function |
| DT | Depth of the tree: 5 & Number of leaves: |
| RFC | Number of trees: 100 |

# 3    Results

## 3.1    Correlation Between Radiomics, Genomics and Overall Survival

Out of the 119 radiomic features extracted, two radiomics showed a significant low positive correlation ($p < 0.05$ & correlation $> 0.3$) with the overall survival in days. These two features are the kurtosis of the enhancement region extracted from T1 contrast and FLAIR MRI modalities. These two features also gave statistically significant ($p < 0.05$) negative coefficients for the Cox proportional hazard analysis. Thus, the large kurtosis of the enhancement is associated with longer survival.

The correlation between the gene expression level of 1023 genes and the overall survival has also been analyzed. 25 genes out of 1023 genes, were significantly correlated with the overall survival. Three of these genes, Endothelin Receptor Type A (EDNRA), Olfactomedin-like protein 3 (OLFML3), and Collagen Type III Alpha 1 Chain (COL3A1), gave a low positive correlation. The rest of the genes showed a low negative correlation. Those genes are given in the Table 2.

Nevertheless, these features were recognized with a Hazard ratio of $> 1$ and $p < 0.05$ with the univariate cox-PH analysis.

**Table 2.** The genes negatively associated with the overall survival obtained from the correlation study.

| Low negatively correlated genes |
| --- |
| Pirin (PIR) |
| Secretogranin-2 (SCG2) |
| Insulin Like Growth Factor Binding Protein 3 (IGFBP3) |
| Mucosa-associated lymphoid tissue lymphoma translocation protein 1 (MALT1) |
| Tubulin alpha-4A (TUBA4A) |
| Growth Differentiation Factor 15 (GDF15) |
| Tetraspanin-13 (TSPAN13) |
| Neural precursor cell expressed developmentally downregulated gene 4-like (NEDD4L) |
| Endoplasmic Reticulum Aminopeptidase 2 (LRAP) |
| Phospholipid Scramblase 1 (PLSCR1) |
| Ankyrin Repeat And MYND Domain Containing 2 (ANKMY2) |
| IQ Motif Containing G (IQCG) |
| Rho Family GTPase 3 (RND3) |
| Radical S-Adenosyl Methionine Domain Containing 2 (RSAD2) |
| Pyruvate Dehydrogenase Kinase 1 (PDK1) |
| Regucalcin (RGN) |
| Dihydrouridine Synthase 4 Like (DUS4L) |
| Oligoadenylate Synthetase 1 (OAS1) |
| FAM3 Metabolism Regulating Signaling Molecule C (FAM3C) |
| Membrane Palmitoylated Protein 6 (MPP6) |

Besides, the correlations between the imaging and genomic markers are also assessed. Thus, the expression level of the TIMP Metallopeptidase Inhibitor 4 (TIMP4) gene showed a moderate positive correlation (correlation $> 0.5$) with the fractal dimension of the necrosis region. Similarly, the necrosis region's extent had a moderate positive relationship with the acyl-CoA oxidase 2 (ACOX2) gene expression level.

## 3.2 Imaging Biomarkers Associated with Molecular Subtypes

Initially, the Kolmogorov-Smirnov test was applied to obtain the normality of the radiomics features. 38 features out of 119 radiomic features, were significantly normally distributed. Thus, for the remaining non-normal features, the Kruskal Wallis test was applied. Therefore, 12 features that were significantly ($p < 0.05$) different between 4 subtypes are identified. These features include the fractal dimensions of the necrosis, whole tumor, and tumor core regions. All these features are given in Table 3, with the test statistic and p-value, obtained.

This suggests that these features were significantly different between some subtypes. To identify those differences between subtypes, the Wilcoxon test was utilized, pairwise. The fractal dimension of the necrosis, tumor core, and whole tumor region showed a significant difference ($p < 0.0001$) between Proneural

**Table 3.** Kruskal Wallis statistics for radiomic features ($p < 0.05$) between 4 subtypes.

| Feature | Test statistic | p value |
|---|---|---|
| Tumor core bounding box 1 | 8.8889 | 0.0308 |
| Tumor core fractal dimension 3 | 7.9312 | 0.0474 |
| Whole tumor fractal dimension 4 | 7.8459 | 0.0493 |
| Whole tumor fractal dimension 5 | 7.9820 | 0.0463 |
| Kurtosis of necrosis - Flair | 9.197 | 0.0267 |
| Bounding box - 1 of necrosis | 9.263 | 0.0259 |
| Bounding box - 3 necrosis | 9.0134 | 0.0291 |
| Fractal dimension 1 of necrosis | 8.887 | 0.0308 |
| Fractal dimension 2 of necrosis | 9.1918 | 0.0268 |
| Fractal dimension 3 of necrosis | 10.418 | 0.0153 |
| Fractal dimension 4 of necrosis | 9.1716 | 0.027 |
| Fractal dimension 5 of necrosis | 8.937 | 0.0301 |

and Classical subtypes and also a considerable difference ($p < 0.0001$) between Proneural and Mesenchymal subtypes. Moreover, the fractal dimension of the whole tumor showed a substantial difference between Classical and Mesenchymal subtypes. The associations and the distributions of the fractal dimensions are shown in the Fig. 1.

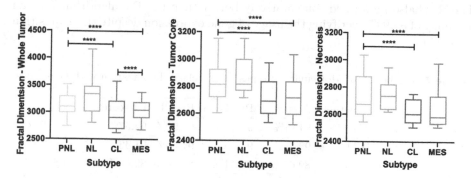

**Fig. 1.** The comparison of the fractal dimensions of whole tumor, tumor core and necrosis regions between 4 subtypes of Glioblastoma.

## 3.3   Subtype Prediction

The significantly different 12 radiomic features identified through the Kruskal-Wallis test was used for this subtype prediction. First, the Mesenchymal subtype (Mesenchymal - 23 cases, Non-Mesenchymal - 36) was predicted with ML tools, and SVM outperformed the other algorithms with an accuracy of 62.7119%, along with 61% precision and 62.7% recall. Next, the Classical subtype (Classical - 12, Non-Classical - 47) is predicted, and the SVM outperformed the other three algorithms with fourfold validation accuracy of 85.3%. Nevertheless, the Prediction of Proneural subtype (Proneural - 16, Non-Proneural - 43) was performed to obtain a four-fold accuracy of 81.82% accuracy with SVM. The performance comparison of the binary classification of each subtype are given in Table 4.

**Table 4.** Prediction of subtypes as a binary classification using Radiomics. Acc, Prec, Rec are denotes for accuracy, precision and recall.

| ML tool | Classical | | | | Proneural | | | | Mesenchymal | | | |
|---|---|---|---|---|---|---|---|---|---|---|---|---|
| | Acc | Prec | Rec | F1 | Acc | Prec | Rec | F1 | Acc | Prec | Rec | F1 |
| l-SVM | 85.3% | 91.4% | 88.8% | 84.5% | 81.8% | 88.8% | 88.8% | 86.3% | 82.0% | 79.2% | 82.0% | 80.2% |
| r-SVM | 82.3% | 84.1% | 81.2% | 81.2% | 83.1% | 83.6% | 85.3% | 84.6% | 81.4% | 83.2% | 80.2% | 78.3% |
| p-SVM | 78.8% | 80.2% | 79.4% | 79.4% | 81.5% | 83.2% | 79.4% | 81.4% | 82.4% | 79.4% | 77.5% | 78.3% |
| DT | 83.1% | 83.1% | 83.1% | 81.9% | 66.1% | 63.3% | 66.1% | 64.7% | 57.6% | 58.7% | 57.6% | 58.7% |
| RFC | 79.7% | 77.3% | 79.7% | 78.3% | 69.4% | 62.7% | 69.5% | 68.6% | 61.0% | 60.2% | 61.0% | 61.4% |
| LR | 77.9% | 80.1% | 78.0% | 76.4% | 64.4% | 65.1% | 64.4% | 65.1% | 57.6% | 56.7% | 57.6% | 55.4% |

The subtype prediction with genomics was executed as a generalized method for predicting any of the 4 subtypes. However, since the Neural subtype no longer exists, this model might require slight changes in current exploration. Thus, the SVM gave the highest accuracy of 94.91% with four-fold cross-validation. The RFC also performed comparatively better than the DT algorithm with an accuracy of 89.93%, verifying the usage of gene expression despite the acquisition (Table 5).

**Table 5.** Prediction of Molecular subtypes as a 4 class classification with Genomics

| ML method | Accuracy | Precision | Recall | F1-score |
|---|---|---|---|---|
| l-SVM | 94.91% | 95.40% | 94.90% | 92.67% |
| r-SVM | 92.47% | 93.29% | 91.50% | 91.43% |
| p-SVM | 89.65% | 90.41% | 88.60% | 89.65% |
| DT | 64.40% | 63.30% | 64.40% | 63.30% |
| RFC | 89.83% | 90.81% | 89.80% | 88.70% |

## 4    Discussion

In our retrospective study, we analyze the associations between radiomics, genomics, and overall survival of GBM patients. Our results showed that the kurtosis of the enhancement region has a positive correlation with survival. Kurtosis represents to what extent the intensity of this particular region deviates from a perfect normal Gaussian distribution. Nevertheless, the enhancement region has shown relationships with the survival, in previously done GBM related studies [1, 7].

While analyzing genes associated with survival, we identified that the COL3A1 gene expression level correlates with overall survival. COL3A1 gene is considered a prognostic marker of GBM patients [6] and have shown associations with GBM prognosis. Further, the TIMP4 gene showed a correlation with the fractal dimension of the necrosis region. According to previous studies, [16], TIMP4 overexpression cause shorter survival in GBM patients. Thus, we can hypothesize that this overexpression in GBM patients can be approximated through the necrosis region's fractal dimension. Another major finding of our study is the differentiation of fractal dimension between 4 subtypes. The fractal dimension provides an assessment of each region's complexity, where we used a box-counting approach to obtain this dimension.

The radiomic features that predict survival provide a suitable platform to predict the subtypes according to our results. Despite the technological advancements, obtaining a consistent gene expression profiles is hard due to the technical shortcomings. Therefore, identifying the subtype with radiomics helps clinicians determine the subtype precisely, with the acquisition of MRI that has been used in clinical practice commonly, followed by a fully automated segmentation and feature extraction.

Originally, GBM is recognized with four subtypes by Verhaak et al. [20]. Recently, Wang et al. [21] define that only Classical, Mesenchymal, and Proneural subtypes exist, and the previously described Neural subtype was identified through contamination with nontumor cells. Therefore, we performed subtype prediction as a binary classification of the Classical, Mesenchymal, and Proneural subtypes separately. Another limitation of our study is the sparse dataset. Yet, we utilized the same dataset to analyze the overall survival of GBM patients with an outperforming accuracy [22]. However, we believe an extended dataset, with both MRI and Gene expression profiling, will lead to a robust subtype predictive model.

## 5  Conclusion

In this study, we address a solution for subtype prediction without employing high dimensional genomics, which is inconsistent with the platform acquired. We identified distinctive radiomics between subtypes, that reflects the underlying molecular level gene alterations between the subtypes. Accordingly, we developed a predictive subtype model, with machine learning for GBM patients. In conclusion, our work delivers a promising subtype predictive model that will lead to better clinical maintenance of GBM patients.

# References

1. Carrillo, J., et al.: Relationship between tumor enhancement, edema, idh1 mutational status, mgmt promoter methylation, and survival in glioblastoma. Am. J. Neuroradiol. **33**(7), 1349–1355 (2012)
2. Chen, Z., Hambardzumyan, D.: Immune microenvironment in glioblastoma subtypes. Front. Immunol. **9**, 1004 (2018)
3. Delgado-López, P.D., Corrales-García, E.M.: Survival in glioblastoma: a review on the impact of treatment modalities. Clin. Transl. Oncol. **18**(11), 1062–1071 (2016). https://doi.org/10.1007/s12094-016-1497-x
4. Dimitriadou, E., Hornik, K., Leisch, F., Meyer, D., Maintainer, A., Leisch@ci, f., Tuwien, A.: At: The e1071 package (2006)
5. Follia, L., et al.: Integrative analysis of novel metabolic subtypes in pancreatic cancer fosters new prognostic biomarkers. Front. Oncol. **9**, 115 (2019)
6. Gao, Y.F., et al.: Col3a1 and snap91: novel glioblastoma markers with diagnostic and prognostic value. Oncotarget **7**(43), 70494 (2016)
7. Gutman, D.A., et al.: MR imaging predictors of molecular profile and survival: multi-institutional study of the TCGA glioblastoma data set. Radiology **267**(2), 560–569 (2013)
8. Hall, M., Frank, E., Holmes, G., Pfahringer, B., Reutemann, P., Witten, I.H.: The WEKA data mining software: an update. SIGKDD Explor. **11**(1), 10–18 (2009)
9. Islam, M., Jose, V.J.M., Ren, H.: Glioma prognosis: segmentation of the tumor and survival prediction using shape, geometric and clinical information. In: Crimi, A., Bakas, S., Kuijf, H., Keyvan, F., Reyes, M., van Walsum, T. (eds.) BrainLes 2018. LNCS, vol. 11384, pp. 142–153. Springer, Cham (2019). https://doi.org/10.1007/978-3-030-11726-9_13
10. Islam, M., Vibashan, V.S., Jose, V.J.M., Wijethilake, N., Utkarsh, U., Ren, H.: Brain tumor segmentation and survival prediction using 3D attention UNet. In: Crimi, A., Bakas, S. (eds.) BrainLes 2019. LNCS, vol. 11992, pp. 262–272. Springer, Cham (2020). https://doi.org/10.1007/978-3-030-46640-4_25
11. Macyszyn, L., et al.: Imaging patterns predict patient survival and molecular subtype in glioblastoma via machine learning techniques. Neuro-oncology **18**(3), 417–425 (2015)
12. Mazurowski, M.A., Zhang, J., Grimm, L.J., Yoon, S.C., Silber, J.I.: Radiogenomic analysis of breast cancer: luminal b molecular subtype is associated with enhancement dynamics at mr imaging. Radiology **273**(2), 365–372 (2014)
13. Naeini, K.M., et al.: Identifying the mesenchymal molecular subtype of glioblastoma using quantitative volumetric analysis of anatomic magnetic resonance images. Neuro-oncology **15**(5), 626–634 (2013)
14. Ostrom, Q.T., Gittleman, H., Truitt, G., Boscia, A., Kruchko, C., Barnholtz-Sloan, J.S.: Cbtrus statistical report: primary brain and other central nervous system tumors diagnosed in the united states in 2011–2015. Neuro-oncology **20**(suppl_4), iv1–iv86 (2018)
15. Pieper, S., Halle, M., Kikinis, R.: 3d slicer. In: 2004 2nd IEEE International Symposium on Biomedical Imaging: Nano to Macro (IEEE Cat No. 04EX821), pp. 632–635. IEEE (2004)
16. Rorive, S., et al.: Timp-4 and cd63: new prognostic biomarkers in human astrocytomas. Modern Pathol. **23**(10), 1418–1428 (2010)

17. Roy, A.G., Navab, N., Wachinger, C.: Concurrent spatial and channel 'squeeze & excitation' in fully convolutional networks. In: Frangi, A.F., Schnabel, J.A., Davatzikos, C., Alberola-López, C., Fichtinger, G. (eds.) MICCAI 2018. LNCS, vol. 11070, pp. 421–429. Springer, Cham (2018). https://doi.org/10.1007/978-3-030-00928-1_48

18. Sidaway, P.: Glioblastoma subtypes revisited. Nat. Rev. Clin. Oncol. 14(10), 587–587 (2017)

19. Sutton, E.J., et al.: Breast cancer molecular subtype classifier that incorporates MRI features. J. Magn. Reson. Imag. 44(1), 122–129 (2016)

20. Verhaak, R.G., et al.: Integrated genomic analysis identifies clinically relevant subtypes of glioblastoma characterized by abnormalities in pdgfra, idh1, egfr, and nf1. Cancer Cell 17(1), 98–110 (2010)

21. Wang, Q., et al.: Tumor evolution of glioma-intrinsic gene expression subtypes associates with immunological changes in the microenvironment. Cancer Cell 32(1), 42–56 (2017)

22. Wijethilake, N., Islam, M., Ren, H.: Radiogenomics model for overall survival prediction of glioblastoma. Med. Biol. Eng. Comput. 58(8), 1767–1777 (2020). https://doi.org/10.1007/s11517-020-02179-9

# Local Binary and Ternary Patterns Based Quantitative Texture Analysis for Assessment of IDH Genotype in Gliomas on Multi-modal MRI

Sonal Gore[1,2], Tanay Chougule[3], Jitender Saini[4], Madhura Ingalhalikar[3], and Jayant Jagtap[1(✉)]

[1] Symbiosis Institute of Technology, Symbiosis International University, Lavale, Pune 412115, India
jayant.jagtap@sitpune.edu.in
[2] Department of Computer Engineering, Pimpri-Chinchwad College of Engineering, Pimpri, Pune 411044, India
[3] Symbiosis Center for Medical Image Analysis, Symbiosis International University, Lavale, Pune 412115, India
[4] Department of Radiology, National Institute of Mental Health and Neurosciences, Bengaluru 560029, India

**Abstract.** Radiomics based multivariate models are potentially valuable prognostic tool in IDH phenotyping in high-grade gliomas. Radiomics generally involves a set of the histogram and standard texture features based on co-occurrence matrix, run-length matrix, size zone matrix, gray tone matrix, and gray level dependence matrix as described by the Imaging Biomarker Standardization Initiative (IBSI). In this work, we introduce 3D local binary patterns (3D LBP) and local ternary patterns (3D LTP) based histogram features in addition to standard radiomics for capturing subtle phenotypic differences to characterize IDH genotype in high-grade gliomas. These textures are rotationally invariant and are robust to image noise as well as can capture the underlying local differences in the tissue architecture. On a dataset of 64 patients with high-grade glioma scanned at a single institution, we illustrate that LBP and LTP features perform at par with radiomics individually and when combined, could facilitate highest testing accuracy of 84.62% (AUROC: 0.78, sensitivity: 0.83 specificity: 0.86, f1-score: 0.83) using random forest classification. Clinical explainability is achieved via feature ranking and selection where the top 5 features are based on LBP and LTP histogram. Overall, our results illustrate that 3D LBP and LTP histogram features are crucial in creating tumor phenotypic signatures and could be included in the standard radiomics pipeline.

**Keywords:** LTP · LBP · Radiomics · IDH · Gliomas

## 1 Introduction

High-grade gliomas (HGG) are a common and aggressive type of brain neoplasms. These tumors can rapidly infiltrate the surrounding healthy tissue making it one of the most

© Springer Nature Switzerland AG 2020
S. M. Kia et al. (Eds.): MLCN 2020/RNO-AI 2020, LNCS 12449, pp. 240–248, 2020.
https://doi.org/10.1007/978-3-030-66843-3_23

disparaging malignancies [1]. The 2016 World Health Organization (WHO) classification of brain tumors acknowledged multiple entities based on genotypes in addition to histological phenotypes [2]. Amongst these, the mutation in isocitrate dehydrogenase 1(IDH1) in high-grade gliomas (HGG) was given utmost importance as these have been shown to relate with longer overall survival [3]. Currently, the IDH diagnosis is based on immunohistochemical analysis following surgical resection. However, developing non-invasive pre-operative markers for identification of the IDH genotype is crucial for early diagnosis and timely management as the pathogenesis of HGGs is highly complex.

Existing literature has illustrated the feasibility of multi-modal MRI images to probe the fundamental tumor type by quantifying the underlying image patterns. Radiomics, that quantify various patterns, textures, and shapes of the tumoral region on the MRI images, have demonstrated potential in characterizing the IDH genotype [4–6]. Multiple studies have demonstrated a potential clinical association and utility of radiomics based genotype prediction using machine learning techniques such as random forests [5], support vector machines [6], etc. Radiomic features are extracted on multimodal MRI that include gadolinium-enhanced T1-weighted (T1ce), T2-weighted, and fluid attenuation inversion recovery (FLAIR) and have shown to boost the predictive outcomes [4–6].

However, with a complex and variable microstructural environment, it is vital to create and employ features that can detect subtle local variations consequently supporting an accurate delineation of the genotype. To this end, our work proposes computation of 3D local binary patterns (3D LBP) and local ternary patterns (3D LTP) based histogram features that are rotationally invariant and are robust to inherent image noise with the capability to extract elusive local patterns [7–9]. We, therefore, evaluate a 3-dimensional version of LBP/LTP based histogram features and its variants in the molecular classification of HGG and provide evidence that these features play an important role in IDH-phenotyping by comparing its performance with five different sets of other texture and radiomic features.

## 2  Method

### 2.1  Study Cohort/Imaging/Image Pre-processing

This was a retrospective study of multi-modal preoperative MRI of 64 patients with high-grade glioma; 39 patients (age 40.30 ± 12.26, 26:13 M: F) with grade III and IV IDH mutation and 25 patients (age 46.72 ± 16.09, 11:14 M: F) were of IDH wildtype. All patients had undergone surgical resection and standard post-surgical care and were identified retrospectively after reviewing the medical records. IDH mutation status was determined after resecting the tumor, via immuno-histochemistry or next-generation sequencing. Patients were scanned at the same institute on 2 different scanners: (1) Philips Achieva 3T MRI scanner where the T1 weighted (T1CE) was acquired using TR/TE of 8.7/3.1 ms using a TFE sequence, fluid attenuation inversion recovery (FLAIR) were acquired using TR/TE/T1 of 11000/125/2800 with an in-plane resolution of 0.5*0.5 mm and T2 weighted imaging was performed using TR/TE = 5500/80 and 0.5*0.5 mm resolution in the axial plane. (2) Siemens 3T scanner with T1CE scans obtained using TR/TE = 2200/2.3 using a T1 MPRAGE sequence with 1*1*1 mm isotropic resolution.

T2 protocol consisted of TR/TE ranging from 5500/90 ms and 0.5*0.5 mm resolution in the axial plane. FLAIR images were acquired using TR/TE/T1 of 11000/125/2800 ms.

All images were resampled to 1*1*1 mm isotropic resolution and co-registered to the patient's T1CE image using affine registration with mutual information similarity metric using ANTs [10]. Next, brain extraction was performed using FSL's brain extraction tool (BET) [11]. Intensity normalization was performed to scale the intensities into standardized ranges for each imaging modality among all subjects.

A convolutional neural network, deepMedic [12] was trained to identify edema and enhancement regions from T1CE and FLAIR images. The images and segmentation labels from BRATS-2018 [13–15] tumor data (https://www.med.upenn.edu/sbia/brats2 018/data.html) were employed for training and validation (training n = 206, validation n = 52). The ROI masks predicted by the model were then corrected manually for each subject and cross-checked by an experienced neuro-radiologist.

## 2.2 Texture Feature Extraction from 3D Local Binary Pattern

The 3-dimensional Local Binary Pattern (3D LBP) method is an extension of original LBPs proposed by Ojala et al. [16]. The LBP describes the local level appearance of an image as a binary pattern by thresholding the local 3D neighborhood with the center voxel as reference. If an intensity of the neighboring voxel is greater than the center-voxel's intensity, then it is coded as 1. Otherwise, it is coded as 0. The resultant binary pattern (or its equivalent decimal code) is the LBP feature descriptor for the center voxel. Likewise, LBP features are computed for the ROIs voxel by voxel which results in a feature vector of 3D image size. For a 26-voxel neighborhood ($3 \times 3 \times 3$ size), $2^{26}$ ($= 67,108,864$) binary patterns for 3D LBP are generated. To reduce the vector size, only uniform and rotationally invariant codes are included [17]. Uniform binary patterns contain a maximum of two bitwise transitions (change in bit value) either from 0 to 1 or from 1 to 0 considering a circular binary pattern. Only 652 combinations of uniform patterns (from $2^{26}$) are possible that conform to the criteria. All other non-uniform patterns (from $2^{26}$), are coded into a single code creating total of 653 LBP codes.

The rotational invariant LBP patterns are achieved from 652 uniform binary patterns by circularly rotating each pattern to the minimum value. For example, the bit sequences 00000000000000000000111110, 00000000000000000000011111, 10000000000000000000001111, 11000000000000000000000111, etc. arise from the different rotations of same local pattern and these all such patterns will map to a single pattern with a minimum value, which in this case would be 00000000000000000000011111. This strategy reduces the number of patterns to 27. All remaining non-uniform patterns are non-rotation invariant, which corresponds to a single LBP code. Therefore, only 28 LBP codes (27 uniform, rotation-invariant and non-uniform) are included in our analysis.

In this study, we compute the LBP image for the region of interest (ROI) and create its histogram. The frequency count for each LBP code is considered as a feature. Therefore, we obtain a total of 168 LBP features; 28 each from 3 scans (T1CE, FLAIR, and T2) each with 2 ROIs (edema and enhancing tumor).

## 2.3 Texture Feature Extraction from 3D Local Ternary Pattern

The local ternary pattern (LTP) [18] extends the original LBP to describe the local level appearance of an image with micro-structures, by generating ternary patterns $(-1, 0$ and $1)$ based on a pre-defined threshold value. The threshold constant $t$ helps in identifying the degree of similarity (with small intensity variations) as a part of a texturally homogenous region.

We use a threshold value of 5 to weigh the intensity difference between the center and its 26 neighboring voxels in the $3 \times 3 \times 3$ neighborhood area. The generalized LTP descriptor computation is given as per the following Eq. 1:

$$LTPV_v = \begin{cases} 1, & G_v - G_c \geq t \\ 0, & |G_v - G_c| < t, v = 0, 1, \ldots, V - 1 \\ -1, & G_v - G_c \leq -t \end{cases} \tag{1}$$

where, '$V$' is the number of neighboring voxels in the neighborhood area of the center-voxel, '$Gv$' $(v = 0\ to\ V)$ is the gray-level intensity of neighboring voxels and '$Gc$' is the intensity value of center voxel, $t$ is the threshold.

Voxel-wise computation as per the above equation results in a vector $(LTPV_v)$ of '$V$' neighboring voxels, which is further converted into two binary patterns known as an upper local ternary pattern- $LTP_{upper}$ and lower local ternary pattern- $LTP_{lower}$ binary descriptors. The decimal code for upper LTP is computed as given in Eq. 2.

$$LTP_{upper} = \sum_{v=0}^{V} 2^v * B_1(LTPV_v) \tag{2}$$

where $B_1(LTPV_v) = 0$ for $LTPV_v = -1$;   otherwise $B_1(LTPV_v) = LTPV_v$

And the decimal code for lower LTP is computed as given in Eq. 3.

$$LTP_{lower} = \sum_{v=0}^{V} 2^v * B_2(LTPV_v) \tag{3}$$

where $B_2(LTPV_v) = 1$ for $LTPV_v = -1$;   and

$B_2(LTPV_v) = 0$ for $LTPV_v = 1$;   otherwise $B_2(LTPV_v) = LTPV_v$

The computation of upper and lower LTP binary descriptors, giving the uniform, rotation invariant binary code for rotations around the x-axis, for the sample center voxel is exemplified in Fig. 1.

The computation method of uniform, rotation-invariant LBP is used in this study to create the upper and lower uniform, rotation-invariant LTP binary patterns (26-bit) for $3 \times 3 \times 3$ local neighborhood (26-voxel) (similar to Sect. 2.2). Finally, a histogram is computed for both upper and lower binary patterns extracted from a region of interest (ROI). The frequency count from the two histograms is used as a feature vector. Therefore, we obtain a total of 336 LTP features; 56 each from 3 scans (T1CE, FLAIR, and T2) each with 2 ROIs (edema and enhancing tumor).

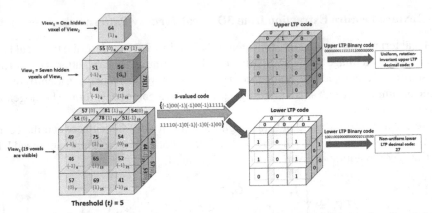

**Fig. 1.** Computation of 3D LTP codes. Sample neighborhood region of size $3 \times 3 \times 3$ containing total 27 voxels is shown on left-side, in which View$_1$ displays 19 voxels, View$_2$ represents 7 voxels which are hidden in View$_1$ and View$_3$ displays hidden voxel of View$_2$. It highlights intensity value of every voxel in bold black color ($G_v$ is an intensity value of 26 neighboring voxels of center voxel with intensity value $G_c$), followed by its value in ternary pattern ($-1/0/1$) (which is generated using threshold ($t = 5$) as per Eq. 1) shown in bracketed red font, followed by its position (shown as a subscript) in 3-valued code pattern. Center voxel (Gc) is shown with box filled in blue color. On the right side, the generated upper and lower LTP binary patterns (as per Eq. 2 & 3) and its corresponding uniform, rotation-invariant or non-uniform decimal codes are shown. (Color figure online)

### 2.4 Radiomics

Radiomic features were extracted from edema and enhancement regions of FLAIR, T1CE, and T2 MRI scans using the open-source PyRadiomics [19] tool (version 2.2.0). Features were extracted after image intensity normalization with a bin width of 32. Extracted features include first-order statistics features (18), grey-level co-occurrence matrix (GLCM) features (24), grey-level run-length matrix (GLRLM) features (16), grey-level size-zone matrix (GLSZM) features (16), gray-level dependence matrix (GLDM) features (14), Neighboring gray-tone difference matrix (NGTDM) features (5). Accordingly, a total of 558 radiomics features were extracted; 93 each from 3 modalities (T1CE, T2, FLAIR), each with 2 regions (Edema and Enhancing).

### 2.5 Multivariate Analysis

Patients were randomly divided with a 4:1 ratio into a training set (51 patients) and a testing set (13 patients). A total of 1062 features were extracted including 558 pyradomics features, 168 3D LBP features, and 336 3D LTP features. These features were employed into a random forest classifier [20] in seven different combinations namely (1) only radiomics (2) only LBP (3) only LTP (4) radiomics + LBP (5) radiomics +LTP (6) LBP + LTP and (7) radiomics +LBP + LTP. The following steps for multivariate analysis were carried out using the scikit-learn library in python [21]. (1) Feature-selection using recursive feature elimination (RFE) with cross-validation was performed to tackle multi-collinearity [22] and reduce dimensionality. (2) Each feature was assigned an elimination rank according to the order-of-elimination at each step of RFE i.e. the last set of retained features had a rank of 1 and so on. (3) Random-forest classifier was tuned using grid-search to optimize the performance over 5-fold cross-validation on the training set. (4) Next, a classifier was trained on a training set using these parameters. (5) Feature importance values for each selected feature was obtained from the trained random forest classifier. (6) Finally, the trained model was used to test on a separate test set (13 cases).

## 3   Results

Tables 1 and 2 provide the comparison of all feature combinations on the testing set and across 5-fold cross validation, respectively. Figure 2(a) shows the Receiver Operating Characteristics (ROC) for all the 7 combinations. It can be observed from Fig. 2(b) that among the features selected after RFE, a majority features belonged to T2 scans and from the radiomics feature set. However, according to the classifier feature importance values (as shown in Fig. 3), the top-5 features belonged to LBP and LTP features from the edema region of T1CE, T2 and FLAIR, scans. The discriminative features from radiomics were only captured from T2 images while LBP and LTP could differentiate the textures of edema region among all three modalities. The top ranked features from the combination mostly include features obtained from edema region in T2 scans. The results obtained by our work are compared with state-of-the-art radiogenomic models and the significance of texture features is proved by observing almost similar findings for AUC value of around 78% for IDH classification [23].

**Table 1.** Comparison of all the feature vector combinations based on classification metrics on testing cohort.

| Feature combinations | Testing cohort | | | | |
|---|---|---|---|---|---|
| | Accuracy | F1 Score | Sensitivity | Specificity | AUROC |
| Pyradiomics Only | 61.54% | 0.62 | 0.67 | 0.57 | 0.64 |
| 3D LBP Features Only | 69.23% | 0.5 | 0.33 | 1 | 0.55 |
| 3D LTP Features Only | 61.54% | 0.55 | 0.5 | 0.71 | 0.62 |
| Pyradiomics + 3D LBP Features | 76.92% | 0.67 | 0.5 | 1 | 0.55 |
| Pyradiomics + 3D LTP Features | 61.54% | 0.55 | 0.5 | 0.71 | 0.63 |
| 3D LBP + 3D LTP Features | 69.23% | 0.5 | 0.33 | 1 | 0.50 |
| **Pyradiomics + 3D LBP + 3D LTP Features** | **84.62%** | **0.83** | **0.83** | **0.86** | **0.78** |

**Table 2.** Comparison of all the feature vector combinations based on average classification metrics across 5-fold cross validation.

| Feature combinations | Cross-Validation (Mean across 5-Folds) | | | |
|---|---|---|---|---|
| | Accuracy | F1 Score | Sensitivity | Specificity |
| Pyradiomics Only | 66.72% | 0.56 | **0.58** | 0.72 |
| 3D LBP Features Only | 54.90% | 0.18 | 0.17 | 0.79 |
| 3D LTP Features Only | 62.36% | 0.48 | 0.52 | 0.69 |
| Pyradiomics + 3D LBP Features | 68.72% | 0.49 | 0.47 | 0.81 |
| Pyradiomics + 3D LTP Features | 68.54% | 0.55 | 0.57 | 0.75 |
| 3D LBP + 3D LTP Features | 62.90% | 0.14 | 0.1 | **0.94** |
| **Pyradiomics + 3D LBP + 3D LTP Features** | **70.36%** | **0.58** | 0.57 | 0.78 |

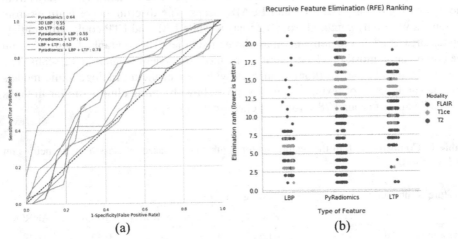

(a)                                                    (b)

**Fig. 2.** (a) Receiver Operating Characteristic (ROC) curves for all seven feature-vector combinations. (b) The distribution of features according to elimination rank obtained from recursive feature elimination. Each point on the graph represents a feature belonging to either FLAIR, T1CE or T2 scan with their respective feature-set on x-axis (LBP, PyRadiomics and LTP). Whereas, the y-axis represents the order of elimination, i.e. features eliminated earlier have a higher rank value compared to the retained features.

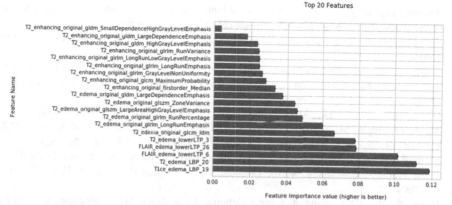

**Fig. 3.** Top 20 features ranked according to feature importance metric. Here, x-axis represents feature importance value obtained from the random forest classifier (higher importance value is better) whereas, the names of the top 20 features are displayed on y-axis.

## 4 Conclusion

Our work evaluated the significance of textures based on 3D LBP and 3D LTP histogram features individually and in combination with standard radiomic features for delineating IDH genotype in HGGs. Our results demonstrated that LBP and LTP features individually performed at par with standard radiomics. Moreover, the combination of radiomics, LBP and LTP features revealed superior accuracy with top ranked features (top 5) from LBP and LTP histograms illustrating the significance of these features. Overall, LBP and LTP histogram features add value in creating IDH phenotypic signatures and can be included in standard radiomics framework.

## References

1. Wank, M., et al.: Human glioma migration and infiltration properties as a target for personalized radiation medicine. Cancers **10**(11), 456 (2018)
2. Louis, D.N., et al.: The 2016 World Health Organization classification of tumors of the central nervous system: a summary. Acta Neuropathol. **131**(6), 803–820 (2016)
3. Houillier, C., et al.: IDH1 or IDH2 mutations predict longer survival and response to temozolomide in low-grade gliomas. Neurology **75**(17), 1560–1566 (2010)
4. Jakola, A., et al.: Quantitative texture analysis in the prediction of IDH status in low-grade gliomas. J. Clin. Neurol. Neurosurg. **164**, 114–120 (2017)
5. Chougule, T., Shinde, S., Santosh, V., Saini, J., Ingalhalikar, M.: On Validating Multimodal MRI Based Stratification of IDH Genotype in High Grade Gliomas Using CNNs and Its Comparison to Radiomics. In: Mohy-ud-Din, H., Rathore, S. (eds.) RNO-AI 2019. LNCS, vol. 11991, pp. 53–60. Springer, Cham (2020). https://doi.org/10.1007/978-3-030-40124-5_6
6. Gore, S., et al.: A review of radiomics and deep predictive modeling in glioma characterization. Academic Radiology, epub ahead of print (2020). https://doi.org/10.1010/j.acra.2020.06.016
7. Zhao, G., et al.: Dynamic texture recognition using local binary patterns with an application to facial expressions. IEEE Trans. Pattern Anal. Mach. Intell. **29**(6), 915–928 (2007)

8.  Ahonen, T., et al.: Face description with local binary patterns: application to face recognition. IEEE Trans. Pattern Anal. Mach. Intell. **28**(12), 2037–2041 (2006)
9.  Samal, A., et al.: Texture as the basis for individual tree identification. Inf. Sci. **176**, 565–576 (2006)
10. Avants, B.B., et al.: Advanced normalization tools (ANTS), Insight j 2.365, pp. 1–35 (2009)
11. Smith, S.M.: Fast robust automated brain extraction. Hum. Brain Mapp. **17**(3), 143–155 (2002)
12. Kamnitsas, K., et al.: DeepMedic for brain tumor segmentation. In: Crimi, A., Menze, B., Maier, O., Reyes, M., Winzeck, S., Handels, H. (eds.) BrainLes 2016. LNCS, vol. 10154, pp. 138–149. Springer, Cham (2016). https://doi.org/10.1007/978-3-319-55524-9_14
13. Menze, B.H., et al.: The multimodal brain tumor image segmentation benchmark (BRATS). IEEE Trans. Med. Imaging **34**(10), 1993–2024 (2015). https://doi.org/10.1109/TMI.2014.2377694
14. Bakas, S., et al.: Advancing the Cancer Genome Atlas glioma MRI collections with expert segmentation labels and radiomic features. Nature Sci. Data **4**, 170117 (2017). https://doi.org/10.1038/sdata.2017.117
15. Bakas, S., et al.: Identifying the Best Machine Learning Algorithms for Brain Tumor Segmentation, Progression Assessment, and Overall Survival Prediction in the BRATS Challenge, arXiv preprint arXiv:1811.02629 (2018)
16. Ojala, T., et al.: A comparative study of texture measures with classification based on feature distributions. Pattern Recogn. **29**(1), 51–59 (1996)
17. Ojala, T., et al.: Multiresolution gray-scale and rotation invariant texture classification with Local Binary Patterns. IEEE Trans. Pattern Anal. Mach. Intell. **24**(7), 971–987 (2002)
18. Tan, X., et al.: Enhanced local texture feature sets for face recognition under difficult lighting conditions. IEEE Trans. Image Process. **19**(6), 1635–1650 (2010)
19. Griethuysen, J.J.M., et al.: Computational radiomics system to decode the radiographic phenotype. Can. Res. **77**(21), e104–e107 (2017)
20. https://www.stat.berkeley.edu/~breiman/randomforest2001.pdf
21. Pedregosa et al.: Scikit-learn: Machine Learning in Python. JMLR **12**, 2825–2830 (2011)
22. Darst, B.F., et al.: Using recursive feature elimination in random forest to account for correlated variables in high dimensional data. BMC Genet. **19**, 65 (2018)
23. Chaddad, A., et al.: Predicting the gene status and survival outcome of lower grade glioma patients with multimodal MRI features. IEEE Access **7**, 75976–75984 (2019). https://doi.org/10.1109/ACCESS.2019.2920396

# Automated Multi-class Brain Tumor Types Detection by Extracting RICA Based Features and Employing Machine Learning Techniques

Sadia Anjum[1], Lal Hussain[2(✉)], Mushtaq Ali[1], and Adeel Ahmed Abbasi[2]

[1] Department of IT, Hazara University, Mansehra, Pakistan
[2] Department of Computer Science and IT, University of Azad Jammu and Kashmir, Muzaffarabad, Pakistan
lall_hussain2008@live.com

**Abstract.** Brain tumor is the leading reason of mortality across the globe. It is obvious that the chances of survival can be increased if the tumor is identified and properly classified at an initial stage. Several factors such as type, texture and location help to categorize the brain tumor. In this study, we extracted reconstruction independent component analysis (RICA) base features from brain tumor types such as glioma, meningioma, pituitary and applied robust machine learning algorithms such as linear discriminant analysis (LDA) and support vector machine (SVM) with linear and quadratic kernels. The jackknife 10-fold cross validation was used for training and testing data validation. The SVM with quadratic kernel gives the highest multiclass detection performance. To detect pituitary, the highest detection performance was obtained with sensitivity (93.85%), specificity (100%), PPV (100%), NPV (97.27%), accuracy (98.07%) and AUC (96.92). To detect glioma, the highest detection performance was obtained with accuracy (94.35%), AUC (0.9508). To detect the meningioma, the highest was obtained with accuracy (96.18%), AUC (0.9095). The findings reveal that proposed methodology based on RICA features to detect multiclass brain tumor types will be very useful for treatment modification to achieve better clinical outcomes.

**Keywords:** Feature extraction · Machine learning · Glioma · Meningioma · Pituitary · Image analysis

## 1 Introduction

Brain tumor is a collection of abnormal cells in the brain or central spinal canal or intracranial hard neoplasms, which can be malignant or benign [1]. In the report 2011–2012 of central brain tumor registry of the United States, about 64,531 cases of the brain are identified as tumors and there are 600,000 people who are suffered with this type of disease [2]. The brain tumor has also increased the mortality rate among children and adults.

To classify the brain tumor into subtypes is more challenging research problem. There are several factors which are related to these challenges. With the advent of the

© Springer Nature Switzerland AG 2020
S. M. Kia et al. (Eds.): MLCN 2020/RNO-AI 2020, LNCS 12449, pp. 249–258, 2020.
https://doi.org/10.1007/978-3-030-66843-3_24

new technology identifying the brain tumor with accuracy is still very challenging task for a specialist. To identify tumor, we need to require a different approach it may see a different. The brain tumor among the other cancer types is one of the deadliest forms due to its heterogenous characteristics, aggressive nature, and low survival rate. The brain tumor is categorized into different types based on the several factors such as texture, type, and location of the tumor (e.g. Meningioma, Acoustic Neuroma, Glioma, Pituitary, CNS Lymphoma etc.) [3]. Among all the brain tumors, clinically the rate of incident of Glioma, Meningioma and Pituitary tumors are approximately 45%, 15% and 15% respectively [4]. The major type of tumor is glioma which has further three types 1) Astrocytomas, 2) Ependymomas, and 3) Oligodendrogliomas. It originates in the glial cells which surround nerve cells it can also classifies according to genetic features and can help to predict the future behavior and treatment. It can affect the function of brain, and deadly for a person. Glioma can detect using CAD techniques which relay on the MRI images of our brain MRI provide more accuracy then CT computer tomography because it provides higher contrast of soft tissue and categorized as malignant tumors. Now a days CAD analysis provide more performance due to deep learning strategies which is vastly use in medical image analysis and other tumor studies [5]. Another type of tumor is meningioma which include in the category of brain tumor. It is most common tumor which originate in brain. It grow so slow without any symptoms and mostly occur in woman's [5]. Another type of tumor is Pituitary tumors that grown and develop in pituitary gland. Pituitary tumors are benign and grows adenomas which remain in surrounding tissue and do not spread in your whole body [5].

In the past, researchers applied different machine learning techniques by extracting features such as Gray Level Co-occurrence Matrix (GLCM) [6–9] and Genetic Algorithm [10] etc. The classification algorithms employed were Random Forest [11], Support Vector Machines (SVM) [6–9, 12–17] etc. In this study, we extracted RICA based features from different brain tumor types (glioma, meningioma and pituitary) and employed multiclass classification using robust machine learning techniques such as LDA, SVM with linear and quadratic kernel.

## 2 Materials and Methods

### 2.1 Data Acquisition

The brain tumor data used in this study were taken from publicly available database provided by the School of Biomedical Engineering, Southern Medical University, Guangzhou, China (https://github.com/chengjun583/brainTumorRetrieval). This detailed illustration of the dataset is described in [18, 19] which contains 3064 T1-weighted contrast enhanced images with three kinds of brain tumor from 233 patients including: meningioma (708 slices), glioma (1426 slices), and pituitary tumor (930 slices). The data is labeled as 1 for meningioma, 2 for glioma, and 3 for pituitary tumor. In MR images, suspicious regions of interest (ROIs) are marked by experienced radiologists.

## 2.2 Feature Extraction

In machine learning, the most important step is to extract the most relevant features for improving the diagnostic performance. The feature extraction methods in different imaging techniques were texture, morphological, scale invariant Fourier transform (SIFT), Elliptic Fourier descriptors (EFDs) and entropy based features [20–25].

## 2.3 Reconstruction Independent Component Analysis (RICA) Based Features

Reconstruction Independent Component Analysis (RICA) is not a supervised learning technique so it does not utilize the class label information. RICA algorithm was introduced to overcome the deficiencies and drawbacks of ICA algorithm. This technique delivered more promising results than ICA. A lot of algorithms have been presented in recent few years to learn sparse features.

Sparse filter can be used to distinguish a huge number of man-made and natural signals, and this feature plays an important role in different machine learning techniques.

The unlabeled data is given as input

$$\{y^i\}_{i=1}^n, y^i \in \mathbb{R}^m, \tag{1}$$

for calculating independent components the problem of optimization of standard ICA [26, 27] can be defined mathematically as:

$$\min_X \frac{1}{n} \sum_{i=1}^n h\left(Xy^i\right) \tag{2}$$

$$Subject\ to \ldots XX^U = I$$

Where, h(.)r represents a nonlinear penalty function, $X \in S^{L \times m}$ is a matrix, L represents the vectors count and identity matrix is represented by I. Furthermore, $XX^U = I$ is used to avoid the vectors in X from becoming degenerate. For this purpose, a smooth penalty function can be used i.e. $h(.) = \log(\cosh(.))$ [27].

On the other hand, some orthonormality constraint hinders the standard ICA from learning an over complete basis. Consequently, this drawback prevents ICA from scaling to high dimensional data. Hence, for the replacement of orthonormality constraints in ICA, soft reconstruction cost is used in RICA. After this replacement, RICA can be represented by the following unconstrained problem as shown in Eq. (3)

$$\min_X \frac{\lambda}{n} \sum_{i=1}^n \left( ||X^U Xy^i - y^i||_2^2 + \sum_{i=1}^n \sum_{k=1}^l h\left(X_k y^i\right) \right) \tag{3}$$

Where parameter $\lambda > 0$ exhibits the tradeoff between sparsity and reconstruction error. After swapping orthonormality constraints with reconstruction penalty, in this way RICA can learn sparse representations even on unwhitened data when X is overcomplete.

However, penalty h can produce sparse representations only, but not invariant [28]. Therefore, RICA [29, 30] swapped it by an additional $L_2$ pooling penalty, which promote pooling features to cluster correlated features together. Moreover, $L_2$ pooling also encourages sparsity for feature learning. $L_2$ pooling [31, 32] is a two-layered network with square nonlinearity in the 1st layer $(.)^2$ and square root nonlinearity in the 2nd layer $\sqrt{(.)}$ as reflected in Eq. (4)

## 2.4  Classification Methods

In this study, we proposed RICA based features extracted from brain tumor types such as glioma, meningioma and pituitary and then employed machine learning techniques such as LDA and SVM with linear and quadratic kernels.

### 2.4.1  Support Vector Machine

In 1979, Vladimir Vapnik proposed Support Vector Machine (SVM). SVMs are state of the art large margin classifiers used in visual pattern recognition [33, 34], medical diagnosis area [35, 36] and machine learning [37] which have gained more popularity recently. SVM is used in many applications such as speech recognition, face expression recognition, text recognition, emotion recognition, biometrics and content-based image retrial etc. SVM is a supervised learning technique that constructs a set of hyper-planes in an infinite dimensional space which is used to distinguish between two sample classes for the classification. Using this hyper-plane separation can be achieved that represents the largest distance to any nearest training data point of any class (sometime known as functional margin). Mostly, larger functional margin represents that the classifier shows lower generalization error. SVM kernel can find a hyper plane that provides the largest minimum distance to the training data point. In support vector machine theory, it is known as margin.

The optimal margin is then calculated for maximized plane. SVM is a two-category classifier which is used to transform data into a hyper-plane.

Consider a hyper plane $u.x + c = 0$, where $x$ is normal and linearly separable data can be labelled as reflected by Eq. (4)

$$\{u_i, v_i\}, u_i \in R^N d, v_i \in \{-1, 1\}, i = 1, 2, 3 \ldots \ldots M \tag{4}$$

Here $v_i$ is the label of two class SVM. Minimizing the objective function, the optimal boundary can be obtained $i.e. S = \|x\|^2$ subject to

$$u_i.x + c \geq 1 \text{ for } v_i = +1$$

$$u_i.x + c \leq 1 \text{ for } v_i = -1$$

After combining the inequalities can be written as shown in Eq. (5)

$$(u_i.c + c)v_i \geq 1 \text{ for all } i \tag{5}$$

When data is not linearly separable, a slack variable $\Xi_i$ can be used to represent the rate of misclassification. Therefore, some new subjective functions are reformulated using Eq. (6)

$$E = \frac{1}{2} = \|x\|^2 + B \sum_i K(\Xi_i) \tag{6}$$

Subject to

$$(u_i.c + c)v_i \geq 1 - \varepsilon_i \text{ for all } i$$

In above mentioned equation, the first term i.e. on the right side it represents regularization that provides SVM an ability to generalize the sparse data. While, the left side can be used for the calculation of empirical risk which shows misclassified within the margin K. K represents the cost function and B is the hyper parameter which represent the trade-off by maximizing the margin and minimizing the empirical risk.

### 2.4.2  Linear Discriminant Analysis (LDA)

LDA is one of the classical algorithms used in pattern recognition systems. by Belhumeur in 1997 [38] introduced this algorithm in the field of artificial intelligence (AI) and pattern recognition systems. The basic idea of LDA is to project high dimensional samples into low dimensional space to achieve the effect of extracting classification information and compressing feature space dimensions. After projection this algorithm, there is a minimum intraclass distance and largest inter-class distance. This is one of the effective feature extraction method. Recently, there are many fields and application areas in which LDA is successfully employed [39–42].

### 2.5  Testing/Training Data Formulation

In this work, Jack-knife 10-fold cross-validation technique has been employed for testing/training data formulation and parameter optimization. It is a well-known and frequently used method to evaluate and validate the accuracy of a classifier. During this research, 2,4,5 and 10-fold cross validations were used to validate the performance of classifiers for different features extracting strategies, but the higher performance was obtained using 10-fold cross validation. Using 10-fold Jack-knife cross validation test, data is divided into 10 folds. 9 folds are used in training and the classes of samples of the remaining fold are predicted based on the training performed on 9 folds. In the test fold, the test samples are purely unseen for the trained model. The entire sampling process is repeated 10 times and each class sample is predicted. Finally, the unseen predicted test samples labels are used to determine the classification accuracy. This Jack-knife process is repeated for each combination of system's parameters and classification performance have been reported for the samples that leads to obtain the maximum classification accuracy on unseen test data.

## 3  Results and Discussion

The Table 1 presents the multi-class classification performance by extracting RICA features from brain tumor types (Glioma, meningioma and pituitary) and employing machine learning techniques such as LDA, SVM with linear and quadratic kernels.

Using LDA, the classification performance to detect Glioma was obtained with sensitivity (100%), specificity (82.45%), PPV (78.85%), NPV (100%), FPR (0.175), accuracy (89.39%) and AUC (0.9122). To detect the meningioma, the performance was obtained with sensitivity (68.74%), specificity (99.36%), PPV (95.92%), NPV (93.60%), FPR (0.006), accuracy (93.89%) and AUC (0.8405). To detect pituitary, the performance was obtained with sensitivity (88.08%), specificity (100%), PPV (100%), NPV (95.10%), FPR (0.00), accuracy (96.48%) and AUC (0.9439).

**Table 1.** Multiclass classification of Brain tumor types (Glioma, meningioma, pituitary) by extracting RICA based features and employing machine learning techniques

| Class | Sens. | Spec. | PPV | NPV | FPR | Acc. | AUC |
|---|---|---|---|---|---|---|---|
| LDA | | | | | | | |
| Glioma | 100% | 82.45% | 78.85% | 100% | 0.175 | 89.39% | 91.22% |
| Meningioma | 68.74% | 99.36% | 95.92% | 93.60% | 0.006 | 93.89% | 84.05% |
| Pituitary | 88.80% | 100% | 100% | 95.10% | 0 | 96.48% | 94.39% |
| SVM linear | | | | | | | |
| Glioma | 100% | 84.56% | 81.30% | 100% | 0.1543 | 90.76% | 92.28% |
| Meningioma | 71.18% | 94.06% | 96.23% | 94.18% | 0.0059 | 94.45% | 85.29% |
| Pituitary | 88.56% | 100% | 100% | 94.77% | 0 | 96.28% | 94.28% |
| SVM quadratic | | | | | | | |
| Glioma | 100% | 90.18% | 88.28% | 100% | 0.098 | 94.35% | 95.08% |
| Meningioma | 82.15% | 99.75% | 98.83% | 95.64% | 0.0024 | 96.18% | 90.95% |
| Pituitary | 93.85% | 100% | 100% | 97.27% | 0 | 98.07% | 96.92% |

Using SVM linear, the classification performance to detect Glioma was obtained with accuracy (90.76%) and AUC (0.9228). While an accuracy of (94.45%) and AUC (0.8529) was yielded to detect meningioma and to detect pituitary an accuracy (96.28%) and AUC (0.9428) was obtained.

Using SVM Quadratic, the classification performance to detect Glioma was obtained with accuracy (94.35%) and AUC (0.9508). An accuracy of (96.18%) and (98.07%) was yielded to detect meningioma and pituitary, respectively.

The Fig. 1 represents the graphical representation for which the AUC are reflected in Table 1.

The researchers extracted various features extraction approaches using machine learning and deep learning techniques for detection binary brain tumor types. To classify brain tumor types, Zacharaki et al. [43] applied LDA and SVM by obtaining sensitivity (75%), specificity (100%) and accuracy (96.4%). Pan et al. [44] applied segmentation and yielded performance in terms of sensitivity (85%), specificity (88%) and accuracy (80%). The highest performance in term of overall accuracy was obtained [19] 91.28%, [45] 84.19%, [46] 86.56%, [47] 90.89%, [48] 84.19%. Using LDA, with multi-class, to detect pituitary the accuracy was obtained (96.48%), meningioma with accuracy (93.89%), glioma with accuracy (89.39%). Using SVM linear, to detect pituitary, the accuracy was obtained (96.28%), to detect meningioma accuracy (94.45%) was obtained, and accuracy (90.76%) was yielded to detect glioma. Moreover, using SVM quadratic, an accuracy of 98.07% was yielded to detect pituitary, an accuracy of 96.18% was obtained to detect meningioma and to detect glioma, an accuracy of 94.35% was obtained. Zia et al. [49] applied window based image cropping and obtained sensitivity (86.26%), specificity (90.90%) and accuracy (85.69%).

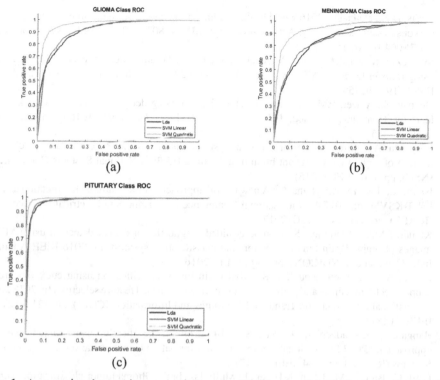

**Fig. 1.** Area under the receiver operating curve (AUC) using Multi-Class classification by extracting RICA features a) Glioma, b) Meningioma, c) Pituitary

## 4  Conclusion and Future Work

We utilized advanced feature extraction methods from MRI scans of brain tumor types (glioma, meningioma, pituitary) patients using multiclass approach. Early identification and classification of brain tumor into their specific grade could be very important to treat the tumor correctly. Automated recognition of tumor in MRI imageries is essential as high accuracy is desired when dealing with the life of a human. With the multiclass approach, the highest detection rate was obtained to detect pituitary followed by meningioma and glioma type. The result reveals that proposed feature extraction approach will be very helpful for early detection of tumor type and to treat the patient for improving the survival rate.

## References

1. Gaikwad, S.B., Joshi, M.S.: Brain tumor classification using principal component analysis and probabilistic neural network. Int. J. Comput. Appl. **120**, 5–9 (2015)
2. Gladis Pushpa Rathi, V.P., Palani, S.: Brain tumor MRI image classification with feature selection and extraction using linear discriminant analysis. Int. J. Comput. Inf. Sci. Eng. **2**, 131–146 (2012)

3. Louis, D.N., et al.: The 2016 world health organization classification of tumors of the central nervous system: a summary. Acta Neuropathol. **131**(6), 803–820 (2016). https://doi.org/10.1007/s00401-016-1545-1
4. Swati, Z.N.K., Zhao, Q., Kabir, M., et al.: Content-based brain tumor retrieval for MR images using transfer learning. IEEE Access **7**, 17809–17822 (2019). https://doi.org/10.1109/ACCESS.2019.2892455
5. Deepak, S., Ameer, P.M.: Brain tumor classification using deep CNN features via transfer learning. Comput. Biol. Med. **111**, 103345 (2019). https://doi.org/10.1016/j.compbiomed.2019.103345
6. Vidyarthi, A., Mittal, N.: Performance analysis of Gabor-Wavelet based features in classification of high grade malignant brain tumors. In: 2015 39th National Systems Conference (NSC), pp. 1–6. IEEE (2015)
7. Islam, A., Hossain, M.F., Saha, C.: A new hybrid approach for brain tumor classification using BWT-KSVM. In: 2017 4th International Conference on Advances in Electrical Engineering (ICAEE), pp. 241–246. IEEE (2017)
8. Kumar, P.M.S., Chatteijee, S.: Computer aided diagnostic for cancer detection using MRI images of brain (Brain tumor detection and classification system). In: 2016 IEEE Annual India Conference (INDICON), pp. 1–6. IEEE (2016)
9. Deepa, A.R., Sam emmanuel, W.R.: MRI brain tumor classification using cuckoo search support vector machines and particle swarm optimization based feature selection. In: 2018 2nd International Conference on Trends in Electronics and Informatics (ICOEI), pp. 1213–1216. IEEE (2018)
10. Bangare, S.L., Pradeepini, G., Patil, S.T.: Brain tumor classification using mixed method approach. In: 2017 International Conference on Information Communication and Embedded Systems (ICICES), pp. 1–4. IEEE (2017)
11. Latif, G., Butt, M.M., Khan, A.H., et al.: Multiclass brain Glioma tumor classification using block-based 3D wavelet features of MR images. In: 2017 4th International Conference on Electrical and Electronic Engineering (ICEEE), pp. 333–337. IEEE (2017)
12. Devi, T.M., Ramani, G., Arockiaraj, S.X.: MR brain tumor classification and segmentation via wavelets. In: 2018 International Conference on Wireless Communications, Signal Processing and Networking (WiSPNET), pp. 1–4. IEEE (2018)
13. Mathew, A.R., Anto, P.B.: Tumor detection and classification of MRI brain image using wavelet transform and SVM. In: 2017 International Conference on Signal Processing and Communication (ICSPC), pp. 75–78. IEEE (2017)
14. Sachdeva, J., Kumar, V., Gupta, I., et al.: Multiclass brain tumor classification using GA-SVM. In: 2011 Developments in E-Systems Engineering, pp. 182–187. IEEE (2011)
15. Abd-Ellah, M.K., Awad, A.I., Khalaf, A.A.M., Hamed, H.F.A.: Design and implementation of a computer-aided diagnosis system for brain tumor classification. In: 2016 28th International Conference on Microelectronics (ICM), pp. 73–76. IEEE (2016)
16. Abdelaziz Ismael, S.A., Mohammed, A., Hefny, H.: An enhanced deep learning approach for brain cancer MRI images classification using residual networks. Artif. Intell. Med. **102**, 101779 (2020). https://doi.org/10.1016/j.artmed.2019.101779
17. Sundararaj, G.K., Balamurugan, V.: Robust classification of primary brain tumor in Computer Tomography images using K-NN and linear SVM. In: 2014 International Conference on Contemporary Computing and Informatics (IC3I), pp. 1315–1319. IEEE (2014)
18. Cheng, J., Yang, W., Huang, M., et al.: Retrieval of brain tumors by adaptive spatial pooling and fisher vector representation. PLoS ONE **11**, e0157112 (2016). https://doi.org/10.1371/journal.pone.0157112
19. Cheng, J., Huang, W., Cao, S., et al.: Enhanced performance of brain tumor classification via tumor region augmentation and partition. PLoS ONE **10**, e0140381 (2015). https://doi.org/10.1371/journal.pone.0140381

20. Friedrich, S.O., von Groote-Bidlingmaier, F., Diacon, A.H.: Xpert MTB/RIF assay for diagnosis of pleural tuberculosis. J. Clin. Microbiol. **49**, 4341–4342 (2011). https://doi.org/10.1128/JCM.05454-11

21. Rathore, S., Hussain, M., Aksam Iftikhar, M., Jalil, A.: Ensemble classification of colon biopsy images based on information rich hybrid features. Comput. Biol. Med. **47**, 76–92 (2014). https://doi.org/10.1016/j.compbiomed.2013.12.010

22. Rathore, S., Hussain, M., Khan, A.: Automated colon cancer detection using hybrid of novel geometric features and some traditional features. Comput. Biol. Med. **65**, 279–296 (2015). https://doi.org/10.1016/j.compbiomed.2015.03.004

23. Rathore, S., Iftikhar, A., Ali, A., Hussain, M., Jalil, A.: Capture largest included circles: an approach for counting red blood cells. In: Chowdhry, B.S., Shaikh, F.K., Hussain, D.M.A., Uqaili, M.A. (eds.) IMTIC 2012. CCIS, vol. 281, pp. 373–384. Springer, Heidelberg (2012). https://doi.org/10.1007/978-3-642-28962-0_36

24. Hussain, L., Ahmed, A., Saeed, S., et al.: Prostate cancer detection using machine learning techniques by employing combination of features extracting strategies. Cancer Biomarkers **21**, 393–413 (2018). https://doi.org/10.3233/CBM-170643

25. Asim, Y., Raza, B., Kamran, A., et al.: A multi-modal, multi-atlas-based approach for Alzheimer detection via machine learning. Int. J. Imaging Syst. Technol. **28**, 113–123 (2018)

26. Hyvärinen, A., Oja, E.: Independent component analysis: algorithms and applications. Neural Netw. **13**, 411–430 (2000). https://doi.org/10.1016/S0893-6080(00)00026-5

27. Xiao, Y., Zhu, Z., Zhao, Y., et al.: Kernel reconstruction ICA for sparse representation. IEEE Trans. Neural Netw. Learn. Syst. **26**, 1222–1232 (2015). https://doi.org/10.1109/TNNLS.2014.2334711

28. Hyvärinen, A., Hurri, J., Hoyer, P.O.: Natural Image Statistics. Computational Imaging and Vision. Springer, London (2009). https://doi.org/10.1007/978-1-84882-491-1

29. Le, Q., Karpenko, A., Ngiam, J., Ng, A.: ICA with reconstruction cost for efficient overcomplete feature learning. Ad. Neural Inf. Process. Syst. **24**, 1017–1025 (2011)

30. Le, Q.V.: Building high-level features using large scale unsupervised learning. In: 2013 IEEE International Conference on Acoustics, Speech and Signal Processing, pp. 8595–8598. IEEE (2013)

31. Boureau, Y.-L., Ponce, J., LeCun, Y.: A theoretical analysis of feature pooling in visual recognition. In: Proceedings of the 27th International Conference on Machine Learning (ICML-10), pp. 111–118 (2010)

32. LeCun, Y.: Learning invariant feature hierarchies. In: Fusiello, A., Murino, V., Cucchiara, R. (eds.) ECCV 2012. LNCS, vol. 7583, pp. 496–505. Springer, Heidelberg (2012). https://doi.org/10.1007/978-3-642-33863-2_51

33. Schmidhuber, J.: Deep learning in neural networks: an overview. Neural Netw. **61**, 85–117 (2015). https://doi.org/10.1016/J.NEUNET.2014.09.003

34. Vapnik, V.N.V.N.: An overview of statistical learning theory. IEEE Trans. Neural Netw. **10**, 988–999 (1999). https://doi.org/10.1109/72.788640

35. Dobrowolski, A.P., Wierzbowski, M., Tomczykiewicz, K.: Multiresolution MUAPs decomposition and SVM-based analysis in the classification of neuromuscular disorders. Comput. Methods Programs Biomed. **107**, 393–403 (2012). https://doi.org/10.1016/j.cmpb.2010.12.006

36. Subasi, A.: Classification of EMG signals using PSO optimized SVM for diagnosis of neuromuscular disorders. Comput. Biol. Med. **43**, 576–586 (2013). https://doi.org/10.1016/j.compbiomed.2013.01.020

37. Gammerman, A.: Publications. 60, 1–18 (2015). https://doi.org/10.1007/s10472-014-9429-3

38. Kambhatla, N., Leen, T.K.: Dimension reduction by local principal component analysis. Neural Comput. **9**, 1493–1516 (1997). https://doi.org/10.1162/neco.1997.9.7.1493

39. Pathak, A., Vohra, B., Gupta, K.: Supervised learning approach towards class separability-linear discriminant analysis. In: 2019 International Conference on Intelligent Computing and Control Systems (ICCS), pp. 1088–1093. IEEE (2019)

40. Piña-Torres, C., Lucero-Gómez, P., Nieto, S., et al.: An analytical strategy based on Fourier transform infrared spectroscopy, principal component analysis and linear discriminant analysis to suggest the botanical origin of resins from Bursera. Application to archaeological Aztec Samples. J. Cult. Herit. **33**, 48–59 (2018). https://doi.org/10.1016/j.culher.2018.02.006

41. Masuda, Y., Yoshida, T., Yamaotsu, N., Hirono, S.: Linear discriminant analysis for the *in Silico* discovery of mechanism-based reversible covalent inhibitors of a serine protease: application of hydration thermodynamics analysis and semi-empirical molecular orbital calculation. Chem. Pharm. Bull. **66**, 399–409 (2018). https://doi.org/10.1248/cpb.c17-00854

42. Quost, B., Denœux, T., Li, S.: Parametric classification with soft labels using the evidential EM algorithm: linear discriminant analysis versus logistic regression. Adv. Data Anal. Classif. **11**(4), 659–690 (2017). https://doi.org/10.1007/s11634-017-0301-2

43. Zacharaki, E.I., Wang, S., Chawla, S., et al.: Classification of brain tumor type and grade using MRI texture and shape in a machine learning scheme. Magn. Reson. Med. **62**, 1609–1618 (2009). https://doi.org/10.1002/mrm.22147

44. Pan, Y., Huang, W., Lin, Z., et al.: Brain tumor grading based on neural networks and convolutional neural networks. In: 2015 37th Annual International Conference of the IEEE Engineering in Medicine and Biology Society (EMBC), pp. 699–702. IEEE (2015)

45. Paul, J.S., Plassard, A.J., Landman, B.A., Fabbri, D.: Deep learning for brain tumor classification. In: Krol, A., Gimi, B. (eds.) p. 1013710 (2017)

46. Afshar, P., Mohammadi, A., Plataniotis, K.N.: Brain tumor type classification via capsule networks. In: 2018 25th IEEE International Conference on Image Processing (ICIP), pp. 3129–3133. IEEE (2018)

47. Afshar, P., Plataniotis, K.N., Mohammadi, A.: Capsule networks for brain tumor classification based on MRI images and coarse tumor boundaries. In: ICASSP 2019 - 2019 IEEE International Conference on Acoustics, Speech and Signal Processing (ICASSP), pp. 1368–1372. IEEE (2019)

48. Abiwinanda, N., Hanif, M., Hesaputra, S.T., Handayani, A., Mengko, T.R.: Brain tumor classification using convolutional neural network. In: Lhotska, L., Sukupova, L., Lacković, I., Ibbott, G.S. (eds.) World Congress on Medical Physics and Biomedical Engineering 2018. IP, vol. 68/1, pp. 183–189. Springer, Singapore (2019). https://doi.org/10.1007/978-981-10-9035-6_33

49. Zia, R., Akhtar, P., Aziz, A.: A new rectangular window based image cropping method for generalization of brain neoplasm classification systems. Int. J. Imaging Syst. Technol. **28**, 153–162 (2018). https://doi.org/10.1002/ima.22266

# Overall Survival Prediction in Gliomas Using Region-Specific Radiomic Features

Asma Shaheen[1], Stefano Burigat[1], Ulas Bagci[2], and Hassan Mohy-ud-Din[3]($\boxtimes$)

[1] Department of Mathematics, Computer Science and Physics, University of Udine,
33100 Udine, Italy
[2] Department of Computer Science, University of Central Florida, Orlando 32826, USA
[3] Department of Electrical Engineering,
Lahore University of Management Sciences, Lahore 54792, Pakistan
hassan.mohyuddin@lums.edu.pk

**Abstract.** In this paper, we explored predictive performance of region-specific radiomic models for overall survival classification task in BraTS 2019 dataset. We independently trained three radiomic models: *single-region* model which included radiomic features from whole tumor (WT) region only, *3-subregions* model which included radiomic features from non-enhancing tumor (NET), enhancing tumor (ET), and edema (ED) subregions, and *6-subregions* model which included features from the left and right cerebral cortex, the left and right cerebral white matter, and the left and right lateral ventricle subregions. A 3-subregions radiomics model relied on a physiology-based subdivision of WT for each subject. A 6-subregions radiomics model relied on an anatomy-based segmentation of tumor-affected regions for each subject which is obtained by a diffeomorphic registration with the Harvard-Oxford subcortical atlas. For each radiomics model, a subset of most predictive features was selected by ElasticNetCV and used to train a Random Forest classifier. Our results showed that a *6-subregions* radiomics model outperformed the *3-subregions* and WT radiomic models on the BraTS 2019 training and validation datasets. A *6-subregions* radiomics model achieved a classification accuracy of 47.1% on the training dataset and a classification accuracy of 55.2% on the validation dataset. Among the single subregion models, Edema radiomics model and Left Lateral Ventricle radiomics model yielded the highest classification accuracy on the training and validation datasets.

## 1 Introduction

Gliomas are brain tumors that originate in the glial cells of the brain [1]. They constitute 80% of malignant brain tumors [2]. Based on the aggressiveness of the tumor, World Health Organization (WHO) classifies them into four grades [3]: WHO Grade II and Grade III gliomas are called Low-Grade Gliomas (LGGs) and WHO Grade IV gliomas are called High-Grade Gliomas (HGGs). Compared to LGGs, HGGs are more aggressive and malignant with a median survival of less than two years [4].

MRI is a non-invasive imaging modality that is routinely used for spatial localization of brain tumors in 3D. Unlike X-ray and CT imaging, MRI provides high resolution

© Springer Nature Switzerland AG 2020
S. M. Kia et al. (Eds.): MLCN 2020/RNO-AI 2020, LNCS 12449, pp. 259–267, 2020.
https://doi.org/10.1007/978-3-030-66843-3_25

images with superior soft tissue contrast without employing ionizing radiation [5]. For diagnosis of brain gliomas, four MRI sequences are acquired, namely, T1-weighted, T1-weighted contrast enhanced (T1ce), T2 weighted, and Fluid Attenuated Inversion Recovery (FLAIR).

In the management of HGGs, overall survival plays an important role in its treatment and surgical planning [6]. Overall survival is defined as the number of days a patient survives after surgery [27]. In the BraTS challenge [7], overall survival prediction in HGGs is formulated as a classification task. The BraTS challenge defined three survival classes namely, short term (<10 months), medium term (10–15 months), and long term (>15 months) survivors.

In the last few years, several radiomics-based approaches have appeared that predict overall survival in brain gliomas directly from MRI scans. These studies are based on the publicly available BraTS dataset [8–12]. Kao et al. [13] extracted morphological, volumetric, and tractographic features from 59 subjects with documented Gross Total Resection status. Discriminatory features were selected by recursive feature elimination and used to train SVM classifier with a linear kernel. Compared to morphological, spatial, and volumetric features, tractography features achieved a high accuracy of 69.7% on the training set but a low accuracy of 35.7% and 41.6% on the validation and test datasets, respectively. Elodie et al. [14] extracted 10 volumetric features from all subjects with Gross Total Resection status. The features were normalized with PCA and used to train 50 Random Forest classifiers. The final prediction was obtained by a majority voting on the 50 outputs from the trained classifiers. The authors reported an accuracy of 54.0% on the training dataset. Pei et al. [15] developed a hybrid machine learning algorithm for overall survival prediction. The authors extracted 1,702 handcrafted features and 737,280 deep features with U-Net-VAE architecture [16]. A subset of most predictive features was selected with LASSO and used to train a linear regression classifier. The study reported an accuracy of 56.0% on the training dataset and 43.0% on the testing dataset. Feng et al. [17] trained a linear regression classifier with a combination of 6 radiomic features and clinical features (including age) for overall survival prediction. The study reported an accuracy of 32.1% on the validation dataset. Islam et al. [18] used PixelNet [19] for glioma segmentation and extracted radiomic features including geometrical, shape, volumetric, and first order features to predict overall survival. The study selected a subset of 50 most predictive features using cross validation followed by training an artificial neural network. The authors reported an accuracy of 46.0% on the test dataset.

In this paper, we explore the power of region-specific radiomic features for overall survival prediction in HGGs using BraTS 2019 dataset. Radiomic features are extracted from tumor-affected regions which makes segmentation of tumor subregions essential [15, 17, 18]. Tumor subregions could be defined based on physiology or anatomy. Physiology-based segmentation divides the tumor into three subregions, namely, peritumoral edema, non-enhancing core, and enhancing core [8]. Anatomy-based segmentation uses a predefined atlas to divide the tumor-affected region into various anatomical regions. Figure 1 shows an axial slice of a FLAIR scan fused with physiology-based manual segmentation and anatomy-based segmentation using a Harvard-Oxford subcortical atlas [20].

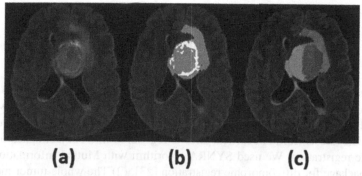

**Fig. 1.** (a) axial slice of FLAIR scan overlaid with (b) physiology-based manual segmentation including peritumoral edema (green), enhancing tumor (yellow), and non-enhancing tumor (orange), and (c) anatomy-based tumor segmentation with *6-subregions* model including left cerebral cortex, right cerebral cortex, left lateral ventricle, right lateral ventricle, left cerebral white matter, and right cerebral white matter. *Note: This figure should be visualized in color.* (Color figure online)

## 2   Materials and Methods

### 2.1   Dataset and Preprocessing

The training dataset is BraTS 2019 challenge data [7] and consists of 259 HGGs with preoperative 3D multiparametric MRI scans (including T1, T2, T1ce, and FLAIR sequences). Manual segmentation of tumor subregions (including peritumoral edema, non-enhancing tumor, and enhancing tumor) are provided and confirmed by expert neuroradiologists [8]. Out of 259 HGGs, complete survival information was provided for 210 subjects and Gross Total Resection status was provided for 101 subjects. The validation dataset from BraTS 2019 consists of 29 HGGs with Gross Total Resection Status. Unlike the training dataset, these subjects only contain preoperative 3D multiparametric MRI scans (including T1, T2, T1ce, and FLAIR sequences).

The 3D MRI scans for each subject were already skull-stripped, registered to T1ce scan, and resampled to an isotropic $1 \times 1 \times 1$ mm$^3$ resolution [8–12]. 3D MRI T1 scan for each subject were preprocessed using N4ITK bias field correction algorithm [21], which is a recommended pre-processing step before performing any image processing in MRI [22].

### 2.2   Tumor Subregion Segmentation Models

We focused on two models for segmentation of tumor subregions in brain gliomas: (1) physiology-based segmentation model and (2) anatomy-based segmentation model.

In physiology-based segmentation model, brain tumor is subdivided into *edema (ED), non-enhancing tumor (NET), and enhancing tumor (ET)*. Further grouping of these subregions provide better representation of tumor for clinical applications [8].

1.  Whole tumor (WT) is a combination of *ED, NET, and ET* subregions.
2.  Tumor core (TC) is a combination of *NET and ET* subregions.
3.  Active tumor only contains the *ET* region.

In this paper, we call this model a *3-subregions* segmentation model.

In anatomy-based segmentation model, the brain tumor is subdivided into anatomical regions with the help of a pre-defined Harvard-Oxford subcortical atlas which has 21 labeled anatomical regions [20]. Anatomy-based segmentation is obtained in four steps: (1) Harvard-Oxford subcortical atlas is registered into subject space using diffeomorphic registration. We used SYNRA algorithm with Mutual Information metric in ANTs package for diffeomorphic registration [23]. (2) The whole tumor mask from manual segmentation is overlaid with the registered atlas to extract the tumor-affected anatomical regions. (3) Volumes of tumor-affected anatomical regions is computed and then ranked in descending order. (4) Finally, the top-most anatomical subregions that combine to occupy more than 90% of WT volume are retained. In this paper, we call this segmentation scheme as *6-subregions* segmentation model where *6* is the number of subregions selected in step 4. Given the two segmentation models, i.e. *3-subregions* and *6-subregions models*, one can extract region-specific radiomic features for classification.

### 2.3  Radiomic Feature Extraction

To compare the predictive power of region-specific radiomic features, we extracted radiomic features, using *PyRadiomics* software package [24], from *3-subregions* model and *6-subregions* model. For each subregion, we extracted shape and volumetric features:

*Shape features* include maximum 3D diameter, major and minor axis length, sphericity, least axis length, elongation, surface to volume ratio, flatness, surface area, maximum 2D diameter along each plane (axial, coronal, and sagittal) of tumor subregions.

*Volumetric features* include volume of tumor subregions obtained from multi-class segmentation maps.

We also evaluated the predictive power of an augmented set of features by including clinical and spatial features:

*Clinical feature* includes age, in years, which is provided for each subject in the BraTS 2019 dataset.

*Spatial features* encode location of tumor within the brain. For each subject, we extracted: (1) Centroid of the WT, TC, and brain mask. These centroids are composed of three coordinate values, one for each axis in a 3D Euclidean space (9 features). (2) Distance and angle of the centroid of WT from the center of the brain mask (2 features). (3) Distance and angle of the centroid of TC from the center of the brain mask (2 features).

In total, we extracted 13 spatial features, 42 shape and volumetric features for the *3-subregions* model, and 84 shape and volumetric features for the *6-subregions* model for each subject.

### 2.4  Feature Selection and Classification

For every feature vector, we replaced NaNs with the mean of the remaining feature values followed by z-score normalization. We employed ElasticNetCV [25] to select a subset of most predictive features. Feature selection was only performed for Whole Tumor (WT), *3-subregions*, and *6-subregions* radiomic models. *Single subregion* radiomic models had few features to begin with and, hence, no feature selection was performed.

A Random Forest classifier (no_of_estimators = 200, max_depth = 2, criterion = gini, min_samples_split = 2, class_weight = balanced, max_features = auto) was trained using the subset of most predictive features and evaluated on the holdout dataset. In our experiments on the training dataset (210 subjects), we conducted a 200-times repeated stratified 5-fold cross validation with 70%–30% split. In our experiments on the validation dataset (29 subjects), a Random Forest classifier was trained on 101 subjects from the training dataset with GTR status. The predictive performance of the classifier was evaluated using an accuracy metric, as suggested by the BraTS 2019 challenge [7]. The code was implemented in Python 3.5 using the scikit-learn package [26].

## 3   Results and Discussion

### 3.1   Evaluation on Training Dataset (210 Subjects)

*3-Subregions Segmentation Model:* We evaluated the predictive power of radiomic features extracted from NET, ET, and ED subregions. We also evaluated the improvement in accuracy achieved by adding clinical and spatial features for overall survival classification task. The obtained results, summarized in Table 1, showed that a combination of shape, volumetric, spatial, and clinical features provided the highest accuracy of 45.7% for the overall survival classification task. We also studied the predictive power of radiomic features extracted from each subregion and found that the ED-radiomics model with shape, volumetric, and clinical features achieved the highest accuracy of 46.8%.

**Table 1.**  Overall Survival classification accuracy with a *3-subregions* radiomics model. Accuracy is reported as a %-age with mean and standard deviation.

| Features | Radiomic Models | | | |
|---|---|---|---|---|
| | 3-subregions | Necrosis | Edema | Enhancing Tumor |
| Shape + Volumetric | $43.7 \pm 5.3$ | $43.6 \pm 5.1$ | $43.9 \pm 5.6$ | $44.6 \pm 5.6$ |
| Shape + Volumetric + Age | $45.1 \pm 5.4$ | $\mathbf{45.8 \pm 5.2}$ | $\mathbf{46.8 \pm 5.8}$ | $44.8 \pm 5.6$ |
| Shape + Volumetric + Spatial + Age | $\mathbf{45.7 \pm 5.3}$ | $44.8 \pm 5.3$ | $45.1 \pm 5.6$ | $\mathbf{45.5 \pm 5.3}$ |

*6-Subregions Segmentation Model:* We evaluated the predictive power of radiomic features extracted from the left and right cerebral cortex, the left and right cerebral white matter, and the left and right lateral ventricle subregions. We also evaluated the improvement in accuracy achieved by adding clinical and spatial features for overall survival classification task. The obtained results, summarized in Table 2, showed that a combination of shape, volumetric, spatial, and clinical features provided the highest accuracy of 47.1% for the overall survival classification task. We also evaluated the predictive power of radiomic features extracted from individual subregions and found that the left Lateral

**Table 2.** Overall Survival classification accuracy with a *6-subregions* radiomics model. Accuracy is reported as a %-age with mean and standard deviation.

| Radiomic Models | Features | | |
|---|---|---|---|
| | Shape + Volumetric | Shape + Volumetric + Age | Shape + Volumetric + Spatial + Age |
| 6-subregions | 34.4 ± 5.5 | 46.2 ± 5.8 | **47.1 ± 5.9** |
| Left Cerebral Cortex | 35.7 ± 5.2 | 43.9 ± 5.6 | **44.6 ± 5.7** |
| Right Cerebral Cortex | 38.8 ± 4.9 | 42.3 ± 5.3 | **43.8 ± 5.7** |
| Left Cerebral White Matter | 36.4 ± 5.0 | 44.4 ± 5.5 | **44.7 ± 5.5** |
| Right Cerebral White Matter | 38.8 ± 5.2 | 44.3 ± 5.8 | **44.2 ± 5.7** |
| Left Lateral Ventricle | 37.3 ± 5.3 | **46.3 ± 5.4** | 44.5 ± 5.7 |
| Right Lateral Ventricle | 36.6 ± 4.4 | 42.6 ± 5.8 | **44.2 ± 5.7** |

Ventricle radiomics model with shape, volumetric, and clinical features, achieved the highest accuracy of 46.3%.

*3-Subregions vs 6-Subregions:* Figure 2 compares predictive performance of three radiomic models i.e. WT model, *3-subregions* model, and *6-subregions* model. With shape and volumetric features only, we found that a *3-subregions* radiomics model yielded the highest classification accuracy of 43.7% followed by WT model, with an accuracy of 41.1%, and *6-subregions model*, with an accuracy of 34.4%. However, augmenting radiomic features with spatial and clinical features significantly boosted

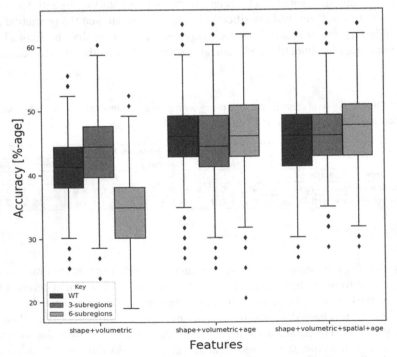

**Fig. 2.** A comparison of overall survival classification performance with three radiomic models, namely, WT, 3-subregions, and 6-subregions models.

the classification performance of *3-subregions*, WT and *6-subregions* radiomic models i.e. improvements of 2.0% in accuracy for the *3-subregions* model, 4.7% in accuracy for the WT model, and 12.7% in accuracy for the *6-subregions* model. These experiments showed that a *6-subregions* radiomics model built on an augmented set of features (including shape, volumetric, spatial, and clinical features) outperformed a WT radiomics model and *3-subregions* radiomics model (in that order).

## 3.2 Evaluation on Validation Dataset (29 Subjects)

The BraTS 2019 validation dataset did not include expert manual segmentations of tumor subregions (including peritumoral edema, non-enhancing tumor, and enhancing tumor). We employed a 2D-slice based U-Net architecture [28, 29] for segmentation of tumor subregions on 3D multiparametric MRI scans. The details of the architecture, training procedure, and associated hyperparameters can be found here [29]. We obtained an average dice score of 86.8% $\pm$ 6.4 for the Whole Tumor, 82.1% $\pm$ 14.2 for the Tumor Core, and 81.8% $\pm$ 12.1 for the Enhancing Tumor subregions. For the overall survival classification task, Table 3 lists the classification accuracy obtained with WT, *3-subregions*, and *6-subregions* radiomic models. Our results showed that a *6-subregions* radiomics provided the highest classification accuracy of 55.2%. Table 4 lists the classification accuracy obtained with single subregion radiomic models. Our results showed that the Edema radiomics model and the Left Lateral Ventricle radiomics model yielded the best classification accuracy (51.7% and 55.2% respectively).

**Table 3.** Overall survival classification accuracy with radiomics models on validation dataset.

| Features | Radiomic Models | | |
|---|---|---|---|
| | WT | 3-subregions | 6-subregions |
| Shape + Volumetric + Spatial + Age | 48.8 | 51.7 | 55.2 |

**Table 4.** Overall survival classification accuracy on individual regions

| Radiomic Models | Features |
|---|---|
| | Shape + Volumetric + Spatial + Age |
| Necrosis | 34.5 |
| Edema | **51.7** |
| Enhancing Tumor | 44.8 |
| Left Cerebral Cortex | 41.4 |
| Right Cerebral Cortex | 48.3 |
| Left Cerebral White Matter | 51.7 |
| Right Cerebral White Matter | 51.7 |
| Left Lateral Ventricle | **55.2** |
| Right Lateral Ventricle | 44.8 |

## 4  Conclusions

In this paper, we comparatively explored three region-specific radiomic models for overall survival classification task in BraTS 2019 dataset. We focused on three radiomic models, namely, *single-region* model which included radiomic features from WT region only, *3-subregions* model which included radiomic features from NET, ET, and ED subregions, and *6-subregions* model which included features from the left and right cerebral cortex, the left and right cerebral white matter, and the left and right lateral ventricle subregions.

A *3-subregions* model defined a physiology-based subdivision of WT and a *6-subregions* model defined an anatomy-based subdivision of WT. The *6-subregions* radiomics model built on shape, volumetric, spatial, and clinical features outperformed *3-subregions* and WT radiomic models on BraTS 2019 training and validation datasets. On the BraTS 2019 training dataset, a *6-subregions* radiomics model achieved the highest classification accuracy of 47.1%, compared to 45.8% for WT and 45.7% for *3-subregions* radiomic models. On the BraTS 2019 validation dataset, a *6-subregions* radiomics model achieved the highest classification accuracy of 55.2%, compared to 48.8% for WT and 51.7% for *3-subregions* radiomic models. Our experiments also demonstrated that single subregion radiomic models, including Edema radiomics model and Left Lateral Ventricle radiomics model, can also be employed for the overall survival classification task.

**Acknowledgement.** This work was in part supported by a grant from the Higher Education Commission of Pakistan that has funded the National Center in Big Data and Cloud Computing and the Clinical and Translational Imaging Lab at LUMS. The authors wish to thank Syed Talha Bukhari in providing the multi-class segmentation maps for the BraTS 2019 validation dataset.

## References

1. Cha, S.: Update on brain tumor imaging: from anatomy to physiology. Am. J. Neuroradiol. **27**(3), 475–487 (2006)
2. Goodenberger, M.L., Jenkins, R.B.: Genetics of adult glioma. Cancer Genet. **205**(12), 613–621 (2012)
3. Louis, D.N., et al.: The 2016 World Health Organization classification of tumors of the central nervous system: a summary. Acta Neuropathologica **131**(6), 803–820 (2016)
4. Bi, W.L., Beroukhim, R.: Beating the odds: extreme long-term survival with glioblastoma. Neuro-Oncol. **16**, 1159–1160 (2014)
5. Banerjee, S., Arora, H.S., Mitra, S.: Ensemble of CNNs for segmentation of glioma subregions with survival prediction. In: Crimi, A., Bakas, S. (eds.) BrainLes 2019. LNCS, vol. 11993, pp. 37–49. Springer, Cham (2020). https://doi.org/10.1007/978-3-030-46643-5_4
6. Sanghani, P., et al.: Overall survival prediction in glioblastoma multiforme patients from volumetric, shape and texture features using machine learning. Surg. Oncol. **27**(4), 709–714 (2018)
7. https://www.med.upenn.edu/cbica/brats2019
8. Menze, B.H., et al.: The multimodal brain tumor image segmentation benchmark (BRATS). IEEE Trans. Med. Imaging **34**(10), 1993–2024 (2014)
9. Bakas, S., et al.: Advancing the cancer genome atlas glioma MRI collections with expert segmentation labels and radiomic features. Sci. Data **4**, 170117 (2017)

10. Bakas, S., et al.: Identifying the best machine learning algorithms for brain tumor segmentation, progression assessment, and overall survival prediction in the BRATS challenge. arXiv preprint arXiv:1811.02629 (2018)
11. Bakas, S., et al.: Segmentation labels and radiomic features for the pre-operative scans of the TCGA-GBM collection. The cancer imaging archive. Nat. Sci. Data **4**, 170117 (2017)
12. Bakas, S., et al.: Segmentation labels and radiomic features for the pre-operative scans of the TCGA-LGG collection. The cancer imaging archive 286 (2017)
13. Kao, P.-Y., Ngo, T., Zhang, A., Chen, J.W., Manjunath, B.S.: Brain tumor segmentation and tractographic feature extraction from structural MR images for overall survival prediction. In: Crimi, A., Bakas, S., Kuijf, H., Keyvan, F., Reyes, M., van Walsum, T. (eds.) BrainLes 2018. LNCS, vol. 11384, pp. 128–141. Springer, Cham (2019). https://doi.org/10.1007/978-3-030-11726-9_12
14. Puybareau, E., Tochon, G., Chazalon, J., Fabrizio, J.: Segmentation of gliomas and prediction of patient overall survival: a simple and fast procedure. In: Crimi, A., Bakas, S., Kuijf, H., Keyvan, F., Reyes, M., van Walsum, T. (eds.) BrainLes 2018. LNCS, vol. 11384, pp. 199–209. Springer, Cham (2019). https://doi.org/10.1007/978-3-030-11726-9_18
15. Pei, L., Vidyaratne, L., Monibor Rahman, M., Shboul, Z.A., Iftekharuddin, K.M.: Multimodal brain tumor segmentation and survival prediction using hybrid machine learning. In: Crimi, A., Bakas, S. (eds.) BrainLes 2019. LNCS, vol. 11993, pp. 73–81. Springer, Cham (2020). https://doi.org/10.1007/978-3-030-46643-5_7
16. Kohl, S., et al.: A probabilistic U-Net for segmentation of ambiguous images. In: Advances in Neural Information Processing Systems (2018)
17. Feng, X., et al.: Brain tumor segmentation using an ensemble of 3D U-Nets and overall survival prediction using radiomic features. Front. Comput. Neurosci. **14**, 25 (2020)
18. Islam, M., Jose, V.J.M., Ren, H.: Glioma prognosis: segmentation of the tumor and survival prediction using shape, geometric and clinical information. In: Crimi, A., Bakas, S., Kuijf, H., Keyvan, F., Reyes, M., van Walsum, T. (eds.) BrainLes 2018. LNCS, vol. 11384, pp. 142–153. Springer, Cham (2019). https://doi.org/10.1007/978-3-030-11726-9_13
19. Islam, M., Ren, H.: Multi-modal PixelNet for brain tumor segmentation. In: Crimi, A., Bakas, S., Kuijf, H., Menze, B., Reyes, M. (eds.) BrainLes 2017. LNCS, vol. 10670, pp. 298–308. Springer, Cham (2018). https://doi.org/10.1007/978-3-319-75238-9_26
20. Desikan, R.S., et al.: An automated labeling system for subdividing the human cerebral cortex on MRI scans into gyral based regions of interest. Neuroimage **31**(3), 968–980 (2006)
21. Tustison, N.J., et al.: N4ITK: improved N3 bias correction. IEEE Trans. Med. Imaging **29**(6), 1310–1320 (2010)
22. https://github.com/ANTsX/ANTs/wiki/Anatomy-of-an-antsRegistration-call
23. Avants, B.B., et al.: A reproducible evaluation of ANTs similarity metric performance in brain image registration. Neuroimage **54**(3), 2033–2044 (2011)
24. Van Griethuysen, J.J.M., et al.: Computational radiomics system to decode the radiographic phenotype. Cancer Res. **77**(21), e104–e107 (2017)
25. https://scikitlearn.org/0.15/modules/generated/sklearn.linear_model.ElasticNetCV.html
26. Pedregosa, F., et al.: Scikit-learn: machine learning in Python. J. Mach. Learn. Res. **12**, 2825–2830 (2011)
27. Macyszyn, L., et al.: Imaging patterns predict patient survival and molecular subtype in glioblastoma via machine learning techniques. Neuro-oncology **18**(3), 417–425 (2015)
28. Dong, H., Yang, G., Liu, F., Mo, Y., Guo, Y.: Automatic brain tumor detection and segmentation using U-Net based fully convolutional networks. In: Valdés Hernández, M., González-Castro, V. (eds.) MIUA 2017. CCIS, vol. 723, pp. 506–517. Springer, Cham (2017). https://doi.org/10.1007/978-3-319-60964-5_44
29. Bukhari, S.T., Mohy-ud-Din, H.: A systematic evaluation of learning rate policies in training CNNs for brain tumor segmentation (2020, under review)

# Using Functional Magnetic Resonance Imaging and Personal Characteristics Features for Detection of Neurological Conditions

Batool Rathore[1], Muhammad Awais[2(✉)], Muhammad Usama Usman[3], Imran Shafi[4], and Waqas Ahmed[5]

[1] Department of Psychology, University of Azad Jammu and Kashmir, Muzaffarabad, Pakistan
[2] Department of Computing, Abasyn University, Islamabad, Pakistan
muhammadawaisrathore@gmail.com
[3] Department of Electrical and Computer Engineering, Florida State University, Tallahassee, FL 32306, USA
[4] National University of Sciences and Technology, Islamabad, Pakistan
[5] Higher Education Department, Punjab, Pakistan

**Abstract.** Neuroimaging-based diagnosis could help clinicians in making accurate diagnosis, accessing accurate prognosis, and deciding faster, more effective, and personalized treatment on an individual person basis. In this research work, we aim to develop a neuro-imaging, i.e. functional magnetic resonance imaging (fMRI), based method to detect attention deficit hyper-activity disorder (ADHD), which is a psychiatric disorder categorized by the impulsive nature, lack of attention, and hyper activeness. We utilized fMRI scans as well as personal characteristic features (PCF) data provided as part of ADHD-200 challenge. We aim to train a machine learning classifier by using fMRI and PCF data to classify each participant into one of the following three classes: healthy control (HC), combined-type ADHD (ADHD-C), or inattentive-type ADHD (ADHD-I). We used participants' PCF and fMRI data separately, and then evaluated the combined use of both the datasets in detecting different classes. Support vector machine classifier with linear kernel was used for the training. The experiments were conducted under two different configurations: (i) 2-way configuration where classification was conducted between HC and ADHD (ADHD-C+ADHD-I) patients, and between ADHD-C and ADHD-I, and (ii) 3-way configuration where data of all the categories (HC, ADHD-C and ADHD-I) was combined together for classification. The 2-way classification approach achieved the diagnostic accuracy of 86.52% and 82.43% in distinguishing HC from ADHD patients, and ADHD-C and ADHD-I, respectively. The 3-way classification revealed classification success rate of 78.59% when both fMRI and PCF data were used together. These results demonstrate the importance of utilizing fMRI data and PCF for the detection of psychiatric disorders.

**Keywords:** Attention deficit hyperactivity disorder · Machine learning · Pattern analysis · Psychiatric disorders

© Springer Nature Switzerland AG 2020
S. M. Kia et al. (Eds.): MLCN 2020/RNO-AI 2020, LNCS 12449, pp. 268–275, 2020.
https://doi.org/10.1007/978-3-030-66843-3_26

# 1   Introduction

Attention deficit hyper-activity disorder (ADHD) is a major psychiatric condition described by thoughtlessness, distraction, and hyper-activity. According to statistical reports, ADHD effects almost 5% of young children and adolescents globally [1]. ADHD not only imposes significant burdens on individuals suffering from the disease and the family members, but also imposes huge economic costs to society. There are three distinctive subtypes of ADHD based on the criterion defined in the Diagnostic and Statistical Manual of Mental Disorders (DSM-IV-TR). These subtypes are (i) hyperactive-impulsive ADHD (ADHD-H), (ii) inattentive ADHD (ADHD-I), and (iii) combined hyperactive-impulsive and inattentive ADHD (ADHD-C).

Previous research in the field of ADHD has investigated the neurobiology of ADHD [2–4]. Majority of existing research has mainly focused on identifying the group-level differences, wherein various characteristics calculated across groups were either compared to each other or to the baseline characteristics. For instance, average fMRI in a certain brain region calculated across a population of ADHD patients might be compared to the corresponding average regional value across a population of healthy controls (HC).

Recently, there has been a mounting interest in applying advanced machine leaning and pattern analysis methods on fMRI data of individual patients to diagnose various psychiatric illnesses [5–8]. Such neuroimaging-based diagnostic methods have the potential to assist the treating psychiatrists in providing better diagnosis and to guide them to select optimal treatment for such patients, thereby leading to the concept of precision medicine [9, 10].

Resting state fMRI (rs-fMRI) is a very useful method for fMRI-based diagnostics of various neurological conditions. In order to acquire a rs-fMRI scan, patient is advised to rest quietly without undergoing through any stimulus presentation or accomplishing any obvious task [11]. Analysis of rs-fMRI scan then allows to examine intrinsic patterns of activation in various brain regions [12, 13]. The rs-fMRI has been used in the past to highlight the differences between different disease groups such as ADHD and HC [14–19]. In these studies, significant differences were found in different brain regions, including prefrontal cortex, putamen, temporal cortex, and cerebellum [15, 20]. The rs-fMRI has also been utilized to diagnose ADHD on an individual patient basis [21, 22]. For example, discriminative analysis of brain function at resting-state was used for detection of ADHD [21], and kernel principal component analysis was employed for dimensionality reduction in fMRI-based diagnosis of ADHD [22].

However, these studies have tested the proposed algorithms on relatively small number of populations [21, 23]. Capitalizing on the recent advances in the field of rs-fMRI based detection, we use rs-fMRI and personal characteristic features (PCF) either singly or in combination. We utilize support vector machine (SVM) to develop the models, and evaluate the performance of the proposed model on publically-available ADHD-200 competition dataset.

## 2  Materials and Methods

### 2.1  Dataset

In this study, ADHD-200 competition dataset was utilized. Each participant was scanned for fMRI and T1-weighted MRI scan at one of the following sites: (i) Peking University, (ii) Kennedy Krieger Institute, (iii) Brown University, (iv) NeuroIMAGE Sample, (v) Oregon Health and Science University, (vi) New York University, (vii) University of Pittsburgh, and (viii) Washington University in St. Louis. In addition to the imaging data, multiple personal characteristic features such as age, gender, handedness, and IQ scores. Data of 776 participants was made available as part of the training dataset, however, the imaging scans (fMRI) of 108 patients were not of sufficient quality, therefore, we utilized data of 668 participants only. The data comprised of healthy control (HC), ADHD type C (ADHD-C), and ADHD type I (ADHD-I). More details on the dataset is in Table 1.

**Table 1.** Details of 688 participants included in this study (a subset of ADHD-200 training dataset). NA stands for Not Available.

|        | Number | Age          | Gender (%) Female-Male | Handedness (%) Left-Right-Ambi.-NA |
|--------|--------|--------------|------------------------|------------------------------------|
| HC     | 429    | 12.4 ± 3.33  | 47.6-52.4              | 2.6-96.3-0.2-0.9                   |
| ADHD-C | 141    | 11.4 ± 3.1   | 17.0-82.3              | 3.5-95.0-0.0-1.4                   |
| ADHD-I | 98     | 12.1 ± 2.5   | 26.5-73.5              | 2.0-98.0-0.0-0.0                   |

### 2.2  Image Preprocessing Applied on the Dataset

In order to preprocess rs-fMRI scans, we used SPM8 fMRI analysis package along with in-house written MATLAB and Python scripts. Preprocessing of each rs-fMRI comprised:

1. Motion correction using 6-parameter rigid body
2. Denoising using adaptive non-local means denoising algorithm [24, 25]
3. Rigid body co-registration of rs-fMRI to patient-specific anatomical scans in SPM8
4. Non-linear estimation and interpolation of each patient's anatomical scan at 1 mm cubic resolution to the MNI T1 template
5. Interpolation of rs-fMRI images to the T1 template at 3 mm cubic resolution using warping parameters of 3rd step
6. 8 mm full width at half maximum Gaussian spatial filtering of rs-fMRI images. After this step, all the patients had same size (57 × 67 × 50 voxels) and spatial resolution (3 cubic mm), however, the temporal resolution was still different across participants depending on the duration and sampling rate of data acquisition at the participating sites.
7. Truncation of all rs-fMRI images to 185 s
8. Temporal linear interpolation of rs-fMRI images into a sampling rate of 1 s volume time.

## 2.3  Dimensionality Reduction and Feature Extraction

In comparison with the high-dimensional imaging data (70,651,500 voxels in each rs-fMRI image), the number of images itself (n = 668) were very small. Therefore, the chance of machine learning algorithm to do overfitting on high-dimensional noisy data compared to learning generic imaging patterns present in the data were very high. Therefore, we adopted several methods to reduce the temporal and spatial dimensionality of the rs-fMRI images before training any machine learning model.

Spatial window averaging was used to reduce the spatial dimensionality of each image by a factor of 3 along each axis., thereby reducing the original size of the image volume from $57 \times 67 \times 50$ (190,950 voxels) to $19 \times 22 \times 16$ (6,688 voxels). We then used a binary mask of the brain to remove all the voxels outside of the brain, which further reduced the size to 3,558 voxels.

We used principal component analysis (PCA) to reduce the temporal dimensions of the rs-fMRI images. We considered the time-course vector (4th dimension of the rs-fMRI image) of each voxel within each image as a stand-alone sample and applied PCA on $i$ images $\times$ $k$ voxels time-courses. We kept first 3–10 principal components (PCs) and projected the time-course of each voxel onto the selected components. This process resulted in reduction of temporal size from $185 \times 3$ to 3 (3 PCs) or from $185 \times 10$ to 10 (10 PCs).

## 2.4  Feature Selection and Predictive Learning

Linear kernel of SVM classifier was utilized to integrate all the rs-fMRI and PCF features via a $k$-fold cross-validation to develop machine learning models predictive of HC and ADHD. The cross-validation scheme assesses the performance of the developed model on any cohort as it was divided in independent and non-related discovery and replication cohorts. In each iteration of $k$-fold cross-validation, it divides the data into discovery ($k$-1 folds) and replication ($k$th fold) subsets and then repeats the process each time by picking a new replication subset until all the samples of all the folds have been tested. In order to ensure robust estimation of the generalizability of the proposed model, classifier's parameter optimization was done on discovery data only which was totally unseen for the replication data. Similarly, feature selection was performed on the discovery data using SVM forward feature selection in each iteration of the $k$-fold cross-validation.

# 3  Results and Application

The fMRI and PCF data was either used alone or in combination to classify HC and ADHD subjects via SVM. Results are separately shown in Sect. 3.1, 3.2, and 3.3 for PCF data, fMRI data, and combined data (PCF+fMRI).

## 3.1  Classification Performance of Predictive Model Using Personal Characteristics Features (PCF)

Table 2 shows classification scores achieved using PCF for the 2-way and 3-way classification tasks. The SVM classifier performed significantly better than the chance in both 2-way and 3-way classification. The classification accuracy using PCF was 79.34% [sensitivity = 82.00%, specificity = 77.86%, balanced accuracy = 79.93%] for HC vs. ADHD, and 76.99% [sensitivity = 77.31%, specificity = 76.53%, balanced accuracy = 76.92%] for ADHD-C vs. ADHD-I. The 3-way classification accuracy was 71.32% when all the data was combined together.

**Table 2.** Performance of the classification model on various configurations using individual and combination datasets

|  | Accuracy | Sensitivity | Specificity | Balanced accuracy |
|---|---|---|---|---|
| Personal characteristic data | | | | |
| HC vs ADHD | 79.34 | 82.00 | 77.86 | 79.93 |
| ADHD-C vs ADHD-I | 76.99 | 77.31 | 76.53 | 76.92 |
| HC vs ADHD-C vs ADHD-I | 71.32 | – | – | – |
| fMRI | | | | |
| HC vs ADHD | 79.79 | 80.33 | 79.49 | 79.91 |
| ADHD-C vs ADHD-I | 78.66 | 78.01 | 79.59 | 78.80 |
| HC vs ADHD-C vs ADHD-I | 72.59 | – | – | – |
| Personal characteristic data + fMRI | | | | |
| HC vs ADHD | 87.13 | 87.87 | 86.71 | 87.29 |
| ADHD-C vs ADHD-I | 84.10 | 82.98 | 85.71 | 84.35 |
| HC vs ADHD-C vs ADHD-I | 78.59 | – | – | – |

The performance of the models developed using PCF was also evaluated using receiver operating characteristic (ROC) analysis, and the corresponding area under the curve (AUC) was 0.83 [standard error (SE) = 0.0179, 95% confidence interval (CI) = 0.7931,0.8631] for HC vs. ADHD and 0.87 [SE = 0.0274, 95% CI = 0.7539,0.8614] for ADHD-E vs. ADHD-I (Fig. 1).

### 3.2 Classification Performance of the Predictive Model Using fMRI Data

PCA-summarized features extracted from fMRI were also used to develop predictive models. Table 2 shows classification scores achieved using fMRI for the 2-way and 3-way classification tasks. Like PCF-based classification, the SVM classifier performed significantly better than the chance in both 2-way and 3-way classification. The developed models yielded classification accuracies of 79.79% [sensitivity = 80.33%, specificity = 79.49%, balanced accuracy = 79.91%] for HC vs. ADHD, and 78.66% [sensitivity = 78.01%, specificity = 79.59%, balanced accuracy = 78.80%] for ADHD-C vs. ADHD-I. AUC of the model was 0.85 [SE = 0.0170, 95% CI = 0.8148,0.8813] for HC vs. ADHD and 0.80 [SE = 0.0279, 95% CI = 0.7456,0.8551] for ADHD-E vs. ADHD-I (Fig. 1). The 3-way classification accuracy was 72.59% when all the data was combined together.

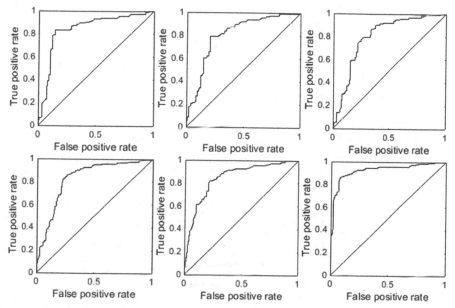

**Fig. 1.** ROC curves. Left-right: PCF, fMRI, and PCF + fMRI. Top-bottom: HC vs. ADHD, and ADHD-C vs. ADHD-I

### 3.3 Classification Performance of the Predictive Model Using Combined fMRI and Personal Characteristics Features (PCF) Data

The model trained on combined data helped improve machine learning results by combining several features such as fMRI and PCF and allowed better predictive rates compared to either of the individual features (fMRI or PCF). The feature combination method not only led to better classification performance but also a unified interpretation by summarizing individual predictions from different feature types. The models developed on fMRI+PCF data yielded classification accuracies of 87.13% [sensitivity = 87.87%, specificity = 86.71%, balanced accuracy = 87.29%] for HC vs. ADHD, and 84.10% [sensitivity = 82.98%, specificity = 85.71%, balanced accuracy = 84.35%] for ADHD-C vs. ADHD-I. AUC of the model was 0.93 [SE: 0.0121, 95% CI = 0.9034,0.9509] for HC vs. ADHD and 0.84 [SE = 0.0249, 95% CI = 0.7928,0.8906] for ADHD-E vs. ADHD-I (Fig. 1). The 3-way classification accuracy was 78.59% when all the data was combined together.

### 3.4 Selection of the Number of Principal Components (PCs)

Selection of an optimal number of PCs was important criteria for developing the classification models. Number of PCs were varied in the range of 3 to 10 with an increment of 1, and corresponding classification accuracy was observed. Classification performance initially increased with an increase in the number of PCs, and then started decreasing after a certain point. Roughly between 6–8, maximum classification performance was observed in all the cases, therefore results corresponding to 7 number of PCs were reported in the paper (Fig. 2).

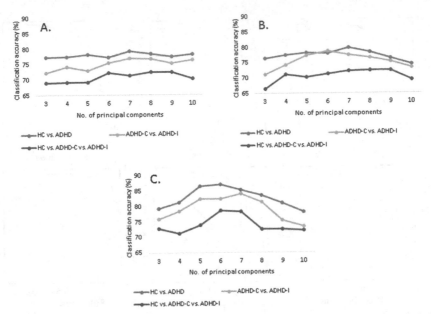

**Fig. 2.** Classification performance as a function of the number of principal components. A. PCF, B. fMRI, and C. fMRI+PCF

## 4   Conclusion

We utilized advanced pattern analysis and machine learning algorithm on rs-fMRIscans to derive an imaging signature of healthy controls and differnet types of ADHD i.e. ADHD-C and ADHD-I. Our results indicate that the synergistic use of rs-fMRI data and PCF data improves detection of HC and ADHD. Moreover, although our proposed signature successfully predicted HC and ADHD participants, the model needs to be evaluated on larger and diverse multi-institutional populations to prove further generalizability of our findings and evaluate the application of our predictive models across various institutional settings. This method holds promise to assist clinical decision-making for selectting ADHD patients for targeted therapeutic approaches and clinical trials.

## References

1. Polanczyk, G., et al.: The worldwide prevalence of ADHD: a systematic review and metaregression analysis. Am. J. Psychiatry **164**, 942–948 (2007)
2. King, J.A., et al.: Neural substrates underlying impulsivity. Ann. N. Y. Acad. Sci. **1008**, 160–169 (2003)
3. Liston, C., et al.: Atypical prefrontal connectivity in attention-deficit/hyperactivity disorder: pathway to disease or pathological end point? Biol. Psychiat. **69**, 1168–1177 (2011)
4. Bush, G., et al.: Functional neuroimaging of attention-deficit/hyperactivity disorder: a review and suggested future directions. Biol. Psychiat. **57**, 1273–1284 (2005)
5. Fan, Y., et al.: Discriminant analysis of functional connectivity patterns on Grassmann manifold. NeuroImage **56**, 2058–2067 (2011)

6. Shen, H., et al.: Discriminative analysis of resting-state functional connectivity patterns of schizophrenia using low dimensional embedding of fMRI. NeuroImage **49**, 3110–3121 (2010)
7. Nouretdinov, I., et al.: Machine learning classification with confidence: application of transductive conformal predictors to MRI-based diagnostic and prognostic markers in depression. NeuroImage **56**, 809–813 (2011)
8. Arribas, J.I., et al.: Automatic Bayesian classification of healthy controls, bipolar disorder, and schizophrenia using intrinsic connectivity maps from fMRI data. IEEE Trans. Biomed. Eng. **57**, 2850–2860 (2010)
9. Rathore, S., et al.: A review on neuroimaging-based classification studies and associated feature extraction methods for Alzheimer's disease and its prodromal stages. NeuroImage **155**, 530–548 (2017)
10. Rathore, S., et al.: Analysis of MRI data in diagnostic neuroradiology. Annu. Rev. Biomed. Data Sci. **3**, 365–390 (2020)
11. Fox, M.D., et al.: The human brain is intrinsically organized into dynamic, anticorrelated functional networks. Proc. Natl. Acad. Sci. U.S.A. **102**, 9673–9678 (2005)
12. Friston, K.J., et al.: Dynamic causal modelling revisited. NeuroImage **199**, 730–744 (2019)
13. Calhoun, V.D., et al.: Spatial and temporal independent component analysis of functional MRI data containing a pair of task-related waveforms. Hum. Brain Mapp. **13**, 43–53 (2001)
14. Cao, X., et al.: Abnormal resting-state functional connectivity patterns of the putamen in medication-naïve children with attention deficit hyperactivity disorder. Brain Res. **1303**, 195–206 (2009)
15. Cao, Q., et al.: Abnormal neural activity in children with attention deficit hyperactivity disorder: a resting-state functional magnetic resonance imaging study. NeuroReport **17**, 1033–1036 (2006)
16. Tian, L., et al.: Enhanced resting-state brain activities in ADHD patients: a fMRI study. Brain Develop. **30**, 342–348 (2008)
17. Zang, Y.F., et al.: Altered baseline brain activity in children with ADHD revealed by resting-state functional MRI. Brain Develop. **29**, 83–91 (2007)
18. Sun, L., et al.: Abnormal functional connectivity between the anterior cingulate and the default mode network in drug-naïve boys with attention deficit hyperactivity disorder. Psychiatry Res. **201**, 120–127 (2012)
19. Qiu, M.G., et al.: Changes of brain structure and function in ADHD children. Brain Topogr. **24**, 243–252 (2011)
20. Tian, L., et al.: Altered resting-state functional connectivity patterns of anterior cingulate cortex in adolescents with attention deficit hyperactivity disorder. Neurosci. Lett. **400**, 39–43 (2006)
21. Zhu, C.Z., et al.: Discriminative analysis of brain function at resting-state for attention-deficit/hyperactivity disorder. In: Duncan, J.S., Gerig, G. (eds.) MICCAI 2005. LNCS, vol. 3750, pp. 468–475. Springer, Heidelberg (2005). https://doi.org/10.1007/11566489_58
22. Sidhu, G., et al.: Kernel Principal Component Analysis for dimensionality reduction in fMRI-based diagnosis of ADHD. Front. Syst. Neurosci. **6**, 74 (2012)
23. Zhu, C.Z., et al.: Fisher discriminative analysis of resting-state brain function for attention-deficit/hyperactivity disorder. NeuroImage **40**, 110–120 (2008)
24. Iftikhar, M.A., et al.: Robust brain MRI denoising and segmentation using enhanced non-local means algorithm. Int. J. Imaging Syst. Technol. **24**, 52–66 (2014)
25. Iftikhar, M.A., et al.: Brain MRI denoizing and segmentation based on improved adaptive nonlocal means. Int. J. Imaging Syst. Technol. **23**, 235–248 (2013)

# Differentiation of Recurrent Glioblastoma from Radiation Necrosis Using Diffusion Radiomics: Machine Learning Model Development and External Validation

Yae Won Park[1], Ji Eun Park[2], Sung Soo Ahn[1(✉)], Hwiyoung Kim[1], Ho Sung Kim[2], and Seung-Koo Lee[1]

[1] Yonsei University College of Medicine, Seoul, Korea
sungsoo@yuhs.ac
[2] University of Ulsan College of Medicine, Seoul, Korea

**Abstract.** We aimed to establish a high-performing radiomics strategy to differentiate recurrent glioblastoma (GBM) from radiation necrosis (RN). Eighty-six patients with posttreatment GBM were enrolled in the training set (63 recurrent GBM and 23 RN). Another 41 patients (23 recurrent GBM and 18 RN) from a different institution were enrolled in the test set. Conventional MRI sequences (T2-weighted and postcontrast T1-weighted images) and ADC were analyzed to extract 263 radiomic features. After feature selection, various machine learning models were trained with combinations of MRI sequences and validated in the test set. In the independent test set, the model using ADC sequence showed the best diagnostic performance, with an AUC, accuracy, sensitivity, specificity of 0.800, 78%, 66.7%, and 87%, respectively. The radiomics models using other MRI sequences showed AUCs ranging from 0.650 to 0.662 in the test set. In conclusion, the diffusion radiomics may be helpful in differentiating recurrent GBM from RN.

**Keywords:** Glioblastoma · Machine learning · Magnetic resonance imaging · Radiomics

## 1 Introduction

Radiation necrosis (RN) usually occurs within 3 years after radiation therapy and is often indistinguishable from recurrent glioblastoma (GBM, World Health Organization [WHO] grade IV) on magnetic resonance imaging (MRI) [1, 2]. Thus, distinguishing between recurrent GBM and RN has clinical importance in deciding the subsequent management; recurrence indicates treatment failure and requires the use of additional anticancer therapies, whereas RN is treated conservatively.

Multiple studies have made efforts to distinguish GBM recurrence from RN using various imaging methods [3–5]. However, there is no gold standard imaging method for the differentiation between recurrence and RN. Currently, the definitive diagnosis is based on histopathology which is both invasive and difficult.

© Springer Nature Switzerland AG 2020
S. M. Kia et al. (Eds.): MLCN 2020/RNO-AI 2020, LNCS 12449, pp. 276–283, 2020.
https://doi.org/10.1007/978-3-030-66843-3_27

Radiomics involves the identification of ample quantitative features within images and the subsequent data mining for information extraction and application [6].

The aim of this study was to develop and validate a high-performing radiomic strategy using machine learning classifiers from conventional imaging and apparent diffusion coefficient (ADC) to differentiate recurrent GBM from RN after concurrent chemoradiotherapy (CCRT) or radiotherapy.

## 2 Materials and Methods

### 2.1 Patient Population

Between February 2016 and February 2019, 90 patients with pathologically diagnosed GBM (WHO grade IV) from our institution were reviewed in this study. The inclusion criteria were as follows: 1) GBM confirmed by histopathology; 2) postoperative CCRT or RT, with a radiation dose ranging from 45 to 70 Gy; 3) subsequent development of a new or enlarging region of contrast enhancement within the radiation field 12 weeks after CCRT or RT; and 4) surgical resection of the enhancing lesion or adequate clinico-radiological follow-up. For clinicoradiological diagnosis, a final diagnosis of recurrent GBM was made if the contrast-enhancing lesions gradually enlarged on more than two subsequent follow-up MRI studies performed at 2–3 month intervals and the clinical symptoms of patients showed gradual deterioration during follow-up. Alternatively, a final diagnosis of RN was made if enhancing lesions gradually decreased on more than two subsequent follow-up MRI studies performed at 2–3 month intervals and clinical symptoms improved during the follow-up period. Exclusion criteria were as follows: 1) processing error (n = 3), 2) absence of MRI sequences (n = 1). Thus, a total of 86 patients were enrolled.

Identical inclusion and exclusion criteria were applied to enroll 41 patients at another tertiary center (***) in the test set for the external validation of the model.

Of the 86 patients in the training set, 63 (73.3%) were classified as recurrent GBM and 23 (26.7%) as RN cases. The 41 patients in the test set consisted of 23 (56.1%) recurrent GBM and 18 (43.9%) RN cases (Table 1).

**Table 1.** Baseline demographic data and clinical characteristics of patients

| Variables | Training set (n = 86) | | | Test set (n = 41) | | | P-value[†] |
|---|---|---|---|---|---|---|---|
| | Recurrent GBM (n = 63) | RN (n = 23) | P-value* | Recurrent GBM (n = 23) | RN (n = 18) | P-value* | |
| Age (years) | 54.4 ± 13.0 | 57.9 ± 10.6 | 0.255 | 60.7 ± 11.8 | 57.0 ± 13.7 | 0.358 | 0.571 |
| Female sex | 20 (31.7) | 7 (30.4) | 0.908 | 10 (43.5) | 8 (44.4) | 0.951 | 0.851 |
| KPS | 73.8 ± 17.0 | 73.9 ± 19.2 | 0.974 | 60.7 ± 11.8 | 57.0 ± 13.7 | 0.394 | 0.961 |
| Extent of resection | | | 0.644 | | | 0.556 | 0.757 |
| Biopsy | 7 (11.1) | 1 (4.3) | | 1 (4.3) | 1 (5.6) | | |

(*continued*)

**Table 1.** (*continued*)

| Variables | Training set (n = 86) | | | Test set (n = 41) | | | P-value† |
|---|---|---|---|---|---|---|---|
| | Recurrent GBM (n = 63) | RN (n = 23) | P-value* | Recurrent GBM (n = 23) | RN (n = 18) | P-value* | |
| Partial | 11 (17.5) | 5 (21.7) | | 7 (30.4) | 3 (16.7) | | |
| Subtotal | 24 (38.1) | 11 (47.8) | | 13 (56.5) | 10 (55.6) | | |
| Total | 21 (33.3) | 6 (26.1) | | 2 (8.7) | 4 (22.2) | | |
| First-line treatment | | | 0.3115 | | | 0.370 | 0.418 |
| CCRT | 60 (93.7) | 20 (87.0) | | 22 (95.7) | 17 (94.4) | | |
| RT alone or RT plus temozolomide | 4 (6.3) | 3 (13.0) | | 1 (4.3) | 1 (5.6) | 0.859 | |
| Total radiation dose (Gy) | 60.2 ± 11.6 | 61.9 ± 16.1 | 0.591 | 56.3 ± 11.4 | 60.7 ± 8.1 | 0.251 | 0.476 |
| IDH1 mutant | 2 (3.2) | 2 (8.7) | 0.282 | 1 (4.3) | 1 (5.6) | 0.859 | 0.342 |
| MGMT promoter methylation | 13 (20.6) | 9 (39.1) | 0.082 | 8 (34.8) | 7 (38.9) | 0.786 | 0.090 |

\* Calculated from Student t test for continuous variables and Chi-square test for categorical variables for comparison of recurrent GBM and RN in training and test sets.
† Calculated from Student t test for continuous variables and Chi-square test for categorical variables for comparison of training and test sets.

## 2.2 Pathological Diagnosis

Twenty-two and 14 patients underwent second-look operations in the training set and test set, respectively. In second-look operations, the pathological diagnoses included 17 recurrent GBM and 5 RN cases in the training set, and 8 recurrent GBM and 6 RN cases in the test set, respectively. The diagnosis was made on the basis of histological findings in contrast-enhancing tissue obtained with surgical tumor resection or image-guided. More than 5% viable tumor diagnosed during the histological examination by neuropathologists, were classified as a recurrent GBM.

## 2.3 MRI Protocol

In the training set, all patients underwent MRI on a 3.0-T MRI scanner (Achieva or Ingenia, Philips Medical Systems) with an 8-channel head coil. The preoperative MRI sequences included T1WI, T2WI (T2), postcontrast T1WI (T1C), as well as ADC scans. After 5–6 min of administration of 0.1 mL/kg of gadolinium-based contrast material (Gadovist; Bayer), T1C were acquired.

In the external validation set, MRI exams were performed using a 3.0-T MRI scanner (Achieva, Philips Medical Systems) with an 8-channel head coil.

## 2.4  Imaging Preprocessing and Radiomics Feature Extraction

N4 bias correction was performed. Signal intensity normalization was used in the T2 and T1C images, by WhiteStripe method [7]. Images were resampled to $1 \times 1 \times 1$ mm. T2 and ADC images were registered to the T1C image. Tumor segmentation was performed through a consensus discussion of two neuroradiologists (with 14 years and 7 years of experience), in order to select the contrast-enhancing solid portion of the tumor on T1C images. Segmentation was performed semiautomatically with an interactive level-set region of interest, using edge-based and threshold-based algorithms. A total of 93 radiomic features, including shape, first order features, and second-order features, were extracted from the mask, with an open-source python-based module (Pyradiomics, version 2.0) [8]. In addition, edge contrast calculation was performed. The final set consisted of 263 radiomic features for each patient. The data were processed using a multi-platform, open-source software package (3D slicer, version 4.6.2-1; http://slicer.org).

## 2.5  Radiomics Feature Selection and Machine Learning

All radiomic features were z-score normalized. For feature selection, the F-score, least absolute shrinkage and selection operator (LASSO), or mutual information (MI) with stratified ten-fold cross-validation were applied. The machine learning classifiers were constructed using k-nearest neighbors (KNN), support vector machine (SVM), or AdaBoost, with stratified ten-fold cross-validation. In addition, to overcome data imbalance, each machine learning model was trained either without subsampling or with synthetic minority over-sampling technique (SMOTE) [8]. Because we wanted to determine which combination of MRI sequence shows the highest performance, the identical process was performed in each sequences (ADC, T2, T1C, and combined ADC, T2, and T1C model). Thus, various combinations of classification models were trained to differentiate recurrent GBM from RN in the training set. The different feature selection, classification methods, and subsampling were computed using MatlabR2014b (Mathworks). Statistical significance was set at $p < .05$ (Fig. 1).

## 2.6  Diagnostic Performance in the Test Set

LASSO Based on the radiomics classification model in the training set, the best combination of feature selection, classification methods, and subsampling in each sequence was used in the test set. The AUC, accuracy, sensitivity, and specificity were obtained.

## 2.7  Availability of Data and Code

Our anonymized data can be obtained by any qualified investigator for the purposes of replicating procedures and results after ethics clearance and approval by all authors. The python code for machine learning can also be obtained by any qualified investigator for the purposes of replicating procedures and results after approval by all authors.

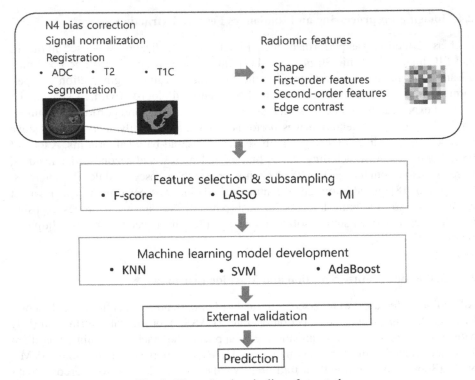

**Fig. 1.** The radiomics pipeline of our study.

## 3 Results

### 3.1 Best Performing Machine Learning Models from Radiomics Features for Differentiating Recurrent GBM from RN

Using radiomic features, in each combination of the selected MRI sequence, the 3 feature selection, 3 classification methods, and 2 subsampling methods was trained.

The performance of each combination of the models is shown in Fig. 2. In the training set, the AUCs of the models showing the best diagnostic performance ranged from 0.859 to 0.932 in each combination. In the ADC sequence, the combination of LASSO feature selection, SVM, and subsampling showed the best diagnostic performance in the training set. The selected 18 features consisted of 3 first-order features, 10 second-order features, and 5 shape features (Detailed information at Table 2). This model demonstrated an AUC, accuracy, sensitivity, specificity of 0.896 (95% confidence interval [CI] 0.841–0.951), 80.5%, 78.3%, and 82.9%, respectively. In the T2 sequence, the combination of LASSO feature selection, SVM, and subsampling showed the best diagnostic performance in the training set with an AUC of 0.859 (95% CI 0.804–0.914). In the T1C sequence, the combination of MI feature selection, SVM, and subsampling showed the best diagnostic performance in the training set with an AUC of 0.906 (95% CI 0.860–0.952). In the combined sequence (ADC + T2 + T1C), the combination of LASSO feature selection,

SVM, and subsampling showed the best diagnostic performance in the training set with an AUC of 0.932 (95% CI 0.892–0.972).

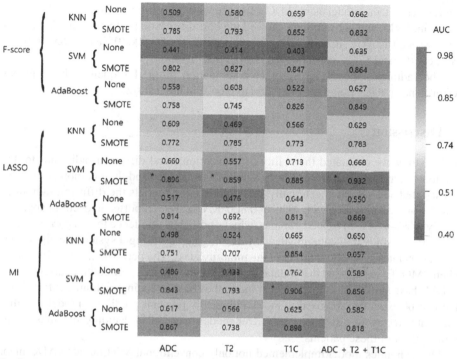

**Fig. 2.** Heatmap depicting the diagnostic performance (AUCs) of combinations of feature selection methods, classifiers, and combination of sequences in the training set.

**Table 2.** Diagnostic performance of the best performing machine learning model in the training set and the test set.

| Sequence | Training set | Test set | | | |
|---|---|---|---|---|---|
| | AUC (95% CI) | AUC (95% CI) | Acc | Sens | Spec |
| ADC | 0.896 (0.841–0.951) | 0.800 (0.654–0.945) | 78 | 66.7 | 87 |
| T2 | 0.859 (0.804–0.914) | 0.650 (0.479–0.821) | 61 | 44.4 | 73.9 |
| T1C | 0.906 (0.860–0.952) | 0.662 (0.491–0.833) | 53.7 | 11.1 | 87 |
| ADC + T2 + T1C | 0.932 (0.892–0.972) | 0.662 (0.487–0.836) | 63.4 | 38.9 | 82.6 |

## 3.2 Robustness of Radiomics Models in the Test Set

Using radiomic features, in each combination of the selected MRI sequence, the 3 feature selection, 3 classification methods, and 2 subsampling methods was trained. In the independent test set, the model using ADC sequence with the combination of LASSO feature selection, SVM, and subsampling showed the best diagnostic performance. This model demonstrated an AUC, accuracy, sensitivity, specificity of 0.800 (95% CI 0.654–0.945), 78%, 66.7%, and 87%, respectively.

The radiomics models using other combination of MRI sequence showed poor performance (AUCs ranging from 0.650 to 0.662) in the test set.

## 4   Discussion

In this study, we evaluated the ability of conventional and diffusion radiomics to differentiate recurrent GBM from RN. Several MR sequences and their combination were investigated and validated externally, and among these models the diffusion radiomics model showed robustness with AUC of 0.800. RN has been reported to occur in approximately 9.8%–44.4% of treated gliomas, which shows low incidence than recurrent GBM [4, 5]. In our study, the data imbalance was mitigated by using a systematic algorithm, which generates synthetic samples in the minority class. The performance was increased when SMOTE was applied in our dataset, showing its efficacy. Although recurrent GBM and RN have similar radiologic appearances, they harbor distinct radiomic information that can be extracted and used to build a clinically relevant predictive model that discriminates recurrent GBM from RN. Our model may aid in deciding the subsequent management of these patients.

Our radiomics model implemented not only conventional MRI but also ADC map, and showed that diffusion radiomics model could robustly differentiate recurrent GBM from RN better than any other radiomics model. ADC maps extract absolute values creating reliable feature extraction, which may be less affected by heterogeneous protocol settings and consequently demonstrated high diagnostic performance in the external validation. In addition, our results may emphasize the importance of domain-specific knowledge in the relatively small data settings of radiomics study [10, 11]. Previous studies have shown that the ADC characteristics are more important than conventional characteristics in differentiating RN from GBM [4]. The diffusion radiomics model is promising for reflecting the tumor microenvironment, since these values can contain biological information. Although ADC value can be affected by various factors, ADC in tumor is generally considered to be an index of tumor cellularity that reflects tumor burden. On histopathological examination, recurrent GBM is characterized by dense glioma cells, which limit water diffusion [4]. In contrast, RN is characterized by extensive fibrinoid necrosis, vascular dilatation, and gliosis [11]. The different histopathology and spatial complexity may be reflected in diffusion radiomics, allowing the differentiation of the two entities. In conclusion, the diffusion radiomics model may be helpful in differentiating recurrent GBM from RN.

Our study has several limitations. First, our study was retrospective with a small data size. Second, dynamic susceptibility (DSC) imaging was not included due to lack of data in a portion of patients. Because DSC data is important in distinguishing recurrent GBM from RN, [12], further radiomics studies implementing DSC data are warranted to evaluate the efficacy. Third, we did not apply various filters such as wavelet transformation for radiomics feature extraction and performance evaluation.

## 5   Conclusion

The diffusion radiomics model may be helpful in differentiating recurrent GBM from RN.

## References

1. Stupp, R., et al.: Radiotherapy plus concomitant and adjuvant temozolomide for glioblastoma. N. Engl. J. Med. **352**, 987–996 (2005)
2. Weller, M., et al.: European Association for Neuro-Oncology (EANO) guideline on the diagnosis and treatment of adult astrocytic and oligodendroglial gliomas. Lancet Oncol. **18**, e315–e329 (2017)
3. Shah, R., et al.: Radiation necrosis in the brain: imaging features and differentiation from tumor recurrence. Radiographics **32**, 1343–1359 (2012)
4. Hein, P.A., et al.: Diffusion-weighted imaging in the follow-up of treated high-grade gliomas: tumor recurrence versus radiation injury. Am. J. Neuroradiol. **25**, 201–209 (2004)
5. Barajas, R.F., et al.: Differentiation of recurrent gliomblastoma multiforme from radiation necrosis after external beam radiation therapy with dynamic susceptibility-weighted contrast-enhanced perfusion MR imaging. Radiology **253**, 486–496 (2009)
6. Gillies, R.J., et al.: Radiomics: images are more than pictures, they are data. Radiology **278**, 563–577 (2015)
7. Shinohara, R.T., et al.: Statistical normalization techniques for magnetic resonance imaging. NeuroImage Clin. **6**, 9–19 (2014)
8. van Griethuysen, J.J.M., Fedorov, A., Parmar, C., et al.: Computational radiomics system to decode the radiograhic phenotype. Can. Res. **77**(21), e104–e107 (2017)
9. Punyakanok, V., et al.: In: IJCAI, pp. 1124–1129
10. Chang, M-W. et al.: In: AAAI, pp. 1513–1518
11. Hopewell, J.W., Calvo, W., Jaenke, R., Reinhold, H.S., Robbins, M.E.C., Whitehouse, E.M.: Microvasculature and radiation damage. In: Hinkelbein, W., Bruggmoser, G., Frommhold, H., Wannenmacher, M. (eds.) Acute and Long-Term Side-Effects of Radiotherapy. Recent Results in Cancer Research, vol. 130, pp. 1–16. Springer, Heidelberg (1993). https://doi.org/10.1007/978-3-642-84892-6_1
12. Hu, L.S., et al.: Reevaluating the imaging definition of tumor progression: perfusion MRI quantifies recurrent glioblastoma tumor fraction, pseudoprogression, and radiation necrosis to predict survival. Neuro-oncology **14**, 919–930 (2012)

# Brain Tumor Survival Prediction Using Radiomics Features

Sobia Yousaf[1], Syed Muhammad Anwar[1(✉)], Harish RaviPrakash[2], and Ulas Bagci[2]

[1] Department of Software Engineering, UET Taxila, Taxila, Pakistan
s.anwar@uettaxila.edu.pk
[2] CRCV, University of Central Florida, Orlando, FL, USA

**Abstract.** Surgery planning in patients diagnosed with brain tumor is dependent on their survival prognosis. A poor prognosis might demand for a more aggressive treatment and therapy plan, while a favorable prognosis might enable a less risky surgery plan. Thus, accurate survival prognosis is an important step in treatment planning. Recently, deep learning approaches have been used extensively for brain tumor segmentation followed by the use of deep features for prognosis. However, radiomics-based studies have shown more promise using engineered/hand-crafted features. In this paper, we propose a three-step approach for multi-class survival prognosis. In the first stage, we extract image slices corresponding to tumor regions from multiple magnetic resonance image modalities. We then extract radiomic features from these 2D slices. Finally, we train machine learning classifiers to perform the classification. We evaluate our proposed approach on the publicly available BraTS 2019 data and achieve an accuracy of **76.5%** and precision of 74.3% using the random forest classifier, which to the best of our knowledge are the highest reported results yet. Further, we identify the most important features that contribute in improving the prediction.

## 1 Introduction

Gliomas are the most common type of brain tumor with over 78% malignant tumors being gliomas [1]. However, not all gliomas are malignant and can be broadly classified into two groups: high-grade glioma (HGG) and low-grade glioma (LGG). According to the World Health Organization guidelines four grades are defined for tumors [9]. Grade I and Grade II tumors are LGG, which are primarily benign and slow growing. Grades III and IV are HGG, which are malignant in nature with a high probability of recurrence. With Grade I tumors being mostly benign, patients tend to have a long term survival rate. Patients with HGG on the other hand, owing to the more aggressive nature of these tumors, have a much lower survival time, sometimes not exceeding a year. An early diagnosis of glioma would help the radiologist in assessing the patient's condition and plan a treatment accordingly. Magnetic resonance images (MRI) provide high contrast for soft tissue and hence represent the heterogeneity of the

© Springer Nature Switzerland AG 2020
S. M. Kia et al. (Eds.): MLCN 2020/RNO-AI 2020, LNCS 12449, pp. 284–293, 2020.
https://doi.org/10.1007/978-3-030-66843-3_28

tumor core, providing a detailed information about the tumor. Different modalities commonly used in radiology include T1-weighted, contrast enhanced T1-weighted, fluid-attenuated inversion recovery (FLAIR), and T2-weighted MRIs. A detailed profile of enhancing tumor region can be described using contrast enhanced T1-weighted MRI as compared to T2-weighted MRI [16]. The hyperintense regions in FLAIR images tend to correspond to regions of edema thus suggesting the need for the use of multi modal images [8]. A quantitative assessment of the brain tumor provides important information about the tumor structure and hence is considered as a vital part for diagnosis [14]. Automatic tumor segmentation of pre-operative multi modal MR Images in this perspective is attractive because it provides the quantitative measurement of the tumor parameters such as shape and volume. This process is also considered as a pre-requisite for survival prediction, because significant features can only be computed from the tumor region. So, this quantitative assessment has a significant importance in the diagnosis process and research. Due to imaging artifacts, ambiguous boundaries, irregular shape and appearance of tumor and its sub-regions, development of automatic tumor segmentation algorithms become challenging.

Over the past few years, several deep learning (DL) based approaches have been introduced especially for medical image analysis [2,4,10,12]. DL models outperform traditional machine learning approaches on numerous applications in computer vision as well as medical image analysis, especially when sufficiently large number of training samples are available [3]. Automatic segmentation alone is not sufficient for diagnosis and treatment, hence survival analysis is also necessary to help determine the treatment and therapy plans. Towards this, traditional machine learning based approaches have shown promising results using hand-crafted features [14]. These features, having been extracted from radiology images, are commonly referred to as radiomic features and help in the characterization of the tumor. Since 2017, the challenge of survival prognosis of glioma patients on BraTS benchmark data has been included. In the task of survival prediction, patients diagnosed with HGG are categorized into short-, mid- and long-term survival groups. The interval of these classes can be decided on the basis of number of days, months, or resection status. While DL algorithms have shown excellent performance on tumor segmentation tasks, in the survival prediction task, they have shown unstable performance [15]. Radiomics are likely to be dominant for precision medicine because of its capability to exploit detailed information of gliomas phenotype [18]. Inspired from these achievements of radiomics features in this challenging task of survival prediction on several modalities, herein we propose to utilize radiomic features for prediction.

## Our Contributions

In this paper we present a machine learning based approach, utilizing radiomic features, for survival prediction on BraTS 2019 data. We extract radiomic features from the tumor regions utilizing the provided ground-truth segmentation masks and train machine learning classifiers to predict the survival class. Our main contributions are

- We identify discriminating features that contributed the most in improving the accuracy and found that Haralick features are more significant for survival prediction task.
- We explore multiple classifiers commonly used in this domain, and found random forest to be the best performing model with state-of-the-art performance when used with the selected radiomics features.

## 2    Proposed Methodology

Our proposed approach towards survival prediction is shown in Fig. 1. It consists of the three main steps. 1) Region of interest (ROI) extraction 2) Radiomic features computation, and 3) Survival prediction The details of these steps are presented in the following sections.

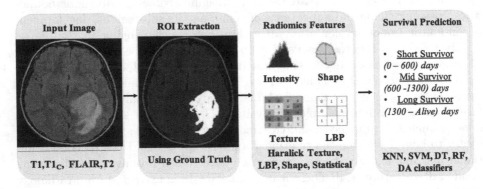

**Fig. 1.** The proposed radiomics features based survival prediction pipeline using BraTS 2019 data.

### 2.1    Image Pre-processing and ROI Extraction

The data were acquired from multiple institutions using different scanners. There could exist different levels of noise in scanners leading to intensity variations that can strongly influence the extracted radiomic features [5]. Hence, bias field correction and normalization steps were applied on the input data to standardize the intensity values. More precisely, the intensity value of each image slice is subtracted from its mean and is divided by the image's intensity standard deviation. In order to extract the ROI, we applied the ground truth of respective patient on all input modalities. As a result we get the complete tumor region from all scans of the patient.

### 2.2    Radiomics Features

Radiomics are the specific kind of features that are primarily computed from radiology images to describe phenotypes of the tumor region. These features can be further used to predict the tumor and can improve the survival prediction. Herein, radiomic features extracted from input modalities are classified into three groups - first order statistics, shape features, and texture features. The details of these features are presented in the following text.

**First-Order Statistics.** These features represent statistical properties such as the average intensity value, median, variance, standard deviation, kurtosis, skewness, entropy, and energy. These features were computed using the intensity values in MR images, such that the gray-level intensity of the tumor region is described accurately. In particular, a total of 10 first order features were extracted from each slice of the four modalities used.

**Shape Features.** Shape features include perimeter, area, convex area, convex perimeter, concavity, diameter, major and minor axis length, circulatory, elongation, and sphericity. Further, we described the tumor shape by using the Fourier descriptor, where the entire shape is represented using minimal numeric values [6].

**Texture Features.** Texture features are considered to be strong in the radiomics field [19]. We computed the Haralick texture features [7], and local binary patterns (LBP). In particular, Haralick features were computed from the gray level co-occurrence matrix (GLCM), which describes the spatial relationship among pixels. Whereas in LBP, a binary encoded representation is used to describe the relationship between pixels of interest with its neighbors [11]. A total of 14 Haralick features (shown in Table 1) and 55 LBP features were extracted from each slice. In particular, G represents the number of gray levels, i and j are indices of the pixels of these gray levels, while $P(i,j)$ denotes the intensities of the pixel in the GLCM matrix. While $\mu$, $\sigma$, and $\sigma^2$ represent the mean, standard deviation, and variance respectively.

## 2.3 Classification Models for Survival Prediction

The survival prediction task is an important but challenging task for BraTS data. One of the reasons could be that only age and MR images are provided, hence this prediction mainly relies on tumor identification within the MRI. To this end, we have used radiomics features for describing tumors within the region of interest. In particular, we computed 90 features (statistical, shape- and texture-based) per subject per slice. These features are computed for complete tumor and fed to five different classifiers including discriminant analysis (DA), decision tree (DT), K-nearest neighbor (k-NN), support vector machine (SVM), and random forest (RF).

k-NN is a simple machine learning algorithm that takes the all data available against defined classes and categorizes the incoming test samples on the basis of distance function or similarity measures. In our experiment, we have used different values of $k$ to evaluate the performance. DA is a statistical approach to find similar patterns or feature combinations to separate two or more data samples. The resultant combination of patterns can be used as a classifier to allocate samples to classes. SVM is a supervised machine learning model which maximizes the hyper-plane margin between different classes. The classifier maps

**Table 1.** Description of Haralick texture feature's used in this study for survival prediction.

| Feature name | Equation |
|---|---|
| Probabilities P(x), P(y) | $P_x(i) = \sum\limits_{i=0}^{G-1} P(i,j), P_y(j) = \sum\limits_{j=0}^{G-1} P(i,j)$ |
| Variance | $Var = \sum\limits_{i=0}^{G-1}\sum\limits_{j=0}^{G-1} (i-\mu)P(i*j)$ |
| Standard deviation | $\sigma_x^2(i) = \sum\limits_{i=0}^{G-1} (P_x(i) - \mu_x(i))^2, \sigma_y^2(j) = \sum\limits_{j=0}^{G-1} (P_y(j) - \mu_y(j))^2$ |
| Homogeneity | $H = \sum\limits_{i=0}^{G-1}\sum\limits_{j=0}^{G-1} [P_x(i,j)]^2$ |
| Contrast | $C = \sum\limits_{i=0}^{G-1} n^2 \sum\limits_{i=1}^{G}\sum\limits_{j=1}^{G} P(i,j), |i-j| = n$ |
| Correlation | $Corr = \sum\limits_{i=0}^{G-1}\sum\limits_{j=0}^{G-1} (i*j)*P(i,j) - (\mu_x * \mu_y)/(\sigma_x * \sigma_y)$ |
| Inverse difference moment | $IDM = \sum\limits_{i=0}^{G-1}\sum\limits_{j=0}^{G-1} P(i,j)/1 + (i-j)^2$ |
| Entropy | $Ent = \sum\limits_{i=0}^{G-1}\sum\limits_{j=0}^{G-1} P(i*j)*log(P(i,j))$ |
| Average sum | $S_A = \sum\limits_{i=0}^{2G-2} iXP_x + y(i)$ |
| Entropy difference | $D_{Ent} = -\sum\limits_{i=0}^{2G-2} P_x + y(i)*log(P_x + y(i))$ |
| Entropy sum | $S_{Ent} = -\sum\limits_{i=0}^{G-} P_x + y(i)*log(P_x + y(i))$ |
| Intertia | $Inr = \sum\limits_{i=0}^{G-1}\sum\limits_{j=0}^{G-1} (i-j)^2 * P(i*j)$ |

input space into a high-dimension linearly separable feature space. Because of the nonlinear problem space we used the radial basis kernel. A DT starts dividing the data into smaller segments, meanwhile the tree is developed incrementally. The final tree contains two types of nodes i.e., decision and leaf nodes. Here every decision node has more than one branches (i.e. low, mid and long survivor) while the leaf node represents the final decision. In particular, we used 10 splits for the DT model. RF is one of the famous machine learning classifiers that is considered to be the best in response to over-fitting problems in large dimensional data. A RF model comprises of several trees that take random decisions on given training samples. For survival prediction, we used an RF with 30 bags and observed that accuracy increased with increasing the number of trees until it plateaued out.

## 3 Experimental Results

### 3.1 Dataset

To evaluate the performance of our proposed method we used BraTS 2019 benchmark data provided by the Cancer Imaging Archive. The dataset comprises of independent training and validation sets. The training data contains 259 subjects diagnosed with HGG and 76 subjects diagnosed with LGG along with ground truth annotations by experts. Moreover, the data comprises of MRI images from 19 different institutions of four MRI modalities (T1-weighted, T2-weighted, T1-contrast enhanced and FLAIR). We selected the CBICA, BraTS 2013 and a single dataset from the TCIA archive resulting in 166 subjects with HGG. The images are pre-processed via skull-stripping, co-registration to a common anatomical template and re-sampling to an isotropic resolution of $1 \times 1 \times 1 \, \text{mm}^3$. The data also includes the survival information in terms of number of days for each patient along with their age. In the BraTS 2019 data, the age range of the HGG cases is from 19 to 86 years and survival information ranges from 0 to 1767 days. It should be noted, that for some patients the survival information was missing, and we treated those as having low survival.

**Table 2.** Performance evaluation of different classifiers for survival prediction using radiomics features. The bold values shows the best results.

| Classifier | Evaluation metrics | | |
|---|---|---|---|
| | Accuracy | Precision | Recall |
| k-NN | 0.388 | 0.379 | 0.365 |
| DA | 0.471 | 0.409 | 0.399 |
| DT | 0.678 | 0.640 | 0.659 |
| SVM | 0.526 | 0.509 | 0.519 |
| **RF** | **0.765** | **0.743** | **0.736** |
| FCNN [17] | 0.515 | – | – |

### 3.2 Survival Prediction Performance

We used the extracted radiomics features combined with clinical features to predict the survival class. All radiomics features were combined with patient age and hence a total of 30632 feature values were obtained from 166 HGG subjects to train five different conventional machine learning classifiers. These included a total of 90 radiomics features extracted per slice per subject, while no feature reduction technique was used. We chose five ML classifiers to evaluate the performance of the extracted radiomics features. We created the class labels by normalizing and dividing the number of survival days into three different regions i.e., short survivor (0–600), medium survivor (600–1300), long survivor (1300–Alive). The measurement criteria followed in literature is to predict the correct number of cases that has survival less than 10 months, between 10 to 15 months and greater than 15 months. We further used precision, recall and accuracy as performance measures for each classifier. Initially, we used first order statistical features and shape-based features, but found that these features could not provide a significant performance in the prediction task. Hence, we incorporated Haralick texture features and Fourier shape descriptor, and observed a significant increase in performance when using conventional classifiers. We used a 10-fold cross-validation approach for classification purpose.

Table 2 shows the performance of machine learning models using accuracy, precision, and recall parameters. A fully connected neural network, with two hidden layers, was used for survival prediction on Brats 2019 training data [17]. For 101 patients, using radiomics features, an accuracy of 0.515% was achieved. We observed that k-NN shows poor performance with k = 3, while RF gives the highest performance with 30 number of bags. The value of $k$ is an important parameter to choose for the k-NN classifier and impacts the overall classification results. Since k-NN performance was not at par when using radiomics features at $k = 3$, we experimented with increasing the value of k, but did not observe a significant improvement in the performance. Our results indicate that random forest was able to learn the data representation from the radiomics features for overall survival prediction. In RF, each tree (total 30 trees) was diverse because it was grown and unpruned fully that's why the feature space was divided into smaller regions. Hence RF learned using the random samples, where a random feature set was selected at every node giving diversity to the model.

**Table 3.** Confusion matrix for random forest classifier (the values represent percentages).

| Predicted class | Actual class | | |
|---|---|---|---|
| | Low survival | Mid survival | Long survival |
| Low survival | 76.52 | 9.04 | 14.44 |
| Mid survival | 24.77 | 75.23 | 0 |
| Long survival | 19.00 | 6.38 | 74.62 |

Since in BraTS 2019 benchmark data, the input modalities have intensity variations and tumor appearance is also heterogeneous, features computed from these modalities are also diverse in nature. We further quantify the importance of all features (statistical, shape-based, and Haralick) as shown in Fig. 2. It was observed that Haralick features (represented on feature index 1 to 14) had an out-of-bag feature importance value ranging between 1–2.5. This was on average higher than all other set of features used and shows the significance of these features in the classification task. This analysis was performed in MATLAB using statistical and machine learning toolbox. A confusion matrix for the best performing classifier (RF) is shown in Table 3, where the values represent percentages.

## 4   Discussion and Conclusion

In this paper, we presented an automatic framework for the prediction of survival in patients diagnosed with glioma using multi modal MRI scans and clinical features. First, ROI radiomics features were extracted, which were then combined with clinical features to predict overall survival. For survival prediction, we extracted shape features, first order statistics, and texture features from the segmented tumor region and then used classification models with 10-fold cross validation for prognosis. In particular, the experimental data were acquired in multi-center setting and hence a cross-validation approach was utilized to test the robustness of our proposed approach in the absence of an independent test cohort. In literature, survival prediction model has been applied on diverse data along with different class labels and resection based clinical feature. For brain tumor, the performance in survival prediction has been lower, for instance an accuracy of 70% was achieved [13]. In particular, 3D features were extracted from the original images and filtered images. Further, feature selection was performed to reduce the 4000+ features down to 14. While, in our proposed approach we utilize slice-based features (90) and majority voting across slices to obtain a final classification. Among five classifiers mentioned above, RF showed the best results using the computed radiomics features. The performance significantly varied among these classifiers, which shows the challenging nature of this prediction. With RF, an accuracy of 0.76, along with precision and recall of 0.74 and 0.73, respectively was achieved. We also predicted subject wise evaluation of RF model where majority voting among slices from each patient was used to assign one of the three classes to the patient. We achieved an accuracy of 0.75 using the subject-wise approach. In future, we intend to extend this work by incorporating more data from the TCIA archive as well as using 3D features extracted from atlas based models for survival prediction. We also intend to use Cox proportional hazards models to better handle data with no survival information provided (missing data).

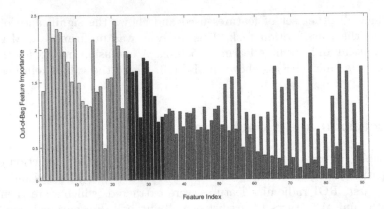

**Fig. 2.** A representation of out-of-bag feature importance for all radiomics features used in this study with different colors, Haralick features (yellow), first order statistics features (green), shape features (blue) and LBP (red). (Color figure online)

# References

1. American association of neurological surgeons. https://www.aans.org/Patients/Neurosurgical-Conditions-and-Treatments/Brain-Tumors. Accessed 07 Dec 2020
2. Anwar, S.M., Altaf, T., Rafique, K., RaviPrakash, H., Mohy-ud-Din, H., Bagci, U.: A survey on recent advancements for AI enabled radiomics in neuro-oncology. In: Mohy-ud-Din, H., Rathore, S. (eds.) RNO-AI 2019. LNCS, vol. 11991, pp. 24–35. Springer, Cham (2020). https://doi.org/10.1007/978-3-030-40124-5_3
3. Anwar, S.M., Majid, M., Qayyum, A., Awais, M., Alnowami, M., Khan, M.K.: Medical image analysis using convolutional neural networks: a review. Journal of medical systems **42**(11), 226 (2018). https://doi.org/10.1007/s10916-018-1088-1
4. Anwar, S.M., Yousaf, S., Majid, M.: Brain tumor segmentation on multimodal MRI scans using EMAP algorithm. In: 2018 40th Annual International Conference of the IEEE Engineering in Medicine and Biology Society (EMBC), pp. 550–553. IEEE (2018)
5. Bakas, S., et al.: Advancing the cancer genome atlas glioma MRI collections with expert segmentation labels and radiomic features. Sci. Data **4**, 170117 (2017)
6. Burger, W., Burge, M.J.: Fourier shape descriptors. In: Principles of Digital Image Processing. Undergraduate Topics in Computer Science, pp. 169–227. Springer, London (2013). https://doi.org/10.1007/978-1-84882-919-0_6
7. Haralick, R.M., Shanmugam, K., Dinstein, I.H.: Textural features for image classification. IEEE Trans. Syst. Man Cybern. **6**, 610–621 (1973)
8. Ho, M.L., Rojas, R., Eisenberg, R.L.: Cerebral edema. Am. J. Roentgenol. **199**(3), W258–W273 (2012)
9. Louis, D.N., et al.: The 2016 world health organization classification of tumors of the central nervous system: a summary. Acta Neuropathol. **131**(6), 803–820 (2016). https://doi.org/10.1007/s00401-016-1545-1
10. Mehreen, A., Anwar, S.M., Haseeb, M., Majid, M., Ullah, M.O.: A hybrid scheme for drowsiness detection using wearable sensors. IEEE Sens. J. **19**(13), 5119–5126 (2019)

11. Polepaka, S., Rao, C.S., Mohan, M.C.: IDSS-based two stage classification of brain tumor using SVM. Health Technol. **10**, 249–258 (2019). https://doi.org/10.1007/s12553-018-00290-4

12. RaviPrakash, H., et al.: Deep learning provides exceptional accuracy to ECoG-based functional language mapping for epilepsy surgery. Front. Neurosci. **14**, 409 (2020)

13. Sun, L., Zhang, S., Chen, H., Luo, L.: Brain tumor segmentation and survival prediction using multimodal MRI scans with deep learning. Front. Neurosci. **13**, 810 (2019)

14. Sun, L., Zhang, S., Luo, L.: Tumor segmentation and survival prediction in glioma with deep learning. In: Crimi, A., Bakas, S., Kuijf, H., Keyvan, F., Reyes, M., van Walsum, T. (eds.) BrainLes 2018. LNCS, vol. 11384, pp. 83–93. Springer, Cham (2019). https://doi.org/10.1007/978-3-030-11726-9_8

15. Suter, Y., et al.: Deep learning versus classical regression for brain tumor patient survival prediction. In: Crimi, A., Bakas, S., Kuijf, H., Keyvan, F., Reyes, M., van Walsum, T. (eds.) BrainLes 2018. LNCS, vol. 11384, pp. 429–440. Springer, Cham (2019). https://doi.org/10.1007/978-3-030-11726-9_38

16. Villanueva-Meyer, J.E., Mabray, M.C., Cha, S.: Current clinical brain tumor imaging. Neurosurgery **81**(3), 397–415 (2017)

17. Wang, F., Jiang, R., Zheng, L., Meng, C., Biswal, B.: 3D U-Net based brain tumor segmentation and survival days prediction. In: Crimi, A., Bakas, S. (eds.) BrainLes 2019. LNCS, vol. 11992, pp. 131–141. Springer, Cham (2020). https://doi.org/10.1007/978-3-030-46640-4_13

18. Weninger, L., Rippel, O., Koppers, S., Merhof, D.: Segmentation of brain tumors and patient survival prediction: methods for the BraTS 2018 challenge. In: Crimi, A., Bakas, S., Kuijf, H., Keyvan, F., Reyes, M., van Walsum, T. (eds.) BrainLes 2018. LNCS, vol. 11384, pp. 3–12. Springer, Cham (2019). https://doi.org/10.1007/978-3-030-11726-9_1

19. Yang, D., Rao, G., Martinez, J., Veeraraghavan, A., Rao, A.: Evaluation of tumor-derived MRI-texture features for discrimination of molecular subtypes and prediction of 12-month survival status in glioblastoma. Med. Phys. **42**(11), 6725–6735 (2015)

# Brain MRI Classification Using Gradient Boosting

Muhammad Tahir$^{(\boxtimes)}$ iD

Department of Computer Science, College of Computing and Informatics,
Saudi Electronic University, Riyadh, Kingdom of Saudi Arabia
m.tahir@seu.edu.sa

**Abstract.** Early detection of Isocitrate Dehydrogenase (IDH) mutations can be used in decision making procedures. We demonstrated the
role of important features identification using extreme gradient boosting
ensemble from MR imagery and their effectiveness in classification of
IDH mutations.

In this work, the MR images are first pre-processed using a number
of image processing techniques. Then features are extracted from the
pre-processed images that are further classified using boosting ensemble.
After, removing very high negative and postive as well as zero valued
attributes from the extracted feature spaces, an increase in the performance accuracy is observed. The proposed technique is simple yet
efficient in classifying IDH mutations from MR imagery. This will help
practitioners to noninvasively diagnose and predict IDH wildtype and
IDH mutants for grades II, III, and IV.

**Keywords:** Glioma · IDH · Gradient boosting · Machine learning

## 1 Introduction

Gliomas, found in patients of all age groups, are the most common primary
brain tumors that affect central nervous system [1, 2]. Isocitrate Dehydrogenase
(IDH) gene product, in its wild-type form, usually transforms isocitrate into
$\alpha$-ketoglutarate ($\alpha - KG$). However, native natural activities are intercepted due
to IDH mutations that eventually transform isocitrate into 2-hydroxyglutarate
(2-HG) instead of $\alpha - KG$ [3]. Due to this condition, natural enzymatic activities
are lost. IDH mutations may cause prostate cancer, acute myeloid leukemia,
colorectal cancer, thyroid carcinoma and melanoma [3].

Therefore, detection of IDH mutations can be used as diagnostic and prognostic tool for the detection of glioma in patients. Early detection and identification of IDH mutations may play key role in decision making process. Gliomas are
graded by the World Health Organization (grades I–IV) according to the clinical
criteria, histopathologic, and MR imaging. IDH status can be predicted noninvasively from MR imagery that is a challenging task. It is due to the fact that some
tumorous tissues may appear normal without applying contrast enhancement.

© Springer Nature Switzerland AG 2020
S. M. Kia et al. (Eds.): MLCN 2020/RNO-AI 2020, LNCS 12449, pp. 294–301, 2020.
https://doi.org/10.1007/978-3-030-66843-3_29

Similarly, contrast enhancing tumor regions may not characterize mutations [2]. Chang et al. [1] have proposed a residual convolution neural network to predict IDH mutations in glioma patients from MR imaging. They utilized three different datasets to train their model. Shboul et al. [4] have developed XGBoost model to predict low-grade gliomas non-invasively from MR imaging. The authors utilized fractal and multi-resolution fractal texture features along with other MR imaging features to develop their model. Ding et al. [5] studied the predictive role of MR imaging features of IDH mutations. Yu et al. [6] proposed to exploit location, intensity, shape, texture and wavelet features of MR images by support vector machine and AdaBoost classifiers through leave-one-out cross-validation protocol to predict the IDH mutation status.

In this study, we develop gradient boosting ensemble strategy to classify IDH positive and negative samples from The Cancer Imaging Archive (TCIA). First, a number of features as detailed in Sect. 2.2 have been extracted, which are then forwarded to gradient boosting ensemble. We also investigated the role of important features in the classification performance. The obtained results have shown the effectiveness of machine learning approaches in the identification of IDH classification from MR imagery.

Rest of the paper is organized as follows. Data used in this study is described in Sect. 2.1. Pre-processing and feature extraction is briefly discussed in Sect. 2.2. Classification algorithm is highlighted in Sect. 2.3.

## 2   Materials and Methods

### 2.1   Dataset

In this work we have utilized pre-operative MRI (T_1, T_2, T_1-Gd, T_2-FLAIR) data from glioma patients from TCIA [1]. Data is pre-processed using a number of image processing techniques listed in the next section. Demographic details about the data is given in Table 1.

**Table 1.** Demographics of the dataset.

|                            | Grade II–III       | Grade IV          |
| -------------------------- | ------------------ | ----------------- |
| **Age** (Mean ± Std. dev.) | 45.43 ± 13.69      | 58.10 ± 13.67     |
| **Gender**                 |                    |                   |
| Male, n                    | 44                 | 55                |
| Female, n                  | 48                 | 45                |
| **IDH mutation**           |                    |                   |
| Available, n               | 92                 | 100               |
| IDH-mutant, n              | 73                 | 05                |
| IDH-wildtype, n            | 19                 | 95                |

The dataset consists of 192 samples in which 114 are normal and 78 are abnormal that shows an uneven distribution.

## 2.2 Pre-processing and Feature Extraction

In this work, MRI data was pre-processed using a number of techniques including intensity noise reduction [7], magnetic-field-inhomogeneity correction [8], affine co-registration [9] with 6 degrees of freedom for $T_1$-Gd against the entire set of remaining sequences of each subject, skull stripping [10] with manual validation when needed. Further, tumors were segmented using ITK-SNAP [11] for the identification of tumorous sub-regions including enhancing tumor (ET), non-enhancing part of the tumor core (NC), and peritumoral edema/infiltrative tumor (ED).

After the pre-processing, features have been extracted using neuro-CaPTk where image specific features were extracted from ET, NC, and ED tumorous sub-regions. Phenotypic characteristics of molecular markers have been captured from all the modalities. Following is the list of image specific features computed in this process.

– multi-parametric imaging signals of different co-registered modalities
– volumetric measurements of different tumor sub-regions
– Gray Level Co-occurrence Matrix based textural features [12]
– Gray Level Run-Length Matrix based textural features [13]
– Gray Level Size Zone Matrix based textural features [13,14]
– Neighborhood Gray-Tone Difference Matrix based textural features [15]
– Local Binary Patterns based textural features [16]
– quantifying characteristics of the local micro-architecture of tissue
– the shape of intensity distributions for detecting functional and anatomical modifications caused by tumors
– tumor's spatial distribution at the anatomical region of interest [17]

## 2.3 Classifier

Decision trees, though easily interpretable, are well known for their inconsistent behaviour in prediction tasks. The high variance, associated with decision trees, is curbed with the help of bagging or boosting aggregation. Bagging strategies can be employed to aggregate decision trees that are produced in parallel and trained with-replacement sampling strategy. On the other hand, boosting strategies produce decision trees in sequential order where every new tree in the sequence learns from the errors of the previous trees and aims for decreasing it. In this way, every tree gets updated form of residual error. Predictive capability of boosting is marginally better than a random classifier where the bias is high in base learners, though each of which has strong contribution towards the ensemble's effective performance. This results in reduced bias and variance. The trees are grown with fewer splits and therefore, easily interpretable in terms of number of trees, the rate of learning, and tree depth. On the contrary, bagging generates trees to the maximum extent that makes interpretation more complex.

The classification performance of multiple weak learners can be enhanced by ensemble learning strategy to improve their overall performance. These weak learners are also known as base learners that can be implemented using either the same algorithm or a different one. Through the ensemble learning strategy, the weaknesses of base learners are complimented by each other and higher performance accuracies are achieved. Decision trees usually use bagging and boosting strategies as base learners of their ensemble.

XGBoost is a library that implements gradient boosting framework. The name XGBoost refers to eXtreme Gradient Boosting that is an ensemble of weak learners. XGBoost curbs overfitting with L1 and L2 regularizations. Further, it can easily handle missing data problem by incorporating sparsity-aware split finding. It can also process weighted data using distributed weighted quantile sketch algorithm. XGBoost also enables parallel processing by sorting and storing the data in memory with block structures. XGBoost can also optimizes the usage of hardware that is achieved by allotting dedicated buffers in each thread. This makes row wise processing of gradient statistics possible. Another key feature of XGBoost is the optimization of disk space availability for manipulating large datasets.

## 3   Results

In this work, we have used eXtreme Gradient Boosting (XGBoost) classifier to predict normal and abnormal brain MRI. One-third of the data is randomly split as testing set whereas two-third is kept for training set. In gradient boosting ensemble, each attribute can be identified for its importance that demonstrates the usefulness of a feature in decision tree construction in a model. Importance score for a certain feature is recorded higher if decision trees are using it frequently in decision making. The attributes are sorted in descending order of importance scores that help in analyzing different attributes. First, importance score of a certain feature is computed for one decision tree considering the performance improvement on each attribute split. Final importance score is calculated by averaging the scores for that feature from all the decision trees.

The performance accuracy of XGBoost classification is 87.5% without performing any kind of post-processing operation on the extracted features. Feature wise importance scores with the original features without any cleansing are depicted in Fig. 1. It is evident that large zone high emphasis features from Gray Level Size Zone Matrix have more influence on the model's performance that is 30%. Since, we have used the original feature space as it is, the performance accuracy is also low. The impact of original data values on the model's out is also shown in Fig. 2.

On the contrary, when we removed the columns having very high negative and positive values as well as the columns containing only zeros, the performance is improved. Overall, 90 such attributes have been removed from the original set.

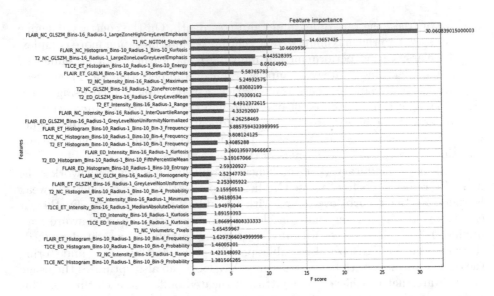

**Fig. 1.** Feature Importance Scores using original data

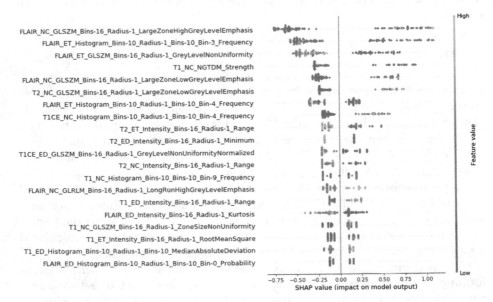

**Fig. 2.** Impact of original data on model's output is shown

In this way, the performance of XGBoost classification reached to 90.6%. The feature importance scores were calculated and depicted again for the modified data as shown in Fig. 3. The same features have high importance scores but now the percentage of its influence is higher i.e. 44.9%.

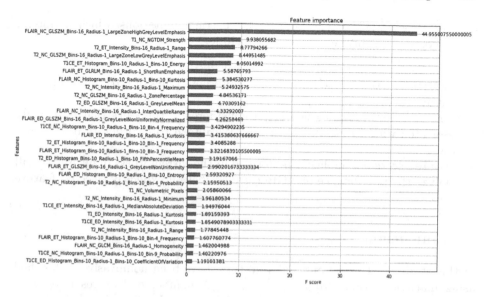

**Fig. 3.** Feature importance scores after removing very high value columns and zero columns

We further investigated the performance of XGBoost classifier on the selected feature space based on the importance scores. The importance scores were calculated from training set that are further used to select features from training set and then the performance is evaluated on the test set. The performance in this way is further enhanced to 92.19% for 47 number of selected features.

## 4   Discussion

In this article, we highlighted the importance of XGBoost algorithm to predict IDH mutation status from MR imagery. Timely identification of IDH mutations is important for decision making in performing clinical procedures. This work predicts IDH mutation status based on MR image features. Hence, prediction of tumor's growth rate can be performed non-invasively. Originally, there were 1338 number of features extracted from MR images that is greater than the number of sample in the dataset. In the first place, we removed features that have zero values, very high positive values or very high negative values. Then classification was performed on the basis of features importance that led to a 47-dimensional selected feature vector with yielded accuracy of 92.1%. The key strengths of the proposed work include:

- XGBoost classifier based simple model for the prediction of IDH mutation status with sufficiently higher accuracy
- Selected feature space is sufficiently smaller with improved prediction performance.

Despite, its good performance, our work has some limitations, which we intend to overcome in our future work. These include:

- Some more in-depth clinical analysis is needed.
- This work does not take into account different grades of IDH mutations separately.
- Currently, 1p/19q co-deletion is not considered in this work that is strongly associated with IDH mutation status. We intend to incorporate it in future work.
- Feature selection is implicitly performed in the current work. In future, we will analyze the performance of XGBoost classifier on explicitly selected feature spaces.

## 5  Conclusion

In this study, IDH mutations and wild-type have been noninvasively classified using machine learning from MR imagery. A number of features have been extracted first and then a gradient boosting ensemble is employed to classify them. Computation of feature importance score can play critical role in identifying key features that effect the classifier's performance.

The proposed method efficiently identified IDH muntants that can assess clinical practitioners in decision making procedures regarding grade II, III, and IV glioma.

## References

1. Chang, K., et al.: Residual convolutional neural network for the determination of IDH status in low-and high-grade gliomas from MR imaging. Clin. Cancer Res. 24(5), 1073–1081 (2018)
2. Biller, A., et al.: Improved brain tumor classification by sodium MR imaging: prediction of IDH mutation status and tumor progression. Am. J. Neuroradiol. 37(1), 66–73 (2016)
3. Guo, C., Pirozzi, C.J., Lopez, G.Y., Yan, H.: Isocitrate dehydrogenase mutations in gliomas: mechanisms, biomarkers and therapeutic target. Curr. Opin. Neurol. 24(6), 648 (2011)
4. Shboul, Z.A., Chen, J., Iftekharuddin, K.M.: Prediction of molecular mutations in diffuse low-grade gliomas using MR imaging features. Sci. Rep. 10(1), 1–13 (2020)
5. Ding, H., et al.: Prediction of IDH status through MRI features and enlightened reflection on the delineation of target volume in low-grade gliomas. Technol. Cancer Res. Treat. 18, 1533033819877167 (2019)
6. Yu, J., et al.: Noninvasive IDH1 mutation estimation based on a quantitative radiomics approach for grade II glioma. Eur. Radiol. 27(8), 3509–3522 (2017)
7. Smith, S.M., Brady, J.M.: Susan—a new approach to low level image processing. Int. J. Comput. Vis. 23(1), 45–78 (1997)
8. Sled, J.G., Zijdenbos, A.P., Evans, A.C.: A nonparametric method for automatic correction of intensity nonuniformity in MRI data. IEEE Trans. Med. Imaging 17(1), 87–97 (1998)

9. Jenkinson, M., Beckmann, C.F., Behrens, T.E., Woolrich, M.W., Smith, S.M.: Fsl. Neuroimage **62**(2), 782–790 (2012)
10. Smith, S.M.: Fast robust automated brain extraction. Hum. Brain Mapp. **17**(3), 143–155 (2002)
11. Yushkevich, P.A., Gao, Y., Gerig, G.: ITK-SNAP: an interactive tool for semi-automatic segmentation of multi-modality biomedical images. In: 2016 38th Annual International Conference of the IEEE Engineering in Medicine and Biology Society (EMBC), pp. 3342–3345. IEEE (2016)
12. Haralick, R.M., Shanmugam, K., Dinstein, I.H.: Textural features for image classification. IEEE Trans. Syst. Man Cybern. **6**, 610–621 (1973)
13. Galloway, M.M.: Texture analysis using gray level run lengths (1975)
14. Tang, X.: Texture information in run-length matrices. IEEE Trans. Image Process. **7**(11), 1602–1609 (1998)
15. Amadasun, M., King, R.: Textural features corresponding to textural properties. IEEE Trans. Syst. Man Cybern. **19**(5), 1264–1274 (1989)
16. Ojala, T., Pietikainen, M., Maenpaa, T.: Multiresolution gray-scale and rotation invariant texture classification with local binary patterns. IEEE Trans. Pattern Anal. Mach. Intell. **24**(7), 971–987 (2002)
17. Bilello, M., et al.: Population-based MRI atlases of spatial distribution are specific to patient and tumor characteristics in glioblastoma. NeuroImage Clin. **12**, 34–40 (2016)

# Author Index